Tiger on the Brink

Tiger on the Brink

Jiang Zemin
and China's New Elite

Bruce Gilley

UNIVERSITY OF CALIFORNIA PRESS
Berkeley · Los Angeles · London

University of California Press
Berkeley and Los Angeles, California

University of California Press, Ltd.
London, England

Library of Congress Cataloging-in-Publication Data

Gilley, Bruce, 1966–
    Tiger on the brink: Jiang Zemin and China's
new elite / Bruce Gilley.
        p.   cm.
    Includes bibliographic references and index.
    ISBN 0-520-21395-5 (alk. paper)
    1. Chiang, Tse-min, 1926–   2. Heads of state—
China—Biography.   3. China—Politics and government—1976–   I. Title.
DS779.29.C477G55   1998
951.05'092—dc21
[B]   97-42753

Printed in the United States of America
9 8 7 6 5 4 3 2 1

The paper used in this publication is both acid-free
and totally chlorine-free (TCF). It meets the minimum
requirements of American Standard for Information
Sciences—Permanence of Paper for Printed Library
Materials, ANSI Z39.48-1984.

For my parents, who gave me wings

Contents

PART 5. BREAKING WITH DENG, 1995–1998

Preface

My first and only encounter with China's president and party chief Jiang Zemin was in a bathroom. Wearied by the deliberations of Guangdong province delegates at the annual session of China's National People's Congress, or parliament, in 1995, I slipped out of a stuffy room in the Great Hall of the People in Beijing and went downstairs to wash my face. Attendants waved me into the nearest men's room, which was empty. But when I went to leave they barred the doors. "Keep that foreigner inside," I heard someone say. Peering out of the opaque windows of the loo, I soon discovered the reason for my temporary incarceration. Out of a nearby conference room burst Jiang Zemin, wiping his forehead with a pink washcloth after a lengthy discourse before delegates from Jilin province. Jiang had obviously sipped too much tea. To the surprise of my captors, he made an abrupt turn and headed straight for my tiled prison. I disengaged my nose from the glass door just in time to be flung against the wall by Jiang, who glanced at me nonchalantly, and a single bodyguard.

One's journalistic instincts evaporate under such stress. I knew my colleagues in the foreign press would want me to take the high road and ask Jiang about some weighty matter of state, such as, "How's the health of patriarch Deng Xiaoping?" But I knew equally well that my colleagues in the Hong Kong and Taiwan press would prefer the low road. "Samples! Samples! Where are the samples?" they would demand of me.

In the end, I was plucked from the bathroom by one of the attendants outside before having to make the invidious choice, emerging into the carpeted foyer only seconds before Jiang, to the astonishment of the assembled Jilin delegates. Jiang brushed past me on the way into an adjoining reception room. The cameras of the mainland press photographers began to flash as he shook hands with each and every one of the Jilin delegates standing in three rows of bleachers.

Although I would not say this book was born in a bathroom, my brush with Jiang did have the effect of making him a living and breathing figure in my mind, an impression sometimes difficult to form from the officially served leader of the Chinese press. It came at a time when I was considering making an exploration of this man's life, which, despite his then six years as general secretary of the Chinese Communist Party, remained a subject barely touched by journalists or scholars. It helped to spur me on.

My purpose in writing this book is to reappraise Jiang, who although bearing all the hallmarks of a weak transitional figure was able to carry on past the death of Deng Xiaoping owing to a combination of personal and historical reasons. In so doing, I hope the book will shed light on the nature of post-1989 and post–Deng Xiaoping politics in China.

As I finish this, it is now almost a decade since Jiang came to power. Deng has died, and there is little to guide us about this man.[1] I hope this book will provide insight into both his personality and China itself. Wary, after years in the Hong Kong press, of the semi-astrological accounts of Chinese politics often reported as news in the territory, I have used only official sources and firsthand information.

The two Hong Kong–based magazines I refer to often, *Jing bao* (Mirror) and *Guangjiaojing* (Wide Angle), are both published by members of the Chinese People's Political Consultative Congress and enjoy official backing. They are the only two such magazines that can be circulated in China, and I take them to be reliable in their information. I treat them, and the Communist-run newspapers *Wen Wei Po* and *Ta Kung Pao* in Hong Kong, as "official" sources.

Given that Jiang Zemin is still in power, this can only be a start in writing his biography. When he eventually falls from power or leaves the stage, more will be needed. New information from reliable sources may perhaps help us understand him better. Until then, I hope readers will tolerate the deficiencies of this first attempt by a Westerner.

I have received no funding or support from any government or institution of any sort for this project. However, I do owe an enormous debt of gratitude to the *Far Eastern Economic Review* for putting up with my topsy-turvy schedule as I completed the manuscript. In particular I would like to thank the editor, Nayan Chanda, and the former regional editor, V. G. Kulkarni. I also benefited greatly at the conception of this project from the advice and support of Maurice Brosseau of the Chinese University of Hong Kong, and later from Jeffrey Wasserstrom of Indiana University. Kenneth Lieberthal of the University of Michigan provided invaluable assistance. All the staff at the incomparable Universities Service Centre at the Chinese University of Hong Kong were, as usual, helpful and friendly. Thanks also to Chris Robyn of the University of California Press, who expressed interest in the project at an early stage and remained its faithful supporter throughout.

PART I

"Son" of a Martyr, 1926–1970

CHAPTER I

Leaving Yangzhou

I

The streets were dark and silent except for the occasional squawk from a Liberation-brand truck roaring through Beijing's suburbs bound for the provinces. It was less than two weeks since the lunar new year celebrations of early February 1997. The cold, somber atmosphere of the capital had yet to be enlivened by the rush of migrant workers seeking jobs in the city after the holiday. Inside a second-floor room at a hospital in the western suburbs, Jiang Zemin, China's highest leader, had convened an emergency meeting of the country's most powerful ruling body, the Politburo standing committee. One floor above the gathering lay the withered corpse of a man whose very presence had seemed to hold this vast country of 1.2 billion people together for the preceding two decades. Deng Xiaoping, a little man from distant Sichuan province and grand designer of the country's successful economic reform program of the 1980s, was dead.

Sitting on the fringes of the grim conclave, Deng's widow, Zhuo Lin, sobbed quietly, while his five children looked on impassively. Following a script laid down many months before, Jiang declared the order and timing of the week-long mourning activities for Deng that would follow. No one dissented. A few hours after midnight, Deng's long-anticipated death was announced to the world.

It was an inauspicious way for Jiang Zemin to begin his unfettered reign as the "core" of China's new leadership. Chinese tradition dictated that nothing unlucky should happen in the two weeks after the lunar new year, until the lantern festival at the appearance of the first full moon. But then again, Deng's death may have been the luckiest possible way for Jiang to ring in the new year. A panda bear of a man, with big round black glasses and a love for the traditional two-stringed Chinese violin, or *erhu*, Jiang had ruled as general secretary of the Chinese Communist Party since being thrust into the role following the 1989 Tiananmen Square protests in Beijing. It was already an unexpectedly long stint at the top for someone often compared to Hua Guofeng, the chosen successor of Communist China's founder, Mao Zedong, who had lasted just five years as head of the party.

By the time of Deng's death, Jiang had already achieved the goal of restoring political stability and economic growth to China following the Tiananmen protests. Foreign investors were on track to pour an astounding U.S.$250 billion in direct investment into the country in the 1990s, compared to just U.S.$15 billion in the 1980s.[1] Beijing's voice in new international organizations such as the Asia-Pacific Economic Cooperation forum, and soon in the World Trade Organization, was loud and influential. Jiang had also by this time established his own authority over the party, over the government that answered to it, and over the military, which kept a keen but distant watch over the whole country. With Deng gone, Jiang could begin to outline his own vision of China's future.

That future was anything but certain. When Jiang began to rule China without the abiding spiritual presence of Deng in February 1997, he was inheriting a country that one Chinese scholar described as a tree-like structure.[2] The roots were China's traditions; the trunk was the Marxist-Leninist and Maoist thought of the first decades after the 1949 Communist takeover; the branches consisted of the economic reforms pioneered by Deng and their attendant social changes; and the leaves were foreign influences. Yet this hybrid variety needed to evolve into a new species that could withstand the test of time.

Jiang favored a gradual transition.[3] He also tended to borrow useful and successful reforms from others and apply them nationwide. He was not, like Mao and, to a lesser extent, Deng, a man with a clear vision of China's future, but by 1997, anyone claiming such a vision would be dismissed as a fraud or an outright danger. Something of an outcome could be guessed at, though. The resulting "tree" would be liberal in some respects (its market economy and growing individualism), but clearly authoritarian in others (its single-party state and media controls). In many ways, it would resemble other Asian "developmental dictatorships" like

Singapore and South Korea. Although it was a less wrenching and spectacular historical change that Jiang was about to preside over, it might be far more important to the great sweep of Chinese history than those overseen by Mao and Deng. China was on the verge of modernization.

Jiang was not the sort of leader disposed to self-glorification, though, even on that frosty evening in a hospital meeting room in western Beijing. As the second eldest son of an intellectual's family from the rich cradle of Chinese tradition along the lower reaches of the Yangtze River, his natural arrogance was tempered by a habitual self-effacement. He had reached his position through a combination of political savvy and public modesty. Like those of his generation who were the first to miss fighting in the civil war that established Communist China, he was pragmatic when it came to the communist creed and more inclined to build consensus than rout enemies. Mourners would stream to Deng's birthplace in Sichuan province following the announcement of the patriarch's death, but the simple gray-brick abode where Jiang grew up in the old part of the city of Yangzhou would remain inhabited by others and unremarked upon by visitors. Jiang, it was said, preferred it that way.

2

The date is 20 October 1996. A torrent of bicycles sweeps past my resolutely planted feet as I stand in the middle of a narrow street called Dongquanmen in the center of old Yangzhou, a sleepy city not far up the Yangtze River from Shanghai. Dongquanmen, the city's former street of notables, still has the *yamen,* or government office, at its western end—now housing the local party committee. But in contrast to the unruffled existence enjoyed by the dozen or so bankers, merchants, and intellectuals who inhabited its large, gray-brick homes in the early part of the century, the street has now been transformed by the clamor of 125 working-class households and several hundred more living in the alleys feeding into it.

Gazing up at the peeling Chinese characters painted in baby blue on a tile signboard, I struggle to read the "Brief description of Dongquanmen." My eyes scan the faint writing with growing intensity. Bells and hoots from cyclists rushing home for lunch seek to dislodge me from the street. Finally, the promised line: "Party General Secretary [unclear] [unclear] Jiang Zemin once lived at Number 16." Nothing more.

I stop two chuckling students mounting their bicycles as they leave the Yangzhou government canteen, on whose wall the sign is affixed.

"What are these two characters?" I ask, pointing to the indistinct pair. The track-suited youths dismount and arch their backs to read the entire line. "Tong-zhi [Comrade]," says one, answering my question. "Jiang Zemin once lived here?" asks the other, startled by the discovery. "Really!" They climb back into their saddles and move back into the lava flow of wheels. "Sure," says the other. "Don't you know? He's a Yangzhou person."

3

The drooping willows and lazy canals of Yangzhou are a welcome respite from the pollution, traffic jams, and stark urban development of much of modern China today. For over a thousand years, they have nurtured an unlikely array of painters, scholars, and philosophers. Walls were first erected here around habitations on the Yangtze River alluvial deposits in the fifth century B.C. The city became one of China's wealthiest at the beginning of the Tang dynasty in the early seventh century A.D. after the completion of the Grand Canal north to Henan province. Historical decline after that was kinder to Yangzhou than to the country as a whole. The salt and iron trades disappeared, and commerce moved to the coast, but more than a thousand years after its initial glory, Yangzhou's beauty remains, its prosperity maintained by its key position at the junction of the Grand Canal and the Yangtze River.

For the young son of a well-off family in the early 1930s, Yangzhou might have been the equivalent of Bath in England or New Haven in the United States. It was a quiet and cultured refuge from the gathering clouds of war and increasing outbreaks of domestic violence: invasion from Japan and attacks on the burgeoning Chinese Communist Party by the insecure Nationalist (Kuomintang or Guomindang) government based upriver at Nanjing.

Jiang Zemin was born in Yangzhou on 17 August 1926 in a book-cluttered house on Tianjia Lane in the old city.[4] His name, Zemin, or "Benefit the People," was taken from the writings of the revered Chinese sage Confucius, who lived in the fifth century B.C. It echoed the name of a young communist, Mao Zedong, or "Benefit the East." At 32, Mao was at this time already teaching peasants in Guangzhou about the Chinese communist movement, which both men would eventually lead.

The swaddled boy was the third of five children and the second son of a prolific writer and part-time electrician, Jiang Shijun, and his peasant wife, Wu Yueqing.[5] We know little about Wu Yueqing. Elders in

Changwei, where she is also remembered by the name Wu Xiaoqing, say she died a broken woman in Yangzhou in the 1980s. But they insist that her younger sister, Wu Yuezhen, who was only ten years older than Jiang, played a greater part in his upbringing than she did.[6]

In the Chinese zodiac, Jiang was born in the year of the tiger. King of the wild animals, the tiger symbolized all that was male in Chinese philosophy—brave enough to drive away demons and strong enough to command the obedience of others. It was a common astrological sign for leaders of men.

The Jiang family was respectable, even honored, in Yangzhou. Jiang's grandfather, Jiang Shixi, was 56 in this year and known throughout the old town for his skills in traditional Chinese medicine. The airy medicine shop near Tianjia Lane where he sent his patients to collect their paper-wrapped mixtures of herbal remedies still stands, adorned in front by groups of chatting elders reclining in wicker chairs.

Jiang Shixi was the link to the family past. The village of Jiang (meaning "river"), from whence their surname came, sat beside a tributary of the Shuxi River, which winds its way through the mist-enshrouded Huangshan mountains in the southern part of the poor inland province of Anhui.[7] Life in this tea-growing region was tranquil but unforgiving. Poverty and famine took the lives of Grandfather Jiang's first two sons, born there in the late 1890s. As prospects for his medical practice were better in the prosperous canal area of the Yangtze River, he moved his family of seven to the town of Xiannu, just outside Yangzhou, in the early 1900s.[8]

Settled outside Yangzhou, Grandfather Jiang Shixi at first made a modest living from the medical secrets he had brought from inland. Better work was soon, however, available on the canal system, which was finding new life in the industrial expansion of the early years of the century. In 1915, at the age of 45, Jiang Shixi took a lucrative job as assistant to the Dada Inland Water Transport Company.[9] The Dada company was based just downriver from Yangzhou at Nantong, the marshaling area for much of the cargo flowing in and out of the Grand Canal. Jiang Shixi was the company representative in Yangzhou. His traditional long gown was discarded in favor of a crumpled linen suit made in Shanghai. In the common parlance, he had "jumped into the sea" of commerce.

With five children, aged 1 through 20, the family moved to Tianjia Lane in Yangzhou's well-to-do Dongguan district. Canals and their attendant freshwater wells run everywhere through the old city, which was doubtless a pleasant change from the need to haul water, if only for short distances, in the suburbs. The move also meant that the education of the family would be assured.

Jiang Shixi spent a lot of time in Nantong at his new job, even taking part in the formulation of an agricultural development plan for the downstream city.[10] Like many intellectuals of his generation, he also devoted himself to national affairs, railing first against foreign incursions into China and then against the weakness of the Qing dynasty and later the Nationalist government. He composed several songs lamenting warlord President Yuan Shikai's infamous concession to Japan's Twenty-one Demands of 1915, ditties that he taught to itinerant Nationalist Party musical troupes organized and funded by the better-off merchants. The demands, which gave Japan control over large swathes of Chinese territory, including the Yangtze Valley, seemed to symbolize the sorry plight of the Chinese nation.[11]

Only a few elders along Tianjia Lane still recall the Jiang household. Grandfather Jiang died in 1933, at which point the family home on Tianjia Lane seems to have been sold. But the enterprising doctor left behind two important legacies, which would be passed on to his four surviving children (his lone daughter, Jiang Shiying, died shortly after marriage), and to their children in turn, at a critical time in the nation's history: an intellectual strain that emphasized action as well as comment, and an indignant nationalism aimed as much at the corrupt Chinese Republic as at the invading Japanese.

4

The first beneficiary of this legacy was the eldest child and son, Jiang Shijun, nicknamed Guanqian, or "Thousand-Time Champion." Born in 1895, this little-known man was later to be confined to official footnotes as merely the "biological father" of Jiang Zemin. But he acquitted himself well at school and managed to gain entry into Lianghuai Middle School on Dongguan Street, a prestigious institution founded in 1902 as the first publicly funded middle school in the city.[12]

Jiang Shijun proved an adept writer at the school, which he attended even though the family was then still residing in the suburbs. As the eldest son, he shared the burdens of family responsibility with his parents, however, and had to forsake his writing career to earn a living wage. Soon after graduation, he accepted a job in Yangzhou with the Nantong Tongming Electric Company.[13]

More inspired by the example set by their father was the sixth child, Jiang Shihou. He was later known by the name Shangqing, or "Rising Youth," acquired because his siblings agreed that he was the family's greatest hope of achieving power and prestige.[14] Born in 1911, when his eldest brother was already 16, Jiang Shangqing and his younger brother, Jiang Shufeng, both attended Nantong Middle School for a year in 1927 because Yangzhou was temporarily in upheaval as a result of Nationalist campaigns against local warlords.[15] There they met Gu Minyuan, a classmate who would later become Nantong's most famous revolutionary son, and by the time they returned to Yangzhou, the brothers had been enlisted by Gu into the underground Chinese Communist Party Youth League.

Jiang Zemin was fortunate as a child in that his father held down a steady job, even as his young uncles got involved in the clandestine Communist movement. For within a year of returning to Yangzhou to continue middle school there, Uncle Jiang Shangqing was arrested for his underground activities at the family's newly acquired home on Jiangjia Bridge Lane.[16] His first incarceration, in a Suzhou jail, lasted only six months. His aging father and his older brother hired lawyers who convinced the courts that he was merely a misled youth.[17] But a year later, in the winter of 1929, he was arrested again after entering the literature department of Shanghai's Fine Arts College. It was not until the summer of 1930 that the Jiang family in Yangzhou learned the news. Elder brother Jiang Shijun was dispatched to find his headstrong younger brother when he did not return for the summer vacation. Informed of the incarceration, his aging father, Jiang Shixi, traveled to Shanghai and won his son's release that winter.

Favoring the traditional long Chinese men's gown over Western garb, Jiang Shangqing cut the perfect figure of an engaged young intellectual, with circular-rimmed glasses, delicate nose, and pursed lips. Undeterred by his year-long jail term—during which he contracted asthma and began to suffer from arthritis—Jiang Shangqing chose to remain in the revolutionary hotbed of Shanghai by entering the social sciences department of the city's Jinan University in the fall of 1931.

The young Jiang Zemin's formal education began at about the same time, but his informal instruction had already been under way for several years. In Chinese tradition, a young man's education, and his later self-cultivation, was based on four arts: music, chess, literature, and calligraphy. Except for the chess, which was the least practical of the quartet, Jiang was shepherded along this traditional path from a young age. From the moment he began to recognize the swirling Chinese characters used before simplification was introduced by the Communists after 1949, Jiang was forced by his father to recite an article of classical Chinese literature each day.[18] Often it was the hated "three-character classic," column after column of three-character sentences that encapsulated the rote learning of Chinese tradition. But just as often it was poetry from the Song or Tang dynasties, masterworks of feeling and ambiguity, peppered with handy aphorisms. These would remain deeply embedded in Jiang's memory for the rest of his life.

Jiang was also forced to learn calligraphy, because, as he explained, "in the old China it was very difficult to find a job if you did not have good handwriting."[19] It would never be his forte; although he never misses a stroke, Jiang's calligraphy is described by most as undisciplined and crude. He still uses the complex pre-1949 characters.

This head start in reading and writing helped win the young boy a place in the prestigious Dongguan Primary School, just a few hundred meters from his Tianjia Lane home.[20] The six years Jiang spent in the school exposed him to a stark contrast in proximate calm and distant turmoil. Dongguan Primary School cultivated a happy environment for its young charges. Days were filled with songs and games, which drew liberally from both Chinese and Western traditions. It was here that Jiang developed his lifelong and comparatively worldly appreciation of music. He was a natural musician. Whatever instrument was placed before him, whether the whining two-stringed Chinese violin played off the knee, the *erhu*, the long bamboo flute, or *dizi*, or even an upright piano, proficiency came easily. "When I was young I loved playing instruments," he would recall. The piano and Western violin seemed to him to be better developed than Chinese instruments, "because their range is wider."[21] He would also at this time develop a lifelong affection for Western classical music, later calling "Ave Maria" "some really beautiful music"[22] and on another occasion asserting that "it's not good if the Chinese people know nothing about Beethoven's Ninth Symphony."[23]

Although his siblings and cousins never excelled as he did in the traditional arts, Jiang would always attribute his aptitude to his cultured upbringing rather than to innate abilities. "Because Yangzhou is a city of culture, and because of the cultured historical background of my family, I am a true lover of music and literature," he would say.[24]

At home, Jiang reveled not only in the doting love of his own mother, Wu Yueqing, but also in that of his aunt, Wang Zhelan, the wife of

Uncle Jiang Shangqing. The two families moved into new quarters on Dongquanmen following the death of Grandfather Jiang Shixi in 1933.[25] In the spacious one-story home, Jiang was the family prodigy. His mother was a simple peasant woman. But Wang Zhelan was able to see the spark in her young nephew and became his earliest mentor. She is said to have loved Jiang most among all the children in the crowded Jiang household on Dongquanmen.[26]

Dongquanmen (now Dongquanmen Street) was Yangzhou's street of the rich. At two meters, it was twice the width of the average street in the old city. The ornately pockmarked iron doors and marble plinths of the houses were the respectable outward displays of wealth and prestige. The irony for Jiang's family was that, just as they reached this distinguished address, the old order on which its distinction was based was about to crumble under the impact of foreign invasion and civil war. It is ironic that the most distinguished street in Yangzhou nurtured the future head of a proletarian state.

5

The din of tambourines and *dizi* inside the happy confines of Dongguan primary school could not entirely muffle the sounds of war outside. In September 1931, Japan's incursion into China began in the distant northeast. Some months later the Nationalist government in Nanjing was briefly forced to relocate north to Luoyang because of the Japanese invasion. Over the following six years, leading up to the outbreak of the Sino-Japanese War, the insecure Nationalist government would launch sporadic assaults on the expanding Communist movement, even as young students protested that "Chinese should not fight Chinese."[27]

Jiang and his young colleagues knew the heavens were shaking. But Yangzhou remained calm. Indeed, the spontaneous welling up of anti-Japanese sentiment at this time brought a seemingly festive atmosphere to the lives of the young boys. "Long before the Japanese marched into Yangzhou, we were already going crazy," Jiang was to recall. "We saw ourselves as Chinese heroes of ancient times, feasting on the blood of the Japanese pirates in the South China Sea!"[28]

For Jiang, in particular, the events outside primary school were vividly told. His young uncle Jiang Shangqing, already suffering from asthma and arthritis at age 21, returned to teach in primary and middle schools in Yangzhou in 1932. There he founded a Communist Party–controlled journal of Marxist literature, *Xin shiji zhoukan* (New World Weekly).[29]

The following five years saw Jiang Shangqing hounded from one
Yangzhou-area school to the next and the magazine shut down by the
local Nationalist authorities. Undaunted, he founded another magazine,
Xiezou yu yuedu (Writing and Reading), with his old classmate Gu
Minyuan and his brother Jiang Shufeng, in 1936.

In December 1936, mutinous Nationalist soldiers in Xian arrested
their president, Chiang Kai-shek (Jiang Jieshi), who seemed bent on wiping out Communist forces rather than repelling Japanese invaders. The
event was a stunning psychological victory for the Communists and their
sympathizers, who had been urging an end to civil strife in order to focus
attention on the threat from Japan. As a result of the coup, Chiang agreed
to call off the anti-Communist extermination campaign (although not
the blockades of Communist-held areas). The event also gave Jiang his
first political lesson. Writing the entrance examination to the prestigious
Yangzhou Middle School in the summer of 1937, he was asked to write
about the Xian Incident.[30] In his essay, he praised the rebellious behavior of Zhang Xueliang, the leader of the Nationalist Northeastern Army,
who had taken his superior hostage. It was Jiang's first political statement in writing; given the influence of his uncles and his grandfather, his
sympathies were never in doubt, however.

Entrance to Yangzhou Middle School was difficult, even for one as
well-bred as Jiang Zemin. The school was compared to Tianjin's famous
Nankai Middle School (which educated future premier Zhou Enlai
among others) in the popular saying: "In the north there is Nankai Middle School, in the south there is Yangzhou Middle School."[31] The white-
stone three-story Shuren teaching hall, built in 1917 and still standing
today, was the grandest classroom in the south. Jiang's father and his
two young revolutionary uncles had all attended the school or its predecessors, but as its reputation improved throughout the 1920s and early
1930s, the competition to enter became acute. In 1936, the year before
Jiang entered, just 10 percent of the 3,000-odd students who wrote the
entrance exam were accepted. In Jiang's year, first-year enrollment was
expanded to 425, but that was still only 10 percent of those seeking admission.[32] Jiang was among those accepted.

The playing fields of Yangzhou Middle School were a symbol of the
fervent and worldly nationalism of youth at the time, which might have
launched China into a development spurt, as it had in Japan seventy years
before. The prestigious academy had already groomed a generation of
leading scholars, politicians, and scientists. Most were men, since women constituted at best a quarter of the student body.[33] Zhu Ziqing, a

Yangzhou writer who would later be eulogized by Mao Zedong for refusing to eat American-supplied "relief grain," graduated in 1916. Hu Qiaomu, later to become Mao's secretary, head of the Xinhua News Agency, and a Politburo member, graduated in 1930.

Students at Yangzhou Middle School were angling for university. After three years in lower middle school, they rushed through the three-year upper-middle-school curriculum in two years and devoted the final year to preparation for university entrance exams.[34] A university education was certainly the expectation when Jiang marched through the gates along the tree-lined avenue that led to the Shuren teaching hall on his first day of classes in the autumn of 1937. But the invading Japanese imperial army, which until now had been confined to the world outside this peaceful city, was soon marching down the same lane.

In July 1937, Japanese troops stationed near the Marco Polo Bridge outside Beijing had bombarded the local Chinese garrison on the pretext that they had been refused entry to a village to search for a missing colleague. Within weeks, an undeclared war was raging between the two countries. By December, Shanghai had fallen under Japanese occupation. A month later, the whole Yangtze valley up to Nanjing, including Yangzhou, was in enemy hands. The results were hugely disruptive, but not disastrous, for the young Jiang's education. Classes were halted after just one month, in October 1937. Hopes of resuming at the school under Japanese occupation were soon dashed. When the Japanese marched into town, their first item of business was to find a large walled compound with plenty of administrative offices and dormitories to serve as a command headquarters. Yangzhou Middle School's new campus in the western Dawangbian area was perfect. The sanctity of the school meant little to the Japanese soldiers. The gymnasium's wooden floor was torn up, and the building was turned into a horse stable. Books were burned for fuel or out of spite. And the students and teachers were all told to search elsewhere for accommodation.[35]

This they did, but they had some difficulty finding it. As with many schools and universities, the Japanese occupation forced Yangzhou Middle School to disperse to a series of far-flung "campuses." It was a grand word for what were little more than exiled teaching colonies. One group went to Sichuan province, another to Shanghai, and two were eventually functioning in the Yangzhou suburbs. Students followed their long-gowned teachers depending on their own circumstances. As a Yangzhou native, Jiang joined one of the groups in the city's suburbs.

The first suburban campus was set up in the autumn of 1938 in Taizhou, along the network of canals feeding into the Grand Canal. Buildings were rented at a local middle school and students billeted with local families. Studies sometimes took place in the canteen.[36] This makeshift beginning to Jiang's education proved a false start. In early 1939, the Japanese authorities briefly imposed a state of emergency on the entire Yangzhou area. Classes came to a halt again, and the students were sent home.[37] By the autumn of 1939, the Japanese occupation was more secure. A new campus was opened in Yang Lane in old Yangzhou, just a stone's throw from Jiang's Dongquanmen home. After a two-year delay, and under the watchful eye of Japanese troops, Jiang's middle-school education finally began in earnest.

The disruption had a critical effect on the nature of Jiang's middle-school education, and indeed on his personal development in these formative years. For no longer was nationalism the preserve of idealistic intellectuals reacting to distant events, as it had been for his uncles and grandfather. Jiang and his teachers saw their nation crumble before their eyes. "Those were the days when the Chinese nation was ridden with disasters," he would recall.[38]

The young boy was inspired in this plight by many people, both past and present. Just north of his home, beside the canal that encircled the old city, lay the simple temple of Shi Kefa, a local Ming dynasty official who had refused to surrender to the invading Qing armies in 1645. Although Shi lost his own life, as well as those of thousands of Yangzhou citizens, for his obstinacy, his dogged loyalty in the face of foreign invasion by the Manchus of the Qing dynasty made him a poignant symbol of Chinese nationalism.

"In those days when I was a student in Yangzhou, I was shocked to see and hear about the evil acts of the Japanese aggressors," Jiang would recall. "Each time I saw the tombstone of Shi Kefa with my classmates I felt a strong anti-Japanese and patriotic emotion and became determined to engage in revolutionary struggle."[39]

Of course, some of this rage may be just so much ex-post facto ritual indignation. The takeover of Yangzhou was largely peaceful—in contrast to the unprovoked massacre of civilians by Japanese soldiers in Nanjing. And, as far as we know, Jiang lost no close family members in the war with Japan. Having school halted only one month into his education may have caused hand-wringing among his elders, but for a boy of 11, faced with a disciplined and taxing course load ahead, it may have been a welcome respite. The following two years of roving education may even have been something of an adventure. The variety nights organized by the school to raise funds to fight the Japanese would have been taken by Jiang, strumming his erhu in accompaniment, as good clean fun rather than serious political involvement. Indeed, Jiang later would not harbor any of the instinctive, visceral anti-Japanese hatred of those as little as five or ten years his senior. He even later regretted not having mastered Japanese when it became a mandatory part of the middle-school curriculum.[40]

The Japanese invasion did, however, spur an ardent desire on the part of Jiang and his classmates to reform their country by catching up to the West, just as the Japanese had done. Ignoring the contemptuous Japanese soldiers patrolling the bridges of the city, Jiang and his classmates redoubled their efforts to learn from the West. It was an act of imitation that was supposed to reflect national pride, not flattery of foreigners, the students were told. "Some people often feel ashamed to be Chinese. They say that even when a foreigner farts, it is a great thing," Jiang's railway engineering teacher, Lu Zuojian, would tell his students. "But we Chinese can do anything foreigners can do. We will even try things that they don't dare!"[41]

Whatever the reasoning, the focus on mastering things Western was quaint. Tired old grammar books from England and monstrously difficult calculus texts from America were used. Jiang's eccentric English teacher, Li Zongyi, even led his charges in repetitions of the speeches of Thomas Jefferson and of Abraham Lincoln's 1863 Gettysburg Address.[42] Jiang was to remember the latter for the rest of his life. He would also long assert that "the English we learned then was better than what even university students of today [learn]."[43] As he later described his middle-school education: "It was mainly an education in British and American cultures."[44]

There were other signs that the national stirrings caused by the Japanese occupation fueled rather than smothered the desire to learn about the outside world. For it was at this time that Jiang began to delve seriously into foreign literature in Chinese translation, in particular offerings from the Soviet Union, which were then widely available, such as Tolstoy's *Anna Karenina* and *War and Peace*.[45] He also read Victor Hugo's *Les Misérables* and *Notre-Dame de Paris*.[46] Jiang scored best in the sciences, but his own interests, plus "family pressures," as he later called them, meant that he absorbed much literature as well.[47]

Besides Russian and French literature, Jiang also took in a strong dose of modern Chinese literature, which was flourishing during his youth.

One of his favorite writers at this time was Zhu Ziqing, a dashing man whose neat, side-parted hair, circular wire-rimmed glasses, and waistcoat concealed a radical within. A native of Jiangsu province, Zhu had grown up in Yangzhou and attended what would become Yangzhou Middle School. While teaching in Beijing, Jiangsu, and Zhejiang in the late 1920s, he helped launch what became known as the "new poetry" movement, which eschewed traditional forms and encouraged topics based on everyday life.

A Communist sympathizer, Zhu would spend nine years from 1937 teaching at the wartime campus of Beijing's Qinghua University in the southwestern city of Kunming, then under Nationalist control. He returned to Beijing in 1946, aged 48, suffering from gastric illness. Two years later, the stomach ailment would take his life, aggravated by his refusal to eat American-supplied relief grain. The refusal would be part of a campus-led protest against the perceived tolerance by the U.S. occupation forces in Japan of resurgent militarism in the vanquished nation.[48]

Zhu explained in his diary that he joined the relief-grain boycott because "we cannot evade our personal responsibilities."[49] For his efforts, Mao Zedong would declare soon afterward that Zhu "embodied the heroic spirit of the Chinese people." Indeed, his death became a symbol for young Chinese like Jiang of the proud obstinacy in the face of foreign pressures that many saw best exemplified by the Communists. The hometown connections Jiang could claim with Zhu Ziqing made the spiritual identification all the stronger. "Zhu Ziqing was full of patriotic moral courage, which makes his writings attractive," a visitor once commented to Jiang. "Right!" came the reply. "I am moved every time I read them."[50]

Zhu seemed to represent two important ideals to Jiang: first, that of the heroic man of letters, a figure his family had taught him to respect, notwithstanding that he himself never became one, having chosen to take up science; and second, the ideal of standing firm on principles in dealings with foreign countries, especially the United States. "Chinese youth should take Zhu Ziqing as a model and not bow obsequiously to and blindly envy the West," Jiang later said.[51] The same sentiments were also expressed by other Chinese writers of the age. "We Chinese have backbone," Lu Xun (1881–1936) wrote famously, a line often quoted by Jiang. "We shall never yield to unreasonable pressure exerted on us by foreigners," he once explained after repeating Lu Xun's affirmation.[52]

Jiang was later to characterize his upbringing in Yangzhou rather inexactly as the "Confucian" phase of his education.[53] To be sure, he was put through the rigors of learning the traditional Chinese skills expected of a nobleman, out of which grew such habits as carving personal seals in fine calligraphy for his classmates.[54] But as we have seen, the combined effects of the Japanese occupation and the worldly nationalism engendered by his teachers exposed Jiang to much more than the traditional "music, chess, literature, and calligraphy" lessons that his description suggests. By the time he graduated from Yangzhou Middle School in the spring of 1943, Jiang was already a cosmopolitan young man, schooled in Western culture and concerned about China's place in the world.

6

For Jiang's two restless young uncles, the war against Japan had been no less a call to intellectual arms. Jiang's father had assumed responsibility for family affairs after the death of Grandfather Jiang Shixi in 1933. This left Jiang Shangqing and Jiang Shufeng free to carry on their work for the still-underground Communist Party cells within the United Front, the on-again, off-again alliance of Nationalist and Communist forces aimed at defeating the Japanese. Separately, the pair would spend most of the war following in the wake of the victorious United Front armies, establishing bases to conduct anti-Japanese education and propaganda. Their long periods away from Yangzhou, fighting the war of ideas on the battlefront, fired the imagination of the young Jiang Zemin.[55]

It was Jiang Shangqing whose exploits were later to attract the most attention. The outbreak of the war against Japan had given a new lease on life to Jiang Shangqing, who had been forced back to Yangzhou by ill-health and anti Communist persecution in 1932. In 1937, he founded yet another new magazine, *Kangdi zhoukan* (Anti-Enemy Weekly), to oppose the Japanese invasion. Soon afterward, he was dispatched to western Anhui province to serve as the contact point and propagandist for the Communist Eighth Route Army. This engagement in official posts seems to have stirred the young writer. He wrote his best poems and essays while on the move with the roving arts troupe he formed in the region at this time.[56] By 1938, he had been made party chief of the Communist cell in the Jiangsu-Anhui border district, and the following year, he began to train United Front cadres at a jointly run college in northern Anhui.[57]

In June 1939, Jiang Shangqing began assisting a specially dispatched young New Fourth Army commander named Zhang Aiping, who would become China's defense minister in the 1980s. Their task was to conceive and make preparations for a new United Front offensive with Sheng Zijin, the Nationalist commander in the Dabie Mountain area of northeastern Anhui. United Front operations were always fraught by the uneasy relationship between the two sides, and this case was no exception. Zhang wanted Sheng to deal first with a rebellious Nationalist administrator across the border in Jiangsu. Sheng preferred to conscript more Communist soldiers for high-risk attacks on the Japanese. In the end, Sheng agreed to visit his mutinous comrade first, provided the Communists supplied an escort.

Jiang Shangqing was chosen to lead the escort, which set off on horseback with Sheng in late July. "When you return, take the road that passes by the horse farm. The other is faster and will keep you out of the river, but it's rife with bandits," Zhang warned the procession as it trotted out of camp. The meeting was uneventful. Sheng won grudging loyalty from the aspiring local warlord by promising more arms. Galloping back in triumph, Sheng opted for the fast route Zhang had scorned. With Jiang Shangqing in the lead, the procession was ambushed by thieves in a village called Little Bay. Sheng dismounted and ran for cover, but Jiang was too slow. He took several bullets to the chest and head. Jolted from his steed by the impact, he hit the ground dead in a pool of blood. He was 28.

News of the death was relayed to the Jiang family in Yangzhou almost immediately. It was shocking for a family that had never sent its sons to war. It also seemed a terrible waste for Jiang Shangqing's life to have been taken by mere local bandits. His wife of four years, Wang Zhelan, was so beside herself with grief that she could not even stand. Jiang Zemin's mother, Wu Yueqing, hired a single-wheeled rickshaw, and the pair made the long, 155-mile journey to the site of the tragedy.[58]

Jiang's father, Shijun, followed behind. As the oldest brother, he presided over the memorial ceremony held on the shores of nearby Hongze Lake. A makeshift grave was dug in Yaji Village, near where Jiang Shangqing had died. Flowers were scattered on the water.

Jiang Shangqing had left behind two baby daughters, aged 1 and 3. This might have seemed a sufficient brood for the family of an intellectual unconcerned about extra hands to help with farmwork. But Chinese tradition died hard, even among supporters of the new anti-feudal Communist ideology. Without a male heir, Jiang Shangqing's family would be left twisting in the wind, or so it seemed to them. Raised in the binding traditions of the Chinese countryside, Wu Yueqing, Jiang Zemin's mother, may have sensed this inadequacy more than others. She is said to have "felt very sympathetic" to her sister-in-law's plight.[59] With three sons of her own, it would be polite to offer the second oldest for adoption by Wang Zhelan. That was Jiang Zemin, then in his final year of lower middle school.

It mattered little that the promising young boy had nursed an intense fear of his passionate uncle, because, as he recalled, "he was very demanding."[60] Later propaganda would assert that "although he did not live long with his foster father, he had a deep affection for him and was deeply influenced by him."[61]

Jiang's misgivings notwithstanding, an adoption ceremony was arranged. He was brought before his widowed young aunt and told to kneel. "Mother!" he cried out to his new mother three times as he kowtowed in respect. Then he stood up and embraced Wang Zhelan. Jiang Zemin was now the adopted son of a Communist Party martyr.

7

By the time Jiang graduated from middle school in the spring of 1943, the defeat of Japan in the Pacific War was already seemingly inevitable. The entry of the United States into the war in December 1941 had brought into the open Washington's hitherto covert support for the Nationalist forces in China. By late 1943, China was assured by the Allied powers of a concerted effort to defeat Japan and fully restore its territories. Challenged by an American-supplied resistance, Japan was forced to devote nearly half its entire soldiery to occupation forces in China.

With the close of war in the offing, intellectuals began to look beyond the immediate concerns of defeating Japan. Questions about the future dominated discussions and periodicals. Which side of the United Front—which began to seriously unravel in 1943—would emerge on top? And how could China rebuild and launch a renewed drive toward modernization?

For a young man graduating from a prestigious, albeit war-battered, middle school at this time, the answer to the first question was far from clear. Nailing one's colors to either the Nationalist or Communist mast was risky. By contrast, being on the winning side of a national modernization drive appeared a safer proposition. A host of European and American-inspired new institutions of science and learning had sprung up in the early part of the century, such as the Science Society of China, established at Cornell University in the United States in 1914. Closer to home, the writings of an American-trained professor, Tao Xingzhi, who was undertaking mass education programs in the Chinese countryside, were also widely disseminated. "Only science can save China," Tao proclaimed.[62]

Jiang had excelled in science at middle school and had been exposed to literature partly because of "family pressures." He cared little for making revolution, despite the influence of his young uncles. Science, for him, was a safe and assured path, as well as one that he would find more engaging than mere propaganda work.

"Every day we were singing anti-Japanese songs and pasting up numerous anti-Japanese slogans and posters," he later recalled. "But I thought I wanted to do something more practical to save the country. So I decided to learn a scientific skill."[63]

Jiang enrolled in the industrial technology and electrical machinery program at Nanjing's Central University after passing an entry examination in the summer of 1943. Under Japanese occupation, the university had been allowed to function normally. The city was quiet, away from the hotbed of revolution in Shanghai, and Jiang would be able to pursue his chosen course in peace. "I believed that twentieth-century engineering science could be the food of the people," he would recall.[64]

Jiang was to claim in the 1990s that he took up the cause of the Chinese Communist Party in earnest the day he walked through the gates of Nanjing Central University.[65] Prior to then, however, the date of his conversion to the revolution was put at 1946.[66] The three-year difference is important. Anyone who joined the Communist cause during the war against Japan is considered a member of China's "first generation" of Communist fighters. Those who joined only when the civil war erupted against the Nationalists are relegated to later generations.

And yet there is no evidence beyond assertion to show that Jiang had anything to do specifically with the Chinese Communist Party while he was in Nanjing. It would have been a risky business, jeopardizing his plan to learn a skill. Indeed, Jiang's very choice of Nanjing Central University, when a diploma from the Yangzhou Middle School would have won him entry to a prestigious Shanghai institution, suggests that he was not inclined toward revolution-making as yet.

Not that Jiang was indifferent to the student activities in Nanjing, organized to relieve famine and expose Japanese atrocities. But such events were invariably jointly organized by both Nationalist and Communist groups on campus. Being a student activist did not mean being a Communist. Any patriotic student could take part, with little or no danger of being branded a Communist.[67]

Fate, though, was to bring Jiang closer to the Communist cause. Two years into his studies, the Japanese surrender brought most of the cities in the lower Yangtze Valley back under the control of the U.S.-assisted Nationalist forces. The scenes of jubilation worldwide as the long war came to an end in Europe and then Asia were not repeated in China. The common ground that had united the Chinese youth movement disappeared in a flash. A civil war loomed, and students were under pressure to take sides.

The new Nationalist administration in the Yangtze Valley was keen to rebuild China's disparate tertiary education system, which the Japanese occupation had left in disarray. In October 1945, two months after the Japanese laid down their arms, Nanjing Central University was formally merged with the Chongqing and Shanghai campuses of Jiaotong University. A new campus for the enlarged institution of 3,000 students was built in Shanghai's Xujiahui area, which today remains the site for Shanghai Jiaotong University.[68]

Jiang and his twenty classmates were to complete their final two years of studies in the electrical machinery program of Shanghai Jiaotong University. Packing their trunks and pressing their short-sleeved white cotton shirts, they must have felt some trepidation. Hailing from Yangzhou, Jiang, like many of his colleagues, spoke the North Jiangsu dialect of Chinese, which was much spurned by the South Jiangsu sophisticates in Shanghai. "You speak better Mandarin than I do. I speak with a Yangzhou accent," he was to tell countless colleagues and guests throughout his later life with barely concealed shame.[69] In Shanghai, the accent was as harsh as the people were cunning. Jiang may have picked up some Shanghai dialect from his uncles, but he probably knew very little upon arrival in Shanghai in the fall of 1945. His status as an outsider in the city was ironic in light of his later image as a Shanghai person.

The fortuitous shift to Shanghai was to have profound effects on Jiang's later life. But it would also have a simple and immediate effect on his education. When they arrived in Shanghai, Jiang and his classmates became part of a class that had grown from twenty-eight to sixty-eight, including three women.[70] Jiang was the youngest. His new teachers were better, more demanding, and the school's ten labs were fully equipped. Teachers at Jiaotong were also sticklers for using the English language for instruction, much more so than in Nanjing. Besides lectures and textbooks, all assignments and tests were also in English.[71]

Jiang seems to have handled the new learning environment better than others in his class. He even had time to enjoy American romantic films like *Gone with the Wind* (1939) and *Waterloo Bridge* (1940).[72]

But he was also the first to admit that he was not a brilliant engineering student. "I threw myself into the study of furnaces along with Zhu Linwu," he would recall, referring to a classmate who would later become one of China's foremost experts in the then still tricky technology. "We banged away with our little hammers [on the furnace casing] to get it just right. It was a profound technology. But I am ashamed to say I never reached his level [of expertise]."[73]

Besides simple streamlining, a second motive in the Nationalist revamping of universities was to weed out and control the underground Communist movement, which had expanded during the Japanese war. The cloak-and-dagger campaign between Nationalist authorities and Communist agitators that ensued would quickly win Jiaotong University a reputation for political struggle—"a hellhole full of spies and secret agents," was how one future chancellor described it.[74]

In September 1945, the Nationalist mayor of Shanghai, Wu Guozhen, announced that six universities in the city, including Jiaotong, would be put through a screening process to ensure there were no "fake students" on campus. Everyone understood this to mean Communist Party members, who at Jiaotong numbered "fewer than ten" at this time.[75] The schools were also to introduce right-wing indoctrination classes that would warn the students about the dangers of communism. Universities in Nanjing and Beijing (then called Beiping) were in for the same.

The screening and reregistration process would take months. Students wrote petitions in protest. "There is no such thing as a fake student, just as there is no such thing as a fake person," they reasoned, perhaps disingenuously.[76] The unflinching attitude of the head of the Nationalist Education Department in Shanghai, Zhu Jiahua, who spurned the appeals, soon provoked the students. Those like Jiang, who had known nothing but disruptions to their education since at least middle school, protested gently at first, but then more vigorously. Seven consecutive student demonstrations erupted in Shanghai in late 1945. Students at the six universities distributed leaflets, held press conferences, and won the support of the city's four major newspapers.[77] Probably more for the sake of getting on with his education than attacking the Nationalist government, Jiang joined the marchers.

As with every major student movement in modern China, what began as a campaign of specific grievances and limited aims soon turned into a wider protest against the style and system of government. "We want freedom. We want democracy," the students chanted in English, Jiang would recall.[78] The slogans would have come easily to the lips of

Jiang given his middle-school rearing on the texts of Jefferson and Lincoln. But they were hardly the words of a budding communist revolutionary. No wonder Jiang would later refer to his days at Jiaotong University as the "bourgeois" stage of his education. "I received a lot of education in capitalism and Western culture," he said.[79]

By March 1946, the Nationalist authorities were willing to compromise. The screening proposal was dropped, but first-year university students were still forced to take two hours per week of indoctrination, now renamed "political studies," based on the writings of Sun Yat-sen, founder of the Republic of China, and President Chiang Kai-shek. For Jiang, it was a first taste of the power of student activism. His first year as a university student in Shanghai had proved two things: that the Nationalist administration was no friend of China's youth, and its educated youth in particular; and that the student movement could achieve results.

8

The establishment in February 1946 of a U.S. military commission in China to keep the feuding Nationalist and Communist forces apart was a last attempt to avert civil war. The bloody swapping of control over the northeastern city of Changchun in April and May 1946 brought tensions to the fore again. Students nationwide appealed to the Nationalist authorities to exercise restraint. On 23 June 1946, Jiang joined tens of thousands of workers, students, and teachers gathered at the north train station in Shanghai to see off a delegation of ten well-known Shanghai student activists on their way to petition the Nanjing government. "End the civil war! Cut military spending! Increase education funds!" the onlookers chanted as the train rolled past the platform to a volley of firecrackers. The so-called Peace Petition Brigade, representing 124 youth groups in Shanghai, was the biggest single group ever amassed by the Communist-controlled alliances in the city.

The representatives did not get far. The moment they arrived at Nanjing's Xiaguan train station, they were detained, beaten, and sent home by Nationalist police. But the growing strength of the underground Communist youth movement was clear. Caught up in the euphoria of what later became known as the "Xiaguan incident," Jiang joined the Chinese Communist Party at the end of June 1946.

We know little of Jiang's motivations in joining the party, but it is worth pausing to consider. Although it would not be until after 1947 that the besieged Nationalists would launch witch-hunts against the student Communists in Shanghai and elsewhere, there were already dangers in 1946. Signing up could spell disaster for Jiang's career and might even threaten his personal safety. Two possible reasons for why he did so, at least, should be considered: job prospects and peer pressure. In surveys carried out in the 1990s, fully a third of all young people joining the party admitted openly that getting a better job was the main reason for signing up.[80] In 1946, though, this was hardly conceivable. The Nationalists were firmly in control of Shanghai, and it was the last place their grip was likely to slip. Nor was peer pressure a likely explanation for Jiang joining the party. Despite later propaganda, the Communist student groups remained very small on campus. Three years after Jiang joined, the Communist group at Jiaotong had a mere 180 members.[81]

Instead, we are left with the more compelling, and straightforward, argument; Jiang sympathized, even identified, with the Communist cause and was willing to apply himself to achieving its goals. Grandfather Jiang Shixi had set his family an example of the engaged intellectual, which was taken up to varying degrees by his sons. Jiang was also now the adopted son of a Communist fighter who had died for the cause. And although no great moralist himself, Jiang clearly felt that the Communists were in the right. He was no ideologue: freedom and democracy were his bywords, and the Western "bourgeois" notion that science was the savior of the nation was his working model. Communism, as understood by the young Jiang, was a revolutionary method for achieving this.

Jiang got in on the ground floor. He joined the party only a month after it had established its first administrative office in the city. Zhou Enlai, whose lone public office of the Chinese Communist Party had been moved from Chongqing to Nanjing in May 1946 along with that of Chiang Kai-shek, directed the underground Shanghai office. Officially, it was simply called "the Zhou Enlai residence." Student activities were under the command of a foreign literature student at Jinan University, Wu Xueqian, later a vice-premier and foreign minister.

Other youths involved in the underground Communist Party movement in Shanghai at the time included an 18-year-old journalist named Qian Qichen and 21-year-old streetcar sweeper named Qiao Shi, who was active in recruiting members from middle schools. Both men would later rise along with Jiang to the citadels of power in the successor to the state they were seeking to overthrow.

Jiang quickly became involved in the movement, but not as a leader. Communist student activities invariably were organized into working groups; a "negotiations" or "leading" group would make the political decisions and lead the activity decided on, and then several subsidiary groups, covering areas like student mobilization, security, propaganda, performances, and pamphlet distribution, would follow in step.[82] With his skills in music and calligraphy, Jiang was naturally drafted into these subsidiary groups. Wang Xiaopeng, a mainland political biographer, writes that Jiang "became known as a 'fortress for democracy.'" "He was as red hot as fire and as scorching white as reed flowers," Wang continues, using an expression of military prowess from the tumultuous Three Kingdoms period (A.D. 220–280).[83] The hyperbole may capture Jiang's enthusiasm, but probably exaggerates his role at the time. More credibly, one of Jiang's classmates, Zhuang Guozhu, recalls that he was known then as "the conductor" because he was frequently seen hammering away on the piano, bowing on an erhu, or acting as impromptu choirmaster for protest sing alongs.[84]

His time-consuming musicianship meant that Jiang was frequently absent from class, but his classmates never asked why. They happily furnished him with notes, a courtesy extended to most student activists. "Only later did we find out he was a Communist party member," Zhuang recalls. The remark is intriguing. As mentioned, the Communist Party group at Jiaotong never grew beyond a few hundred members, the highest estimate being 400.[85] And although it played a crucial role, the Communist Party was not the sole organizer of the student movement in Shanghai. As in Nanjing, being a student activist in Shanghai did not mean being a Communist. In any case, Communist youth were still under orders to keep a low profile and cultivate goodwill in the Nationalist-dominated Shanghai environment. Nobody wanted to be the victim of a late-night assault by Nationalist thugs wielding the notorious "wolf's teeth clubs," wooden planks with protruding nails that ended many a promising university career.[86] Although Jiang joined the party in June 1946, his role in the tumultuous year ahead was surely not as prominent as later official portraits would suggest.

Jiang's artistic skills from his Yangzhou primary and middle school days were put to good use in the year of protest that rounded out his formal education. In January 1947, when students nationwide protested the alleged rape of a Beijing University student by a U.S. soldier, Jiang was assigned to draw large caricature posters. In his cartoons, the student victim represented China and the soldier symbolized the villainous U.S. and Nationalist forces.[87] In April, Jiang played the erhu in a student-run opera in Shanghai organized to protest an alleged hit-and-run accident involving an American merchant that resulted in the death of a Jiaotong science student, Jia Zigan.

It was the nationwide spring 1947 student protests against the Nanjing government that Jiang was to recall most vividly though. Education spending by the Nationalist government had fallen to 3.6 percent of expenditures by 1946 under the pressures of inflation and rearmament. Sporadic clashes with Communist forces and a growing famine in the countryside added to the concerns of students. In addition to peace, they wanted education spending to rise to 15 percent of the budget.[88]

As early as 1946, Shanghai student activities had been organized to deal with the rapidly deteriorating financial situation of the universities as a result of funding cuts and inflation. The Student Aid Movement in January 1946 handed out grants to 10,000 tertiary students on the verge of dropping out for a lack of money. In May and June, another fund-raising movement, called "Respect Teachers," brought similar relief to impoverished professors.

At Jiaotong University, the situation was grim indeed. Chancellor Wu Baofeng was a weak-willed man, appointed by the director of the city's education department, Zhu Jiahua, and unable to prevent him from cutting back on school funding. By early 1947, the school had a staff of 460 but was only receiving salaries for 300. Funding for operations was only a fifth of that needed.[89] Zhu Jiahua's response to complaints was simple: plans were initiated to ax all but the engineering-related departments at Jiaotong.

The liberal arts students who led the Communist movement at Jiaotong mobilized their 3,000 fellow students to protest the miserable state of the educational system in general and the downsizing plans in particular. On 13 May, the throng climbed into sixty-five trucks provided by sympathetic local merchants and headed for Nanjing. The scenes of departure on the lawn in front of the stately Jiaotong library were jubilant: girls strutted before the trucks in high heels and their best dresses. Men, many wearing Western suit coats, waved from the trucks' crammed running boards. The whole campus was abuzz. Parading through Shanghai, the students won applause from onlookers. "Save our school!" "No coming back unless we succeed!" they chanted. Other students commandeered a passenger train from the north station and set off along the sabotaged tracks for Nanjing, draping the steam engine's nose in a banner reading: "Long Live Jiaotong University!" The atmosphere was festive, even intoxicating.

"That was really a time when we were not afraid to die," Jiang would recall. "We didn't even think of our personal safety."[90]

Their efforts were again rewarded. Within hours of their departure for Nanjing, Zhu had capitulated to their demands. Jiaotong was saved and the victorious trucks returned to the university that same evening.

Similar sentiments were firing students throughout the lower Yangtze Valley. The next day, an even larger trek to Nanjing began, involving 7,000 students from Shanghai, Suzhou, Hangzhou, and Nanjing itself. All faced straitened circumstances and their demand for an end to the civil war was echoed throughout the land. The renewed student unrest dramatized the unease of a nation entering into a three-year civil war that would claim the lives of over a million soldiers and countless hundreds of thousands of civilians.

Historians say that this second procession marked the onset of a truly mass national movement against the Nationalist government.[91] But the thrilling scenes as disparate student groups linked up on the road to the capital were short-lived. Nationalist police and soldiers were dispatched to break up the procession before it reached Nanjing. On 20 May, more than fifty students were arrested as armed police halted the ragged protesters strung out along the long road.[92] Many watched helpless as their colleagues were beaten on the head with billy clubs and leather belts or sent scurrying by fire-hose spray. Jiang was also witness to the crackdown. Student protest, he saw, was not all singing and dancing after all.

9

Late one night in June 1947, shortly before graduation, Jiang heard a knock on the door of his dormitory room. It was his classmate and fellow party member, Lei Tianyue, wearing a dark overcoat and carrying two bundles and a simple duffel bag. "I've got to leave in a hurry. I'm in danger of arrest," Lei explained, looking nervously over his shoulder. Jiang barely had time to shake his classmate's hand. Lei turned and disappeared down the darkened corridor.[93]

A year earlier, when Jiang had joined the party, the Communists were in the ascendant among the students of Shanghai. At the negotiating table in Nanjing, meanwhile, Communist negotiators were also holding their own in the knotty three-way talks with the Americans and the Nationalists.

That had all changed in the interim. At the onset of the civil war, the Nationalists could do no wrong. Their army of 3.7 million was roughly double the size of that fielded by the Communists.[94] Nearly 200 towns and cities and 174,000 square kilometers of territory were seized from the retreating Communist forces in the latter half of 1946. About 18 million of the roughly 140 million people under Communist control were lost to Nationalist forces. With a national population of just under 500 million, the Communists were in danger of utter defeat. The fall of the Communist capital Yanan to the Nationalists in March 1947 was the nadir of the war for the Communists.

At the top political level, the rising Nationalist fortunes dashed any hopes that the Communists might win some sort of power-sharing in a coalition government. The results for the underground student movement in Shanghai were baleful. Police hounded the young activists through the narrow streets of the old city, where they frequently met. In the wake of the breakup of the joint march on Nanjing, Nationalist thugs in Shanghai gratuitously attacked youths suspected of Communist sympathies.[95] After a brief dance in the daylight, the city's Communist movement dove headlong back into the deep underground, fleeing persecution.

Although his involvement as a student probably lasted only one year, Jiang was to recall this underground experience vividly. The Communist students were organized along lines used by the city's notorious organized criminal groups, or triad societies, and a number of the triad expressions proved apposite. Many would find their way into Jiang's own vocabulary, try as he might to replace them with refined references to classical poetry. In later life, he would frequently blurt out old triad expressions. "You take the open road, I'll go across my special wooden bridge," was one phrase he often used to indicate mutual respect between non-Communist (non-triad) and Communist leaders.[96] One anecdote has Jiang eluding arrest by hiding in the trunk of the car of Jiaotong's chancellor, Wu Baofeng.[97]

For a young man beginning his working life under Nationalist rule, these cloak-and-dagger experiences were of little use, though. The tide of the war was only beginning to turn when Jiang graduated in mid 1947. Fortunately, his one year in the party had not converted him into a raving Marxist. He had enrolled in electrical machinery studies with the expressed purpose of "doing something practical" for his country. Eschewing the dangerous Communist agitation work pursued by his uncles, Jiang had opted for a safer route. It was the open road more than the special wooden bridge that he followed.

The Communist-organized protest activities, after all, were less about promoting communism than about defeating the Nationalists.

"The street demonstrations, the tens of thousands involved in protest marches, produced very few Marxists," noted the great sinologist Laszlo Ladany. "The reason that the Communists stirred up the mobs was not to convert demonstrators to Marxism, but to destroy the credibility of the Nationalist government."[98] Jiang himself preferred to speak of "revolution" rather than "communism" in recalling his role at the time: "In order to spread revolutionary thinking, we were often putting on street performances," he would recall. "I played the erhu as accompaniment."[99]

Although later propaganda would assert that Jiang helped "lead" the student Communist movement in his final year, there is no evidence that this was true. Unlike Qian Qichen and Qiao Shi, Jiang never had an official post in the student wing. Certainly, he took part. But the erhu and paintbrush he wielded suggest support rather than leadership roles. Indeed, Jiang never so much as got detained during his final year of university as an active party member. His impunity is odd, given that the Communist propaganda brigades from Jiaotong University, where he played a role, were frequently arrested at the beginning of the class boycott movement that followed the repression of the march on Nanjing.[100]

Perhaps the most damning evidence showing that Jiang played only a peripheral role in the Communist student movement is the lack of any reference to him in the two official Jiaotong University histories of the period.[101] While he had joined the party, his participation was on the fringes at best.

Whatever difficulties that meant for his later political career, it bode well for Jiang's adjustment to living and working "on the open road" under Nationalist rule when he graduated in 1947. When his class gathered for their graduation photo, the only student missing was Lei Tianyue, already on his way to Hong Kong. The photo is the earliest so far released of Jiang. The large forehead and back-combed hair stand out. Small, circular glasses train in from his wide temples.

Clutching an engineering degree and wearing freshly pressed linen trousers, the adopted son of a Communist martyr was being forced out onto the open road.

CHAPTER 2

Mao's China

I

As Nationalist fortunes deteriorated over the period 1947 to 1949, the persecution of suspected Communist groups in the cities intensified. Nowhere was this more true than in Shanghai, where student groups made a natural target. Those caught were pinioned in the street by police using cheap hemp rope and led immediately away to the execution ground. "Your students are spending all their time dancing and singing about liberation as if they lived in a Communist concession," Shanghai's mayor Wu Guozhen fumed to the newly appointed U.S.-educated chancellor of Jiaotong University, Cheng Xiaogang, in 1948. Cheng, a suspected Communist sympathizer, remained defiant. "If you send armed troops or police to the school to cause trouble, I'll roll up my bedding and follow them out the door," he warned.[1]

Leaving the heated campus environment just as the persecution of Communist student groups turned ugly may have been a stroke of good luck for Jiang Zemin. Graduating with a technical degree in mid 1947, his obvious choice was to remain in Shanghai. Despite the war, the city remained China's most open and technologically advanced commercial center. His first job was not a glamorous one, however. He was assigned to watch two 300-horsepower diesel engines as an engineer in the power-supply department of the U.S.-owned Hai Ning Company's factory in northern Hongkou district,² which made several canned food products, but was perhaps best known for its Pretty Lady brand popsicles. From the sublime to the ridiculous, Jiang had left a national liberation movement for a popsicle stand.

Later propaganda would assert that Jiang was "sent" to Hai Ning by the party as a sort of Communist mole. Hongkou district was a squalid, bombed-out factory area, teeming with migrant workers from Jiang's native northern Jiangsu, the explanation goes, and he was expected to form underground Communist unions among them. "Although his official post was with Hai Ning, Jiang's principal energies were devoted to underground party activities," one sympathetic Hong Kong biographer explains.³ It was hardly an assignment that Jiang would have relished, given his low profile in the campus movement. Nor do we hear Jiang himself ever speak of the two years he worked for Hai Ning. His official résumé simply skips the period altogether. "Jiang graduated in 1947. After China's liberation in 1949, he . . . ," is the common refrain.⁴

Fitful bouts of amnesia are nothing new to the Communist Party in dealing with its history. Episodes viewed as somehow unbecoming to a party that prides itself on a glorious history are simply airbrushed from memory. This appears to be the case with Jiang's first job. Founded in 1913, the Hai Ning Company had survived warlords, revolution, Japanese occupation, and civil strife by bending to the wishes of the authorities of the day. Its American bosses had installed a Chinese comprador as manager by the time Jiang joined and simply drew profits. They were a perfect example of the "foreign adventurers" the Communists were determined to chase out of Shanghai.

By 1948, as food shortages appeared in the city, the Nationalist garrison cast its covetous eyes on the food factory. The winter of 1947–48 had been bitter and long, resulting in the deaths of about 500 people in Shanghai alone.⁵ With little choice, the U.S. owners sold out for U.S.$300,000. Jiang was now working for the Nationalists. The renamed Number One Army Provisions Plant was ordered to crank up production of cereal-based foods to feed the retreating Nationalist armies. Shanghai was to become one of the major departure points for their flight to Taiwan, and Jiang's factory would help them stave off hunger as they waited to embark.

One Communist elder, Zhang Zhiyi, maintains that Jiang was "installed as a secret agent" to remain in the Nationalist-owned factory in anticipation of its confiscation by the Communists.⁶ To be sure, that day was not far off. But the fact remains that Jiang's first two bosses were the Americans and the Nationalists in turn, "exploiters" and "reactionaries" respectively in Communist jargon. Little mention is made of the fact now, except amongst overseas Chinese intellectuals, some of whom have cast biting, Communist-style aspersions on Jiang for his brief flirtation with the foes of Marxism: it was, they say, the *bu guangcai*, or "undistinguished" phase, of his career.[7]

Fortunately, it was also short-lived. Confident of the support of the vast Chinese peasantry, Mao Zedong predicted in 1946 that it would take five years for the Communists to defeat the Nationalists. In the event, even Mao was too pessimistic. The tide of war began to turn in mid 1947. Thenceforth Communist forces inflicted heavy losses on the Nationalists in running battles across Henan, Shandong, and Anhui provinces, assisted by the fact that their popular support in the countryside alleviated the need for large occupation forces in conquered territories.

The final turning point may have come in August 1947, when about 200,000 troops under a 43-year-old commander named Deng Xiaoping drove south to establish a base in the strategically important Dabie mountain area along the Anhui-Jiangsu border. It was the same district where Jiang Zemin's foster father, Jiang Shangqing, had been killed eight years earlier.

After the Nationalists lost nearly half a million troops in the bloody Manchurian campaign of September and October 1948, the Communists had the most soldiers, and the end was nigh. In late April 1949, the People's Liberation Army (PLA) began massing on the outskirts of Shanghai after crossing the Yangtze River and chasing the Nationalist government out of Nanjing. Nationalist authorities in Shanghai reacted by venting their anger on the helpless Communist youth groups in the city. Jiaotong University's two party martyrs, the students Shi Xiaowen and Mu Hanxiang, were both executed in a police station on Fuzhou Road on 20 May. "The Shanghai student movement was most hard-pressed during that month," Wu Xueqian recalled.[8] To all intents, the civil war ended in Shanghai on 25 May, when PLA forces marched into the Xujiahui district, containing Jiaotong University. Two days later, the entire city was under Communist control. The 3,000 students and teachers forced to evacuate the Jiaotong University campus by the pitched battle reclaimed their "heavenly peach garden" amid scenes of jubilation.

The Nationalist forces would take eight months more to flee from China to their new republic on the island of Taiwan off the southeast coast. In the two-week siege that preceded the PLA entry into Shanghai,

Jiang and his colleagues feared the Nationalists might try to strip the equipment from the Number One Army Provisions Plant for evacuation to Taiwan. "I won't let them take it away," Jiang, now elevated to power department chief, told the workers. "It would leave us with nothing to eat but the bitter northwest wind."[9] As it happened, the frightened and disorganized Nationalists in Shanghai had no such intention. Jiang and his workers gathered on the streets to herald the arrival of the straw-shod PLA soldiers.

Within a month of the takeover, the Communist Party's Shanghai Military Control Commission annexed the factory as part of the spoils of victory. The name was changed to the Yimin ("Benefit the People") Foodstuffs Factory, which was roughly the same as Jiang's given name. As the only party member in the factory, Jiang was given the added title of chief of administration. Changing bosses was not as easy as all that, though, even for party members. Ideological disputes and civil war had left the Communist Party with a heightened fear of spies in its midst by the time the People's Republic was founded. Jiang was a party member, but, as we have seen, he had not played a leading role in party activities in the three years since the issuing of his card. Indeed, the war-hardened Communist commanders from northern China could hardly have trusted their pampered Shanghai comrades, with their well-oiled hair and shiny shoes.

"We wear homespun cloth, but you wear nicely pressed Western style clothing," commented Commander Chen Yi, one of the Shanghai military commission members, shortly after marching into the city. "How can you serve the people? You are still people of the old society!"[10]

The order soon came down that all underground party members in Shanghai must undergo "training and rectification." The one-on-one interrogation sessions, to be held in the town of Songjiang, twenty-five miles southwest of Shanghai, were aimed at weeding out suspected Nationalist agents and checking for bourgeois tendencies in others. Crash courses in party organization principles were also to be arranged for those who passed muster.

"It's going to be a tough winter," Jiang is reported to have muttered to his colleagues in North Jiangsu dialect as they marched out of town. It appeared they were in for a long spell in the rural town. "Ideological rectification is not easy," Jiang remarked.[11]

There is no record of what transpired in Songjiang, much less of how Jiang fared during what turned out to be only a month-long inquisition. But the evidence suggests that he passed with flying colors. By the end of July, Jiang was back in the Yimin factory with two new titles to his name. One, first deputy factory director, probably just reflected his status in the administrative hierarchy. But the other, party branch chief, was more important. It was his first leadership role in the Chinese Communist Party.

There is a minor irony here. If Jiang's factory had not been seized by the Nationalists in the first place, it might have remained in foreign hands for a few years yet. The Communist takeover of China's biggest capitalist enclave was gentle at first. Capitalists were able to hold on to their factories until mass nationalization began in 1954. But as chance had it, Jiang found himself sitting on top of a key state enterprise the moment the Communists walked in the door. Overnight, he became a key cadre in the party-controlled Shanghai industrial sector.

Factory work was the new way up the ladder of the Communist hierarchy that would distinguish Jiang's "third" generation from its predecessors. The "second generation," as represented by Deng, gained influence on the battlefield. The "first generation" under Mao emerged out of rancorous ideological debates. Distinction in the new era would be achieved in the grimy world of Soviet-style industrial development.

But Jiang was suited to the new battleground. Since leaving Yangzhou for university at the age of 17, he had matured from the bookish son of small-time rural intellectuals into a junior party organizer in China's most cosmopolitan city. At the age of just 23, he was already showing signs of the irrepressible good nature that would serve him well in the difficult years of Maoist China. That nature, born of a happy childhood, would later develop into something approaching buffoonery, but in the early 1950s, it was perfectly suited for an industrial cadre.

Accordingly, life at the Yimin Foodstuffs Factory quickly changed under Jiang's leadership. The Pretty Lady brand name was replaced by the Glorious (*guangming*) brand product line. Rousing renditions of Communist worker songs became part of the daily routine during work breaks. In 1950, when repeated power shortages occurred as power supply was nationalized, Jiang rallied the workers with Communist standards like "We Workers Have the Power," a ditty he would later belt out whenever he visited a major state factory.

Yimin was at first put under the auspices of the national defense industry, since it had been owned by the Nationalist army. This at least assured it of a captive market for many of its canned foods, some of which were shipped to North Korea during the Korean War. At home, confusion abounded about how to behave in the planned economy being introduced piecemeal by Beijing. "I remember having to advertise our Glorious-brand products," Jiang would recall. "We took aim at consumers and came up with new ideas in order to grab a bigger market share. Everything depended on making an effort."[12]

The crash course in marketing in a Stalinist economy did not last long. A year later, Jiang was pulled from Yimin and sent to help take over a former British concern in Shanghai, the China Soap Factory. The factory had been operating at only half capacity, and at a loss, since its expatriate managers had fled in 1949. Jiang became first deputy director.[13] Although hardly salutary, the transfer did have one important spin-off for Jiang. It brought him into contact with Wang Daohan, the 36-year-old head of the East China Industry Department, to which the newly nationalized soap factory belonged. Wang, a short, stocky Anhui native, had fought in the Jiangsu-Anhui border area where Jiang's uncle had died. He had also graduated from Jiaotong University.

It appears that Wang saw something he liked in Jiang very early. Whether because of their historical ties or because Jiang simply impressed him, Wang staked his claim to Jiang right away. It turned out to be Jiang's ticket out of the state factory ghetto. The moment he was made vice-minister of the newly created First Machine-Building Ministry in Beijing in 1952, Wang sent Jiang to the ministry's Number Two Design Bureau in Shanghai as head of a new electrical power equipment department.

The design bureau was one of several set up as part of a Soviet-style industrialization effort and would receive ample funding. The move for Jiang was not a promotion in rank. Coming under the nurturing and protective wing of Wang Daohan, however, was an important change. It was the beginning of a patronage that would last for four decades.

2

For all his promise in the party, Jiang Zemin was no Adonis. He was short, had bad eyes, and still spoke in the disdained accent of North Jiangsu. In his lengthy stay in Shanghai, he appears to have had little luck romancing the emancipated belles of the cosmopolitan city. As models of a new "socialist lifestyle," young party cadres were expected to marry early, however, and Jiang's decision in December 1949 to wed his high-school sweetheart, Wang Yeping, a stout, chipmunk-faced woman of about his own age, was perhaps all but inevitable.[14]

Jiang claims that he had been deeply in love with Wang since their
youthful days playing together along Yangzhou's willow-lined canals.
"There was an innocent affection between them from childhood," says
one official report.[15] Other motives were probably also present, however. Ties between the two families were already strong. Wang was the
niece of Jiang's foster mother, Wang Zhelan. [16] Jiang, of course, had been
handed over to Wang Zhelan after the death of Jiang Shangqing in order to be the family heir. That meant he needed a wife; if she was from
within the extended family, then all the better. We know that Jiang's
grandmother "took the lead" in introducing Wang Zhelan to Jiang
Shangqing, a loaded phrase in Chinese, indicating that the marriage was
pre-arranged.[17] It would make sense for Wang Zhelan to have done the
same for her niece and adopted son.

Jiang's wife turned out to be a quiet and unassuming woman. One
mainland writer explains their differences this way: "He has a wide range
of interests, is clever and open-minded, has organizational ability and
likes to show off, whereas she is introverted, accommodating, kind, and
hospitable."[18] Still, Wang was not the kind of uneducated rural girl favored by leaders like Mao. Her father owned a small stationery and crafts
shop in Yangzhou, "earning not very much, but enabling him to support
his family and to put his daughter through middle school," one report
explains.[19] It was no mean accomplishment in that era. In turn, it won
Wang entrance to Shanghai's Foreign Languages College at the same time
that Jiang entered university there. Jiang often stayed with Wang's family while he was studying in Shanghai.

After the nuptials, Jiang's factory dormitory was their first matrimo-
nial home. Wang's mother moved in along with them.[20] Family planning in the early 1950s existed but was only loosely enforced. Still
ahead was Mao's disastrous appeal to the nation to bear more children,
which caused a population explosion and forced the introduction of the
hated one-child policy in 1979. In the 1950s, family planning was
aimed more at ensuring healthy babies. In 1952, the same year that
Jiang's career took a critical turn with his transfer to the Shanghai design bureau, his first son, named Mianheng, or "Gentle and Persever-
ing," was born. It was the year of the dragon, symbol of power. Two
years later came another son, named Miankang, or "Gentle and
Healthy."[21] In the China of Jiang's youth, having two sons was a iron-
clad guarantee of a happy old age. Although he had been schooled in
Western science and was struggling to master the tenets of Marxism, it

could not have escaped Jiang's attention that his life was awash with auspicious signs.

3

The early years of the People's Republic sent confusing signals to the millions of Chinese who had fled to Taiwan and elsewhere abroad. Witch-hunts were launched against "counterrevolutionaries, enemy agents, and political bandits." At the same time, the Communists took an accommodating line on capitalist enterprises in hopes of resurrecting the country's war-battered economy. Not until 1952, when Leninist dictates began to drive economic policy as well, were hopes of a mixed economy and a moderate communist state thoroughly dashed.

In addition to the rapid nationalization of private concerns, the party in December 1952 began drawing up a Soviet-style five-year plan to run from 1953 to 1957. There was a lot of catching up to do. Industry accounted for only a quarter of the national economy, compared to nearly half in the Soviet Union. The state sector, meanwhile, was only a fifth of the national economy, versus an official 100 percent in the Soviet model. If China were to join the ranks of the industrialized world via socialism, both these ratios would have to grow rapidly. "We can make tables and chairs, teacups and teapots, grind grain into flour, and make paper, but we cannot make even a single car, plane, tank, or tractor," Mao complained.[22]

Wrangling delayed the completion of the plan as output targets for items like steel became bogged down in political infighting. After five major revisions, the plan was finalized in September 1954 and formally approved in July 1955. By then, it was half expired.[23]

As macroeconomic targets were agreed on, each ministry was asked to draw up its own mini-plan. Already known as a "red expert," or loyal party member with technical skills, Jiang Zemin was summoned to Beijing in early 1954 to help draw up the First Machine Building Ministry's blueprint for the period. Like his earlier transfer to the design bureau in Shanghai, on paper, it was not a promotion. But taking part in the drafting team did suggest that he was marked for greater things.

The transfer came at an inconvenient time: Jiang's second son had only recently been born. But questioning job assignments was politically risky then, and Jiang could count himself lucky not to have been sent to one of the inland areas targeted for much of the new industrialization. In any case, he was not the only member of his extended family to leave home to heed the call to national economic development. His youngest foster sister, Jiang Zehui, was sent to the Soviet Union for training in agriculture in 1955 at the age of 17, and his younger brother, Jiang Zekuan, had been assigned to the Zhenjiang Canned Foods Factory, across the river from Yangzhou.[24] Even his stepmother, Wang Zhelan, came to Shanghai to take up a job in a bank.[25]

Jiang may have reckoned on a short stay in Beijing, but being at the nerve center of the ministry's planning—and directly under the nose of his patron, Wang Daohan—he was soon rotated onto other projects as well. One of these, the Number One Vehicle Plant, was taking shape in Changchun, a frigid and featureless northeastern city that had bene-fited from extensive railway development early in the century and from heavy industry construction as the capital of Japan's puppet state of Manchukuo from 1933 to 1945.

The Changchun plant was one of hundreds of projects built under the auspices of a pact of proletarian solidarity signed with the Soviet Union in 1950. Mao described the bond as "lasting, unbreakable, and invinci-ble," but it would unravel with fury in less than a decade. Before then, though, China would reap huge dividends as the Cold Warrior of the East. Beginning in 1954, more than 400,000 Soviet industrial experts poured into the country to assemble an industrial sector that would sat-isfy Mao's desire to make more than just teapots. In addition, 10,000 Chinese were sent to the Soviet Union to learn and train. Even China's propaganda billboards—featuring belching factories, soaring space-ships, and spanner-clenching workers in overalls—were copied whole-sale from those in the Soviet Union.

The plans and technology for the Changchun plant came from the mammoth Stalin (later renamed Lihachov) Autoworks in Moscow. Dur-ing construction of the plant, more than 700 Chinese technicians were sent to Moscow to train at the Stalin works.[26] Among the pioneers set-ting up the plant was a 22-year-old commerce graduate from Fudan Uni-versity in Shanghai named Li Lanqing, who would later become a mem-ber of Jiang's Politburo standing committee.

Construction of the Changchun plant began in 1953. By October 1956, the first vehicle, a Liberation-brand truck, finally trundled off the line. A few years later, the plant would produce China's first sedan car, the East Wind, and a luxury line of sedans and limousines called Red Flag. The range of revolutionary-sounding brands was an unmistakable sign of China's confidence in its new Communist system. An elated Mao would herald the cars as the end of the "teapots and paper" era of

Chinese industry. "Finally," he would cry after zooming around the Zhongnanhai leaders' compound in Bejing at the wheel of an East Wind, "I am sitting in a car made by Chinese people!"[27]

Jiang was formally assigned to the Number One Vehicle Plant project in November 1954, a sign that he was on his way to Changchun. First, though, he would have to learn the power-supply system of the new factory inside and out. That meant a spell at the mother factory in Moscow.

Although Jiang had been fond of Russian literature in his youth, he had read it in Chinese translation, and learning Russian had come far behind English for most of his school days. After a four-month crash course in the language taught by Russian experts in Changchun, however, Jiang and a dozen fellow technicians from the plant boarded the Trans-Siberian Railway for Moscow in April 1955.[28]

It was Jiang's first time outside China, and he was already 28. Deng, by comparison, had boarded a liner for Marseilles on his own initiative in 1920, at the tender age of 16, to take part in a one-year work-study program in France, which turned into six years. Deng's was the generation that still believed in using Western ideas to scorch a sun-baked castle out of the "loose dish of sand" that was the Chinese nation, as Sun Yat-sen had described it. Jiang, by contrast, grew up in a generation that was less enamored of the West. The technology it possessed was valuable, but its organizing ideas could never be adopted by China, they believed. American support for the Nationalists and supposed toleration by the United States of Japan's remnant militarism were fresh in their youthful memories.

Jiang himself was also less eager to travel abroad than Deng, who had grown up thirsting to know about the world beyond the poor peasant household in inland Sichuan province where he was raised. While Jiang could claim an intellectual's affinity for Western music and literature, he had lived comfortably as a youth in the prosperous and educated milieu of the Yangtze River Delta region. Many Western delights were in any case available to him there. It took a job assignment to force Jiang from his homeland.

Jiang was nonetheless to remember his time in Moscow fondly. The city seems to have appealed to his worldliness; its culture and music were a welcome relief from the ravages the civil war had left behind at home. He strolled in the city's parks, striking up conversations with whomever came into sight. "We have to get past this language barrier by talking more and listening more," he told his less garrulous colleagues. "Don't

be so afraid of being embarrassed!"[29] Heavy Russian food also appealed
to his hearty appetite. The black bread called *khleb* was a favorite, a
dozen loaves costing only a few rubles.[30] Many years later, he would rise
at a diplomatic dinner for visiting Russian leaders in Harbin to belt out
the solo part of the popular Stalin-era song "Doleko, Doleko." "We have
been deprived of a great opera star!" Russian President Boris Yeltsin
would declare.[31]

At work in the vast Stalin Autoworks, Jiang sat patiently on a stool
in the central control room monitoring the power-supply instruments. It
was the closest he had been to such advanced technology. Although he
had not studied hard at university, he was learning far more as an up-
and-coming party cadre than were many of his more studious classmates,
now stuck in ancient factories at home. There was also a useful lesson
in sexual equality, since most of the technicians Jiang worked with were
female. For someone whose university class had been virtually all male,
it must have come as an eye-opener. When he visited the factory many
years later, it was these same women—many still in the same jobs—
whom he would remember best.[32]

After less than a year in Moscow, however, Jiang was a little homesick. With a wife and two young sons fending for themselves in Shanghai, his desire to return to China grew. When he gathered with the other
Chinese workers at the Stalin works, Jiang would take out the erhu he
had brought along and entertain them with old standards like the melan-
choly "Ballad of Liang Xiao." "An endless feeling for the motherland
would surge into my mind," he would recall.[33]

The homesick technicians were fortunately all brought back to
Changchun in early 1956 in order to help prepare for the plant's formal opening that summer. Jiang's position was deputy director of the
power office, subordinate only to a Russian technician and to the office
head, Chen Yunqu.[34] Chen, who had been a part-time engineering
teacher and model worker in Tianjin before being drafted to the
Changchun plant, was an "expert" plain and simple, not a party member. As the most senior party member in the office, Jiang therefore became the office's party chief.

Wang Yeping soon moved to Changchun, bringing their two sons.
There was a dilemma about what Wang would do. As a university graduate, she was entitled to a state job. But besides the auto plant,
Changchun offered very little else. The military's August 1st Film Studio, which made propaganda films, was the only major employer that
might have used her language skills. Jiang's contacts in Beijing helped

here. Wang was given a job as a researcher in First Machine-Building Ministry's Changchun Institute of Optical, Mechanical, and Electrical Studies, despite the fact that she had no background in science. Wang became a sort of "barefoot scientist," learning as she went, just like the novice medics known as "barefoot doctors" who were then spreading basic medical knowledge across the countryside. She would henceforth be officially described as a scientist.

Life was good for the Jiang family in Changchun. As a key technician in a key national industrial project, Jiang was assigned a three-room flat that was among the best China could offer, with a gas stove, a private toilet, and wooden floors, central heating, and double glazing to keep out the cold in winter, when temperatures in Changchun averaged minus 14°C (7°F).[35] One of the rooms was soon taken over by a young technician from the gas-works shop, who had come to Jiang complaining that he could not marry because he had no flat.[36]

The plant's other 30,000 workers were all accommodated in redbrick dormitories, which still serve the purpose today (although the workforce has expanded to 280,000). Kindergartens, shops, and hospitals, later to be considered an insufferable burden on state firms, were part of the social contract at the Changchun plant.

Jiang's first months in Changchun were the best. The spanking new plant churned out its quota of vehicles. He got along well with his Russian tutor, picking up Russian folk songs from him as they worked. After hours, Jiang and his men would play bridge or ping-pong. The carefree days would not last long, though. If Jiang had ever had hopes of being insulated from politics at the huge Changchun plant, these were quickly dashed by the movement against alleged "rightists" that broke out in 1956.

Mao had encouraged intellectuals to criticize the state. When many obliged by offering forthright opinions on the party's mistakes, Mao turned on half a million of them. Initially, there were to be only 4,000 "rightists" subjected to criticism nationwide. But by the end of the "anti-rightist campaign," over 550,000 had been dismissed from their posts, beaten, sent home, and sometimes maimed or killed.

The campaign came as a shock to Jiang. "I am a person who appreciates ability," he declared on joining the power office in Changchun. As party chief, Jiang had promoted several technicians who had grown up in the families of small merchants or landowners. "If his father was a capitalist, what does that have to do with him?" he wondered out loud.

The orders from party center were clear, however. As party chief of the power office, Jiang was told to "ferret out" a given quota of rightists from among his staff. A co-worker recalls that Jiang was not enthusiastic about the idea. "How can there be so many rightists here?" he complained to the union chief, Shen Yongyan. "All these young people were brought up and sent through university by the party itself!"[37]

The appeals had no effect. Jiang, "under pressure from upper levels," his co-worker Guang Yu explains, duly labeled two technicians in his power office as rightists. They were soon relieved of their jobs and sent away to the countryside for "socialist education," a byword for communist boot camp, where many were simply allowed to die. Jiang is said to have urged leniency for one of the victims he purged, a young man fresh out of college.

Jiang's apparent distaste for the task was understandable. As the adopted son of a party martyr and veteran of the Shanghai underground student movement, his own credentials were beyond reproach. But he had been brought up in a family that was bourgeois in all but name and educated, by his own admission, in a bourgeois education system. Moreover, his wife was the daughter of a merchant, although that was apparently never an issue in Jiang's case.

His revulsion at the campaign may also have been a result of the sufferings inflicted on his elder sister, Jiang Zefen, who had taken up teaching after graduating from middle school in Yangzhou a year before Jiang and had been assigned in 1949 to work at the primary school in Jiangduo, about 50 miles east of Yangzhou.[38] Her "crime" in 1957 was to speak up in defense of a man whom she believed had been unfairly branded a rightist. The price she paid for this selfless act was immediate reassignment to a makeshift peasants' school for a year. After that, she was sent home with a monthly stipend of just eight yuan.[39]

Jiang must have known of his sister's fate. But his relations with his siblings even then seem to have been distant, and he may simply have accepted it. Over two decades later, the party would seek to redress the injustices of the anti-rightist campaign. Those like Jiang Zefen whose cases had never been "documented" did not benefit, however. Not until Jiang rose to undreamed-of power over thirty years later would Jiang Zefen's monthly stipend finally be raised, in line with the prescribed policy, from thirty to seventy yuan per month.

Worse than the anti-rightist movement was to come. But it is worth pausing to consider how events had already changed Jiang. In his first decade as a party member, he had stood on the sidelines during party infighting, content to saw on his erhu while the ambitious engaged in faction building. Jiang even reportedly grumbled out loud about being sent to Songjiang for interrogation. He may have carried out some purges as party chief at the Yimin and China Soap factories in Shanghai, but these were apparently selective and comparatively mild.

. But now he was part of a mass movement. The psychology was different: don't question on principle, and make others pay to save yourself. Did this make Jiang a party hard-liner at age 30? Hardly. His grumbling and his own background suggest that he had serious reservations, although these were held in check. Like millions of other fresh-faced party members who had emerged during the civil war, Jiang saw that the rules of the game were changing. Being "red" was becoming more important than being "expert," and if Jiang and his family wanted to survive, he would have to lash out at the "dangerous elements" as viciously as the party required. Jiang was not a party hard-liner; he was simply learning to survive in Mao's China.

4

During the debate over the first five-year plan, Mao complained that other top leaders were too timid in setting economic goals—"tottering along like a woman with bound feet," as he called it. Indeed, the early years of the plan suggested that more impressive results could be attained; industrial growth averaged 18 percent between 1952 and 1957, about four percentage points above the planned rate.[40] This gave Mao the justification he needed to imagine what none had dared. The party, despite the purges of its first decade in power, was riding a wave of prestige in the country, and revolutionary élan was everywhere apparent. Touring the country in the spring and summer of 1958, Mao called for a "great leap forward" in economic development. China, he said, should catch up to Britain as an industrial power in fifteen years. By that fall, China was gripped by such a spasm of economic activity that some thought this might actually happen. It seemed as if the country was poised to jump into an economic time machine and emerge a century ahead of where it had left.

Mao's "great leap" bandwagon rolled into the Changchun car plant in February 1958. His visit was a parable of the period. Plant managers fell over themselves to set ambitious production targets. They pledged to quadruple production to 40,000 trucks a year, and halve unit costs. Five years later, they pledged, output would be up eightfold, and the range of models would be precisely seventy-three.[41]

These plans were clearly unattainable. But those who questioned them were branded "rightists" or "conservatives" and sent away for reeducation. Jiang, as usual, appears to have muttered under his breath about such travesties. "Jiang thought that those being branded conservatives had played an important role in raising different opinions about the [rapid] development and production plans," Guang Yu recalls. "He was very unhappy about it."

The smile on his young face obviously never wavered, though. When a new power plant was built in mid 1958 to attain the fantastical targets set in Mao's presence, Jiang was appointed director. It was a two-step promotion, because of the important role the plant was supposed to play in meeting the targets.[42] Making cars required huge amounts of steel, which the Changchun plant rolled and cut from steel billets itself. This in turn ate up inordinate amounts of power. As the vehicle production targets were ratcheted up to please Mao, power supply became the tightest bottleneck. Pushing the transformers beyond their limits, Jiang's power plant on one day reportedly rolled out over 112 tons of steel. This still fell short of the demand, however, and much of the resulting steel, to quote Li Shizheng, a worker at the time, who later became the plant's information head, was "useless for making cars."[43]

As steel shortages grew, plant managers devised ingenious methods to ensure that Chairman Mao would not be disappointed. Air pumps were made from wood, and car bodies were fashioned out of bamboo. Small steel beams were welded together for trucks when there were no long beams, an improvisation that Jiang later laughed about: "We plodded away small piece after small piece in order to complete a big piece," he said. "While the spirit we showed should be commended, it was not a scientific method and was eventually canceled."[44]

As a key state enterprise entitled to whatever resources it needed, the Changchun works might have been able to attain the targets set for Mao given enough time. But by late 1958, signs of economic calamity resulting from the spasm of misguided industrialization were beginning to emerge nationwide. Under Mao's call to "take steel as the key link," peasants and soldiers had scoured the mountains for ore to smelt and wood to burn. By the end of the year steel output had soared to 11 million tons. But more than three-quarters of it was substandard. Meanwhile, many sectors of the economy—such as services and transport—had been neglected. In the countryside, peasants were quickly reorganized into 26,000 supposedly high-efficiency communes with the aim of increasing grain yields by half. But they had neither the knowledge nor the means to engage in large-scale farming.

The combined effects of inappropriate industrial production and unsuccessful rural collectivization were devastating. Reports of famine were widespread by early 1959. The three years of starvation that followed claimed between twenty and fifty million lives—some say more. Food supplies reached the Changchun works, but the quality and quantity of all foods, even staples, fell precipitously. "We were very happy just to eat a pound of grain per day," Li Shizheng recalled.[45]

As reports of the scorched earth in the countryside poured in, workers at the Changchun works were dispatched to offer assistance. In the summer, they fought floods. In the winter, they repaired dikes. Jiang sat in the back of the trucks with his men on the way to nearby disaster areas, grimly leading songs to bolster their flagging spirits. It was a far cry from the spotless high-tech jobs they had been promised as workers at one of China's showcase industrial facilities.

Further calamity resulted from the withdrawal of all Soviet experts in 1959–60. Jiang's power plant lost several. Perhaps as a favor, the chief Russian engineer left Jiang a manual in Russian on energy conservation at car plants in the USSR, written by Jiang's former tutor at the Stalin works. Faced with sudden technical illiteracy, Jiang began feverishly translating this work, "The Rational Use of Electrical Power in Machine-Building Factories," in his spare time.

Jiang never finished the translation. When he left the power plant, he passed it on half-done to his successor as its director, Shen Yongyan. Shen eventually completed the translation, but the Cultural Revolution was to make publication impossible. It would be thirty years before Jiang's work was finally published, his only known book.[46] By then, he had moved well beyond the narrow academic confines of his earlier preoccupation, and the technology described was in any case hopelessly out-of-date. Most copies, priced at a mere Rmb3 each, were simply shipped to Changchun as mementos. Nonetheless, the book came to symbolize Jiang's single-minded attention to duty at a time when the country was experiencing economic collapse and social catastrophe. As befitted this symbolism, Jiang donated the minuscule proceeds to the Shanghai children's welfare fund.

By 1961, the Changchun plant was in a sorry state. Workers were doubling over on the production line from hunger. Little had been done to alleviate the steel shortages. And worst of all, the central government decided that the Changchun plant would have to help bear the burden of national fuel shortages. The original power generators at Changchun

ran on refined oil and coal, resources plentiful in the Soviet Union but
scarce in China. The first well in the huge Daqing oil field in nearby Heilongjiang province had gushed in 1960, but output of the refined products needed at the Changchun works was minimal. Coal from Datong
in Shanxi province, meanwhile, was apportioned on a strictly egalitar-
ian basis among major state enterprises.

As a last resort, Zhou Jiannan, deputy minister of the First Machine-
Building Ministry, decided to convert the power plants of several large
factories—including Changchun—to heavy crude oil. It was a wildly audacious decision in retrospect, but at the time it seemed to make sense.
If successful, it would keep the factories running, while at the same time
conserving scarce refined products. But no one in China knew how to
burn unrefined oil in power plants. It was a new technology and the Russians, who might have helped, had walked out in a diplomatic huff.

Jiang was given two months to convert almost the entire Changchun
power plant to burning crude oil, leaving only a small portion still burning coal. He quickly assembled a working group of plant experts for the
project. At their first planning meeting, he faced a torrent of complaints.

"This is crazy! We might cause a serious accident," Zhou Huaifei, the
deputy director of the technology department, said.[47]

"Don't let the pressure get to you," Jiang replied. "If we show some
determination, even the most unfamiliar technologies can be mastered."

Few were convinced. Hadn't many workers been killed at the Daqing
field because of unsafe handling of crude oil? Jiang finally admitted the
risk: "Maybe some problems will occur that we had not expected," he
said. "But the party and the people will forgive us. They'll understand."

Over the next few months, four towering fuel tanks, each with a capacity of 1,000 cubic meters, were built to handle the new oil supplies.
Using manuals left behind by the Russians, the novice technicians refit-
ted the power plant and set up what they hoped would be a safe supply
mechanism. Progress was slow, but Jiang was desperate to meet the two-
month deadline. Three shifts of workers were thrown at the project around the clock to fulfill a work schedule usually handled by four
shifts. When workers fell ill, Jiang drew replacements from other parts
of the plant.

In the end, it took three and a half months. But the conversion was
completed and became a model for other enterprises struggling to meet
the same demands from Beijing. The unrelenting schedule left Jiang with
acute stomach problems, though. For much of the hectic period, he had
eaten on the run or not at all. Colleagues often saw him massaging his

stomach with his right hand.[48] Blood began to show up in his urine.[49] For the rest of his life, he would be unable to eat the cold steamed buns common in workers' canteens. "Don't ignore food," he would tell workers in the Datong coal mine many years later, after learning that they were skipping meals to save money. "I did that during the Great Leap Forward and have suffered ever since."[50]

Beginning in late 1961, party leaders began a belated attempt to mitigate the disastrous results of Mao's failed Great Leap Forward. Cadres at every level had been touring the country since the beginning of the year and reporting in no uncertain terms the tragedy they saw. The reports, sent up to Beijing, allowed leaders like Chen Yun and Deng Xiaoping to urge a partial undoing of the collectives thrown together with such undue haste.

By late 1961, private vegetable gardens, free markets, and results-based pay were reintroduced within limits in rural areas. And state factory managers who had exaggerated their production were being sacked or demoted. In early 1962, Jiang was finally transferred away from the Changchun plant back to a research institute in Shanghai. It was a promotion, and there is no evidence that he was being punished as one of the "leftists" who had overestimated the potential of the "Great Leap Forward" at the Changchun works.

Years later, Jiang would be chauffeured around the precincts of Beijing in a sporty black V-6 sedan made at the Changchun plant in a joint venture with the German concern Audi GmBH. By then, production of all models at the plant would be around 300,000 vehicles a year, ten times the number in Jiang's day and many more than the targets set for Mao. Jiang's spiritual and collegial contacts with the plant would remain strong. He would invariably show up at plant anniversaries and would frequently swap stories about his Changchun days with Russian and Chinese friends.

Jiang's six-year stint in Changchun was salutary from many perspectives. He had visited Moscow, leapt up the promotions ladder, and emerged with a reputation as a reliable technician who could organize and lead others. More interesting, the period at Changchun witnessed Jiang's emergence as what we might call an "everyman leader." A master of the possible, he soldiered on even when others were hesitant. He did not try to lead by eliminating opponents. If others disagreed, he let them sit on the sidelines and went ahead on his own.

His appeals were not by reference to high-sounding objectives but by a slightly imperious personal suasion. A buffoon who broke into Russian song without request to rally the workers, he threatened no one and amused many. His lasting reputation at the plant was that of a man not afraid to lose face to get the job done or break down personal barriers. These traits were hardly likely to inspire awe. But then Jiang had no illusions of grandeur.

"When he lost at ping-pong with the workers, he would go to the end of the line to wait his turn to play again," Guang Yu recalled. "He was not at all pompous. . . . That's why people liked him."[51]

5

In the eight years Jiang was assigned to the Changchun plant, Wang Daohan had clung tenaciously to his vice-ministership in the First Machine-Building Ministry. His experience was similar to Jiang's, at first reluctantly helping to purge a quota of rightists and then vying with colleagues to set the most outrageous output goals for ministry factories. In 1962, as the economy was being pulled back from near collapse, Wang decided that he wanted his bright researcher back. His invisible hand brought Jiang out of Changchun and into the ministry's Shanghai Electrical Equipment Research Institute as deputy director.

The three years Jiang spent at the institute are a sort of blank in the official memory, like his earlier "undistinguished" period working for foreign and Nationalist factory bosses. The hush may be simply because of the short period he was there. But it may also relate to the sensitive nature of the work the institute was conducting. One Hong Kong report has said that the projects involved military radar and electronic communications under instructions from both the ministry and the PLA.[52] That would explain why, as newly promoted institute director in early 1965, Jiang made his first trip to Hong Kong, China's main conduit for purchases of sensitive technology. It was only his second time outside the country.

The new Jiang family home was in the Caoyang new town in the northwestern suburbs of Shanghai, a one-hour bus ride from the institute. It was a relief for the family to be back in the city. Changchun had been a hardship posting, and although the new family quarters were more cramped, the city was livable in most other respects. Jiang's eldest son, Mianheng, was ready for first grade, while Miankang was entering kindergarten. And Wang Yeping's mother was getting too old to live in the harsh environment of Changchun.

Wang Yeping's switch to scientific research while in Changchun meant she could also rely on the munificence of Wang Daohan for a new job. Since Jiang's institute was expanding, she was given a post there as general affairs secretary. Although her husband would soon move on, Wang would remain at the institute for more than twenty years, rising to deputy director and then director of research before retiring.[53]

Riding through the streets of Shanghai on their way to work each day, lunchboxes in hand, as inseparable as the Mandarin ducks that symbolize devoted couples in Chinese culture, Jiang and Wang must have looked a loving pair. It turned out to be the golden time in their marriage. Ahead was an almost two-decade separation, which would leave Wang weary and sick. Just as the family bliss attending Jiang's arrival in Changchun had heralded political turmoil ahead, his joyous return to Shanghai portended a coming period of strife.

Indeed, Jiang or Wang might have seen the first sign of this while they bounced their way to work on their bus on the morning of 10 November 1965. Scanning the morning edition of Shanghai's *Wenhui bao* (Wenhui Daily) newspaper, they would have found a stridently worded commentary on the play *Hai Rui Dismissed from Office*, a new historical drama by a vice-mayor of Beijing, Wu Han.

In the commentary, an obscure writer in the Shanghai propaganda department, Yao Wenyuan, censured the play as a barely veiled attack on Mao's own rule. The commentary was unusual on two counts. For one, Mao himself had urged cadres in 1959 to learn from the example set by Hai Rui, a Ming dynasty official who had returned land confiscated from peasants and scolded the emperor to his face for ruling badly, losing his job as a result. In addition, the review attacked Wu Han by name and suggested he had been put up to writing the play by more senior party leaders. Ideological politics in China rarely transgressed the unwritten rule of not attacking people by name. The breach was an ill omen.

Sure enough, Yao had not acted in isolation in writing the commentary. Egging him on were Mao's third wife, a mediocre Shanghai actress named Jiang Qing, and Zhang Chunqiao, another Shanghai propaganda hack. Along with a factory worker named Wang Hongwen, they were to make up the notorious Gang of Four, which would bring China closer to anarchy than it had known this century.

The Hai Rui editorial was soon reprinted nationwide. It was one of the most obvious, but by no means the only, incident that fed Mao's swelling paranoia about being surrounded by enemies within the party.

By March 1966, he was so convinced of a conspiracy to subvert his rule that he urged local party organizations to rise up and "assault" the party's Central Committee, "the palace of hell," as he called it. The "Cultural Revolution" that his devious appeal set off would engulf the country for the next three years and ruin millions of lives and careers.

As the rumblings of the Cultural Revolution grew in May 1966, Jiang was transferred to a newly established Thermal Power Machinery Research Institute under the First Machine-Building Ministry, up the Yangtze River in Wuhan. Again, Wang Daohan seems to have been behind the move. Partly, it may have been a prescient attempt to protect his protégé from the coming political storm by stealing him out of Shanghai. It may also have been because as director and party chief of the Wuhan institute, Jiang would be given the enviable role of helping launch China into the age of nuclear power.

China had detonated its first atomic bomb two years earlier, but its progress in harnessing this unimaginable power for civilian use had been spotty. Not until 1991 would the country's first nuclear power plant open, at Qinshan on Hangzhou Bay, south of Shanghai.

This move to a completely new field of research was not unusual for those days. Faced with international isolation, China had to reinvent every wheel, and anyone with a modicum of knowledge to offer was deployed to assist with each spoke. It was an enviable position to be in. Jiang had the opportunity to make his name as one of the fathers of China's civilian nuclear industry.

The gathering ferocity of the Cultural Revolution ended such hopes. The first gusts lashed the First Machine-Building Ministry in November, when the minister since 1960, Duan Junyi, was fired for being a "capitalist roader." Within days, the storm struck the rest of the ministry. Vice-ministers Zhou Zijian and Zhou Jiannan were forced to stand down. Stranded in Wuhan with little information on the situation in Beijing, Jiang took advantage of the month of home leave to which he was entitled to apprise himself of the situation. The route he took during that month is unclear. By one account, he first traveled to Beijing to compare notes with colleagues in the ministry headquarters.[54] Wang Daohan had been sent to the countryside along with Duan and would not reappear for over a decade. But Jiang may have had other, less vulnerable contacts whom he trusted. Armed with information on the parlous situation in Beijing, Jiang is said to have headed for Shanghai, where he was in any case supposed to be visiting his family. The scenes there were worse. When he arrived, Red Guards were massing in front of the municipal party office on a daily basis demanding the removal of the municipal party chief, Chen Pixian, and the mayor, Cao Diqiu. Dressed down in an old army tunic and a floppy-eared cotton hat, Jiang is said to have witnessed the ugly Kangping Road Incident on 30 December, the overrunning of the party office that marked the onset of the violent stage of the Cultural Revolution. Chen Pixian was subjected to three "struggle and criticism" sessions broadcast live on national television over the next four months. He would then disappear for over a decade.

We have no official reports to confirm that Jiang was making the rounds to get a reading on the political situation at this time. Later events would show him to be just as low-key and keen to avoid politics as ever. But as party chief of the Wuhan institute, Jiang was already a lower-ranking member of the party's ruling elite, a mere thirteen grades below Chairman Mao himself. Although he had served the capricious dictates of the party as best he could, he could become a target of criticism merely for being the director. It would have made sense for him to prepare by taking the pulse of the movement.

"As the Cultural Revolution approached, Jiang was bound to be attacked," Wang Xiaopeng, a mainland biographer, points out. "He was a technical expert with the makings of a leading cadre. It was inevitable that he would be forced to stand down."[55]

Returning to Wuhan in January 1967, Jiang was probably little surprised to find the institute buildings plastered with "big character" posters denouncing his workstyle. "Jiang Zemin is expert but not red!" said one of the posters, which were usually daubed in black ink on red or white paper. "Jiang Zemin worships foreign things!" accused another. The charges were standard for the day. Youthful Red Guards were everywhere instructed to rise up against those in power. Scant consideration was given to differences among individuals. Jiang, though, was not exactly vulnerable to criticism. As the adopted son of a revolutionary martyr, his provenance was beyond reproach. And although he displayed little of the revolutionary fervor of other cadres, he was also not one to speak out against the party.

The same reticence was not shared by an elderly man surnamed Yang who headed the institute's general office. A former security guard in the Zhonghanhai leaders' complex in Beijing, Yang had written three letters to the Central Committee criticizing the emerging Gang of Four for being unreasonable over the Hai Rui affair. That won him the serious label of "reactionary," a charge not leveled against the tight-lipped Jiang.

"Old Yang, listen to me," Jiang commiserated with his comrade in disrepute, hoping to keep Yang's tongue in check. "You're a good comrade. Have faith that as long as there are party elders in good health and an army to back them up, it's not the end of the world. Your problem will be solved eventually."[56]

Jiang's vulnerable points were superficial. For one thing, he was a graduate of the elitist Yangzhou Middle School, which had been overrun at the onset of the Cultural Revolution by Red Guards, who painted huge slogans in red paint on the two-story, gray-brick teaching buildings urging a "thoroughgoing reform" of its "feudal teaching." They also plastered over the foundation stone on the elegant Shuren teaching hall because the year was given according to the old Nationalist calendar, and boarded over the sign of the old gymnasium because the letters were written in traditional Chinese characters.[57] Jiang's fellow Yangzhou Middle School alumnus Hu Qiaomu, by then the number two in charge of party propaganda, was publicly humiliated in January 1967 for being the son of a wealthy landlord.

Jiang's heroic efforts at the Changchun car plant and his humble lifestyle probably helped save him. The sum total of his possessions in Wuhan, aside from clothes, books, and personal hygiene items, were an old leather suitcase, a kerosene stove, and a transistor radio. Colleagues recalled his insistence on not using the institute's kerosene supplies when refilling his stove. "Public property is public property, and private property is private property," Jiang explained. "We have to keep the distinction clear."[58]

More incriminating, comically enough, was his hair. Since university days, Jiang had worn his mane long, as was the style then in Shanghai. Brushed straight back from his long, sloping forehead, it suited his broad face. By then, too, Jiang had also developed an almost compulsive habit of combing his hair, keeping a small wooden comb and a vial of oil in his breast pocket for the purpose like talismans. "His hairstyle and wide-rimmed glasses made him look quite distinguished," a colleague recalls. "But it brought him trouble when someone suggested: 'It's nearly the 1970s and he still wears his hair in the 1930s style!'"[59]

Sensing that his plumage was under suspicion, Jiang ducked into a local barber shop on returning to Wuhan. When the first cropping failed to appease the critics, Jiang went back to the barber and ordered a bristly brush cut. "You need long hair to look good. Don't do this!" the barber urged. "I won't be off the hook until it's short," Jiang replied. "I have to adapt to the situation."[60]

When Jiang returned to his dormitory patting his fuzzy pate, his room-mate laughed out loud. "No need to worry about any hair-splitting over your problems now," the roommate joked, guffawing at his own humor. "You'll definitely pass the test!"[61]

When that test came, Jiang was ready for anything. His temporary suspension had remained in force pending an "examination." When the examination day came, Jiang had little truck with the interrogator, an unlucky student named Liu Zhenhua. The exchange between them was short and sharp. Short-haired and wrapped in an old woolen coat, Jiang rejected charges of leading a bourgeois lifestyle. "Outrageous!" he cried. "My dormitory blanket is worm-eaten. My synthetic leather purse is falling apart. Look for yourselves!"

Liu shuffled his feet.

"You young students should cool down and learn how to analyze problems," Jiang continued. "Use your brains for God's sake! Then you'll see something of the truth!"[62]

Jiang obviously got off without much difficulty. Cutting his hair and standing up to the frightened youth with the misfortune to confront him seems to have got him through the difficulties. But his suspension would remain in force for a few years yet. At 41, at a time when his career had just begun to take off, Jiang was left twiddling his thumbs.

He had little to do for the next year. Research at the institute was brought to a virtual standstill while Red Guard factions battled it out in the streets of Wuhan. In July 1967, Wuhan would be the site of an up-rising by a rebel faction in the army that threatened to plunge the whole country into armed conflict. When curious young researchers at the institute asked Jiang to join them as spectators of the pitched street battles, he demurred. "You'd be better off using this time to learn new things," he urged in his avuncular way. "I've seen the advanced societies of the world and their level of development. We won't get anywhere without culture and knowledge."[63]

Practicing what he preached, Jiang appears to have become something of a one-man college in all the spare time afforded by his suspension. By day, he offered language tutorials in English and Russian to young re-searchers. "Given the chaotic situation in 1967, it was a miracle that he could get any teaching done at all," Wang Xiaopeng notes.[64] By night, Jiang read Mao's collected works in English, a politically correct way of maintaining his competence in the language. He also studied books on nuclear reactors, hoping that some day the research he was supposed to be undertaking would resume.[65]

Being sidelined also meant that Jiang was treated like any other worker. The single room he was allotted at first was soon occupied by another young researcher. Soon, two more joined them. When the wife of one of the researchers came to visit, the thoughtful Jiang suggested to his roommates that they leave the sex-starved couple alone for a few nights. "We all left to find other beds to sleep in," one of the evicted roommates recalled. "What else could we say?"[66]

Worse was in store for Jiang. By his own admission, the most depressing moment he experienced came on 9 October 1967, when Premier Zhou Enlai arrived in Wuhan accompanying the visiting Albanian prime minister, General Mehmet Shehu. In the minds of millions of intellectuals like Jiang, Zhou represented a small bud of hope flowering in the vast and bleak Maoist landscape. Zhou was at this time trying to rein in the Red Guards, just as he had earlier attempted to alleviate the excesses of the Great Leap Forward. Few people yet blamed Mao directly for either catastrophe—believing them to be either aberrational errors by the Great Helmsman or evidence of insubordination. Zhou was admired because he was seen as a true defender of Mao's fundamentally beneficent rule, not as an opponent.

When Zhou arrived in the city to take Shehu to see the Wuhan Boiler Factory, all the staff at Jiang's nearby institute were called out to line the streets in welcome. But six senior staff sidelined by the Cultural Revolution, including Jiang, were locked up in an empty storage room instead.

"Up to this very day, my biggest regret is not having been allowed to see Premier Zhou that day," Jiang is quoted as saying. The memory apparently elicits a despondency rarely seen in the normally upbeat Jiang. "It's rare to see Jiang get so depressed and troubled about something," Wang Xiaopeng notes.[67]

Other members of Jiang's family suffered more. His uncle, Jiang Shixiong, was killed by Red Guards in Shanghai early in the Cultural Revolution.[68] He was probably only in his mid to late fifties at the time, and there is no information on the circumstances of his death. More mysterious was the death of his father, Jiang Shijun, who died in 1973, aged 78.[69] Since being adopted by his uncle, Jiang had ceased making mention of his true father. Either they lost contact, or else Jiang was simply keen to pass himself off as the "son" of a revolutionary martyr. In any case, no mention was made of his father's death when it occurred. Given his age, Jiang's father may have died peacefully. But at least three family members had come in for political criticism in the previous decade, and it is natural to be suspicious about the circumstances surrounding this death as well.

The uncertain future faced by Jiang's two sons, who visited their father in Wuhan frequently while he sat it out in the political wilderness, was a more immediate question. The Cultural Revolution was as disruptive to the education and careers of the boys as the Japanese invasion and civil war had been to that of their father. When Jiang's eldest son, Mianheng, graduated from lower middle school aged 14 in 1966, further studies were impossible for him. Instead, he was sent to the countryside as one of the 16 million "educated youths" detailed to improve their lifestyles through rustication.[70] Three years later, the party began breaking up the entire higher education system, putting factories and local revolutionary committees in charge of universities. Within two years, the number of tertiary institutions had fallen by a quarter, to 328. University places were allocated only to peasants and workers. As the son of a sidelined cadre, Mianheng didn't stand a chance. With little else to do, he took a job in the warehouse of a state grain store in Shanghai.[71] His younger brother Miankang, meanwhile, shrugged his shoulders on leaving lower middle school in 1968 and joined the army. Not until the reintroduction of university exams in 1979 would both boys finally enter college.

6

Probably half a million people out of an urban population of around 135 million died as a direct result of the Cultural Revolution.[72] They were thrown from windows, beaten senseless in the street, or died from heart attacks under the daily threats and humiliation they were forced to endure. Many simply took their own lives.

Jiang would later call the Cultural Revolution "a period of unprecedented destruction." He could count himself lucky in some respects. He had escaped being sent to the countryside and was spared the casual physical and psychological violence inflicted on others. His fate was similar to that of Deng Xiaoping, who after being named the "number two enemy" in the party in 1967 was confined to his home but spared gratuitous abuse.

More interesting is the comparison of Jiang's fate with those of the men whom he would later join at the citadel of power. His then fellow power industry worker, Li Peng, later premier, escaped virtually unscathed as head of the Beijing municipal power administration. Mainly, this was because Li was the son of a party martyr, Li Shuoxun, who had been decapitated on Hainan island in 1931 after being arrested by the

Nationalists. Li Peng had also studied in Moscow and headed the student Communist association there, which gave him "both red roots and straight shoots," as the revolutionary saying went.[73]

Less fortunate was a straight-talking young engineer from Hunan province named Zhu Rongji, later to succeed Li Peng as premier. Zhu had been expelled from the party during the anti-rightist campaign in 1957, but kept his job in the State Planning Commission until the Cultural Revolution, when he was packed off to an agricultural labor camp for five years. Meanwhile, the then party secretary of Guangdong province, Zhao Ziyang, later party general secretary, was put under house arrest for four years and later forced to work in Inner Mongolia for another year.

As a commonsense rule of thumb, the more a person suffered during the Cultural Revolution, the more liberal their political views seemed to be later. By this rule, Jiang would be expected to be in the middle. He did suffer, but only mildly. His faith in the party was tried but not shaken.

Without a doubt, though, the Cultural Revolution changed Jiang. Ten years earlier, on leaving the Changchun plant, he was emerging as an "everyman's leader." He bore the burden of responsibility handed him by the party in a good-natured and humble way. He rarely engaged in politics. He was heroic, or at least he wanted to be. He was building China. The Jiang Zemin whom we see emerge after being bullied by Red Guards is more politically astute. The buffoonery surfaces less often, and criticism is taken more personally. Contacts are cultivated more assiduously in Beijing.

As his career progressed, Jiang continued to bear these scars of the Cultural Revolution. And if there was one outward manifestation in him of the end of the Cultural Revolution, it was this: Jiang immediately grew his hair long again and would thereafter spend a small fortune keeping it jet black, well oiled, and combed to perfection.

As his barber said: "You look better that way."

PART 2

Mr. Tiger Balm, 1970–1988

CHAPTER 3

Foot Soldier for Deng

I

If there was one salutary legacy of Jiang's time on the sidelines during the Cultural Revolution, it was that he finally learned to swim. After a lifetime of failed attempts, floundering first in the canals of Yangzhou and later at the Jiaotong University swimming pool, Jiang finally paddled to success along the inviting shores of Donghu Lake in eastern Wuhan.[1] It was a perfect way to while away the tribulations of his suspension and a symbolic gesture of his desire to return to work.

In July 1966, over a year before Jiang mastered the waves, Mao Zedong had made a public display of his own vigor by plunging into the Yangtze River and swimming a distance at "four times world record speed."[2] Going for a dip came to prefigure political comebacks in Chinese politics and would be used for this purpose by Deng Xiaoping and the future premier Li Peng in later years.

Jiang was ready to return too. But the road back from state crisis was long and twisted. With the breakup of the Central Cultural Revolution Group under Jiang Qing in late 1969, the worst excesses of the turmoil were past. Over the next seven years, tentative steps toward rebuilding the state would be made on the ground even as court politics in Beijing remained as divided as ever. Jiang Qing's Gang of Four would seize control of the Central Committee at the party's tenth congress in 1973. But

by then her enemies were too numerous, and Mao's health was too feeble, to permit her wild dictates to be implemented. Three years later, the
Gang would be arrested, tried, and jailed.

At the party's ninth congress in April 1969, several former ministers
and vice-ministers were partially rehabilitated. The clearing of the skies
after the stormy years at the First Machine-Building Ministry was
patchy at first but never in doubt. Among those brought back in late
1969 were the former vice-ministers Zhou Zijian and Rao Bin, who
were made vice-chairmen of its "revolutionary committee." As a vice-
minister of the State Economic Commission in the 1950s, Rao had su-
pervised the construction and early operation of the Changchun auto
plant.[3] Meanwhile, the former minister, Duan Junyi, popped up as
Sichuan party secretary in 1971.

Jiang Zemin's comeback began in 1970. More than three years after
being sidelined, he was summoned to Beijing by the newly restored ministry leadership. It was still the twilight of the Cultural Revolution, so
Jiang's reassignment at first was under the pretense of enduring "labor
and thought reform" at the ministry's 7 May Cadres School.[4] Ironically,
even though it was a halfway house to rehabilitation, Jiang seems to have
endured his greatest Cultural Revolution deprivations while at the
school. Since it was a model of the ministry's revolutionary fervor, he enjoyed none of the little favors from sympathetic colleagues that had made
life bearable in Wuhan. "During my days at the 7 May Cadres School,"
he would recall, "we did not even have folding stools to sit on. When
we ate, we just squatted and gulped noodles from big bowls."[5]

The adversity lasted only a few months. Jiang was soon given a new
posting in the ministry's expanding Foreign Affairs Bureau. There is some
speculation that Premier Zhou Enlai personally approved the promotion. One report had him meeting Jiang for an hour to discuss the promotion. "That's minister material," Zhou was reputed to have said afterward.[6] There is no doubt that the promotion would have required the
endorsement of those in charge of China's diplomacy, which Zhou had
been given the unenviable task of maintaining in some semblance of nor-
mality during the Cultural Revolution. At least he would have known
of the appointment. For Jiang, even that was some recompense for having had to glimpse Zhou's procession through the steamed-up window
of a locked storeroom door in Wuhan.

Whoever it was who made the decision to bring Jiang into the Foreign Affairs Bureau, one thing is clear: Wang Daohan was nowhere in
sight. Wang had left the machine-building sector for a Foreign Trade

Ministry posting shortly before the Cultural Revolution and no longer had a direct say in the First Machine-Building Ministry's personnel decisions. Even an indirect say was unlikely, since at the time of Jiang's rescue, Wang was still toiling in the countryside. The families remained closely tied; Jiang's wife, for example, reportedly offered shelter to Wang's daughter when he was sent to the countryside.[7] But for once Jiang had to rely on other allies. Most likely, the newly rehabilitated leaders in the ministry simply shared Wang Daohan's glowing overall assessment of Jiang, a useful reminder that his career did not depend on the patronage of one man alone.

The move to Beijing was significant for Jiang as the end of what he would later call "my twenty-three years at the grass roots." Since graduating from university, he had served in factories and research institutes, but never in government offices. His party promotions had come step by step, but more as an adjunct to each job transfer. Jiang the official had always been subordinate to Jiang the engineer. That now changed.

There were, of course, practical reasons for Jiang's promotion to the Foreign Affairs Bureau. In the wake of the split with the Soviet Union, China was in a position of unprecedented international isolation and needed all the friends it could get. Checkbook diplomacy was a favored way to make friends, especially among the less-developed countries of Africa and Eastern Europe. Jiang's foreign-language skills and his experience working in Moscow would be useful.

One of the first beneficiaries of this new diplomacy was Romania. Premier Zhou visited the country in June 1969 to offer long-term, interest-free loans and the construction of several large industrial projects. Several ministries in the Chinese government were brought into the Romanian aid program. Headed by Jiang, a team from the First Machine-Building Ministry drew up plans to build fifteen machinery plants in the country. After a hastily arranged month-long tutorial in the Romanian language, the team flew to Bucharest at the end of 1970.

Jiang's Romanian adventure was different from his Moscow stint in two ways. For one, the Chinese were now the masters, not the apprentices. Despite the political turmoil of the intervening years, the Chinese economy had continued to advance, although slowly, and Chinese technologies were soon surpassing those in stagnant Eastern Europe. Jiang's personal role had also changed. Although his technical knowledge was put to use, his overriding responsibility this time was a diplomatic one. That meant that he would share in whatever blame or praise was handed out after the diplomatic gains of the projects were assessed.

That is probably why Jiang recalls the Romanian tour as being frantically busy, in contrast to his leisurely days in Moscow. One of the factories the team overhauled, the Bucharest Heavy-Duty Machinery Plant in the city's southern suburbs, was just seven years old and barely able to make a simple press when the Chinese arrived. By the time they left, plans had been set in motion to turn it into Romania's biggest machinery plant, making everything from railway-track equipment to towering heavy-duty cranes.[8]

Jiang fudged his way through the Romanian language, just as he had Russian, earning himself a reputation for speaking "North Jiangsu Romanian" but blustering on "for the sake of foreign relations."[9] When he revisited Romania a quarter-century later, he would speak in English, despite official assertions that he was "fluent" in Romanian.[10] The country's strong European and Latin flavor tweaked his interest, however. "That trip really opened my eyes to the world," he would recall.[11]

It seems the trip was also chalked up as a diplomatic success. Within two years of his return to China, in 1974, Jiang was made deputy director of the ministry's Foreign Affairs Bureau. By 1976, he was director, just two steps away from ministerial rank in the central government.[12]

We have little record of Jiang's time in the Foreign Affairs Bureau. We do know that since his own family remained stubbornly in Shanghai, he dined every Sunday night at one vice-minister's home.[13] The prestige of working in the diplomatic office was probably little recompense for the miserable conditions as a cog in the central government machinery in the 1970s. The dormitories the bureaucrats inhabited were so shabby that when an American-Chinese businessman came to visit one of Jiang's colleagues, ministry leaders asked the colleague to shift temporarily from the run-down dormitory to a more luxurious one in order to save face. Jiang thought this window dressing ridiculous. "It's silly to cover up the truth," he said. "The situation of intellectuals is like that. We have to face the facts."[14]

History was not long in rescuing Jiang from drudgery at the First Machine-Building Ministry, where he had seemed stranded.

2

The year 1976 brought momentous changes to China following the death of its two senior statesmen. Zhou Enlai, who had delivered his last speech a year earlier, gray and gaunt from cancer despite six major surgeries, died on 8 January. Mao, who had been mostly bedridden for the past two years, his ankles and legs swollen, his sight gone, finally succumbed on 9 September.

Within a month of Mao's death, on the night of 6 October, the Gang of Four were arrested at the Zhongnanhai complex in a midnight coup. Fears of an insurrection led by their allies were centered on Shanghai, which had remained under the strong influence of Jiang Qing ever since the appearance of the Hai Rui commentary a decade earlier. Restoring authority in the country meant first wresting back control over Shanghai.

"Shanghai was the most important stronghold of the Gang of Four," an official account recalls. "It was their second armed force, a fortress of stubborn reactionaries."[15]

Within days of the coup, the Shanghai revolutionary committee deployed 33,000 troops and militia on the streets and took over local media organs, ordering them not to broadcast any news supplied from Beijing. Days later, the Shanghai leaders were invited to Beijing for peace talks and offered an amnesty if they dropped their opposition to the coup. When the meeting took place in Beijing on 12 October, preparations were already under way to dispatch a team to Shanghai to occupy the party and government offices there. The team—led by the deputy commander of the navy, Su Zhenhua, and the Jiangsu party secretary, Peng Chong—was hastily thrown together. Su and then Peng would hold the post of Shanghai party secretary from 1976 until normalcy was restored in 1980.

Most Chinese did not learn of the arrest of the Gang of Four until the news was issued on 24 October. But when Jiang arrived at work on 16 October, there was already a message on his desk to report immediately to the office of the central party secretariat. Hustling down Fuxingmen Avenue from his office near the Deep Pool of Jade in the western district, Jiang could not have guessed his fate.

"There's a big job in Shanghai. You're being seconded," he was told by the secretariat staff. With his knowledge of industry and his experience in the city, Jiang was to join the fourteen-person "Central Committee Shanghai Work Group" that would nurse the city back to health.[16] The team flew to Shanghai on 19 October in a navy plane, hours after the city's revolutionary leaders had capitulated in Beijing.

It was by far the most politically sensitive task Jiang had ever undertaken. The group's aim, according to one of the only official histories of the period, was "to control the situation" in Shanghai.[17] Jiang was in charge of restoring the city's transport system and getting industry back on its feet.

The most delicate task, though, was sifting through the files of those whom the Gang of Four had put under house arrest or simply sidelined (who totaled 106,000 in the city as a whole) and deciding whom to rehabilitate. This also entailed dismissing cadres elevated unfairly. For the third time in his party career, Jiang was conducting the invidious task of "ferreting out" reactionaries. As in Shanghai just after the civil war and in Changchun during the anti-rightist movement, he did not prove an enthusiastic inquisitor.

The first move was to restore the former director and party chief of the Shanghai Bureau of Machinery, Jiang Shou and Xu Nianyi, respectively. At the same time, Jiang dismissed several of those promoted under the Gang of Four.[18] Old work rules were brought back into force— for example, allowing workers to don tough canvas overalls rather than impractical revolutionary tunics for their grimy tasks. Thousands of old production workers were rehired. The Shanghai work group was making similar amends at the top. Chen Pixian, the deposed Shanghai party chief, whom Jiang had reputedly visited at the onset of the Cultural Revolution, was given a new posting as party chief of Yunnan province.

Jiang's brief return to Shanghai lasted less than a year, during which he lived with his family in their flat in Caoyang new town. Although he would return to the First Machine-Building Ministry in Beijing, this spell with the Shanghai work group was significant, in that it showed that Jiang was slowly sloughing off his engineering past and emerging as a party leader. Again, historic changes would provide the next rung up the ladder.

3

Despite the seeming return to normalcy, Chinese politics remained in a mist of uncertainty in the two years after the arrest of the Gang of Four. Mao's chosen successor as party chairman, Hua Guofeng, seemed unable to lead the country anywhere but back to its pre–Cultural Revolution past. The sound of knives sharpening was everywhere audible. In July 1977, Deng Xiaoping, who fifteen months earlier had been dismissed by the Gang of Four, with Mao's barely conscious consent, won back his leading posts.

Jiang returned to Beijing in mid 1977. His mission in Shanghai had been ably handled, and the clean-out of Cultural Revolution cadres in the First Machine-Building Ministry was proceeding apace. Vice minis-

ter Zhou Zijian was soon elevated to minister, replacing the army officer who had headed the ministry's "revolutionary committee."

Jiang's position as director of the ministry's Foreign Affairs Bureau
was secure, but he appeared to have hit a glass ceiling in his career.[19] A
cast of old characters was reappearing at the top levels of the ministry,
choking up the promotions ladder. When two vice-ministerial posts
opened up in 1979, they were quickly filled by the heads of technical bureaus in the ministry. At the same time, foreign business dealings were
still the jealously guarded preserve of each ministry; Jiang seemed to
stand little chance of using his skills with another ministry.

Two events in late 1978 were to give his stalled career new life. The
first was the reappearance of Wang Daohan in his old post as vice-minister for foreign economic relations in September. The second was Deng's
triumphant maneuvering at a party conference in December to jettison
"class struggle" as the party's main objective and replace it with economic development, termed "socialist modernization."

These events furnished Jiang with both the personal backing and the
political environment he needed to put his abilities to better use. As a loyal
party member for thirty years, Jiang had already acquired a reputation
for competence and leadership. He had suffered personal humiliation but
not physical or psychological injury during the Cultural Revolution, sitting on the fringes of the main battles first in Wuhan and later in Romania. At 52, he was both expert and worldly and looking for new vistas.

These appeared soon after Deng swung the party around to the task
of economic development. Under Deng, first peasants and then foreign
investors—those two suppressed economic agents that would become
engines of the subsequent Chinese economic boom—were encouraged
to let their entrepreneurial skills rip. In the countryside, the commune
structure was stripped of its essentials and a new system introduced, in
which families contracted land to farm for profit. The results surprised
everyone. Between 1978 and 1984, total grain output rose by a third, to
over 400 million tons, while real incomes in the countryside bounded
ahead at an annual clip of 18 percent.[20]

More tricky was the reopening of the Chinese economy to foreign investment. Mao was dead, and Deng's slogan "Opening and Reform" was
gaining currency as the zeitgeist of the new China. But the memory of colonial treaty ports died hard. Welcoming back the sort of Chinese com-
pradors and "foreign adventurers" who had invariably managed foreign
trade and investment in prerevolutionary days required a politically astute
leadership.

These swirling winds finally caught the sails of Jiang's becalmed patron, Wang Daohan, who was appointed executive vice-chairman of two
new commissions established in August 1979 to handle foreign trade and
investment. Jiang's erstwhile vice-minister and fellow Jiangsu native
Zhou Jiannan also was made a vice-chairman of both.[21]

With his smattering of experience in foreign economic dealings and
his foreign-language abilities, Jiang was an obvious candidate to join the
commissions. After less than a year in his new posts, Wang Daohan was
made mayor and party chief of Shanghai, now fully back under central
government control. Before leaving Beijing, Wang recommended that
Jiang be made a vice-chairman of both commissions.[22]

It may have been Wang's simple way of saying thanks to Jiang for protecting his daughter during the Cultural Revolution. In any case, the rec-
ommendation was easily justified on grounds of merit and won immediate support. Besides his proven competence in handling politically
sensitive economic issues, Jiang was also ten years younger than the other
vice-chairmen on the commissions. This probably helped, since as part
of his political reforms at the time, Deng was trying to clear out the dead-
wood in the top echelons of the party and government. "The temple is
not big enough for too many gods. Unless the old withdraw, there will
be no room for the young," Deng had said in mid 1979.[23] A year later,
when Deng's admonition was carved in stone as a policy of "finding and
promoting excellent young cadres" for top posts, Jiang was an immediate beneficiary.

The promotions to the foreign trade and investment commissions
meant that after a four-year plateau, Jiang's status was finally raised another notch, to vice-ministerial level. Perhaps more important, after more
than three decades working in the machinery sector, he had finally made
the switch to a different field. Jiang the official had now completely replaced Jiang the engineer.

As their names suggest, the State Foreign Investment Control Commission and the State Import/Export Control Commission were less than
friendly to foreign businessmen. Their aim was to ensure that the reopening of the Chinese economy did not undermine socialism. To this
end, the commissions were charged with drawing up plans for four "special economic zones" (SEZs) to be located in Guangdong and Fujian
provinces. They would be windows on the world, chutes along the Great
Wall of socialism through which capitalist money, goods, and knowledge could be passed. But they would be limited in number and sepa-

rated from the rest of the country by barbed-wire fences and German shepherd dogs.

The idea for the zones originated in the similar enclaves set up around the developing world throughout the 1970s. In February 1979, Baoan district in the city of Shenzhen, abutting Hong Kong, was declared an "export commodities production base." It would be a laboratory in which the competing fears and claims about foreign trade and investment could be tested. Preliminary planning for the four SEZs began shortly thereafter. By the time Jiang joined the commissions in August 1980, the initial plans for the SEZs were nearly complete. Putting his name to the edict passed by the National People's Congress (NPC), or parliament, the same month as the zones were established seems somewhat presumptuous in retrospect. But work on the zones was just beginning, and Jiang would be expected to ensure that they were a success.

Within a month, he was already reaping the fruits of his new assignment. For hardly had he moved his inkstone and brushes to a new desk than he was sent as the head of a nine-person study group to visit the export-processing zones of a dozen countries. The delegation—comprising the mayors of the four SEZ cities plus assorted finance, tax, and legal officials from the central government—left at the end of September. The trip was paid for and organized by the United Nations Industrial Development Organization, which left the uninitiated cadres free to take notes and enjoy themselves.

If Jiang could gush that a year in Romania had "really opened my eyes to the world," the next seven weeks must have brought sensory overload. The first arc of their trip took in Sri Lanka, Malaysia, Singapore, the Philippines, and Hong Kong. This was followed by stops in Japan and the United States before a visit to Mexico. From there, the travelers headed for Ireland and Britain and then to a UN briefing in Geneva. "Many members of our delegation were going abroad for the first time," Jiang would recall. "Everything was new to them."[24]

New. And impressive. While China had been engaging in internecine ideological warfare for the past ten years, the capitalist world had vaulted ahead. Mao's hopes of catching up with Britain were now so much nonsense. Jiang was especially impressed with the Shannon free-trade zone in Ireland and the Jurong industrial estate in Singapore.

"It certainly broadened our horizons!" he recalled.

A few foreign specialists assembled by the UN in Geneva doubted the efficacy of the SEZs. "But the conclusions we arrived at were different," Jiang said. "Seeing the state of international economic development, it only strengthened our confidence in setting up the SEZs."

On their return to China, the group wrote a report for the Politburo that advocated vesting local governments with powers to offer tax breaks, grant land leases, and even approve small-scale foreign investment projects. Foreign investors would be allowed to hire and fire Chinese wage workers at will.

The recommendations were a challenge to many in Beijing; to the ideologues opposed to any reintroduction of foreign capital; to the bureaucracy, which was to be shorn of some approval powers; and to conservative economists like Chen Yun, who worried out loud that the zones could cause serious payment imbalances and undermine domestic industry.[25]

Jiang and the mayors held fast. "Stones from other hills can be used to polish the jade on this one," they argued in allegory. Adopting the methods used by capitalist countries, they meant, would not undermine socialism in China, but would help strengthen it. The debate soon came to be seen as a test case internally for whether the anti-capitalist and anti-Western rantings of the Maoist era could be forgotten. "Our party elders were correcting the 'leftist' mistakes of the past and urging people to liberate their thinking at that time," Jiang recalled. "That meant putting stress on learning useful things from abroad."

Jiang appeared before the NPC standing committee in November 1981 to explain the proposed SEZ policies. After long debate, a divided standing committee finally gave its grudging approval. It was a triumphant conclusion to Jiang's first task in his new job. After biding his time for almost a decade on a lumbering economic exchange program with Romania, he was now engaged in a project that would fundamentally alter China's foreign economic relations. He could now rightfully claim to be one of the founders of the SEZs and a key general on the battlefront for Deng's economic reforms.

The prominent role he played in the SEZ fight brought Jiang quick and extensive exposure to senior leaders. It also placed him on the right side of the debate as doubters fell from power in the face of the impressive economic results being racked up by the reform policies. Zhao Ziyang and Hu Yaobang, two reformers brought in from the provinces, took over as premier and party chairman (later general secretary) in the early 1980s.

In March 1982, the four separate ministries and commissions handling foreign economic relations were amalgamated into one newly formed body, the Ministry of Foreign Economic Relations and Trade. Jiang lost his job in the revamp, but he was hardly likely to fall through the cracks. Other administrative changes were also under way, among them the creation of a new Ministry of Electronics Industry, where Jiang was made a vice-minister.[26]

4

Although seemingly a return to his roots, the move to the rapidly changing world of electronics was as novel for Jiang as his brief flirtation with foreign trade and investment had been. By this time, however, he was already adept at switching from one sector to another. Every successful Chinese leader was expected to handle new portfolios as they came, and Jiang seemed to relish the challenge. "My work involved the engineering, electronics, and power industries, as well as the import-export business," he would recall later. "It was my habit to learn on the job."[27]

Indeed, learning on the job was actually what Jiang was best at. As a self-professed failure at mastering complex subjects—everything from blast furnaces to the Japanese language—his aptitude was in being able to learn just enough to get by. In private, Jiang would at this time even start to call himself "Mr. Tiger Balm" (wan jin you), a Shanghai expression alluding to a popular peppermint-scented liniment that relieves all manner of aches and pains.[28] Used self-deprecatingly, the term is roughly equivalent to the English phrase "jack of all trades and master of none." The self-appellation perfectly reflected the fact that Jiang's career was now more tied up with the party than with any specific economic sector or government ministry. The cadre's role was to solve problems and offer succor. It did not require brilliance in any particular field. Jiang was now a bureaucratic dilettante and a party specialist.

Henceforth, Jiang's party rank became a better indicator of the state of his career than his official government post. The change was subtle but important. When he joined the electronics ministry as a vice-minister, he was also made deputy party secretary, a sort of minister-in-waiting moniker. That meant he was senior enough in the party ranks to be elevated into the outer sanctum of true power, the roughly 200-member Central Committee, which he joined at the party's twelfth congress in September 1982. It was not unusual for vice-ministers to be on the Central Committee. But the move put Jiang firmly in the running to be one of the so-called "third generation" of leaders who would follow the era of Deng Xiaoping. Within a year, he was made minister of electronics, as expected, the second time that Deng's drive to promote "young and excellent" cadres had aided his career.

As electronics minister, Jiang presided over 1,400 ministry-run enterprises employing 75,000 ministry workers and a total workforce—including bureaucrats, local enterprises, and military affiliates—of close to three million.[29] He was also in charge of a sector that Premier Zhao had singled out for special attention in the five-year plan ending in 1985.

The creation of the Ministry of Electronics reflected a perceived need for China to catch up on two trends in the world economy; the rapid spread of computers, and the growing importance of consumer electronics in world trade. But China's electronics industry was in a sorry state when Jiang took over, and he did not try to hide the fact. "The output, quality, and reliability of products is low, and most of the sector loses money," he said on taking office. "The factories are scattered and the research is backward."[30] Jiang estimated when he took over that the country's industrial electronics products were fifteen years behind the world's best. Electronics imports were five times exports, and only six joint ventures had been signed in the sector. "There is a big problem with foreign investment, which has not been thriving in recent years," he commented.[31] As part of his planning, Jiang visited the Massachusetts Institute of Technology in Boston, commenting later that, but for his party career, he would have liked to have pursued doctoral studies there.[32]

His rescue plan, presented to the State Council in late 1983, called for a massive drive to bring China into the information age. Electronics industry output was to increase eightfold, to 3 percent of GDP, by the year 2000.[33] Black and white TVs would be replaced by color ones, radio production would fall, telephone output would rise. The old Soviet product standards would be phased out in favor of new international ones. Industrial electronics, meanwhile, would take the lion's share of new investment. "In order to promote China's new technological revolution," he said, "the electronics industry first has to undergo its own revolution."[34]

The approval of the development strategy in early 1984 gave Jiang a virtual free hand in running the ministry's business empire. In this, he proved purely mercenary. Exports were dumped on foreign markets to raise market shares. Joint ventures, meanwhile, were at first allowed to sell their products domestically in order to attract their foreign technology, but once the technology was acquired, those privileges were withdrawn. "We cannot allow our products to be excluded abroad and then let foreigners run our factories to make money," he said.[35]

Jiang took in briefs on everything from microcomputers to hotel management systems. He also had substantial exposure to the military electronics sector, one of three targeted development areas, along with integrated circuits and computers. Most exciting, though, was the launch of China's first satellite, which Jiang predicted blandly "will lead to considerably higher production of TVs."[36] After fourteen trial launches in as many years, China successfully launched its first geostationary communications satellite from the Xichang launch base in Sichuan province on 8 April 1984. After standing in the swirl of smoke at the launch pad, Jiang received congratulations from the entire State Council and the Politburo. Like the decision to establish the SEZs, it was something he had just walked into. But by now, Jiang was a master of the moment. Mr. Tiger Balm was winning praise everywhere he went.

5

At the end of his stint as electronics minister, Jiang was to admit defeat. "I tried to develop our country's electronics industry, but it was not accomplished in line with my original hopes," he admitted years later.[37] The "internal revolution" in making microcircuitry and semiconductors simply never took place, he explained. But by then, Jiang's feats as a government official were less important than his performance within the party. And in this area, he had made big strides. Away from the public world of microcomputers and pocket calculators, Jiang was proving his mettle in the arcane world of Chinese high politics.

The importance of factions and faction-building in Chinese high politics is well known. In essence, this theory argues that the informal politics of personal connections and shifting alliances is far more important than the formal legislative process in the Chinese political system. In principle, the preference among senior Chinese leaders is for a friendly consensus on all issues, the sinologist Lowell Dittmer explains. "But meanwhile, the search for personal security generates a ceaseless countermobilization of informal loyalty networks."[38]

Factions often have recognizable features (such as common home provinces, university alma maters, etc.) and can often be discerned battling it out in public. But for the most part, they are subtle, indistinct, and changing entities. The building of such "loyalty networks" is as old as China itself. Asked about how to build personal relationships, the sage Confucius once explained: "It may be possible to learn with someone but not to achieve results with them. It may be possible to achieve results with someone but not to go along with everything they do. It may be possible to go along with everything they do but not to rule with them."[39] In other words, every person is a potential ally to one degree or other.

When Jiang was elevated to the Central Committee, there were several immediate allies at hand. Also elevated to the Central Committee in 1982 was Qiao Shi, Jiang's one-time fellow student agitator in Shanghai. Qiao's rise in the party hierarchy was to precede Jiang's. Within a few years of joining the Central Committee, Qiao was a Politburo member and head of the party's powerful Organization Department, responsible for personnel changes. Although there is little evidence of contact between the two men after 1949, later evidence was to prove they had maintained close contacts since then. As a member of the party's International Liaison Department since 1963, Qiao had paved the way for the Romanian projects Jiang worked on. Later, as a top advisor to the party's general secretary, Hu Yaobang, Qiao was to recommend Jiang for higher posts.

In the major government reshuffle of June 1983 that won Jiang his ministership, more potential allies cropped up. Qian Qichen, another one-time Shanghai student dissident, became a vice-foreign minister. Li Xiannian, who had fought in the Civil War alongside Jiang's foster father, was made state president. It would, of course, be up to Jiang to breathe life into these potential personal allies. Following the Confucian schema of progressively closer relations—"learning, achieving, following, and ruling"—Jiang would have to probe the limits of cooperation with each.

One elder, whose support Jiang would later enjoy at a critical time, literally sought him out. One day in early 1984, Jiang received a call from the office of Chen Yun, a fellow native of Jiangsu province, who was perhaps second only to Deng in the overall hierarchy, asking him to come over for a chat about electronics development. On 3 March, Jiang and two colleagues from the ministry stopped by Chen's house as requested, carting along a microscope, a microprocessor, and some integrated circuit boards. When they arrived, a *People's Daily* reporter and another from the Xinhua News Agency were already on hand to record the proceedings. Realizing the import of the moment, Jiang adopted a more formal mien, buttoning up his dark blue Mao tunic and adjusting his pen so that it was visible in the left breast pocket, the accepted symbol of a diligent grassroots worker. Chen sat in his comfortable chair and peered through the ancient microscope at the densely printed circuit board as the cameras flashed. Jiang commentated on what the hoary elder was seeing, while his assistant stood at the ready with a magnifying glass. "This is a real eye-opener," Chen said at last, sitting up from the microscope. "I think that our government cadres have no idea about the urgency of learning this new technology."[40]

The next day, the visit was reported by the *People's Daily* at the top of page one, with an accompanying photograph. "Jiang gave a report to Chen Yun on the development and requirements of our country's integrated circuit and computer industries," the Xinhua report read. The brief encounter would create a lasting political pact between the two. The mixture of practical and tribal motivations at work was summed up by a comment on the visit by *Guangjiaojing* (Wide Angle) magazine: "Chen Yun naturally views Jiang Zemin in a more favorable light since Jiang understands technology and since they both come from Jiangsu province."[41]

In other areas, Jiang took the initiative to ally himself with the winning side. In an important first for his party career, Jiang wrote an article for the *People's Daily* in May 1984 with the unpromising title of "Carry Out Party Rectification in a Thorough Way by Constantly Seeking Unity of Thinking."[42] It was a dutiful response to the three-year "consolidation" and "rectification" of party ranks reluctantly launched in late 1983 by Hu Yaobang after mild outbreaks of open dissidence in the late 1970s and early 1980s. Jiang's article of support was long and dull. Little in it was worthy of note. He blamed slow progress in his own ministry on bad ideology rather than bad leadership. The article's significance lay in its high-profile expression of support for Hu's drive—*biaotai*, or "making known one's stance in public," a well-used signaling device in high Chinese politics. Jiang was now doing more than just going along with the party line. As a Central Committee member, he was expected to run with the ball, to "explain" the party line. In doing so, he could signal through nuance his own political views and hope to build factional support. It was an essential feature of Chinese politics.

One more ally came into sight at this time. In September 1984, an interministry "leading group" was set up to coordinate the ambitious plans for the electronics industry laid down a year earlier. Li Peng, who had become a vice-premier in 1983, was the group's head, and Jiang was the deputy. Their duet as group leaders was short. But they seemed to work well together, even to appreciate each other's talents. As with Chen Yun, the "harmonious relations" Jiang established during this brief liaison would prove crucial to him years later.[43]

CHAPTER 4

Shanghai's Chief Clerk

I

In the days before the Third Field Army marched into Shanghai and declared it part of the Communist state in 1949, the sprawling city at the mouth of the Yangtze River was among the most cosmopolitan in Asia. But incompetent and corrupt rule by the Nationalists during the civil war, followed by three decades of communist-style industrialization, had left it impoverished and ugly. When Wang Daohan took over as mayor in 1981, it was merely one of several drab industrial cities along the Chinese coast.

In retrospect, the appointment of a reliable yet uninspired cadre like Wang Daohan to lead the city at the outset of the economic reforms was a mistake. The post was a sinecure for services rendered. Already 65 when he became mayor, Wang was neither able nor willing to remake the city. By the end of 1983, Shanghai had attracted only twenty-three foreign investment projects, worth a pledged U.S.$220 million. It was declared an "open city" for foreign investment, along with thirteen other coastal cities, in 1984. But by then, other places that had been faster off the mark were leaving the lumbering metropolis far behind. The once-great center of the Orient had become a city in decline along a Chinese coast that farther south was already reverberating to the beat of Deng's reforms.

Shanghai's sad state was reflected in the fact that its share of national exports fell by half, to just 12 percent, between 1980 and 1985.[1] The port was so congested that local officials regularly called out PLA soldiers to help load and unload ships in midstream. "Made in Shanghai," a label that had once signified quality and workmanship, was now a byword for ill-made and outdated relics of the socialist past.

"We did not take the intellectual advantages of Shanghai into account," Deng would later say to explain Beijing's overlooking of the city in the early 1980s. "If we had decided to establish a special economic zone here, the city would look very different now."[2]

Belated efforts by the central leadership to resuscitate the listless giant did little at first. Beijing allowed the municipality to retain slightly more of its tax revenues as the 1980s progressed, but it still skimmed off an inordinate share of the city's wealth. Shanghai spent from its own budget just 17 percent of the total revenues generated in the city in 1985, compared to 56 percent in Tianjin. This was despite the fact that locally owned state firms accounted for more than two-thirds of the revenues.[3]

Wang Daohan was probably lucky to turn 70 when his first term as mayor expired in mid 1985. His advanced age gave the increasingly anxious Beijing leadership a polite excuse to replace him with a younger, more economically astute leader. Beijing was considering a successor as early as mid 1984. Wang, of course, had his say in the matter, and it came as no surprise to those already familiar with his loyalty network that his first choice was Jiang Zemin.[4] Jiang at this time was having little success trying to steer the country into the computer age as electronics minister, and he jumped at the prospect. As mayor of Shanghai, he would be in charge of all government departments and second overall only to the city's party chief, a stark contrast to the overlapping bureaucratic gridlock that had prevented him from taking radical action as electronics minister. The city of his past was ripe for development, and the central government was obviously ready to offer support. A clearly frustrated Wang did sound one note of caution when he met Jiang in Beijing to offer him the post: "Being the mayor of Shanghai is like being the chief clerk of a general affairs office," he warned.[5] Jiang thought for a moment, then replied: "I'd be thrilled with the idea of being the chief clerk for 12 million people!"[6]

Beijing appears to have agreed to the appointment as early as December 1984. In that month, Premier Zhao Ziyang took Jiang along as the only minister in a central government delegation to Shanghai to draw up a new economic development strategy for the city. From then until his formal appointment, Jiang would have almost six months to prepare. His ministry duties left with subordinates, Jiang spent much of that time just walking around the city, disguised in a black leather jacket and a duck-billed baseball cap in order to elude public attention.[7]

Since his last stint in the city in the mid 1960s, Jiang had returned only sporadically. Passing through Shanghai's markets, riding the buses, and glancing at school buildings, he was startled by the decrepitude. An old Shanghai expression came to mind that described the jerry-built city unfolding before his eyes: "If there are too many noodles in the pot, add water. If there is too much water, add noodles."[8] When a major fire broke out at the Second Light Industry Bureau, Jiang remarked with dismay that the ladder truck on the scene still had the words "Police Bureau" stenciled on the side: it was a relic of the pre-1949 Nationalist government![9]

It was not squalor; Communist China would rarely allow showcase urban areas to descend to the levels of the shantytowns in other developing countries. But glancing out of the dust-smudged windows of a cross-town trolleybus, Jiang knew he had his work cut out for him. "On a blank sheet of paper free from any mark, . . . the freshest and most beautiful pictures can be painted," Mao Zedong had written before launching the disastrous crash industrialization drive of the 1950s.[10] The challenge for Jiang, by contrast, was to draw a fresh, beautiful picture on a canvas already thickly encrusted with four decades of paint.

His sidekick in the endeavor was the city's new party secretary, Rui Xingwen, a former minister of urban construction and environment. The Communist-run newspaper in Hong Kong, Wen Wei Po, broke the news of their appointments in June 1985. The paper noted pointedly that the outgoing leadership duo of Wang and party chief Chen Guodong had "failed to bring about radical change" because they "lacked energy." Jiang and Rui, by contrast, were "in the prime of their lives" and it was "an opportune moment for them to display their talents." The paper's evaluation of the challenges the pair faced is illuminating:

> Rui Xingwen and Jiang Zemin are confronted with an extremely tough task. Shanghai people expect the new leaders to give them new hope. At present there are many problems in Shanghai, like environmental pollution, traffic congestion, and overcrowded housing. Although these problems have been a concern for many years, it has been hard to shed old habits in a hurry. . . . The people of Shanghai are not yet satisfied, and the local parliamentary delegates have lodged scores of complaints.[11]

On the day Jiang formally became mayor in July 1985, he invited journalists to a press briefing. Rather than make a speech, as Wang used to do, he simply invited them to ask questions. Sitting forward earnestly on a lace-backed sofa and wearing only an informal summer safari shirt, Jiang contrasted sharply with the old man he had replaced. The clutter of microphones and tape recorders around him symbolized a city aching for competent leadership. "We know it will be a tough job with a lot of responsibility," he said. "Comrade Rui and I have already heard a lot of opinions on what needs to be done."[12]

Jiang promised "less empty talk and more concrete actions" as mayor.[13] Concrete actions, indeed. His first plan was to pour thousands of tons of fresh concrete to rebuild the city's decrepit infrastructure. Nothing could be achieved until the city functioned properly again, he said. Nine projects had already been put on the agenda in April in line with the central government's new five-year development strategy for the city. These included a new train station, a subway, a bridge across the Huangpu River, a better phone system, and an airport extension.

There would also be ports, elevated expressways, and a new exhibition center. Once the transport problems were solved around the river-side strip known as the Bund, the party and government would withdraw to inner-city offices, allowing foreign financial institutions to rent the old buildings. Better housing would eventually be needed too. Then would come improved health and education facilities. It would take a long time. "You can't get fat just by having a single big meal," Jiang joked, pointing to his own expanding girth.[14] By the year 2000, the total cost would exceed U.S.$8 billion, not including industrial projects.[15]

It was a heady beginning to Jiang's term of office. Not since he had worked night and day to convert the Changchun Auto Works power factory to crude oil nearly a quarter century earlier had he been so fired up. As a petty technocrat in a large central bureaucracy in Beijing, he had been uninspired, even frustrated. Now he was again reveling in being in charge.

It was not long, however, before Jiang the visionary was brought thumping back down to Earth by Jiang the chief office clerk, just as Wang Daohan had warned. One of his first official acts as Shanghai mayor was to organize disposal bins for the millions of watermelon rinds discarded on the city's streets every day by overheated residents. The stench of the rinds in the summer of 1985 was terrific, worse than before. Jiang phoned around to see if they could be used as fertilizer, but finally decided to simply ship them away. "What can you do with all those watermelon rinds?" he asked a foreign reporter. "You can't just turn them into useful products."[16]

More serious was the strong typhoon that swept across the city in the early hours of 1 August 1985, flooding thousands of homes and factories. Jiang's first official inspection of the city ended up as a disaster relief effort. "It's because of my name," he joked after the deluge, noting that *ze min* could be translated as "inundate the people." The remark elicited uncomfortable laughter from cadres attending a safety meeting. "It's rare to hear high-ranking Chinese Communist Party officials daring to joke about themselves in public," one commentator noted.[17]

Still, nuisance chores like disposing of watermelon rinds and rescuing flood victims did confirm to Jiang, and probably to the rest of the new city leadership, the importance of rebuilding the city's insufficient infrastructure. It also reminded Jiang of the truth of Wang Daohan's words. "Shortly after I took over in Shanghai, torrential rains fell, and I had to deal with all the problems that arose then," he would recall. Then he added an unexpected note of nostalgia for his previous post. "You don't have to deal with such matters when you're a minister."[18]

2

Jiang's return to Shanghai marked the end of a nearly two-decade separation from his wife and family. Aside from the brief return to the city in 1976 as a member of the post–Gang of Four cleanup crew, he had lived away since being sent to Wuhan in 1966. The contrast between his family life before and after he returned to Shanghai is stark.

While in Beijing, Jiang seems effectively to have lived like a bachelor. His old leather suitcase stuffed with a trove of books, and his colleagues in the bureaucracy were his main sources of company in his off hours. The only respite came in the three years, from 1979 to 1981, when his sister, Jiang Zefen, and her family moved into his spacious and barely used apartment off Cuilu Road in western Beijing. "He kept up a pretty hard-working and simple lifestyle in the days when he was in Beijing," Jiang Zefen recalled. "He would often come home very late from work, after we had finished eating dinner. I would hurriedly say: 'We've eaten everything. Let me make you something!' He would just ask for a bowl of noodles."[19]

The extended severance of Jiang from his wife was not entirely of necessity. Party regulations would have allowed Wang Yeping to move to Beijing when he reached the level of deputy director of a department in 1974. Her decision to remain in Shanghai suggests that the couple were by this time not close. They may have been more intimate in earlier days, although the likelihood that their marriage was an arranged one suggests otherwise. But the lengthy time they spent apart when married quarters were available in Beijing is the best evidence we have of an estranged relationship. Among other things, it meant that Jiang could offer his ample Beijing residence to his long-suffering sister Jiang Zefen, who had been persecuted during the anti-rightist movement of the 1950s and sent home on a pittance of a pension.

Wang had her own reasons for staying in Shanghai, of course. Her health began to deteriorate in the early 1980s, and the dry, cold Beijing climate would not have helped matters. In addition, her feeble mother needed attention, and her sons were making their careers in the city. Jiang, for his part, may have preferred the unfettered life in Beijing to the mesh of family obligations and suppliant relatives in his native area. After all, he was the natural patriarch of the extended family of Grandfather Jiang Shixi—the second son of his biological father, the patriarch of the previous generation, and the adopted eldest son of the family hero, Jiang Shangqing. Moreover, his rising official status gave him an added responsibility toward his family that at times would conflict with his determination to avoid suspicions of favoritism and nepotism. Keeping a distance from Shanghai seemed to suit him fine.

That all changed when he returned to the city. For one thing, Wang was now called out to appear with her husband on the newly repaved Shanghai diplomatic circuit of the 1980s. Having a spouse had been of little importance when Jiang was electronics minister. His foreign trips to Eastern Europe and the United States had been brief and businesslike. But as Shanghai mayor, he hosted a stream of foreign delegations, official and otherwise, fascinated by the country's plans to put the polish back on the tarnished Pearl of the Orient. Mayors from the seventeen cities that Shanghai had signed sister-city agreements with were frequently in town with large delegations. So, too, were the heads of several states, including the British monarch, Queen Elizabeth II, who came through in October 1986. Amidst the toasts and banquets, Jiang and Wang became a couple again.

Jiang's return to Shanghai also brought him back into touch with his family past. Within a month of taking office as mayor, his foster mother, Wang Zhelan, died in Yangzhou. She had been retired for two decades and living in the care of her eldest daughter (Jiang's foster sister), Jiang Zeling. By the time of her death, she had lived as a widow for almost half a century since the shocking news of the shooting of her husband, Jiang Shangqing, had brought her grief-stricken to the shores of Hongze Lake.

It was not clear at first whether Jiang would attend the funeral, even though Wang had been his foster mother and an aunt of his wife. His pedigree as the "son" of a revolutionary martyr had not always been a blessing after all. During the Cultural Revolution, the patron of Jiang Shangqing's martyrdom, General Zhang Aiping, was accused of being a counterrevolutionary and relieved of all his posts. As a result, Jiang Shangqing's exploits were also relieved of their position in the annals of the party. On the anniversary of Jiang Shangqing's death in 1969, his tiny grave in Jiangsu province's Yaji village was desecrated by Red Guards. Jiang did not brag of the fact that he was the adopted son of Jiang Shangqing while he was sidelined during the Cultural Revolution, even though the Red Guards in Wuhan did not seem to consider this martyr as illegitimate.[20] Although he had assailed the notion that a person should be blamed for the faults of their ancestors, Jiang had little choice if he was to survive.

The end of the Cultural Revolution allowed family members to hold a low-key memorial service in Yangzhou on the fortieth anniversary of Jiang Shangqing's death in 1979.[21] After General Zhang was appointed minister of national defense in 1982, he ordered the local government to build a proper memorial to the fallen martyr.[22] But Jiang—then newly appointed electronics vice-minister—appears to have been the only close family member who did not attend the opening of the memorial, a domed structure set on a hillock surrounded by cypress trees and wild flowers.[23]

On returning to Shanghai, Jiang's pride in his pedigree seems to have been rekindled. As a Central Committee member, he was now competing against several other sons of martyrs, among them Li Peng, the future premier. He could not afford to overlook this feather in his genealogical cap. A month before taking office, in April 1985, he made his first visit to the new tomb of Jiang Shangqing to sweep his foster father's grave. Local officials crowded around the "son," as they called him, of their most famous martyr, and assisted the filial mission.[24] Then, when Wang Zhelan died, Jiang attended her funeral and used the return visit to Yangzhou to meet long-forgotten relatives.[25] Thenceforth, he made a point of returning to Yangzhou every spring to sweep their graves during the traditional festival for the dead, Qingming ("Pure Brightness").[26]

Being the acknowledged "son" of a revolutionary martyr would stand Jiang in good stead in later years. It was much preferable to being the son of a current party leader, like the group of well-connected up-and-comers called "red princes," who would attract growing popular resentment in the 1980s. Indeed, when a rumor began circulating in

Shanghai shortly after Jiang arrived that he was the son-in-law of President Li Xiannian, he went to inordinate lengths to scotch it. "Today, I wish solemnly to tell you that this is simply rumor and sheer nonsense," he told a specially convened meeting of city cadres in late 1985. "My wife's name is Wang not Li!"[27] Later, when the rumor surfaced again, his cousin Jiang Zeren was called out to deliver the refutation. "Jiang's only relative of any standing was the martyr Jiang Shangqing, who died holding the rank equivalent to a local party chief," she asserted. "That is his only political background."[28]

Jiang's family, both past and present, had been an aspect of his private life that he had shunned while rising quickly through the lower ranks of the party. Now that he was Shanghai's mayor and a Central Committee member, it became an indispensable part of his future.

3

Jiang had little knowledge of economics when he took over as Shanghai's mayor. Only during his brief tenure working on the SEZs had he grappled with such issues. Yet they would absorb most of his energies as mayor of Shanghai. Everything from livelihood concerns about inflation to new issues such as foreign investment and international banking were the responsibility of the city's "chief clerk."

In the debate over the SEZs, Jiang had shown himself to be an avid economic reformer, keen to follow international practice and willing to take short-term risks to try out new policies. Whether because of his experiences in Moscow and Bucharest, his other travels abroad, or just plain instinct, Jiang had little faith in the planned economy that China had copied wholesale from the Soviet Union. "We cannot stick to the Soviet model forever," he told a foreign reporter while Shanghai's mayor.[29]

In late 1984, under a grand plan to create a "planned commodity economy," the party had decided to allow market prices a greater say in the urban economy. The changes would gradually increase urban purchasing power and living standards, but the immediate effects were negative; inflation rose abruptly, and official profiteering to exploit the difference between state and market prices, known as *guandao,* became rampant. After rising at less than 3 percent a year since 1981, national urban living costs jumped by over 12 percent in 1985 as producers rushed to price their goods according to what the market would bear. It came as a rude shock to a country where prices had been virtually frozen for thirty years. Senior leaders—who prided themselves on having ended the inflationary problems of the Republican era—grew uneasy. Elders like Chen Yun warned that reforms must be slowed and price controls used to ensure social stability, but at the March 1985 meeting of the National People's Congress, Premier Zhao Ziyang pledged to stay the course of reform despite these "temporary difficulties." Local leaders like Jiang were forced to take sides.

In Shanghai, retail prices rose by 17 percent in 1985, compared to just 2 percent the year before.[30] Everything from train tickets to clothing suddenly became dearer. Zhao had warned city cadres earlier that the following two years might be "the most difficult the city would face" because of plans to lift controls on prices of raw materials and energy. He was said, however, to have brought "gifts and not whips" to city leaders: they were permitted to apply price controls selectively if necessary.[31] At a meeting on economic work in Shanghai in August 1985, Jiang indicated that he was leaning toward Zhao's side of the argument. "Some of the difficulties we have encountered are problems on our road of progress," he told cadres. "The most fundamental way to solve these problems is to carry out reforms."[32]

He took the same message to restless students at Tongji University, where he spoke in late October 1985 to pacify growing campus concern about the soaring costs of living. Sporadic student protest marches had taken place in Beijing since September. Although ostensibly aimed at various noneconomic issues (such as Japanese militarism, the stationing of soldiers on campus, etc.), the protests were seen more generally as reflecting discontent about the inequalities arising from the nascent urban reform program.[33] Zhao Ziyang's characteristic response to the disquiet on campus was one of reconciliation. Local leaders, including Jiang, were instructed to meet with students and explain the policies—such as the lifting of price controls—that had caused inflation. When Jiang visited Tongji, an estimated crowd of 10,000 students and teachers listened politely to his defense of the reform policies.[34] It was Jiang's first encounter with popular discontent, and he made a convincing spokesman.

Indeed, the jitters over stability seemed only to increase Jiang's determination to ensure that the policies stuck. "Shanghai has never before experienced such big increases in retail prices," he admitted to city cadres shortly after the Tongji meeting. The solution, however, was to increase supplies, especially of foods, not to impose price controls. "Suburban counties must pay greater attention to Comrade Chen Yun's call to ensure adequate production of agricultural products," he said, making an ironic appeal to the pleas of one of the harshest critics of the price reforms.[35]

Food prices would fall slightly as the new year began, but nonfood price rises continued apace. Jiang never sought to reinstate price controls, though, despite Zhao's consent. It was an unmistakable sign that Jiang's liberal economic instincts were genuine. In less than a year since taking over as Shanghai's mayor, he had propelled himself squarely into the ranks of the Zhao camp, which was taunting the naysayers who warned of the dire consequences of reforms. The 1980s were a decade in which the senior Chinese leadership could be roughly divided into those who supported such flirtations with the market and those who were opposed to them. Jiang's political instinct was to be cagey, but he had at least dispelled the idea that his economic views were vague or capricious. He tacked his colors firmly to the mast of Zhao Ziyang's market experiments in the cities. For better or for worse, senior leaders in Beijing took note.

4

When Deng Xiaoping launched his dramatic economic reforms, one of the biggest worries was how the indoctrinated youth of this long-closed country would react to the sudden onslaught of ideas and influences from the West. At first Deng downplayed the possible effects. Any "decadent" influences would be mere rivulets, lost in the sea of China's established socialist ideological system, he argued. "There's nothing to be afraid of," he said in 1980.[36] But the force and extent of the foreign cultural invasion caught everyone by surprise. By 1983, even Deng was beginning to backtrack. "In recent years we have witnessed an influx of books, films, music, dances and audio and video recordings that even in Western countries are regarded as pernicious junk," he said. "This corruption of our young people by the decadent, bourgeois culture of the West is no longer tolerable."[37]

Over the next three years, high politics in China would be almost entirely dominated by the question of Western influences—coded in Marxist terminology as "bourgeois liberalization"—and the prescribed antidote for them, the building of a "socialist spiritual culture."[38] Local leaders like Jiang could mostly busy themselves with economic development. But the swirling currents of the anti-bourgeois liberalization campaign in Beijing eventually demanded at least lip service from local leaders. Jiang and Rui convened a seminar to draw up a "cultural development strategy" for Shanghai to complement its ambitious economic plans in May 1986, an apparent attempt to show hard-liners in

Beijing that the port city was not abjuring old-style indoctrination in its attempt to regain its former glory. But it was difficult to make much progress when the senior leadership in Beijing was itself deeply divided over the issue. The party plenum that convened in September 1986 papered over the differences by condemning bourgeois liberalization on the one hand but promoting the notions of intellectual freedom and learning from capitalist countries on the other.

Not until the fiery orations of Fang Lizhi, an astrophysicist at the National Science and Technology University in Hefei, stirred up a nationwide student protest movement did the high-level differences come into the open. In a series of speeches to college students in Shanghai in November 1986, the frumpy-looking Fang set campuses ablaze. "Some people do not dare to challenge our leaders, but I have found that if you challenge them, they dare not do anything against you," he told students at Jiang's alma mater, Jiaotong University, on 6 November. "Democracy granted by top leaders is not true democracy," he added. The call to challenge authority was followed a few weeks later by another startling statement. "I am here to tell you that the socialist movement has been a failure," Fang told Tongji University students gathered in a campus park on 18 November. "Complete Westernization is the only way to modernize."[39]

When he returned to Hefei in late November, Fang was already something of a campus hero. Although his starkly pro-Western views were probably shared by only a small minority of them—most students cared more about issues such as better cafeteria food and more course choice—the students were spoiling for a fight with the Communist authorities. Fang's oratory had galvanized their energies. Almost anything could have caused the nationwide student demonstrations that followed. Injustices were everywhere visible, and students needed only one excuse to urge their colleagues into the streets. The first street demonstrations, by about 2,000 students, took place in Hefei on 9 December after the provincial authorities reneged on promises to allow greater popular participation in elections to local people's congresses. Shanghai was the slowest major city to respond to the Hefei protests, even though it was later to become the focal point of the movement. Sympathy posters appeared on notice boards on the campuses of Tongji, Jiaotong, and Fudan universities in the week after the initial outbreaks in Hefei, the first time such "big character" posters had been seen in public since the right to post them had been removed from the constitution in 1979.

Open disobedience was limited at first; the posters in Shanghai complained mostly about student life and called for faster democratic change. Student gatherings remained sporadic and peaceful. But a rumor soon spread that a graduate student from Jiaotong University had been beaten senseless by a policeman on 9 December while attending a rock concert. The small spark was all that was needed to engulf the entire city in protest. "This aroused the indignation of students. They organized meetings on campus and called for the assailants to be punished with the full force of the law," an official report would say.[40]

By 15 December, the campus posters had taken up the cause of the student, whose name was never given. The clusters of students milling about the billboards grew to thousands. Premier Hu Yaobang, whose calls for political reform had in many ways inspired the students in Shanghai, adopted a policy of "mediation and discussion" (shutong, duihua). He was loathe to suppress a movement that might conceivably strengthen his hand against the hard-liners in Beijing. The public security minister, Ruan Chongwu, a former Shanghai vice-mayor, was sent to the city to ensure that the gatherings were handled leniently, in line with the instructions.[41]

Student sentiment was most volatile at Jiaotong University, where school authorities were facing a daily battle to remove notices relaying information on the protest movement in other cities from billboards. The school's party secretary, Deng Xuchu, warned Ruan and Jiang that the gatherings might spill into the streets at any time. One of the students' demands was for a meeting with Jiang. Given his year-earlier appearance at Tongji University, the students took it as their natural prerogative to summon the mayor again. Jiang agreed, and a public assembly was hastily arranged for the afternoon of Thursday, 18 December, at Jiaotong University.

The irony would not have been lost on Jiang as he prepared for the showdown. Exactly forty years earlier, he had joined student protests at Jiaotong University after a female student from Beijing University had allegedly been raped by an American soldier. That incident had become a rallying point for opposition to the Nationalists. Now, a similar incident was drawing youthful fire down on the Communists.

Jiang's car drove through the gates of Jiaotong University shortly after 1 P.M. on the appointed day. The auditorium was halfway across campus, and it took the mobbed car twenty minutes to reach the building. Jiang had been briefed beforehand by Deng Xuchu. The student grievances about living conditions could probably be allayed with promises of money or investigations, they agreed. But others were less tractable; political reform was going nowhere, the press was muzzled, and police brutality was on the rise. Jiang would be hard-pressed to make promises of change in these areas.

As he stepped from his car, Jiang glanced at a nearby billboard. Written on one red poster in black ink were the famous words of Lincoln's Gettysburg Address, which Jiang had memorized as a middle school student: "Of the people, by the people, for the people." Jiang made a mental note and stepped into the packed hall.

The mood inside was raucous. Jiang climbed onto the stage, and thunderous applause erupted. It was a type of applause typical in China; not a sign of approval or support, but an excited, nervous reaction to the conspicuous behavior of others. What would Jiang say?

Taking a wad of folded city government stationery covered in his arthritic-looking scrawl from his breast pocket, Jiang switched to his reading glasses and began to speak. At first the 3,000 students lining the walls and seats of the room listened politely. But within minutes, they realized that Jiang had no intention of holding a dialogue. He was simply going to lecture them.

"You should listen to us first! We are not here to listen to a speech!" one student leader burst out from the back.[42]

Jiang looked up startled. More students chimed in. "Let us speak first!" "Conduct an honest dialogue as equals!"

Jiang ignored their pleas and began to read again. But the students continued to boo and hiss. "Who dares to boo once more?" Jiang finally demanded, looking up from his paper. Several students booed again. Jiang pointed to one in the front row. "If you won't listen to me, how about you standing up here and talking?" The student was reluctant under the sudden glare of attention. But his colleagues urged him on, and he took the microphone.

After a few minutes, the students were happily taking the microphone in turn and badgering their mayor with questions. Why was the press not free to report on the demonstrations? And why was Jiang mayor? "Who elected you? Was it the people of Shanghai?" one student asked flippantly.

Jiang was tongue-tied with anger. The insolence of the student had caught him off guard. "What's your name? What class are you in?" he demanded. Boos erupted as students reacted to the menacing gesture. Jiang was supposed to be listening and conciliating; instead, he was making threats.[43]

At last Deng Xuchu came to Jiang's aid. "The mayor is very busy and does not have time to engage each one of you in dialogue," he said. Deng suggested the students raise several questions at once and then give Jiang time to respond to them all.

The students then calmed down. For the next three and a half hours, until around 5 P.M., another twenty-five managed to speak. Their leader presented four specific demands: press freedom, meaning press coverage of their demonstrations; the right to put up wall posters for free and open debates; official recognition that the demonstrations were legal; and a guarantee that no action would be taken against participants.

When he finally spoke, Jiang could not offer much consolation on the specific problems. The press, he said, "is the mouthpiece of the party. The reports must benefit the interests of the people, the reforms and the open policy."[44] He promised, however, to look into the alleged beating of the student, agreed that the demonstrations were constitutional, and promised that there would be no retribution against participants.[45] The students needed to be patient, however. Nothing would be solved by street protest, he said.

Jiang then made a clumsy attempt to cow the students into submission. "As I was walking in, I noticed the words of Lincoln on the notice board outside," he ventured with a smug air of assurance. "But you are really too superficial in your use of these words," he charged. "You need to understand the full meaning of what Lincoln said."[46] Jiang then began to recite the entire Gettysburg speech. Within minutes the students grew restless and began to boo again. "Of the people, by the people, and for the people!" they chanted. Jiang finally gave up in frustration. He called for calm, wiping his forehead with a soiled handkerchief. "You guys just want to put on the clothes of Western democracy and freedom but you have no idea about the real situation of China," he shouted above the din, jabbing his finger in accusation. "You're really too shallow!"[47]

It was too much. The booing and hissing grew to a crescendo. Deng Xuchu leapt onto the stage. "I think we've had enough dialogue for today. The mayor is very busy," he said. Jiang was bundled off the stage and into his waiting car. Class cadres cleared the auditorium.

Official reports put a positive spin on Jiang's performance. "Jiang affirmed the students' concern about democracy, reform, and school life, but expressed the hope that their actions would abide by the constitution. He advised the students not to take to the streets and disrupt public order," the official Xinhua News Agency said in the first official report on the Shanghai protests.[48] Local radio told a similar story: "Jiang urged them to exercise their democratic rights correctly and cherish the current excellent situation to safeguard political unity and stability."[49]

But Jiang's belligerent attitude seemed to inflame student sentiment. Posters appeared the same evening at Jiaotong demanding press coverage of the demonstrations and faster democratic change. When they were torn down, new ones appeared with a more confrontational message: "The voice of the people cannot be ripped down."[50]

Maybe Jiang could have stopped the demonstrations that followed. Lu Qiang, a leader of Shanghai's autonomous student federation, said later that if Jiang had given "satisfactory" replies that afternoon, no street demonstrations would have taken place.[51] Certainly, Jiang's appearance did not alleviate the situation. But it would have taken a Herculean effort, not to mention lavish and politically risky promises, to subdue the entire student movement in a single meeting. Indeed, even as Jiang was trapped inside the Jiaotong auditorium with his young detractors, over 1,000 students were already breaching the barricades across town at Tongji University, marching onto the streets with banners calling for freedom, democracy, and human rights.[52]

By evening, the students were resolved to air their grievances on the streets. A short poem appeared on the Jiaotong University campus in the form of an open letter tacked to a bulletin board:

> The masses have yet to awake.
> We walk forward alone,
> Like orphans into a den of wolves.
> When we die,
> There will be no burial place for us.[53]

5

Few students bothered to show up at classes on Friday morning, 19 December. News of Jiang's run-in with students the previous day was splashed across campus notice boards, where students gathered and chatted. What they read only incited further action. On the one hand, Jiang had admitted that the protests were constitutional and had promised no retribution against those who took part. On the other hand, he had further incensed the students by condemning their "shallow motives" and denying them press coverage. The morning papers, as expected, carried no news of the meeting. It was a recipe for open protest.

By noon, student leaders were rallying the disaffected to join street marches. More than 5,000, some said 10,000, from the three largest universities poured into the streets in the afternoon.[54] First they gathered at the People's Square and the nearby Municipal People's Congress building. Many students jumped the iron fence of the congress building and slapped posters on the walls inside. Others handed out leaflets to passersby. Police stood by impassively, awaiting orders. By late afternoon, the parade had moved to the front of the municipal party and government office along the Bund.

The doors of the government office were chained shut and barricaded with heavy timbers. Two policemen with fixed bayonets stood sentry, while others surrounded the building. A pair of state security officers filmed the crowds from an upper balcony.[55] "Come out Mayor Jiang! Come out Secretary Rui!" the students chanted.

Inside the neoclassical building, the attitude of the Shanghai leadership continued to be guided by Hu Yaobang's conciliatory guidelines: mediation and discussion were the bywords. Deputy Mayor Ye Gongqi was finally pushed out of the door to meet the students as dusk fell on the cold day. He urged them to leave before 5:30 P.M., when rush hour traffic would peak. Buses were already halted along seventeen routes engulfed by the protesters. Some students took Ye's advice and boarded the buses mustered to take them back to campus. But about 2,000 held fast as darkness enveloped the scene.

Jiang was clearly reluctant to face the students again. His ordeal at Jiaotong University the previous day had ended in uproar. Now the students were returning the visit in a defiant mood. Not until shortly after midnight, as the sit-in continued, did Jiang meet student leaders. Official reports said he "rushed to the scene" after finishing his daily work. We know now, however, that he was at home in the Kangping Road party compound before setting out.[56] Rather than take his normal sedan car, which he worried would attract attention, Jiang ordered a truck to take him to the Bund. The ploy succeeded in getting him to the site on time. But the truck driver was obviously less adroit than Jiang's chauffeur. As the truck neared the Bund, the driver swerved to miss a group of students. Jiang was thrown against the half-opened window and cut his head. "Blood was flowing everywhere," he recalled.[57]

Jiang entered the building through a side door. He was waiting slumped in a cushioned chair with a bandage on his head as the students were led through the metal barricades hastily erected on the steps of the building and into the conference hall. The formal setting was obviously more to Jiang's liking after the chaotic scenes at Jiaotong University.

"I was trying to talk some sense into them," he would recall. "I was also trying to teach them a powerful lesson."[58]

First, he struck a conciliatory tone. "We understand that you want reforms and faster democratization," he said. "But this kind of street demonstration is intolerable."[59] The students disagreed. They wanted the government to declare the movement patriotic. And they repeated their demand for press coverage. Jiang winced. "Newspapers have the freedom to select their own stories. I can't tell them what to publish," he insisted, changing tack from his previous explanation for the press gag.[60] No one would be punished, but the students had to stay within the law. "Watch out for the few troublemakers within your midst," he warned.[61]

Emerging from the meeting, one student leader used a bullhorn from the steps to inform the others of the proceedings. Jiang had been as inflexible as ever. It was certainly not enough to encourage the students to go home, and they remained steadfast as dawn approached.

By this time, despite his easy demeanor in the meeting, Jiang was by his own admission eager to use force to clear the students. "Things were very tense," he recalled. "Traffic jams always occurred before work, and if the students were not cleared away before 6 A.M., cars would pile up. There would be an accident." If the students were stubborn, Jiang had mustered sufficient force to clear them away. "I had 2,000 policemen standing by to take administrative measures," he recalled.[62]

Those measures were implemented just before 6 A.M. on 20 December. "After repeated warnings, the civilian police took action to disperse the students," local radio said.[63] The action was gentle. Police carried no weapons or equipment of any sort. They were merely instructed to get the students onto buses. In the mêlée that ensued, each side accused the other of brutality. The Xinhua News Agency insisted that the students had beaten up 31 policemen, "but not one returned a single blow."[64] Students, meanwhile, said that 200 of their number had been detained.[65] Neither report was ever confirmed.

Despite the scuffles, the word from Beijing was still to use conciliation. Shanghai officials were told to recognize the "patriotism" of the students and disperse the movement through dialogue. The soft line was understandable. Despite stirrings at dozens of colleges across the country in the wake of Fang Lizhi's movement in Hefei, every other city, including Beijing itself, was mostly calm by now. Everyone was watching Shanghai.

The early morning clearance of students from the Bund got the traffic moving again. But it also seemed to encourage more demonstrations, since the city authorities were clearly reluctant to use force. The kicks and blows delivered to some students as they were stuffed onto buses became a new source of grievance. For the next two days—Saturday, 21 December, and Sunday, 22 December—larger crowds, estimated at between 10,000 and 25,000, camped along the Bund. This time they carried banners calling for more freedom and democracy. Students from Shanghai's prestigious Institute of Mechanical Engineering carried a banner that read: "We Want to Be Free Men. We Don't Want to Be Mechanical Men."[66]

The crowds swelled as pedestrians stopped and watched. One foreign news agency estimated that 70,000 gathered on Saturday, most in the People's Square, but many in front of the party office on the Bund.[67] On Sunday, official estimates said that 30,000 were on the streets, including 10,000 students.[68] They were by far the largest protests in China since the economic reform movement had begun at the end of the 1970s.

The inclusion of workers and peasants in the movement made the situation more volatile; at about 8 P.M. on Sunday, for example, workers swarmed around a Toyota minivan and car sitting near the party office along the Bund that they believed belonged to the police. They rocked the vehicles until they turned over. Gasoline began to spill out. Fire fighters hosed the vehicles furiously to prevent them from being set alight.

That night, along with Rui Xingwen and Ruan Chongwu, Jiang presided over an emergency meeting of 8,000 cadres from all city government departments in the Shanghai coliseum, nursing his head wound.[69] Orders were issued to staunch the movement; rural cadres were to ensure that the 10,000 middle-school youths working in the fields did not return to the city when holidays began on 26 December; new regulations were to be prepared tightening controls on demonstrations; and bus companies were ordered to cancel all staff leave so that extra services could be run. A Xinhua report issued that evening complained: "We have just gained some peace since the Cultural Revolution. Was that suffering not enough?"[70]

In the end, the frantic preparations for worse unrest proved unnecessary. By Sunday night, the demonstrations were already losing momentum. The Bund was empty by 11 P.M. as students and workers returned home to prepare for the week ahead. The next day, most students returned to classes. Large numbers of police had been brought into the city from surrounding areas overnight,[71] but by then, they were not needed.

Two new regulations were announced that day effectively banning further demonstrations and threatening protesters with punishment. Students were also warned they should not "encircle, sneer at, insult, abuse, or beat state functionaries such as cadres and people's police."[72] A Shanghai spokesman, in a clear departure from the govenment's earlier tone, even called some of the protest posters "reactionary."[73] Nonetheless, he said, "the municipal government adhered constantly to the principle of dialogue."[74] Jiang, attending a work safety meeting that day, appeared already to be considering how to prevent future unrest. "With respect to those factors unfavorable to social stability," he said, "organizations at various levels must do a good job in ideological education in a just and forceful manner."[75]

By 3 A.M. on Tuesday morning, the last of the demonstrators had left the People's Square. One official report chirped merrily that students at Jiaotong University were attending classes and wrapping Christmas presents.[76] The next day, Shanghai officials staged a meeting with fifteen hand-picked "student leaders" from the top universities, at which the most important student complaints were glossed over. The government retracted the charge that 31 policemen had been beaten, one of several demands put forward by some 5,000 students during a meeting Tuesday with city education officials at Tongji University. In return, the students agreed to hold no further demonstrations.[77] Although the fifteen student leaders were hardly representative of the movement—Lu Qiang, the head of the city's autonomous student federation, for example, was not among them—the radical students had already lost their drive. The meeting was a face-saving gesture for both sides.

Could Jiang take credit for the rapid dousing of the Shanghai movement? To be sure, he had little sympathy with the students. "They were very simple-minded, all those students in 1986," he would recall in comparing them with his own experiences as a student. "It was nothing like us in 1946."[78] Given his dismissive attitude, he barely stayed within the limits imposed by Hu Yaobang's appeal for "mediation and dialogue" with the students. Police surrounded the students everywhere they went. As the days passed, they also erected barricades in the People's Square and in front of the Bund. These had the effect of corralling the students, isolating them from passers-by who in other circumstances might have joined in. Certainly, Jiang was leaning toward using force. But the measures his government took proved adequate in the face of a flagging student movement in the chill of winter. Shanghai students made their point and went back to class.

The Shanghai government was quick to tabulate the disruption caused by the four days of protest: 3 million people missed their buses, and 2,600 people missed their trains. "Old, weak, sick, and disabled passengers had to stand for several hours in cold winds to wait for the normalization of public transport services," the Xinhua News Agency complained.[79] Six men were put to death for alleged hooliganism. Two of them had allegedly been involved in the overturning of the Toyota van, while another had pushed over a row of bicycles. The other three included a peasant from nearby Jiangsu province who had allegedly groped four young women in the crowds. "None of the six is a university student," a government spokesman said emphatically, apparently seeking to emphasize that Jiang had kept his promise to the students.[80]

Students were threatened with "administrative punishment" by police, which could mean up to three years in a labor camp.[81] But in the aftermath of the protests, university officials concentrated mainly on party purity; 127 student members of the party were expelled at Jiaotong University alone.

The protests were the first setback for the Communist government since the end of the Cultural Revolution. Up to then, the social consequences of Deng's economic reforms had been largely contained or deflected. But the sight of thousands of students and workers parading through the streets calling for rapid democratic changes left senior leaders seething, even if they maintained an outward composure. One of Deng's first acts was to expel Fang Lizhi from the party, along with a dissident writer in Shanghai, Wang Ruowang. This was only window dressing though. Knives were being sharpened at the top as well.

It was difficult for Deng simultaneously to save his beleaguered party chief, Hu Yaobang, and to prevent incipient liberalism from taking his reforms further than intended. At a meeting on 30 December, Deng criticized Hu for not taking a tougher stance on the students. "In Shanghai, people are even saying that the party center has no mettle," Deng complained.[82] Hu was given one last chance to save his job with a vigorous self-criticism at the end of December. But it was like throwing a beachball to a man drowning in a hurricane. On 4 January, Deng met Zhao and several party and army elders at his residence, and together they decided that Hu had to go. Zhao would take over as party secretary, and Li Peng would be designated premier. After a five-day internal inquisition, which was little more than a prelude to his dismissal, Hu was sacked on 16 January. The announcement was made on that evening's television news.[83]

Even as party elders were preparing to oust Hu in Beijing, Jiang sensed the shifting winds and began trimming his sails accordingly. "We must take a clear-cut stand against bourgeois liberalization," he told a meeting on 6 January. "We should persist in taking the Chinese-style socialist road . . . without ever returning to the capitalist road."[84] A week later, a start-up Shanghai newspaper, *Shanghai shehui bao* (Shanghai Society News), was shut down for having covered the protests sympathetically. Meanwhile, two party cadres from the city's propaganda department were installed in the editorial office of the *Shijie jingji daobao,* or *World Economic Herald*, a lively weekly set up with Wang Daohan's blessing in 1980. The *Herald* would return to prominence during the 1989 protests, but even then, its liberal views were the subject of several critical letters by local party elders attached to the Shanghai Retired Cadres Bureau.[85]

From January to March, Jiang and Rui also organized three consecutive "study and report" meetings aimed at reading the riot act to cadres who might have taken up the cause of the students, even if only in their hearts. "Historical experience tells us that capitalism won't work in China," Jiang asserted. "We must march forward unswervingly along the road of Chinese-style socialism."[86]

If the 1985 unrest had shown Jiang to be a staunch economic reformer, the events of December 1986 proved that he was an equally staunch political conservative. If not for the restraining influence of Hu Yaobang, Jiang might even have overplayed his hand and used greater force against the students. As it was, having extinguished the movement with little more than a few scuffles, Jiang and the rest of the Shanghai leadership appealed to liberals and conservatives alike. It was a high ground worth staking out as politics in Beijing grew increasingly rancorous. Whatever combination of skill and luck was used, one thing was clear: Jiang looked good. The largest and most potentially damaging student demonstrations since the Cultural Revolution had effectively been stifled in Shanghai. Jiang had met the students twice, fulfilling Hu's request, but at the same time had not budged on any position of principle. Hu's dialogue became Jiang's lectures. Li Guoqiang, an official biographer, paid Jiang this backhanded compliment in the wake of his handling of the Tiananmen Square protests three years later: "People remember him more for the way he handled the 1986 protests."[87]

6

Jiang's insistence during the December 1986 protests that press reports "must benefit the interests of the people, the reforms and the open policy" marked the emergence of a new dimension of his character as a party leader. Although he may have preferred frank, factual reporting as electronics minister, now that he was the mayor of a major city, he had to consider more than just the media's role in conveying facts.

As a child, Jiang had witnessed the political power of the press in the activities of his two prolific uncles, Jiang Shangqing and Jiang Shufeng. The battery of party newspapers and magazines they published during the late 1930s and early 1940s may have helped instill into him very early a sense of the media as a tool of the party's work. Although he never fought in the civil war, Jiang later showed that he shared the civil war mentality of the earlier generations, at least when it came to the press.

This eventually surfaced when he ran Shanghai. During his nearly five years as mayor and later party secretary of the city, Jiang displayed an extraordinary concern—perhaps bordering on paranoia—about what was in the press. The closure of the *Shanghai shehui bao* and the reorganization of the *World Economic Herald* after the December 1986 protests were just two early examples.

Signs of Jiang's fastidious treatment of the media had emerged soon after he became mayor. An article in *Jiefang ribao* (Liberation Daily) on his plans for new infrastructure quoted Jiang promising to change three landmarks of the city—namely, the airport, the train station, and the port passenger terminal.[88] In a typically pretentious display, Jiang had sought during his press conference to use the English word "faces" in place of the Chinese word for landmark, *mianmao*. When *Jiefang ribao* duly reported his vision using the Chinese word the next day, Jiang was enraged. His attempt to flaunt his English, incorrect as it was, had been thwarted by know-it-alls in the media. Jiang had his private secretary phone the newspaper in protest. "It would have been better if you had written the English word 'face,'" his secretary lectured the blameless journalist. "That would be more in keeping with Mayor Jiang's meaning."[89]

Beginning in 1986, Jiang held regular meetings with the senior editors of all the main media organizations in the city. It was a departure from the normal method of media control, where propaganda officials were normally deputed to handle such work. No other mayor had done this before.[90] The purpose was to cast a wider net of control over the media in his own kingdom. "Jiang paid very close attention to his relationship with the media and reporters," notes Wang Xiaopeng.[91]

Jiang's sensitivity about press reports was heightened by the nature of his job. Shanghai was crowded and run-down, and its people were famous for their short tempers. Even the least incident could spark minor protests. When a fire broke out at a government building on the Huangpu

River in October 1986, Jiang admitted that city leaders "could not conceal their anxiety."[92] A hundred homes were built cheek by jowl around the flaming building, and firefighters raced to soak the structure before sparks leapt to the adjoining houses. The fire was soon contained, but the sudden and huge demand on the city's ancient water system resulted in mains bursting all along bustling Nanjing Road. Parts of the central transport route were inundated.

Shanghai Television rushed to the scene of both accidents, giving viewers a solid two days of nothing but disaster. The TV reports made city authorities look like the bumbling Keystone Cops. Jiang was angered by the unflattering coverage. "Reports like this should not just alarm people," he charged at a fire-prevention meeting a week later. "They should enable people to understand the problems of Shanghai's infrastructure, as well as see that improvements are gradually being made."[93]

A similar problem that arose over poor infrastructure soon provoked Jiang's worst run-in with the local media. On 4 May 1987, following a meeting with local People's Congress delegates, Jiang was accosted by one harried delegate, who told him a sorry tale. A water pipe near the new train station had been spewing into the street for close to a year after being severed by careless workers. Several letters from the delegate to the Zhabei district authorities had received only polite replies. "The matter is being handled by relevant departments," they read. The broken pipe was, of course, affecting the image of one of Jiang's own showcase "face" projects. Back in his office, he patched through to the local water supplies department. "Get someone to fix that pipe now!" he hollered. It was done the same day.

The incident might have passed unremarked. But a few weeks later, Xu Jingen, a star reporter for *Jiefang ribao*, asked the delegate about his campaign to fix the pipe and was told the story of Jiang's personal intervention in the matter. An average reporter for the mainland press might have written a story praising Jiang's respect for the "suggestion" of the People's Congress delegate. But other ideas crossed Xu's mind. The issue was important enough, he thought, to be written up in the "Weekly Forum" column on the front page of the *People's Daily*. Editors there, familiar with Xu's work, agreed immediately.

The column appeared on 6 July 1987.[94] Entitled "The Other Side of Doing Things Yourself," the column was a stinging indictment of Jiang's high-handed meddling in what should have been an administrative affair. "It is totally abnormal for leading cadres to get involved in sorting out every little problem," the column read. "All it will do is encourage a mentality of dependence and procrastination among those at the lower levels."

Jiang was furious. Although it did not mention him by name, the article left little doubt that he was the "principal city leader" of Shanghai under discussion. The last sentence made the connection even stronger by making a reference to one of Jiang's earlier attempts to hold down taxi fares in Shanghai. "Some newspapers around the country constantly run articles praising the mayors of certain cities for resolving the high costs of taxis," it read. "But what's the point of having a director of the price bureau or a general manager of the taxi company if this kind of thing goes on?"

Jiang was being held up for public ridicule on the front page of the party's flagship national newspaper. Xu's biting sarcasm made a point that the *People's Daily* felt was fair. But Jiang was offended. His assiduous efforts to run this creaky, sprawling city were being dismissed as petty meddling by an insolent young reporter. It wouldn't do.

On 10 July, Jiang convened a special meeting of all party and government officials in Shanghai involved in propaganda. "Xu Jingen has not the slightest idea of what it's like to run this city," Jiang charged, pounding his fist on the table. "This supposedly skillful writer really thinks he's impressive," he continued. "Well, I think he should get out of his office more often and have a look around!"[95] Editors from *Jiefang ribao* sat at the meeting hanging their heads in shame. The meeting had turned into a forum for a torrent of abuse against Xu and his superiors.

Jiang by this time was sufficiently aware of the power of the media—even in its heavily controlled form in China—to influence public opinion in favor of or against the government. Not only his effectiveness as mayor but also his image in Beijing depended on keeping close tabs on the press. After lambasting Xu, he proceeded to enumerate the various reasons why he had intervened over the broken pipe. No one spoke a word.

When the meeting adjourned, the editors returned to the newspaper office and informed Xu of his transgression. There was no point debating. Only by showing contrition could Xu hope to save his job. A letter of apology was the first step. On his editors' advice, Xu worked through the night fashioning an apology to Jiang and delivered it by hand the next morning.

It seems that Jiang was not after Xu's head. Indeed, he appears to have been caught off guard by the repentant appeal. "After you've been around me a little longer, you'll realize that I always encourage comrades to appraise each in an open-hearted way," Jiang responded in a letter to Xu. "But I have this one fault: sometimes my attitude is a little too harsh. Please excuse me."

It seemed magnanimous. Jiang was admitting that he had gone overboard in calling the special struggle session. But he had made his point. Jiang was the chief clerk of the city's general affairs office, as Wang Daohan had predicted, and he was determined not to be held to blame for the bureaucratic sclerosis that forced him to intervene in such cases. The chastened Shanghai media never again dared to comment on his style of governance.

7

Near the end of an otherwise routine National Day soirée at the Shanghai Sports Stadium on 1 October 1987, Jiang Zemin suddenly rose from his seat on the VIP rostrum and approached the stage. The bemused audience expected their pudgy mayor to make one of his dull speeches. But instead, Jiang hopped onto the conductor's dais and asked for the baton. Spinning around to face the full symphony orchestra, he lifted his hands and began conducting a rousing rendition of the "Internationale," the world communist anthem. Red and green lights flashed from above the stage, and clouds of vapor rose from floor outlets. Jiang beamed from ear to ear when the surprised audience of 20,000 hooted, "Hao! Hao! [Good! Good!]"[96] Months earlier, on a tour of the Melbourne opera house in Australia, he had leapt onto the stage and broken into song before his amused hosts.[97]

Jiang by this time exuded confidence as Shanghai's mayor. He had developed a reputation for being both politically astute and administratively competent. The egomania that would later characterize his leadership style was already beginning to show. The exuberant displays may also have been induced by advance knowledge of more good things to come. At the party's thirteenth congress in late October, Jiang was made a member of China's inner sanctum of power, the 15-member Politburo. In a single bound, he had joined the ranks of the country's ruling elite.

He was not the only mayor who made the exclusive cut. Li Ruihuan, mayor of another provincial-level city, Tianjin, was also elevated to the Politburo at the congress. Like Jiang, Li had served only one term on the Central Committee before the promotion. And like Jiang, he would also switch posts from mayor to party chief of his city at this time.[98] Positions had opened up on the Politburo with the departure of eight party elders, including Jiang's fellow Yangzhou Middle School graduate Hu Qiaomu, earlier in the year. Deng's creation in 1982 of a halfway house for retiring party elders, the Central Advisory Commission, was finally having the intended effects. Two younger members of the Politburo, Qiao Shi and Li Peng, were bumped upstairs to its standing committee.

Still, there were dozens of other promising young local leaders among the 300-odd Central Committee members who might have merited inclusion in the Politburo. Why choose Jiang? Many ascribed the promotion to a Machiavellian "Shanghai faction" maneuvering to promote its kind to Beijing, a tired old Chinese political theory. This is unlikely, however, both on practical and theoretical grounds. In fact, the proportion of cadres on the Central Committee raised or having worked in Shanghai had actually fallen continuously ever since the establishment of the People's Republic, and would continue to do so throughout the 1990s.[99] Jiang was the first Shanghai leader promoted to the Politburo since 1976.

In fact, the theory probably has things back to front. Rather than being a stepping stone to later promotion to Beijing, evidence suggested that Shanghai was more like an incubator for high-flying cadres whom party leaders had *already* decided merited future promotion. Cadres like Jiang and Rui Xingwen (who was appointed to the party secretariat at this time) were most likely already in line for promotion before they were sent to the city.[100]

Jiang's eminence had first manifested itself when he was attached to the central work group sent to regain control over Shanghai in 1976. His appointment to the Central Committee in 1982, at the youngish age of 56, confirmed that he was marked for higher things. But, in retrospect, it was his appointment to Shanghai that most strongly indicated that he was finding favor in the right circles in Beijing. Since he had acquitted himself well in his first two years in Shanghai, promotion to the Politburo was almost a matter of course.

As a Politburo member, Jiang was now treated as an equal when senior leaders from Beijing came to visit Shanghai. As early as August 1987, when Jiang accompanied Acting Premier Li Peng on a tour of the city, for example, he did not have to "present a report" (*hui bao*), as local leaders usually do. In December of that year, he enjoyed the same exemption while entertaining the party elders Yao Yilin and Li Xiannian.

Taking on new responsibilities in the party's core of power also meant that Jiang would have to forsake his cherished role as chief clerk of Shanghai. He probably had few regrets about leaving the mayoralty, though. By this time, he was complaining long and loud about the burdens of the post. For one thing, there was the inexhaustible store of seemingly trivial issues he had to solve; besides dealing with broken pipes and watermelon rinds, Jiang had also been forced to intervene to restore electricity to the city's only vinegar factory during a power outage shortly before the 1986 lunar new year festival, when the condiment is doused liberally on traditional dumplings.[101] The endless stream of foreign and domestic visitors always clogging up his waiting room seeking an audience was another annoyance. "I can't refuse to see these people. But it means these activities are occupying all my time," Jiang had complained. "The only time left to read important documents in my average day is from 9 P.M. until midnight. I'm already overwhelmed by new things as it is and I have no time to study. . . . To be honest, it's a real pain in the neck."[102] Even Jiang, it seems, wearied of being Shanghai's chief clerk. Membership of the Politburo had its advantages.

At a meeting in December 1987, Jiang introduced the assembled Shanghai cadres to the man who would replace him as mayor, Zhu Rongji. Little known to the Shanghai crowd, Zhu had worked in central government ministries virtually all his life since graduation from Beijing's prestigious Qinghua University in 1951. His assignment to Shanghai was another example of the city's incubator role, since he would later serve as premier. One report said that when Zhu was introduced, "the applause was so sparse that Jiang's clapping seemed especially loud."[103] A native of Hunan province, Zhu had struggled to put himself through secondary school and university; his father had died before his birth and his mother shortly afterward. His self-acknowledged "background of suffering" gave him a blunt demeanor that ingratiated him to common people but often rubbed colleagues the wrong way. Cadres from more privileged backgrounds, like Jiang, found his unwillingness to mince words alarming. Unlike Mao, the greatest communist son of Hunan, Zhu was not a bumpkin. (He was well read in modern literature.) Neither, however, was he impressed by fancy talk. Zhu's introductions to conferences were short and snappy. If cadres showed up at meetings unprepared with loads of statistics, he would kick them out. Those late for official ceremonies would be told to skip the banquet afterward.[104] It was a stark contrast to Jiang's more affected and cordial manner. But they would prove a formidable team.[105]

Few were willing to openly suggest good riddance when Jiang left the mayoralty. Certainly, starts had been made on a number of key urban infrastructure projects, and foreign investment was starting to pick up.

The economy was growing at around 6–8 percent. But there was a clear sense that more could be done. "The people of Shanghai feel that Zhu is bolder and more decisive than Jiang, and that many of Shanghai's problems have been somewhat alleviated only since Zhu became mayor," an official report would note in retrospect.[106]

Zhu, of course, had history on his side. For in the same way that Jiang had walked into a favorable situation compared to his predecessor, Wang Daohan, so too would Zhu enjoy an external boost just as he assumed office. Beijing had announced a series of preferential foreign investment policies specially for Shanghai, which came into effect in 1987.[107] In the same year, the central government adopted a strategic policy of speeding up the development of all coastal areas, which would remain in force for eight years, before widening income gaps forced a shift in focus to impoverished inland areas. While the coastal-based development strategy lasted, the economic story of places like Shanghai was one of huge inflows of foreign investment and a booming local economy.

Shanghai's share of national exports slipped further from 10 percent in 1985 to 8 percent by 1989.[108] But a different tale was told on the foreign investment front. Direct foreign investment rose from U.S.$58 million in the entire period 1979 to 1985 to U.S.$1 billion in the next four years, including U.S.$422 million in 1989 alone. The city's share of the national total over that period rose from 1 percent in 1985 to 12 percent in 1989.[109] It was remarkable considering that it was not until 1990 that an SEZ-like development area was opened in Pudong, on the east bank of Shanghai's Huangpu River.

Most of the one billion dollars of foreign investment attracted to Shanghai in the second half of the 1980s went into real estate and hotels. As mayor, Jiang had been in charge of the city's first joint-venture hotel, the Sheraton, opened at the end of 1986. After the Sheraton was opened, he allotted land for another luxury hotel, the Shanghai Hilton.[110] He worked with Prescott Bush, the brother of George Bush, then U.S. vice president, to build a golf course in Shanghai. And he presided as mayor over the opening of the then-biggest ever Sino–U.S. joint venture, for the assembly of McDonnell Douglas airplanes.

Jiang enjoyed rubbing shoulders with wealthy foreign investors. He would ply them with technical questions and emit off-the-cuff remarks in English. When serious talks began, he would retreat to the safety of translated Chinese. "We have to let foreign investors make money," he told foreign diplomats stationed in Shanghai, "and make more money than we do."[111]

With Zhu as his eager sidekick and Beijing pressing for an acceleration of Shanghai's economic opening, Jiang made a symbolic trip to Guangdong's booming Pearl River Delta region at the head of an 11-member city delegation in January 1988. It required enormous humility for the proud Shanghaiese to stoop to the level of seeking answers from the Cantonese. "It is natural for Shanghai to feel humiliated in sending such a large group of officials to Guangzhou," the vice-chairman of the city's economic commission, Jiang Yiren, told a foreign reporter. "But leaders have always urged us not to be arrogant toward other areas."[112] On his return from the trip, Jiang held a meeting for 10,000 cadres, at which he said they must "learn humbly" from Guangdong. "We should no longer be blind or self-content," Jiang said. "Everyone from the top down has to adapt to the needs of the commodity economy."[113]

Jiang's southern tour provided the momentum and the political will to carry out a large reduction in red tape for foreign investors that eventually won both Jiang and Zhu plaudits from abroad and purring praise from Beijing. The vast economic planning structure associated with Shanghai's 4,000 state-run industrial enterprises made the city bureaucratic even by China's standards. Faced with a maze of government offices, all demanding their say in a project, foreign investors often turned elsewhere. Attempts had been made by Jiang while mayor to cut out layers of government, but with only modest success.

The worsening situation was brought to light by an article in the Beijing-based *Jingji ribao* (Economic Daily) in March 1988, which described the "official chop travels" of foreign managers of a small joint venture being set up in Shanghai's rural Baoshan district. The article described how it took the managers fifteen months to get a mind-boggling 126 official "chops" (approvals) from nineteen different government bureaus and fourteen government commissions in quest of a green light for their start-up. By the time they gave up and complained to city leaders, more approvals were still being demanded.

"I felt deeply ashamed when I was told about this case," Jiang admitted in mid March. "When I visited Dongguan [Guangdong province] in January, they told me they approve these contracts in an hour. How can we expect foreigners to put up with all this red tape?"[114]

The timing of the "official chop travels" article could not have been better. Jiang's immediate response was to convene a now-famous "denounce red tape" meeting. Zhu—more inclined toward solving problems rather than merely bewailing them—suggested practical changes, which were immediately approved. Within two months, Zhu had set up

Shanghai's first one-stop foreign investment center. The new Shanghai Foreign Investment Commission was authorized by Beijing to approve projects worth up to U.S.$30 million. More important, obtaining the commission's approval would obviate the need for other official chops. Henceforth, Shanghai's new mayor, and China's future premier, would be known as "one-chop Zhu."

8

In April 1988, Shanghai's local TV station teamed up with the Shanghai women's federation to revive the "Miss Shanghai" beauty pageant, which had last been staged in 1947. Another beauty pageant was already being planned in Beijing, where organizers were appealing to the worldwide popularity of such events for justification. The costs of staging the Shanghai contest would be Rmb450,000, including Rmb5,000 for the winner.

Torn between a natural aversion to popular culture, but an outward desire to be seen as a reformist, Jiang said nothing at first. Within days of the announcement, however, party elders in the city were flooding his office with complaints. They called the expenditure "inappropriate" at a time when many Shanghai residents were being squeezed by inflation on one hand and inadequate public spending on social welfare on the other. A few delegates to the municipal parliament meeting in May tabled a motion calling for the contest to be called off. That was all the pressure Jiang needed to ban it on 10 May. "Conditions are not yet ripe," he said.[115] "As long as I'm party secretary of Shanghai, there will be no beauty pageants here." Jiang took the step with some reluctance, knowing that the city was trying to project a modern image abroad. Probably for that reason, he forbade the local press from reporting the move. "People guessed that this was either to avoid embarrassing the sponsors or to ensure that people abroad did not mistakenly assume he was too 'hard-line,'" an official biography notes.[116]

For all his aspirations to worldliness, Jiang remained a social conservative even in the liberal heyday of the late 1980s in China. At the time, he could easily have justified the beauty contest on the grounds of Shanghai's aspirations to regain its lost shine as the Pearl of the Orient. But with just a little persuasion, he lowered the boom. His clampdown on media coverage suggests that he knew that the move might paint him as an ideological hard-liner abroad and in Beijing.

But Jiang's social conservatism was not rooted in party dogma, an obvious reason why he recoiled from being associated with ideological conservatives. He never called the beauty pageant bourgeois frippery. Rather, he was a natural conservative. His traditional upbringing had instilled into him a paternalistic view of the role of the party and of the government, something like the sensibility of a Victorian do-gooder. His final years in Shanghai would be characterized by a fatherly and often patronizing concern for the common people and their cultural life. Freed from the burdens of handling the economy and day-to-day city affairs, Jiang developed into a true father figure.

The thirteenth congress had appealed for more direct dialogue between the people and the party, and Jiang responded with relish by convening a series of roundtable discussions with hand-picked city residents. Jiang was comfortable in large groups, especially when he was the center of attention. Far from feeling threatened by dialogue, he warmed to the opportunity to deliver fatherly lectures on his view of the world. The egomaniac and the paternalist were always at work. "Discussions with city residents have made me one of their close friends," he told Xinhua in December 1987 after meeting twenty local notables, including professors and factory directors.[117] Jiang insisted that the meetings were "not paying lip service" to the party line, but were "aimed at helping people solve difficulties so we can win their confidence." Descriptions of the meetings suggest, however, that he was falling into his old habit of lecturing those he was supposed to be sounding out. "Some angry residents raised questions about traffic congestion during one meeting, but were satisfied after the mayor explained the problem and quoted statistics on the government's efforts in this area," Xinhua reported.

Jiang's newfound adherence to the idea of "helping the people" found expression in a number of bizarre ways. On the eve of lunar new year in February 1988, for example, he sent a special plane to Guangzhou to collect 140 stranded Shanghai natives who were unable to get flights home for the traditional family festival. The act of benevolence "incurred a financial loss," the local *Wenhui bao* newspaper noted, but Jiang did not seem to mind. It showed he "cared for his people."[118]

If more proof were needed of the traditional rather than ideological roots of Jiang's conservatism, it could be seen in the nonchalant attitude he took toward Marxism. The thirteenth congress had also called for a further refinement (some would say watering down) of Marxism to meet the needs of contemporary China, and Jiang took just as eagerly to this task. "There should be no forbidden zones for theoretical study and researchers should be allowed to say anything they want," he told an academic conference in March 1988. "We should never condemn or label theoretical faults, or keep a record of them."[119]

Jiang admitted he was "always confused" by a number of issues, such as whether greater democracy would compromise economic efficiency and whether the booming semi-private rural firms were eroding the state's hold on the economy. They were not the type of questions asked by a committed Marxist. But by now Jiang was starting to see and create the world in his own image. Not according to the dictates of a long-dead German philosopher, but more according to the aristocratic highbrow traditions of his native Yangtze River Delta area. Miss Shanghai was not an affront to Marx, he believed. She was an affront to Shanghai itself.

9

The price rises set off by the renewed drive for economic reform endorsed by the October 1987 party congress caught everyone by surprise. National retail prices and urban living costs both soared nearly 20 percent in 1988, more than double the previous year's increase. Monthly retail price rises rose from 19 percent in June to a post-1949 high of 26 percent in October. By the end of the year, the average national market price of steel was two and a half times the government-controlled price.[120]

Inflationary bouts were, of course, common in the 1980s. Rapid economic growth, averaging 8.9 percent in the decade, masked a rollercoaster ride of policy reversals, which helped to exacerbate the normal economic cycle. Inflation fell and then rose to consecutively higher peaks in 1980, 1985, and 1988. The 1988 blight was particularly acute in Shanghai, where both food and general retail prices rose 21 percent over the year.[121] Sectors long characterized by supply shortages fared even worse; the price of a typical high-rise apartment in the city's urban areas, for example, zoomed upward by 44 percent in 1988.[122] In a symbolic gesture, on 1 May, to alleviate the impact of rocketing food prices on blue-collar workers, the city government began paying every resident a food stipend of Rmb10 a month.[123] It had little effect on calming fears of hyperinflation. In the last two weeks of August, more than Rmb100 million was withdrawn from banks in Shanghai. Runs on textiles, salt, and gold were reported in the latter half of the year.[124]

Jiang seemed to be reaching for the trigger as fears of social unrest increased. At a meeting with the Shanghai garrison on 9 August, he warned of "unstable social factors" in the city. Shanghai police had barely coped with the four days of mass demonstrations in December 1986, he said, and city leaders were pinning their hopes on stronger contingents of militia (citizens trained in military operations) and reserves (part-time military personnel subject to call for active duty in emergencies) to prevent renewed disturbances. "To eliminate the unstable social factors in Shanghai, we must give full play to the backbone role of the militia in maintaining social order," he told the local army commanders. "Our army and militia have played a great role in cases of emergency. By attaching importance to building the militia and reserve forces, we can use them at critical moments."[125]

The inflationary swell gradually assumed greater prominence in national politics. By the time senior leaders, including Jiang, met to discuss the situation in the northern seaside resort of Beidaihe in mid August 1988, buying panics had already broken out in several major cities. At issue at the Beidaihe meeting were Zhao Ziyang's plans for wide-ranging decontrol of most prices over the following five years. A Politburo meeting a month earlier had approved the idea of further price decontrol as the best way to root out inflation for good. Zhao Ziyang now presented a "preliminary plan for price and salary reforms" that would solve the most egregious price distortions in the economy. The Beidaihe meetings were given unusually extensive publicity, and between the lines the Chinese people could see the internal strife that beset economic policy-making. Zhao's plan was approved "in principle," signifying that dissent remained. The official party history later described the decision as "improper."[126] More panic buying ensued as consumers sought to beat imminent price hikes.

It took only a few weeks for party leaders to realize their mistake. On 31 August, all the arguments made at Beidaihe were put back on the table at a State Council standing committee meeting in Beijing. Premier Li Peng's conservative instincts finally won the day. Retail prices were to be frozen in the second half of the year, inflation indexing was introduced for bank deposits of three or more years, and construction of new offices and hotels was halted. Within two months, over 10,000 building projects worth Rmb33 billion were stopped.[127] The party plenum in late September 1988 put its official stamp of approval on Li Peng's austerity program. For the next two years, taming the economy would be the primary task. Reforms, meanwhile, were to be "comprehensive" rather than piecemeal—code for the ditching of Zhao Ziyang's ambitious price decontrol package.

It was clear that Zhao was being blamed for the economic mess. Local leaders like Jiang who had lavished fulsome praise on Zhao's planned reforms when those reforms appeared to be in the ascendancy now found themselves uncomfortably exposed. Jiang had supported Zhao's coastal development strategy and even made his own "imperial tour" to Guangdong to show his adherence to Zhao's economic agenda. On several occasions, he had trumpeted the Zhaoist slogans "Reform is the driving force behind everything" and "Frictions that arise in the course of reforms can only be solved by more reforms."[128]

But as an ancient Chinese saying goes, "When the tree falls, the monkeys scatter" (*Shu dao, husun san*). Local leaders like Jiang, who had once sat peaceably in Zhao's tree of bold reforms, now began to scamper from its boughs. Jiang called together a group of scholars in mid October 1988 to discuss how to stick to the letter of the plenum's new guidelines for reining in the economy over the following two years. "The economic reforms must be guided and orderly," Jiang told the assembly.[129] Coming the same day that an embattled Zhao invited academics in Beijing to a meeting to criticize the plenum guidelines, Jiang's switch in allegiances could not have been more obvious. But he was not the only official making a climbdown, and, probably for that reason, he would still be remembered by those who mattered in Beijing as an economic reformer at heart. By late 1988, the gathering storm of court strife in Beijing made it safe for Jiang to switch sides with his reputation intact.

As inflation roared in late 1988, concerns about *guandao,* or official profiteering, also grew. Responding to a growing popular outcry, the State Council issued new regulations in October 1988 on "cleaning up and rectifying companies." At the top level, senior retired cadres were forbidden to work for companies. Lower down, all private companies were ordered to sever their links with party and government organizations. So-called "reversible sign" companies—which were really just government offices that called themselves companies in order to levy fees—were also to be cast off or closed down.

Jiang's position was precarious in the campaign against *guandao,* because to a large extent he had abetted the practice in Shanghai. Under reforms he had introduced in early 1988 to help city finances, government and party departments were encouraged to "actively organize reasonable income," and to operate enterprises as long as they were not "purely commercial." Such income, Jiang argued, could help improve the living conditions of bureaucrats and cadres.[130] Zhao Ziyang was furious at Jiang's encouragement of such blatant bureaucratic capitalism.

He telephoned Jiang several times in the first half of 1988 to demand an end to these money-making activities. "I made special phone calls to Comrade Jiang asking him to correct this mistake," Zhao would reveal in his extraordinary self-defense of the following spring.[131]

Zhao's appeals apparently had little effect. Not until the State Council regulations came out in October did Jiang close the shutters on the aspiring mandarin-entrepreneurs in Shanghai. By then it was clear that Zhao was losing influence; hard-liners were now in the ascendant in Beijing.

10

It becomes virtually impossible to follow Jiang's stint as Shanghai party secretary in even modest isolation from national events after late 1988. From then on, soaring inflation and growing reports of official corruption led to a spiral of discontent, which dominated local and national politics. What do we know of Jiang on the eve of this maelstrom?

By early 1989, he had completed, by his own reckoning, "nineteen years in leading organs" of the party and government since his rescue from the penumbra of the Cultural Revolution in 1970. Nicknames applied to him by snide Shanghai residents suggested a leader who was all show and no substance. "Panda Bear" and "Flowerpot" were just two of these unflattering sobriquets. To a large extent, the slurs were fair comment. Jiang was not a capable economic manager, even though he was an avid economic reformer. On foreign investment, for example, Jiang had all the right instincts but pursued none of the right policies. It had taken the likes of Zhu Rongji to put in place a one-stop investment-approval office. Infrastructure plans were set in motion under Jiang. But only the new train station was completed during his term, while other projects were bogged down in financial and engineering difficulties.

Jiang's proclivity to micromanage also meant that he showed up a lot in the daily press but never seemed to get at the root of the problems. He sent a plane to retrieve stranded cadres. He intervened to fix a broken water pipe or restore electricity to a vinegar factory. But this tendency to hurl himself into minor matters might have taken away from broader planning efforts. Wang Daohan had warned him about the travails of managing such a large city, but Jiang found it suited his style just fine. When he was taken to task for this fault on the front page of the *People's Daily,* he denounced the writer as an ignoramus.

Another nickname given to Jiang while he was in Shanghai was "Weathercock," suggesting that he turned in whatever direction the political wind was blowing. To some extent this was true of every successful Chinese leader. But Jiang may have been more capricious than most. He turned against Hu Yaobang after the 1986 student protests and against Zhao Ziyang after the 1988 inflation in an obviously self-serving way. This may have made him a weather vane, but it also showed his acumen in playing high politics. Indeed, Jiang used his stint in Shanghai to build a modest array of top-level personal relationships that would serve him well later. In 1988, Deng Xiaoping began a tradition of visiting the city every lunar new year, which he would carry on for seven years until 1994, when he made his last public appearance. The 1988 trip gave Jiang a chance to play host to the nation's economic savior at the happiest time in the year. Jiang's elevation to the Politburo further enhanced his status in Beijing.

Shanghai had also provided Jiang with the chance to hone his diplomatic skills, which would prove crucial in later years. While ignored or used as mere photo opportunities in Western countries, the formalities of diplomacy were a staple ingredient of the state-controlled media in China. They were also a carefully watched indicator of the "openness" of up-and-coming leaders. "As a person, he was one of the most 'Western' leaders I ever met in China," recalled U.S. Senator Dianne Feinstein, a former mayor of San Francisco, who traded several official visits with Jiang.[132] The *Washington Post* praised Jiang as "an energetic, bespectacled former minister of electronics, [who] is representative of the new type of educated, technically competent leader whom the country's top leadership is trying to promote."[133] Jiang even impressed U.S. reporters by donning a Chicago Cubs baseball cap given to him by a visiting delegation from that city in September 1985. "It's very beautiful," he said graciously as he puzzled over the plain-looking cap.[134]

Jiang's conviviality with foreigners came naturally. Indeed, he seemed to become more animated when talking with outsiders. "He struck me as a very progressive administrator, intent on bringing China into modern society," the late San Francisco city councilor Gordon Lau recalled. Lau even recalled a splendid example of Jiang's "openness" while the pair stopped over in Hawaii on their way to San Francisco in 1986:

> We started out at 8 A.M. and kept going until 1 A.M. the next morning. He ate a breakfast that would have knocked out an elephant. Then we toured Oahu a while, and moved on to an enormous traditional Hawaiian lunch. At dinner, he showed up in a Hawaiian shirt. The next morning, Jiang was up by 6 A.M., for a swim at Waikiki, and another breakfast at the Royal Hawaiian [Hotel].[135]

The impression Jiang left was almost always favorable, if not exactly suave or polished. And if that was the summation of his time in Shanghai, it could be counted a profitable experience. At 62, he was a member of the Politburo and in charge of the Yangtze River city that had been the reviving center of intellectual and commercial life of his youth.

Most cadres might have considered it a worthwhile career. Jiang was three years from possible retirement (although as a Politburo member he could continue past 70), and his wife and family were comfortably settled in Shanghai.

It would take a national crisis to sweep him from this comfortable roost.

PART 3

Called in a Time of Danger, 1989–1992

CHAPTER 5

Tiananmen

I

With his big ears and clown face, Hu Yaobang perfectly looked the part he was forced to play in the Politburo after being stripped of the post of general secretary of the Chinese Communist Party in 1987. He was a court jester, an outsider forced to remain in the palace for the edification of the party leaders. To have purged him completely for mere "errors of judgment" after the late 1986 student protests would have sent a bad signal to the outside world that China was unstable. It also would have embittered liberals and intellectuals in China, for whom Hu remained a hero.

As a result, Hu sat on the council, but as little more than a source of amusement. This humiliating role took a heavy toll on his health. In 1988, at the age of 73, he suffered a mild heart attack, and he spent most of the following winter fighting off a bad attack of flu. On 8 April 1989, he attended his last Politburo meeting. Forty minutes into the proceedings, people seated near Hu noticed that he was looking pale. Before anyone could offer help, he keeled over in the throes of another heart attack.

Jiang Zemin, sitting just four seats away, was the first to rush toward his gasping colleague. Now well known to his Politburo colleagues, Jiang had been entrusted by Hu's wife with nitroglycerin tablets to revive her husband in just such an emergency, tablets the obstinate Hu had refused to carry himself.[1] Jiang pushed his way through the commotion toward

Hu, fumbling for the tablets in his pocket. After several attempts at opening the child-proof package, he handed it to Song Ping, who succeeded
in popping open the lid and placing two tablets in Hu's mouth. The
ghostly figure soon revived. For a week, it looked as though Hu might
recover under the careful attention of doctors at the Beijing Hospital,
east of Tiananmen Square. But on the morning of 15 April, he succumbed to another massive heart attack. Family members were at his
bedside when he died. The loss was announced on the national TV news
that night.

When Zhou Enlai died in 1976, spontaneous memorial activities had
taken place in Tiananmen Square, the 49-hectare (121-acre) concrete
desert that stands to the south of the Forbidden City in the center of Beijing intersected by the Avenue of Eternal Peace. Zhou, like Hu, was seen
as a champion of liberal values, and the crowd who gathered to pay him
their last respects were later declared by the party to be "patriotic."

Students in 1989 had every reason to expect similar party tolerance
of their outpourings in remembrance of Hu. The day after his death was
announced, a contingent of Beijing University students bearing a flower
wreath for this fallen hero of liberalism converged on the square. Students in other cities followed suit in their own city centers. The acts of
remembrance for Hu were soon transformed into demands that the party
reevaluate his record, and in turn into demands for wider goals: more
press freedom, more democracy, and an end to official corruption.

In Shanghai, on 17 April, students from East China Normal University, led by an economics professor, Chen Qiwei, were among the first to
take to the streets. That night, the Shanghai government issued its first
statement on the nascent movement. A radio broadcast called on students to keep order and told workers to "transform grief into strength"
to carry on reforms. A mild warning came last: "One must be alert and
on guard against evildoers, who may try to seize the opportunity to stir
up trouble and carry out sabotage."[2] From the beginning, the protests
in Shanghai were less organized and less confrontational than those in
Beijing, although the demands voiced were similar. As in 1986, officials
in Shanghai seemed to take the movement in stride at first. When police
and paramilitary personnel moved in to disperse hundreds of students
gathered in front of the municipal party office on the Bund on the night
of 19 April, *Wen Wei Po* reported, "their attitude was gentle, and there
was no clash with students or onlookers."[3]

Demonstrations would continue every day in Beijing from 16 April
until 9 June. In those fifty-five days, China's other cities were to varying

extents also gripped by student-led unrest. Shanghai recorded forty-six days of demonstrations, second only to the capital.[4] "Rain came to Shanghai as soon as winds blew in Beijing," the official report on the Shanghai demonstrations would recount.[5]

2

At the center of the Shanghai movement that Jiang Zemin would grapple with was the weekly newspaper called *Shijie jingji daobao,* the *World Economic Herald.* Founded in 1980 with the backing of Wang Daohan, Shanghai's newly appointed mayor, the *Herald* soon gained a reputation as the redoubt of liberal social scientists throughout the country. Even official reports on the *Herald* admitted that it had "published some fairly good articles" and that university students read it religiously "for the latest news and for theoretical guidance."[6] The paper's chief editor and founder, Qin Benli, 70 in 1989, was the party branch head and deputy director of the Shanghai Academy of Social Science's World Economics Institute. At first the *Herald* was placed under the administrative purview of the academy. But Mayor Wang, who was honorary chairman of the newspaper, had it upgraded in 1983 to an official department-level organ of the Shanghai government. Its growing circulation was printed on spare press capacity of the city's *Jiefang ribao* (Liberation Daily). This official backing sat at odds with its claim to exemption from party media controls as "the only nongovernmental newspaper in China."[7] Jiang's appointment of two overseers at the newspaper in the wake of the 1986 protests had been more symbolic than effective. In the three years that followed, it continued to attract and publish an array of dissenting views on the course of reform. Circulation reached 300,000 by the time of the Tiananmen Square movement, when it again found itself at the forefront of a national student-led protest movement.[8]

Almost as soon as Hu Yaobang's death was announced, editors at the *Herald* began planning a conference in Beijing. The ostensible purpose was to honor Hu, but the liberals connected with the paper also intended to challenge the official line that Hu had made mistakes and that his removal had been constitutional. Zhang Weiguo, who headed the paper's Beijing office, was in charge of organizing the conference in cooperation with another outspoken magazine in the capital, *Xin guancha* (New Observer). It was a star-studded lineup of thirty-three intellectuals in attendance when the conference, entitled "Comrade Yaobang Lives in Our Hearts," opened in a committee room of the Ministry of Culture on the morning of 19 April. Besides Hu's eldest son, Hu Deping, and his former top theoretical advisor, a vice-president of the party's Chinese Academy of Socialism, Wu Jiang, the meeting was attended by some of the most prominent liberal critics of the regime. They included Dai Qing, a Shanghai journalist and environmental activist; Chen Ziming, later to be branded a "black hand" of the Tiananmen student movement; and Yan Jiaqi, a political philosopher and consultant to Zhao Ziyang on government reform.

The reminiscences and praise of Hu that poured out at the meeting ran counter to the official verdict on his career. In a reference to the two most prominent hard-line party ideology czars, Deng Liqun and Hu Qiaomu, who were planning to attend Hu's funeral on 22 April, Yan declared: "Some people who were in charge of ideology have no right to mourn Hu. They stabbed him in the back. They should be tried by history."[9] The meeting soon veered into several other sensitive political areas. Participants called for greater democracy and repeated appeals carried in the *Herald* two weeks earlier for government leaders to reveal their incomes.

In Shanghai, the *Herald*'s editor, Qin Benli, planned to publish excerpts from the seminar speeches as a special issue of the newspaper's 24 April edition.[10] But barely had the conference ended than a call came through from Jiang's office warning that the edition would have to be carefully screened. There are two accounts of how Jiang found out about the plans ahead of time. One version holds that Liu Ji, deputy propaganda chief in Shanghai and head of the city's economic reform office, attended the seminar in Beijing. Before it was over, the story goes, he slipped out to phone Jiang in Shanghai.[11] The other version asserts that Jiang's attention was drawn to the plans by a report carried in the 17 April edition of the *Huaqiao ribao* (Overseas Chinese Daily) newspaper in Hong Kong. The report was relayed to Jiang by the Xinhua News Agency in Hong Kong, according to this version, via its "internal reference" reprints of local press stories.[12]

Probably the second version is true. Before leaving for Beijing on 21 April to attend Hu Yaobang's funeral, Jiang ordered his deputy party chief, Zeng Qinghong, to obtain drafts of the proposed issue from Qin. Zeng in turn deputed the city's propaganda chief, "iron lady" Chen Zhili, to secure the proofs. According to staff accounts, Chen telephoned the newspaper office with the request the same day. "A Hong Kong newspaper said that you would dedicate several pages to Hu Yaobang and we were a little curious about the contents," she said.[13] The *Herald*'s editors obligingly delivered the proofs to her that day. Predictably, Qin was dragged into the party office a day later and given a dressing down by Zeng and Chen.

"Students are already on the streets," Zeng said. "This edition could worsen the public opinion climate and jeopardize stability," he continued, pointing to the speech by Yan Jiaqi warning that "problems" might arise if the verdict on Hu Yaobang were not reversed.[14]

"Don't worry, I'll take personal responsibility," replied Qin, always wearing a smile and smoking a cigarette.[15]

"It's not a question of personal responsibility, it's a question of the social effect of the articles," Zeng stammered, rising to his feet.

"All we ask is that you delete a few hundred characters. There's no problem with the rest," Chen entreated.

"No deal," Qin said at length, rising to leave. "If you think Deng Xiaoping wants to examine this, then let him come here and do it himself. At least then he would gain some popular support."[16]

The flat refusal embarrassed Zeng and Chen, who would now have to appeal to their superiors to bring more pressure to bear on the impudent newspaper. Their only option was to call in Jiang and Wang Daohan. It would be a sorry admission of their own ineffectiveness, but it was preferable to the consequences if the 24 April edition appeared uncensored. "We didn't want to disturb Jiang because he'd been so busy late into the night dealing with so many calls from the [Shanghai] universities," Chen recalled. "But we thought we should tell him anyways [sic]."[17]

Jiang attended Hu's funeral in the Great Hall of the People on the morning of 22 April. By then, tens of thousands of students and citizens were already camped out in Tiananmen Square. Like sandbags holding back a flood, 10,000 soldiers sat around the Great Hall of the People sheltering the proceedings inside. Leaders were becoming nervous. At an emergency meeting of the Politburo that afternoon, which Jiang attended, it was decided to terminate the official mourning period for Hu. "This is no ordinary student movement," Deng declared.[18]

Jiang flew back to Shanghai that night. His biggest concern, given the clearly nervous attitude in Beijing, was to head off the special edition of the *Herald*. Informed on arrival by Zeng of the failed attempt at persuasion, Jiang lost no time. After a frantic search, Qin was found meeting with fellow *Herald* editors in the Jinjiang Hotel. Along with Wang Daohan, Jiang went to the hotel and sat in private with Qin for two hours. "Jiang was very upset and angry with Qin," Chen recalled. The official Xinhua version added: "Jiang seriously criticized Qin Benli's erroneous viewpoint and acts of ignoring party discipline."[19] After making his denunciation, Chen recalled, Jiang left the hotel, asking Wang to settle the matter with Qin. "Wang Daohan read the [Yan Jiaqi] story until about 1 A.M. He said it should be deleted, and that since Qin is a party member, he should show some party discipline. Qin then agreed to drop the offending passages."[20] The deal was made; a revised "version B" would be put together that afternoon (23 April) and issued the next morning, on schedule.

Jiang had to tread carefully. The *Herald* was respected among more than just a handful of radical liberals in the country. Indeed, later analysis shows that it was a platform for the elitist "technocratic" movement sweeping the country in the 1980s, which argued that only the educated were qualified to rule.[21] As such, it had many adherents both inside and outside the party. Wang Daohan had fought hard in 1983 to have it upgraded to department-level status and remained its honorary chairman. Ba Jin, doyen of the official literary establishment and a writer deeply respected by Jiang, described himself as a "faithful reader" of the newspaper.[22] Even Jiang himself was probably a modest admirer. He is said to have held the late-night meeting at the Jinjiang with Qin "hoping to protect the *Herald*" rather than cause it harm.[23] Perhaps more than other factors, this tacit official support explains why the newspaper had survived despite its increasingly open attacks on the party beginning in late 1988.

The deletion of the offending passages in the 24 April issue might have proved an amicable solution. Qin, a wiry man in a gray double-breasted Mao jacket, remained a loyal party member despite having suffered in one political campaign after another. He openly opposed the radical behavior of some students on hunger strike in Tiananmen Square, arguing instead for dialogue with the authorities. The deal he struck with the avuncular Wang Daohan would have allowed the *Herald* to continue, and there was every indication that he intended to keep his word.

Unfortunately, the young firebrands in Qin's office dissented. More than 160,000 copies of the original "version A" were printed on the morning of 23 April, and a few hundred were sent to Beijing. *Herald* editors insisted in a meeting with Qin that morning that "version B" should not even be printed. "There is nothing wrong with 'version A'; it says just what we intended," Qin admitted. But a deal was a deal, he added. The thirty-something editors, emboldened by years of impunity and spoiling for a showdown with the party over press freedom, suggested stalling. Qin agreed. He would disappear from sight at the suburban Yinghua Holiday Village for a few days. In the meantime, as many of the "version A" copies already printed as possible would be distributed. The editors would then sit tight, hoping that the Shanghai leadership would let it pass. Some even suggested that the leadership in Beijing—under pressure from mounting demonstrations—would soon agree to reevaluate the official verdict on Hu Yaobang. The *Herald* would then be exonerated.

It was a big mistake. When "version B" failed to appear on the streets of Shanghai on the afternoon of 23 April, Jiang felt betrayed. More than 20,000 copies of "version A" were confiscated at the printing plant in Shanghai, but it was too late. Reports were soon trickling into Jiang's office that "version A" had appeared in Beijing. Calls to the *Herald*'s office elicited calm assurances that "version B" would be printed. When it failed to appear, it was clear that Qin's word had been broken. Wang and Jiang were furious.

"If you can't keep your promise to me, then I want nothing more to do with you," Wang fumed on the telephone to Qin. "I'll resign my position as chairman."

The three met again on the evening of 23 April at Qin's house. Qin explained that he had tried to have the "version A" print run stopped and that overanxious subordinates had acted on their own initiative. He pledged to have the revised edition out by the next day, 24 April.[24] Again, it failed to appear. *Herald* editors wrote to the Shanghai party committee on 25 April saying that Qin was ill and could not produce the revised "version B" as promised. In any case, the letter continued revealingly, the possibility of a reversal of the Hu Yaobang verdict made the printing of "version A" more "appropriate."

It was a great moment in bad timing. The act of defiance by the *Herald* coincided with a clear hardening of official attitudes in Beijing. Zhao Ziyang was on a week-long visit to North Korea, and Li Peng's inflexible stance was gaining sway. On the evening television news on 25 April, the contents of a *People's Daily* editorial to be printed the next day were announced. "It Is Necessary to Take a Clear-Cut Stand to Oppose the Turmoil" ran the banner headline on the editorial, which accused unnamed plotters of seeking to throw the country into chaos and undermine the political system. "Turmoil," *dongluan*, was a serious charge. Even the 1986 protests had been classed as mere disturbances (*naoshi*).

Jiang saw copies of the *People's Daily* editorial and the defiant letter from the *Herald* staff at about the same time on the evening of 25 April.

He had sought a solution, but his hand was clearly being forced. Wavering now might cost him his job. Together with Wang, he decided that the time for gentle persuasion had passed. He summoned Zeng, Chen, and Liu Ji to his residence the next morning and showed them the letter.

"We felt insulted," Chen recalled. "The letter was titled 'For Your Information'. They weren't seeking our approval, they were just stating that they would print the original version."[25]

Jiang then informed his aides-de-camp of his decision. Qin would be dismissed as the *Herald*'s chief editor for "serious violations of discipline," while remaining free to visit the paper's office as he wished. Meanwhile, a five-person task force headed by Liu and a former editor of the local *Wenhui bao* newspaper, Ma Daren, would be sent in to supervise future editions.

"The staff at the *Herald* have done a good job running the newspaper. They've run a lot of good articles on the reforms," Jiang said. "The responsibility for this should rest with Qin Benli alone."[26]

The decision to shake up the *Herald* was announced the next day, 27 April, before a packed crowd of 14,000 city cadres at the Shanghai Sports Stadium. "Some people are trying to use overseas public opinion to put pressure on us over this affair," Jiang said, referring to overseas news reports that decried the clampdown on press freedoms. "Well, I can tell you they won't succeed."[27] Polite applause resounded through the metal rafters.

The meeting, or "rally," as it was officially described, was ostensibly called to show support for the *People's Daily* editorial. Jiang said the situation in Shanghai was "grim." Big character posters that attacked state leaders or were "too far off" should be torn down posthaste, he added. But it was his announcement of the *Herald* shakeup that made headlines. The action was immediately seized upon by both the mainland and foreign media as a sign of his "hard-line" credentials. Jiang seemed to have taken up the cause of the *People's Daily* editorial with incredible alacrity. But, as we have seen, it was purely coincidental that the *Herald* affair came to a head just when the editorial came out. What's more, Jiang intended the changes at the newspaper to be modest. Qin would be the fall guy, and two moderates would sit in his place. The newspaper could continue in its outspoken ways.

Unlike in his handling of the beauty pageant in early 1988, Jiang did not suppress this symbol of Shanghai's reviving cosmopolitanism willingly. He tried compromise first and might have held off longer if the official climate had not changed in Beijing. The Scylla of swelling conservative opinion in the capital reduced the wide berth he wanted to allow the Charybdis of outspoken opinion at the *Herald*. Jiang now navigated between the two as best he could. But he was still far from open waters.

Despite an approving *People's Daily* report on 28 April, Jiang's reprisal against the *Herald* was by no means assured of success. Both practically and politically, the changes at the newspaper looked as though they might backfire. Liu, Ma, and the three other members of the *Herald* task force got a predictably chilly reception when they arrived at the newspaper office on the morning of 27 April. "If you change the style or the contents, then the *Herald* will be dead," one editor said. "The only way to solve this problem is for you to reinstate Qin Benli and leave."[28] That was unlikely. Instead, an uneasy peace finally settled on the newsroom. The office walls were arrayed in black gauze, over which staffers posted letters of support pouring in from around the country. "Officially, the task force is meant to help us bring out the newspaper," the deputy editor, Zhu Xingqing, told a foreign reporter. "In practice, their main task is to see that we do not contradict the line of the local authorities."[29]

Judging from the newspaper's next two editions, the task force was making little attempt radically to change or censor the feisty journal. Black mastheads were used to protest Qin's dismissal, and articles by many of the regular contributors were carried, most in unedited form. On 1 May, the paper carried an article on press freedom entitled "We Need an Environment Where We Can Speak Freely," alluding to the unfairness of Qin's dismissal. Other articles also ran as planned. "Although the task force objected to some of the contents, it still allowed publication after taking into consideration the overall situation," Xinhua would later report.[30] An article entitled "Without Press Freedom There Is No Genuine Stability," written by Hu Jiwei, a former director of the *People's Daily*, ran inside the 8 May edition, from which only an open letter to Jiang from a group of Chinese scholars in the United States protesting Qin's dismissal was censored.[31]

Politically as well, Jiang was on the defensive over the incident in both Shanghai and Beijing. The dismissal of Qin had prompted an unexpected series of demonstrations by journalists from virtually every major media organization on the streets of the two cities. The *Herald* became a cause célèbre. Calls for Jiang to step down over the incident resounded the length and breadth of the Bund. Banners hung at the entrance to the paper's cramped street-level office on Middle Huai Hai Road called for Qin's immediate reinstatement. As he held court in the Jinjiang Hotel each evening, this gentle old man became the focus of nationwide concern about press freedom.

The Shanghai party committee finally met on the evening of 3 May to "discuss" the handling of the *Herald*. The day before, Shanghai had been rocked by its most serious protests to date; 7,000 students and many times that number of workers and onlookers had jammed the streets for most of the day before being dispersed by police around 10 P.M. Many in the party committee, openly or under their breath, were blaming Jiang for the worsening unrest. Two issues were at stake in the 3 May meeting: whether the sacking of Qin was legal, and whether it was politically wise. "Iron Lady" Chen Zhili told the cadres that because the newspaper was under the Shanghai Academy of Social Sciences, the government had the right to dismiss Qin. Few dissented from that view, even though *Herald* editors would later insist that the newspaper had no links to the government or party.[32] But many of the assembled cadres were unconvinced about the advisability of the move. "Concerned persons are reserving their views to some extent," the official media reported. "The municipal party committee never clarified whether the punishment of the newspaper was correct."[33]

The next day, 6,000 students took to the streets in what would turn into a 24-hour march and protest.[34] The banners were varied, calling for an end to corruption and official profiteering, better pay for teachers, rule by law, and more democracy. A few new banners had also appeared: "Newspapers Must Tell the Truth"; "Give Us Back Our *Herald*."[35] During the day, student leaders sent three representatives to the party office asking for formal talks with Jiang. The efforts were partly rewarded for the 300 stragglers who made it to the party office on the Bund early in the morning of 5 May. A government representative came out and agreed to hold talks on several issues, including the handling of the *Herald*.[36] It was clear that Jiang lacked broad support for the move on both sides of the Doric pillars and unadorned frieze of the party building.

In Beijing, Jiang appeared to be in even deeper political waters over the *Herald* incident. When he returned from North Korea on 30 April, Zhao Ziyang was furious at the clampdown on the liberal newspaper, which later propaganda asserted had been a mouthpiece for Zhao's think-tank members in Beijing.[37] "This is shocking," Zhao clamored. "Jiang has really messed things up now. He's put the whole party on the defensive."[38]

The outburst probably reflected Zhao's own frustration at his own gradual debilitation in the Beijing power struggle. The *Herald* incident was becoming an ideological football in the increasingly divided Politburo.

On 4 May, in response to the hard-liners, Zhao urged conciliatory handling of the student demonstrations at a meeting of the Asian Development Bank in Beijing. "The reasonable demands of the students must be met through democratic and legal means," he said.[39] It was taken as a sign that Deng was giving Zhao one last chance to calm the situation. If he succeeded, Zhao would regain the upper hand over Li Peng, and possibly purge him. Jiang would also be in danger, inasmuch as it would appear that he had acted too rashly against the *Herald*. "Two men, one pair of trousers" was the popular assessment of Jiang's relationship with Li. They were dangerous clothes to be wearing.

Jiang was called to Beijing to explain his handling of the *Herald* before the entire Politburo and the mayors of major cities on 10 May. Liu Ji and Zeng Qinghong went along to provide moral support, but the subjugation of the newspaper had been Jiang's decision, and it would be his alone to defend. At the meeting, Zhao defended the *Herald* and dragged Jiang over the coals, while the rest of the Politburo looked on in silence. "With this sort of support [from Zhao] in Beijing, it's no wonder a handful of *Herald* staff threw caution to the wind and blew the matter all out of proportion so that it became part of the social upheaval," the official report on the student movement would contend.[40]

Foreign media reports guessed that Jiang's standing had been considerably weakened by the run-in with Zhao.[41] But the silence of the rest of the Politburo may not have been as deafening as all that. Little remarked on at the time, Jiang remained in Beijing for two days after the Politburo meeting, not returning to Shanghai until 13 May. One can only assume that he stayed behind for further consultations with senior leaders. At some point during these talks, he appears to have won a silent nod from someone more senior than Zhao—possibly Deng—to keep a firm grip on the *Herald,* even at the risk of incurring Zhao's further wrath. That became clear the moment he got back to Shanghai.

While he was away, a furious argument had broken out between the paper's original editors and the official task force over the edition due out on 15 May. The editors planned to devote two pages to domestic and foreign reports critical of Jiang's dismissal of Qin and the appointment of a task force. Included would be excerpts from some of the letters of support for Qin received from more than sixty media organs, representing six hundred journalists in China.[42] Advertisements in support of Qin had been taken out by organizations as diverse as the mainland's *Jingji ribao* (Economic Daily) and a Chinese chamber of commerce in the western United States.[43]

Foreign press reports that Jiang had taken a drubbing at the enlarged Politburo meeting must have emboldened the *Herald's* editors. But for the task force to have allowed the issue to go ahead would have been to admit that Jiang was wrong. Although there were clearly doubts among the city's leaders about the sagacity of the *Herald* clampdown, Liu Ji and Ma Daren stood firm. The page proofs for the 15 May edition did not leave the office. Jiang approved the postponement of the issue the moment he got back. His attitude was even more unyielding than before the Politburo meeting. The *Herald,* he declared, would be suspended until the editors agreed to drop their plans.

When the issue failed to appear as scheduled on 15 May, the *Herald's* four-phone "switchboard" was flooded with calls of concern. The Shanghai evening paper *Xinwen bao* (News Bulletin), which carried a front-page item explaining the standoff, sold out in an hour, necessitating the printing of an extra 1,000 copies.[44] The Shanghai protesters—especially journalists and intellectuals—now feared for the *Herald's* survival. The next two days saw an unprecedented outpouring of support for the suspended publication. About 230 artists and scholars presented a petition demanding that the task force be withdrawn, that Qin be restored to office, and that there be dialogue between the *Herald* editors and Jiang. China's grand old man of letters, Ba Jin, expressed support for Qin from his hospital bed in Shanghai. "I know Qin Benli and appreciate his way of thinking," said Ba, then aged 84. "He has also shown daring and resolution in running the *Herald.*"[45]

It was all to no avail. Jiang held to his position that Qin could regain his post only if he admitted he had been wrong in seeking to publish the contents of the conference on Hu Yaobang. Qin refused, arguing that the clampdown on the newspaper had inflamed sentiment both inside and outside the municipal party. "Such perverse behavior is simply turning a deaf ear to public opinion," he argued in a petition submitted on 17 May.[46] Rumors circulated in the days after the *Herald's* suspension that Jiang's line was softening, and that Qin might be reinstated within days. In retrospect, there was little chance of that. Notwithstanding the soft line being advocated by Zhao in Beijing, Jiang had been given the green light to deal firmly with the *Herald.* The absolute silence that greeted the chorus of protest over the newspaper's suspension only shows how blinding that green light must have been.

A year later, the *Herald* was officially closed. At the same time, Qin was admitted to hospital suffering from terminal stomach cancer, after a year under house arrest at home. He was given a private room in the

Huadong Hospital, where he was treated with respect and allowed to see most visitors, except foreign ones.[47] The doyen of Shanghai journalism and the center of a brief period of press freedom in Communist China was now rarely mentioned, however, even in private. After a further year's battle with the gnawing illness, Qin died on 15 April 1991, exactly two years after the passing of Hu Yaobang. A brief obituary on Shanghai Radio referred to Qin as a "veteran journalist" and refrained from casting aspersions on the defunct *Herald*.[48] Radicals on both sides had forced Jiang and Qin to act in ways that they probably would have preferred to avoid. The brief but conciliatory obituary brought a fittingly sad close to the story of the *World Economic Herald*.

3

In Beijing, Zhao Ziyang's formal position on the student-led demonstrations gripping the country by mid May 1989 remained one of conciliation. Just as Hu Yaobang had done three years before, Zhao advised local leaders to placate the movement through dialogue. Many, like Jiang, must already have sensed that Zhao was losing influence. But until the mollification policy was officially abandoned, they were obliged to form "dialogue teams" to engage the fresh-faced petitioners.

On 15 and 16 May, more than 4,000 students and teachers took to the streets of Shanghai in support of hunger strikers in Tiananmen Square. The mood was subdued in the unseasonable drizzle and cold that had settled on the city. Students who stayed overnight in front of the party office were visited in the small hours by the deputy party secretaries Huang Ju and Zeng Qinghong. A few hundred even began their own hunger strike. The fresh wave of protests finally paid off on the afternoon of 16 May, when the Shanghai government announced plans to hold formal talks with the students for the first time the following day. Many hunger strikers remained in front of the Bund building keeping a silent vigil through the night until the talks could begin. A repeat visit from city leaders failed to budge them.

The dialogue took place on the afternoon of 17 May at the Shanghai Exhibition Center. Thirty hand-picked student representatives from seventeen institutions took part in the four-hour meeting. Opposite them sat five senior city leaders, including the deputy party secretary, Wu Bangguo, and the propaganda chief, Chen Zhili. Neither Jiang nor Mayor Zhu Rongji attended, perhaps an indication that they expected the official line from Beijing to change. The handling of the *Herald* occupied

much of the discussions. Chen insisted that newspapers must not devi-
ate from the party line, but allowed that there was dissent over Jiang's
clampdown. "Differing views on the handling of the *Herald* should be
judged by time and history," she said.[49] More animated debate erupted
over political reforms and official profiteering. The students eventually
called an end to the talks and demanded another round that would be
broadcast live on television. As they emerged from the Soviet-style exhibition center, more than 10,000 protesters were already choking the
streets in a third consecutive day of mass protest.

Jiang's failure to appear at the first round of talks caused widespread
consternation. Banners reading "Put Jiang on trial" began to appear.[50]
More worrisome, signs of insubordination grew. In an unprecedented step,
eighty-seven cadres from the municipal party's Organization Department signed a petition saying that they were "shocked and distressed"
by the protests and called on Jiang to take steps to meet the legitimate
demands of the students. "We suggest that Comrade Jiang Zemin immediately hold a dialogue with students on the spot and declare the student movement to be a patriotic and democratic movement," read the
petition.[51] The same appeal was heard from the local branches of the five
noncommunist political parties.[52]

Jiang remained out of sight. In the end, his caution was well rewarded. The standoff in Beijing between Zhao Ziyang and Li Peng over
how to handle the demonstrations was finally ended at a meeting in
Deng's residence on the night of 17 May. Members of the Politburo's
standing committee plus a handful of party elders, including Chen Yun
and Li Xiannian, overruled Zhao's objections in light of reports indicating a gradual radicalization of the protest movement and voted to implement martial law in the capital. Zhao was the only known dissenter.

While the leadership had already resolved to suppress the movement,
it was not immediately apparent. In the early hours of 18 May, Zhao,
Li, Qiao Shi, and Hu Qili visited hospitalized hunger strikers from
Tiananmen Square. The same day, in the afternoon, Li Peng hosted a
televised debate with student leaders in the Great Hall of the People. The
acts of reconciliation may have simply been a strategic attempt to deflate
the movement and isolate the radical student leaders from the less-de-
termined majority. After a last-ditch attempt to persuade Deng to hold
off on martial law on 19 May, Zhao had himself driven to Tiananmen
Square, where he bade a tearful farewell to the students. "We've come
too late," rang his famous admission. After returning to his car, Zhao
was not seen again.

Li Peng arrived in the square at the same time as Zhao. It was a symbol of the new order dawning. After a stiff march past a few protest tents, Li left the square without a word. That evening, at a televised forum held in an army auditorium in southwest Beijing, Li declared martial law in the capital. Over 100,000 troops from military regions across the country moved into Beijing under cover of darkness and were in position and waiting by early morning.

As the soldiers were moving into the capital, Jiang followed the lead in Beijing and made a last-ditch effort in the early hours of 20 May to persuade the Shanghai students to end their protest. Wading through the crowds along the Bund for the first time with all the city's top leaders, including Zhu Rongji and Zeng Qinghong, in tow, his tone was moderate. "Your patriotism and aspirations are admirable," he said through a bullhorn. "Your views have a positive significance for the improvement of our work and for speeding up reforms and economic development."[53] The assertions met the demands of the students that their movement be recognized and that no participants be punished. Just as in 1986, Jiang knew where to give in and where to hold fast. Before leaving the throngs, he told the students that he was "always ready to hold all kinds of meeting and dialogues with you to discuss your views about the party and the government." The promise cost him little to make. Jiang, after all, had been holding informal roundtable talks with journalists and citizens ever since coming to Shanghai. They were not necessarily free and fair discussions, but at least the offer was on the table.

The unusually moderate tone of Jiang's late-night stroll on the Bund suggests tantalizingly that he was already thinking about how history would judge his role in the upcoming crackdown on the movement. If so, he had at least succeeded in making it clear that confrontation with the students was not the preferred solution in Shanghai, no matter what was being contemplated in Beijing.

The Soviet leader Mikhail Gorbachev had arrived in Beijing on 15 May for a three-day visit that was to end in Shanghai, bringing in his wake hundreds of foreign journalists anxious to cover the historic resumption of friendly Sino-Soviet ties after thirty years of discord. If not for the protests, the visit would have been Jiang's best chance in Shanghai to act as a national statesman since joining the Politburo. But there was little he could do to stop foreign reporters from stumbling upon the student-led protests and deciding they were a better story. "We welcome Gorbachev, but our parade has nothing to do with him," an editor of the *Xinmin wanbao* (Xinmin Evening News) remarked to one foreign

reporter.[54] Gorbachev skirted the scenes of protest in Shanghai to visit
an elevator factory and lay a wreath on a monument to the Russian poet
Aleksandr Pushkin. "Even though the monument occupies only a very
small area, we still had to go out of our way to ensure Comrade Gorbachev
could fulfill his wish," Jiang would recall.[55]

With Gorbachev and his foreign press brigade out of the country and
PLA troops massing on the outskirts of Beijing under martial law orders,
the stage was set for suppression of the student movement nationwide.
The enforcement of martial law in Beijing beginning on 20 May changed
the nature of the Tiananmen Square movement dramatically. The threat
of force against the peaceful demonstrators in the capital had the effect
of radicalizing parts of the movement across the country. The rifts that
began to emerge as a result were easily exploited by authorities. Hard-
core demonstrators soon found themselves isolated and under intense
pressure to capitulate.

Rumors of an impending army crackdown in several cities sent students onto the streets to block traffic and conduct random identity
checks. Scattered incidents of violence against soldiers and police and
the sabotage of public facilities began to occur. One of the worst affected national arteries, the Xuzhou train junction in northern Jiangsu
province, became an almost comical clutter of Beijing-bound trains waiting on sidings after being stopped by university students lying across the
tracks. In Shanghai, Hong Kong press clippings posted in the windows
of the *Herald* office excited rumors of a crackdown in the city. The grassy
"Five Corner Field" intersection near Fudan University in northeastern
Shanghai was opened and closed like a valve by nervous students.

On the morning of 20 May, just a few hours after his conciliatory visit
to the students camped outside the municipal party offices, Jiang was
one of the first local leaders to express support for Li Peng's declaration
of martial law. At 8:30 A.M., he convened a meeting of the Shanghai party
standing committee where members "expressed their unanimous support" for Li's speech.[56] But it was clear that the Shanghai leadership under Jiang would continue to use persuasion rather than force to deal with
its own students. The chancellors and party chiefs of all the major universities were asked "to persuade students taking part in marches and
petitions to resume classes unconditionally." The next day, local radio
broadcast a "letter to citizens" saying that the government "hoped" that
students would return to classes and that citizens would not follow the
protest marches or act as onlookers. It promised continued dialogue with
students "to improve our work." There were no threats.[57]

Jiang and Zhu had also drafted a longer version of the "letter to citizens" to be broadcast on television. Although supporting the Li Peng speech, it also took a conciliatory line toward the demonstrators. "When students take to the streets, we shall try to persuade them to stop their marches and return to campus," it said. Citizens were "asked" not to overturn cars, storm government offices, or block intersections, but no threats were made against miscreants. Mixed in were several homely appeals to the sensibilities of affected groups such as women with babies and residents needing charcoal briquettes.

On the same morning, 21 May, Jiang summoned eighty members of noncommunist political groups to hear their opinions on the proposed television message. The soft tone was immediately endorsed. It was clear that there was no support for the hard-line stance being peddled in Beijing. "The members hoped that the party and government would continue to hold dialogues with the students and take good care of them," local radio reported of the meeting. "Before making any major decisions," they added, in an apparent allusion to the possible use of force in Beijing, "democracy must be fully exercised and opinions from all circles sought."[58]

Zhu's "letter to citizens" was prerecorded that afternoon and broadcast the next day, 22 May. If nothing else, it managed to deflect criticism toward Beijing. About 600 journalists and writers who took to the streets that afternoon, including Qin Benli, chanted "Li Peng step down" as they marched through heavy rain. An "emergency letter" issued by the intellectuals, including Ba Jin, captured the mood of near-hysteria Li Peng's speech had created:

> We appeal to the officers and men of the armed forces carrying out martial law in Beijing to remember that you are facing patriotic students, patriotic workers, and ordinary citizens who have loved and trusted you. Can you open fire on them? Can you allow the military flag to be stained with shame and with spots that will never be washed away? You should never do so under any circumstances![59]

In all the commotion, it was not surprising that Jiang's sudden absence was not noticed. For unbeknownst to everyone except his closest associates in the Shanghai leadership, Jiang had flown back to Beijing in secret.

4

The fall of Zhao Ziyang was probably inevitable long before the Tiananmen protests began. Zhao's commitment to economic reforms at almost any cost made him unique, even among the reformists running China in the late 1980s. When opponents of his price reforms had hissed their displeasure in late 1987, Zhao accused them of wanting to reinstate "leftist" economic policies. "If the old leftist ways prevail again, the whole country will instantly be in turmoil and the economy will be brought to its knees," he had warned. "The consequences will be far graver than students shouting 'freedom and democracy' in the streets."[60] Zhao was alone, though, in this nonchalant attitude to social unrest. Premier Li Peng's reversal of his bold price-liberalization package in August 1988—just a few weeks after it had been approved in principle—was the beginning of the end for Zhao's courageous attempts at change. "Zhao's downfall was clear by the end of 1988," *Wen Wei Po* would comment.[61]

Indeed, it is reasonable to assume, given the anti-Zhao swing that began in late 1988, that Deng Xiaoping was thinking seriously about a replacement by early 1989, several months before the Tiananmen protests began. It was an odious responsibility for Deng. He had dearly wanted to avoid Mao's example of clinging to power into his dotage by handing on the torch of supreme power to the "core" of a "third generation" of leaders in good time. In 1984, when Hu Yaobang and Zhao Ziyang took over as national party chief and premier respectively, Deng proclaimed that the youngish duo would hold their positions "even if the sky falls down."[62] In 1987, despite the sacking of Hu, Deng had resigned from the Politburo standing committee when Zhao was formally appointed party general secretary, hoping at long last to fade into the background. Now his best-laid plans were again in a shambles. He had already been obliged to remove Hu for letting inflation and Western influences spread unchecked. Now he was on the verge of casting out Zhao as well. "Hu and Zhao did not have their own unique styles . . . I had no choice but to replace them," Deng was to tell party elders later.[63]

When Deng repaired to Shanghai for his annual lunar new year retreat in late February 1989, there were already signs that the change of leadership weighed heavily on his mind. He is said to have consulted there on the matter with Li Xiannian and with the military strongman Yang Shangkun, his successor as state president.[64] But there were no signs of an imminent decision. Zhao was in Shanghai in early March and was accorded a cordial welcome by Deng, holding court at a guesthouse in the western suburbs. Deng may have hoped that he could retain Zhao at least until the party congress that fall. Price rises were gradually slowing, and Zhao's predictions of student protest if reforms were slowed had not yet come to pass. That all changed, though, once the protests began. By the time Zhao disappeared after his tearful last visit to Tiananmen Square on 19 May, it was only the formal end of a reign as party general secretary that was by then already seriously attenuated.

We are told that Deng made his final choice of a replacement only after "thorough consideration and planning" and "a lot of searching."[65] That comes as no surprise, since finding a "core" for a third generation of leaders had cropped up in Deng's speeches increasingly in the late 1980s. What was Deng looking for?[66] Someone who would last more than just a few years, so that the architect of reform could get on with his hoped-for retirement, seems the simple answer. In turn, that meant someone who was firmer—in deed if not in word—against the stirrings of liberal dissent that had brought down both Hu and Zhao. At the same time, they needed to be tenacious economic reformers, like Hu and Zhao. It was an odd mixture of political conservative and economic liberal who would fit the bill. If anything, Deng wanted the economic liberal in the new party general secretary to be better known than the political conservative. "The new central bodies should present an entirely new look so that people will feel there is a promising new lineup that will carry out reforms," he explained. "If the people feel that the leadership is hidebound, conservative or mediocre . . . there will be many more disturbances and never any peace."[67]

More immediately, Deng knew that anyone associated with the impending crackdown in Beijing would be tarred at home and feathered abroad. As much was clear from the immediate and negative reaction to Li Peng's 19 May speech. It confirmed to Deng that whatever happened, the future party general secretary had to have some hope of reconciling the nation. "The change in leadership was not based on the contributions of different leaders to the crackdown on the [student] rebellion," the Beijing-backed *Jing bao* (Mirror) magazine in Hong Kong noted later.[68] That probably ruled out all of the Politburo standing committee, the premier, and his vice-premiers, as well as most leaders of the Beijing municipality. The new general secretary would have to be someone in a central government or party department who had played no role in the Beijing crackdown, or a local leader whose handling of the students was deemed moderate.

Those were Deng's own criteria. But the wily old soldier knew from past experience that the successor to Zhao would also have to be broadly acceptable to those who were passed over for the job and to conservative party elders like Chen Yun and Peng Zhen. Unless these other senior leaders coagulated around the chosen one, the "core" would be more like a "cavity" at the center of the 50-million-member party and the vast government structure it led. Given the deep rifts driven through the leadership over the past decade, finding a broadly acceptable candidate was difficult. Deng admitted in private that he should have clamped down on factional infighting earlier. "I need someone who does not deal in factions," he said.[69] A fresh face would solve this problem. Unallied to any faction in Beijing, such a person could be more easily sold to doubters.

There were several fresh faces Deng was probably considering who met all these criteria, and a few seem to have been in the running right up to the last minute. In particular, Li Ruihuan, the Tianjin party secretary, and Ding Guangen, vice-minister in the State Planning Commission, both still in their fifties, were among the top choices.

But it was an owl-faced figure with straight, back-combed hair, wearing a gray tunic, who stepped from a plane door at Beijing's military-run Nanyuan airport on the morning of 22 May and was immediately bustled into a waiting black Volkswagen Santana. The unmistakable figure would become familiar to the whole nation in coming years. Deng had chosen Jiang Zemin to be China's next party general secretary.

Why Jiang? For one thing, Jiang had displayed precisely the political instincts in dealing with dissent that Deng was seeking, most recently in his handling of the *Herald*. Jiang, like Deng, was often called a "silk-covered needle" (*mianli cangzhen*) because of these instincts. It was a conservative disposition aimed almost exclusively at preserving the party's monopoly on power, as outlined by Deng's own "four cardinal principles," and one that did not spill over into economic policy. "Deng regarded Jiang's handling of the *Herald* as adhering to the four cardinal principles," *Wen Wei Po* would note.[70] A later Xinhua biography chimed in: "In matters of principle, Jiang stands firm. A case in point was his treatment of the *World Economic Herald* editor Qin Benli in 1989."[71] They were ironic laurels to bestow on Jiang. He had suspended the *Herald* reluctantly and only after trying to find solutions that might gloss over the newspaper's political mistakes. From Beijing, however, it looked as though he was tough when necessary.

Jiang was also distinguished by his attempts at moderation in handling the Shanghai students, both in 1986 and in 1989. Although portrayed by protesters as a hard-liner—"wearing the same trousers" as Li Peng—within the party, where it counted, Jiang was viewed as having adopted a moderate, even mildly maverick style. His last-minute foray into the crowds of students on the Bund and the conciliatory tone of Zhu Rongji's 22 May speech were ample proof. "The Shanghai authorities did not actively intensify frictions with the students. Instead, they prepared teams of workers rather than resorting to the threat of military force," *Wen Wei Po* wrote.[72] Another mainland biographer, Wang Xiaopeng, was more effusive: "During the disturbance, Jiang showed the courage and the resourcefulness of a mature politician and super-human abilities in dealing with important political matters. He won a great reputation for himself."[73] Even the carefully worded official Xinhua biography noted that the "persuasion work" done by teams of workers organized by Jiang and Zhu "succeeded in maintaining stability in Shanghai."[74]

But would Jiang gain the support of the entire senior leadership? Deng admitted that this would require some lobbying on his part. Jiang's old mentors, like Wang Daohan and Chen Pixian (now on the standing committee of the Central Advisory Commission), would stand behind their long-time friend. But it would be necessary to have virtually every political heavyweight on board for the decision to stick. At this crucial time, Jiang's earlier cultivation of broad ties within the party elite since at least the early 1980s finally paid off. Li Peng and Chen Yun, for example, had worked with Jiang. He could also count on his historical affiliations with Qiao Shi, Qian Qichen, Li Xiannian, and others. Jiang's support was wide, but not deep. An official report would say that Deng favored Jiang because although his relationship with Chen was good, he "had not been so deeply involved" as others up for the post.[75]

For all his friendly ties, Jiang had no factional base of his own. He had been bounced from one sector to another since leaving the First Machine-Building Ministry in 1980. Now, it was precisely this shallow factional support that was at once his greatest strength and his greatest weakness: a strength because it made him acceptable to Deng and not strongly opposed by others, but a weakness because it threatened to render him a lame duck, especially if Deng, then 84, should die within a few years.

On arriving in Beijing on 22 May, Jiang was told that he would meet Deng the next day. With a day to spare, he allegedly dressed himself as a doctor to get into Tiananmen Square, where protest leaders were checking unfamiliar faces.[76] For the first time, Jiang saw the haggard but spirited demonstrators who had shaken the nation. Jiang walked quickly around before leaving from the south side of the square. The next day at the Western Hills Villas outside Beijing, Deng formally offered him the job of party general secretary.[77]

We know little else of what transpired there, but judging from Jiang's subsequent return to Shanghai to seek advice from friends and family, he was overwhelmed and even surprised by the offer. "I was being handed the post in a difficult situation," he told an American academic later. "I was totally unprepared."[78] Deng explained his logic and pledged to support Jiang against the restless factions that would no doubt be his greatest challenge. With this assurance, he sent the stunned Jiang back to Shanghai to make what preparations he could.

5

Back in Shanghai, Wang Yeping burst into tears the moment Jiang broke the news. "More than just your future is at stake," she wailed, hoping to dissuade her husband from accepting the post. "If you don't do a good job, it's not just the country that will suffer. It will be a personal disaster for you, and there'll be a lot of troubles for our family."[79]

Wang doubtless had personal reasons for recoiling at the prospect of becoming China's first lady. She would never be allowed to remain in Shanghai, as she had for almost two decades. Yet her health had continued to deteriorate, and she dreaded having to compete for influence among the formidable array of spouses in the capital. Li Peng's wife, Zhu Lin, was a powerful businesswoman. How could an ungainly scientist from the south survive in such circles?

Her reaction played upon Jiang's own doubts. He was happy as Shanghai's party chief. Having his own kingdom amid the self-assured and cosmopolitan Shanghaiese appealed more than the secrecy and intrigue of politics in the capital. "I was greatly influenced by my days in Shanghai," he told a visitor later. "I found there was a big difference between local and central officials."[80] Taking leave of Shanghai would be distressing for personal reasons as well. Jiang was not a Shanghaiese, but the city had nurtured him, both in youth and in maturity. "I can't bear to leave!" he would tell old colleagues at an evening tea party some months later.[81]

Jiang may also have doubted his intellectual capacity to lead a country where ideological virtuosity and political nous counted for so much.[82] Others in Shanghai also warned Jiang of the perils of high politics in Beijing. He would later tell staff at the Chinese embassy in Germany that he was "indifferent" to being an official: "Those in high places don't survive the winter," he would say.[83]

To have refused Deng's offer, though, would have been equally dangerous. As at many times in the past, it fell to Jiang's longtime mentor, Wang Daohan, to dispel Jiang's doubts and embolden his brooding protégé. Jiang

telephoned Wang, who was in Beijing at the time. It was a breach of con-
fidentiality to reveal the offer to Wang, but his stolid longtime mentor
deserved to know. Wang's response was immediate and unequivocal. The
nation was in crisis, he said, and Jiang should take up the baton. Wang
was reminded of Lin Zexu, an imperial commissioner appointed by the
Qing emperor in 1838 to halt the opium trade in Guangzhou. Girding
himself against entrenched British and local Chinese interests, Lin had
waged a one-man battle against a scourge he feared would cripple the
Chinese nation. His detention of several opium traders and confiscation
and destruction of over 20,000 chests of opium in early 1839 brought
about the Opium Wars and China's loss of control over several port cities.
Yet Lin had come forward to answer a national call despite dangers to
himself and attempted dissuasion by friends. "For the sake of the country, one should not fear death," Wang said, quoting a well-known phrase
from Lin's diaries. "Still less should one consider one's own well-being
or misery and hide one's head when difficulties are faced. Does one only
step forward when times are good?"[84]

Jiang, of course, owed most of his promotions since leaving university to the erstwhile Shanghai mayor. How could he reject his advice
now? The decision was made. Jiang would accept the post as China's
next party general secretary. Later, in his office, he would keep an in-
scription of Lin Zexu's nationalistic appeal. "When he read out this quotation in his Yangzhou accent, the modulating tones brought out his
northern Jiangsu provincial flavor," Professor Chao Hao-sheng of Yale
University would recall after meeting Jiang sometime later. "It conveyed
a clear impression of his sincerity and loyalty as a man entrusted with
an important mission by the nation in dire peril."[85]

6

The first official to be told of Jiang's new job was Zeng Qinghong.
With his gentle smile and square-rimmed glasses, Zeng might have been
mistaken for a middle-school math teacher. Yet behind the amiable
façade and the jaunty black leather jacket was the mind of a strict party
functionary. Zeng's father, Zeng Shan, had been a Central Committee
member and the head of several ministries before his death in 1972. His
mother, Deng Liujin, had been a party worker in Mao Zedong's early
Jiangxi soviet in the 1930s. Born in Jiangxi, Zeng, aged 50 in 1989, had
worked his way through the national petroleum industry after graduating from college in Beijing, before being transferred to Shanghai in 1984.

Jiang arrived the next year, and the pair struck up an immediate and natural friendship. Although sharing little in background—Jiang was an intellectual from the south, Zeng a red prince from the north—the two complemented each other; Jiang liked the limelight, Zeng preferred to be in the background. Zeng took over propaganda work in the city in 1988 and became deputy party secretary the same year.

Within a day of Jiang's decision to accept the post of party general secretary, Zeng was on a plane to Beijing, where he would act as Jiang's point man in the coming tumultuous weeks.[86] Although still in Shanghai, Jiang now effectively became an emperor-in-waiting, taking instructions from Deng and from his future Politburo.

One of Jiang's first duties as party general secretary–designate literally flew into his lap. In the first week after the declaration of martial law in Beijing, leaders of the national parliament, or National People's Congress (NPC), had acted swiftly to avert a military crackdown. Three petitions bearing the signatures of 57 of the 156 standing committee members were delivered to the office of the NPC's chairman, Wan Li, seeking an emergency meeting of the body. Dissent by the NPC risked hobbling the party leadership in its mounting desire to crush the student movement. Wan, then on a visit to Canada, pledged to "firmly protect the patriotic enthusiasm of the young people of China" and cut short his trip to return.[87] Li Peng told him to stay in Canada, but to no avail.[88]

Wan's private plane landed in the small hours of 25 May at Shanghai's military-run Changbai airport in eastern Yangpu district. The plane was expected to stop for an hour to refuel before continuing on its way to Beijing. But when Wan disembarked for a breath of air, he found Jiang waiting on the tarmac. As he descended the stairs, blocks were already being slipped under the plane's wheels. Wan knew he would not leave. A telegram from Li Peng to the Shanghai party committee while Wan was airborne had instructed the local leadership to detain him "until he makes public his stand regarding the student movement."[89] Wan was under pressure to capitulate and support martial law.

Jiang put Wan under virtual house arrest at Shanghai's Western Suburbs Guesthouse—where Mao had used to stay while in the city. The official reason was that he had taken ill.[90] But Jiang would not release his charge until Wan disavowed any plans to launch an NPC revolt against martial law. On 27 May, national television announced that Wan would support martial law and had decided to delay the next NPC standing committee meeting until late June. Four days later, he was allowed to return to Beijing, a crushed man. In detaining Wan, Jiang had made his first "contribution" to the crackdown on the demonstrations in Beijing.

Although he could not have foreseen the events that followed, it was clear that Jiang knew that force would be used to end the protests in Beijing. His last public statement before the crackdown came on 26 May. It was fittingly prosaic for this engineer, who claimed that his background did not equip him for the rigors of high politics, to bid farewell to his past at Shanghai's giant Minhang power station. "The people will remember your deeds," Jiang told workers as he toured the plant, which provided a third of the city's electricity, wearing an orange hard hat. Before leaving, he offered an unintentional but symbolic riposte to Hu Jiwei's claim in the last edition of the *Herald* that "without press freedom there can be no genuine stability." Jiang by now was thinking less about dialogue and conciliation and more about putting in good order the country he was about to rule. Press freedom was now as nothing compared to a healthy economy. "Without electric power," he declared, "Shanghai cannot have stability."[91]

Still, the situation in Shanghai was improving. On 26 May, as Shanghai students and workers continued to block northbound trains suspected of carrying soldiers to the capital, the city government warned that "organizers and ringleaders will have their criminal responsibilities investigated."[92] The warnings seemed to have some effect. Although fewer than ten thousand protesters remained in Tiananmen Square, student organizations on campus continued to advocate a boycott of classes to show solidarity with them. However, an order on 29 May for teaching to resume at institutions of tertiary education in Shanghai brought about thirty of the fifty schools back to class. The traffic began to flow again. "Shanghai people are once again enjoying peace and tranquillity," observed the official China News Service, which had covered the protests with unaccustomed balance.[93]

In private, Jiang called together a "study meeting" of the municipal party committee on 30 May. Ostensibly, it was to "study the central spirit of opposing the counterrevolutionary turmoil" in Beijing, and Jiang offered advice on handling further disturbances in Shanghai. They were the last instructions he would issue in his capacity of Shanghai party boss.[94] After the meeting, Jiang told Zhu Rongji of his imminent promotion to Beijing.[95] Zhu would be left in charge of handling the fizzling protests in Shanghai. In happier times, Jiang had deferred out of modesty

to Zhu's superior abilities in handling economic issues. Now he was asking Zhu to take over out of pure necessity.

Meanwhile, as military leaders in Beijing stood in tents marking out
a planned assault on the peaceful protesters on huge wall maps, Deng
was busy mustering the support of party elders for Jiang's appointment.
Chen Yun and Li Xiannian had supported the decision soon after Deng
made it known to Jiang on 22 May. Jiang had established their trust early
at a personal level and had shown an apparent conservatism on political issues that they admired. Deng gave Chen and Li the assurance that
Jiang would not be allowed to tamper with "even a single word" of the
two sacred texts of the reform era, namely, the 1979 party plenum document that had made economic development the overriding objective
and the 1987 party congress document that had put political reform on
the agenda.[96]

Securing the support of the elders was critical. After that, Deng had
merely to continue down the line to "pass on" the news. On 31 May, he
met Li Peng and Vice-Premier Yao Yilin at his home. (Other reports say
that a party secretariat member, Qiao Shi, was also there, taking notes.)
They were told to refrain from taking advantage of Jiang's relative lack
of experience in the party center to score political or personal points.[97]
"We must have a core leader . . . creating factions never works," he lectured the trio. "I want you to bear Jiang's leadership closely in mind."[98]
Jiang had worked briefly but happily with Li in the 1980s and had known
Qiao in the pre-1949 days of the Shanghai student movement. Neither
had any reason to oppose the appointment. With their fealty secured,
Deng's third party general secretary was ready for action.

At this stage, Deng was on the brink of another masterful handling
of a difficult situation. Protests were abating across the country, foreign
journalists were going home, and Deng's choice as successor to Zhao
was winning support where it counted. If the leadership had remained
patient with the protest movement, it might have petered out harmlessly
just as in 1986. Tragically, their patience ran out.

7

In the first three days of June, soldiers on foot and in buses gradually
infiltrated the central areas of Beijing, inciting alarm among and drawing
sporadic attacks from protesters. From about 6 P.M. on 3 June, motor-
ized infantry units and tanks followed in their paths, breaking down
blockades and crushing anyone rash enough to stand firm. In the approx-

imately twelve hours that followed, the capital was virtually at war. Mao Zedong, who had stood on the balcony of Tiananmen Gate to declare the founding of the People's Republic forty years before, looked down on the scene from his huge portrait on the gate, his impassive smile seeming to bless the carnage below.

Along the two-kilometer stretch of the western Avenue of Eternal Peace, the army lost sixty-five trucks and forty-seven armored vehicles to enraged protesters, in addition to the lives of six soldiers. Figures for civilian injuries were never compiled, but the scale of the battles that raged through the night can be surmised from the more than 6,000 injuries reported by the army and police.[99] The official death toll from the crackdown in Beijing was "over 200 civilians, including 36 students." Better estimates put the toll at over 1,000. One Beijing professor alone, who lost her son in the battles, compiled the names of 96 young people killed.[100] When the Chinese defense minister Chi Haotian later made the controversial assertion in the United States that "not a single person lost their life in Tiananmen Square," he was playing with the truth; most of the killing occurred in the surrounding streets, where even Chi admitted there were "disturbances" on that fateful night.[101]

The suppression of the movement need not have been so bloody. In places like South Korea and Indonesia, police properly equipped with tear gas, rubber bullets, and water cannon regularly sent restless students scurrying back to their campuses. But the PLA and the paramilitary People's Armed Police (PAP) lacked such equipment. When they pulled the trigger, they fired deadly bullets. Scores of protesters fell in their path.

For most of the week leading up to and during the Tiananmen massacre, Jiang's movements remain unconfirmed. Most agree, though, that he probably returned to Beijing from Shanghai before tanks and soldiers shot their way into the capital's central areas. He was last seen in Shanghai on 29 May.[102] In Beijing, he was housed in the Central Committee guesthouse on the central lake of Zhongnanhai. Virtually ignored by party leaders, he spent most of his time on the phone to Shanghai. In his haste to reach Beijing, he had forgotten to bring enough clothes and was obliged to send an orderly to buy new ones.[103]

Jiang was almost certainly close to the fighting, or at the command headquarters, on the night of 3 June. "At first, soldiers began carrying out their orders [to enforce martial law in Tiananmen Square]. They were not allowed to open fire at first," he has recalled. "Then tanks were burned and soldiers were beaten to death. We had no choice. So we let them open fire."[104]

The order to end the protests, by bloodshed if necessary, doubtless came from Deng himself after consulting with elders, especially his fellow Long March veteran Yang Shangkun. Many years later, the party's eulogy to the architect of reform would describe how the movement was crushed "with the firm and strong support of Comrade Deng Xiaoping and other senior comrades."[105]

The official reasoning, as explained by Jiang, was simple. For one thing, the protests were beginning seriously to affect daily life in the capital, and by implication the dignity of the state. "Tiananmen symbolizes the capital of our country, and the party central leadership is just close by," Jiang would explain. "For nearly two months it was occupied by students. . . . If only a tenth the number of the student camps [in Tiananmen] had been sitting in front of the White House, [No. 10] Downing Street or the Elysée Palace, no sovereign government would have allowed it for long."[106]

Jiang would claim that the party had shown "maximum patience" with the movement in Beijing because of the awful implications of resorting to armed force. But that tolerance had been seized upon by the protesters as a sign of weakness, he said. "This plus the divergence of views emerging in the top leadership led to a delay of action at a critical moment," he explained.[107] Action in, say, mid May, he seemed to be saying, could have reduced or even prevented the bloodshed.

The divergence of views that had delayed early and possibly more peaceable action was blamed squarely on Zhao Ziyang, who was officially accused of "supporting the turmoil and splitting the party." His hair turning a buff silver and his facial skin sagging, Zhao would ever after be confined to his simple traditional courtyard-house residence near Tiananmen Square.[108] "At that time, it was as if there were two command headquarters," Jiang would recall. "If we had been unanimous . . . there's no way we would have been forced to move troops into Beijing."[109]

The question of what finally provoked the crackdown would be debated for years. The radicalization of the students and the involvement of workers in the movement in late May clearly encouraged Deng to act. Some pointed to the arrival from Hong Kong on 28 May of thousands of brightly colored tents, sleeping bags, and jackets, as well as fresh injections of cash for the bedraggled protesters from the more than U.S.$2 million raised at a pop charity concert in the colony the previous weekend. The supplies boosted the flagging spirits of the students and gave the movement a material ability to hold out for weeks more.[110]

Others pointed to the appearance of a 35-foot statue of a woman bearing a torch in her two upstretched arms, known as the Goddess of Democracy, which was wheeled into the square in front of the watchful portrait of Mao Zedong on 30 May. The blatant challenge to party authority may have been too much for Deng. The next day, Beijing's mayor, Chen Xitong, promised children that they would "soon" be able to lay wreaths on the monument to Communist martyrs in the middle of the square.[111] If his ominous pledge was to be fulfilled, force would be needed.

But there is another factor staring us in the face based on this narrative. The internal party agreement by the end of May to have Jiang succeed Zhao as general secretary may have encouraged Deng to use force earlier. For one thing, Deng may have felt greater urgency, because factional support for Jiang might waver if too much time passed. Deng and his commanders may also have been more reckless in the deployment of armed force in the knowledge that whatever methods were adopted to crush the Beijing movement, Jiang would be spared blame.

Given that the crackdown brought him to power, it was hardly surprising that Jiang would famously tell his first press conference: "We do not consider [the suppression of the student movement] to be a tragedy."[112] But his support in principle and his insistence that it was not tragic were betrayed by frequent expressions of regret about the way it was handled. "We feel regret for the families of those killed and injured and those injured accidentally," he has said.[113] Jiang did not, after all, feel part of the team that had ordered the attack on the students. He did not have a guilty conscience about Tiananmen. That was what distinguished him from many of his future colleagues. "All party members must firmly bear in mind this bloody lesson [xuede jiaoxun]," he pointedly told a media conference shortly after the massacre. "We must prevent it from happening again."[114]

Two main lessons suggested themselves to Jiang. Most obvious was the need to improve the equipment and training of the PAP to deal with social unrest. This would be high on his agenda as party general secretary. "We should learn to use methods usually adopted in some Western countries," he would tell American television. "We should build up an adequate riot police force and acquire nonlethal weapons for maintaining public security."[115] Although his comments would not be reported for four years, Jiang would also suggest shortly after the massacre that the PLA should not have been used at all. "Under normal circumstances in dealing with threats to social stability, we should mainly rely on our police force and our armed police," he told an internal security meeting.[116]

Tighter controls should also have been slapped on the foreign press in Beijing, Jiang said. This would have helped contain the nationwide backlash that erupted as foreign reports of the events in Beijing were picked up around the country. "When June 4th occurred, there were no [mainland] Chinese reporters on the scene. They were all foreign and Taiwan reporters. The head of the New York Police department once told me that when an incident occurs there, reporters are not allowed on the scene. But here in Beijing, they were all staying at the Beijing Hotel [overlooking Tiananmen Square]. It was better than sitting in a reviewing stand! As a result they all exaggerated their stories."[117]

Jiang was a shameless apologist for the action, as he had to be. But he was also clearly appalled by the results and could speak plainly about the lessons to be learned without a sense of guilt. He would even admit at Harvard University several years later that the use of force might have been a mistake. "Our policy is to promote dialogue," he would respond to a question about the massacre. "It goes without saying that naturally we may have shortcomings and even make some mistakes [*chuxian quedian rengzhi cuowu*] in our work."[118]

In these ways, Jiang gave himself room for beginning a process in later years of reevaluating the party's handling of the movement. That reevaluation, when it came, was likely to reaffirm the decision to remove the protesters from Tiananmen Square. But it would criticize the use of lethal weaponry, which had resulted in so many deaths. In this way, the party's "correct" decision to end the protests would be portrayed as having been carried out by crude, overzealous soldiers. The policy was correct, but the implementation was badly flawed. If anyone were tried for the tragedy, it would likely be an army officer, not a party leader. Jiang's clear conscience over the affair allowed him to make this distinction. Those like Li Peng who had ordered the crackdown, by contrast, could never admit to "shortcomings" or "mistakes" in this galling chapter of the government's "work."

For Jiang, there were even twinges of guilt about his support for the policy of ending the protests, although as the leader of the party that had made the decision, he could never hope to question it without fatally weakening his hold on power. On occasion in the company of friends, these twinges would surface. With a fine sense of irony and subtle suggestions of regret, Jiang would wonder privately whether his support for the Tiananmen massacre was at odds with his own participation in protests for "freedom and democracy" as a student in the 1940s. "Have

I come full circle compared to back then?" he would ask academics from Taiwan sometime later. No one in the room, Jiang included, dared offer a reply.[119]

8

Within hours of the massacre in Beijing, Shanghai students erupted in indignation. By early morning on 4 June, roadblocks had been set up at forty-seven major intersections, and half of the city's bus lines were suspended.[120]

Jiang had left the handling of the Shanghai protests in the capable hands of Zhu Rongji, an intellectual like himself, whom he could trust to act in moderation. Zhu was aided by the deputy party secretaries Huang Ju and Wu Bangguo. In constant contact with Jiang in Beijing, the trio were told to stabilize the situation in Shanghai as soon as possible. But that situation was growing steadily worse as reports of the Beijing massacre trickled in. The events in Beijing had brought the Shanghai movement back to life with a vengeance. With the capital under virtual military control, Shanghai students took up the tattered standard of the democracy movement. Tires were slashed, radio stations seized, and trains leaving the city brought to a complete standstill. "Shanghai is now at a critical juncture, from which we may maintain stability or land ourselves in turmoil," the Shanghai government warned on 5 June. "We want to give a serious message to leaders of illegal organizations and plotters of sabotage: pull back from the brink of the precipice . . . otherwise you will be severely punished."[121]

Shanghai was the first local government to express support for the crackdown in Beijing, an alacrity that probably owed something to Jiang's presence in the capital.[122] But determined not to follow the confrontational example of Beijing, the Shanghai government brought 40,000 citizens and cadres onto the streets on 7 June to remove roadblocks at major intersections.[123] Over the coming week, these so-called "mobile pickets" would prove effective in gradually curtailing the efforts of students to block traffic. Both Zhu and Jiang would win plaudits for this tactic, although Jiang could have had at best an indirect role in its adoption. "Why couldn't Beijing have thought a little and adopted the same method?" one official newspaper would ask plaintively.[124]

The contrast between the two major cities in these days was stark. While soldiers in Beijing patrolled the smoking, war-torn streets of the

capital, flashing their guns and bayonets, Shanghai was still awash with
students and angry workers. But the Shanghai government never threatened to deploy the army. A statement issued early on the morning of 6
June said merely that there were "limits to the tolerance and restraint of
the party, the government, and the masses."[125] Asked directly about the
possible use of military force against the students, a city spokesman said:
"The so-called readiness [of the PLA] to move into central areas of the
city to enforce martial law is sheer nonsense."[126]

Instead, Shanghai unleashed its formidable police force on the sometimes wanton violence taking place on the fringes of the student protests.
In an ironic sort of way, Shanghai's lack of recourse to military force
seemed to make its already notorious police force more ruthless. If peaceful protesters were declared immune, then those committing even minor
infractions of law would be mercilessly dealt with. On 7 and 8 June, forty
"criminals" were arrested, most accused of disorderly behavior such as
deflating tires and blocking roads. Another group of eleven men, none
of them students, were soon arrested for their part in a mêlée at a rail-
road crossing north of the city on 6 June, where half a dozen students
lying across the tracks had been crushed under the wheels of a Beijing-
bound train.[127] The arrests were the first in the country related to the
pro-democracy demonstrations.

Zhu Rongji came on the radio on the night of 8 June.[128] "My heart
is burning with anxiety," he said, sounding tired and ragged. "As mayor
of Shanghai I have felt very sorry and guilty in recent days because I
could not protect the personal safety of my people." His tone was conciliatory. Some cadres had urged him to use force to restore order, he
said, but this would risk innocent lives and the lives of students who had
simply "lost their reason." "I tell you now. I have never considered using troops or exercising military control. This is the honest truth." As to
events in Beijing, Zhu seemed to share the outrage of his fellow citizens.
"Things that occurred in Beijing are history," he said. "No one can conceal history. The truth will eventually come to light."

The "soft" crackdown in Shanghai was then unleashed with fury.
Over 160 people were arrested in the coming week, a fifth of them for
"organizing illegal organizations and inciting unrest."[129] Within two
weeks, 126 student leaders were detained. Three men accused of leading the railroad-crossing riot were sentenced to death on 15 June, and
the executions were carried out six days later. They were the first in the
country related to the pro-democracy movement, coming a day earlier
than the first executions in Beijing.

Although he was not in Shanghai at the time, Jiang would boast frequently of the peaceful way in which the city's protests had been handled. "In Shanghai we did not need to use armed force," he told American television. "It's a question of unanimous thinking within the leading organs. We were unanimous in Shanghai."[130] Doubtless, the consensus among leaders in Shanghai helped matters. But the fact that it was not the national capital and the focus of protest also helped. More important, just as action in Beijing may have been more severe because of the knowledge that Jiang would not be blamed, it may have been unusually restrained in Shanghai for the same reason. Although Jiang was in Beijing, the moderate handling of the Shanghai situation would still be important to his image after the movement had been suppressed. For national political reasons, Shanghai may have been stuck with having to control unruly mobs using only citizen groups and mostly unarmed police. Although little more than a bystander in this watershed event in modern Chinese history, Jiang Zemin may have played a key role in the way it was handled merely by agreeing to succeed Zhao Ziyang.

9

The ordination of Jiang Zemin in the wake of the killings in Beijing on 4 June was slow and methodical. Deng appeared for the first time on national television on the evening of 9 June at a meeting in Zhongnanhai stacked with party and military elders. President Yang Shangkun and Premier Li Peng were surrounded at the head of the table near Deng by half a dozen retired party leaders. Further down the table were the elder military commanders who had overseen the Tiananmen massacre. It was clear that, with the exception of Li Peng and the remotely seated Qiao Shi, the "second generation" of leaders was still calling the shots.

Deng's task now that he had secured Jiang's promotion was to ensure that overall party policy was not affected. "This storm was bound to happen sooner or later," Deng said. "If there is any shortcoming, then I'd say it is that our reforms and opening have not proceeded adequately. . . . Perhaps this bad thing will enable us to go ahead with reforms and opening at a more steady, better, even faster pace."[131] In a private meeting a week later with eight senior party members, Deng was ready to take his first step toward retirement. Like a young boy crouching by the lakeside giving a gentle nudge to his toy sailboat as it nosed its way into the small ripples, he gave his final instructions. "You should make an effort to protect the core—Comrade Jiang Zemin, as you have agreed," he said.[132] With Jiang at the helm, Deng would be content to stand by the shoreline watching the boat, perhaps making a few helpful splashes when needed. "I will no longer concern myself with your affairs or interfere with them," he said. "If you want to consult me, I won't turn you down, but it won't be the way it used to be."[133]

The direction he wanted to see the new leadership take was already well known from his internal speeches since mid May. The most pressing task, Deng said, was to regain the people's trust. This might be accomplished for a start by fighting corruption and speeding up economic reforms. Political reforms, meanwhile, would be subsumed within these objectives: "The highest objective of our political restructuring is to keep the environment stable," he said.[134]

The stage was now set for Jiang's formal nomination and election to the highest post in the land. An enlarged Politburo meeting was held from 19 to 21 June, where the formal vote was taken. It was endorsed at a party plenum a few days later. In a show of unanimity, the 276 members and alternate members of the Central Committee were joined at the plenum by the 184 party elders of the Central Advisory Commission. The probable second choice to Jiang, Tianjin's mayor, Li Ruihuan, was added to the Politburo standing committee, along with the head of the party's Personnel Department, Song Ping. The probable third choice, the State Planning Commission vice-minister Ding Guangen, joined the party secretariat.

It had been nearly a month since Jiang had appeared in public. Some in Shanghai were still guessing that his handling of the *Herald* had landed him in permanent perdition. But on the night of 24 June 1989, his image flashed across the nation sitting at the center of a dais in a gray Mao tunic surrounded by the other five members of the revamped Politburo standing committee. After Jiang, the hierarchy was signified by the order in which the names were read: Li Peng, Qiao Shi, Yao Yilin, Song Ping, and Li Ruihuan.

Immediate reaction at home and abroad was one of disbelief. "Jiang's selection to the nation's most powerful post came as a surprise to many China-watchers," commented the Associated Press. "Although he has the experience and the right political stance for the job, he lacks a power base."[135] Indeed, it was this apparent lack of strong factional support that landed Jiang with the tag of a "transitional figure" almost immediately. "Even if Deng really wanted to help Jiang turn himself into a genuinely strong and charismatic successor," said the Taiwan journal *Issues and Studies*, "he will not have enough time given that there are so many strong leaders already."[136]

The "transitional figure" label would gradually peel off as the years passed. But certainly on that muggy summer evening, with Soviet-designed tanks still roaming Beijing's streets, Jiang was barely in charge. In the month since Zhao's tearful farewell in Tiananmen Square, Deng had made the big decisions, while day-to-day matters had been handled by a triumvirate consisting of two of the three remaining Politburo standing committee members, Li Peng and Qiao Shi, and the state president, Yang Shangkun.[137] It was this trio, for example, that had replaced the liberal *People's Daily* director Qian Liren and his chief editor Tan Wenrui with more conservative editors in mid June.[138] Qiao Shi was being referred to officially during the interregnum as "[a] Chinese Communist Party leader,"[139] while Li Peng's proximity to Deng at the meeting on 9 June showed that he was in control of the government. Yang meanwhile had taken over from Zhao as first vice-chairman of the Central Military Commission, making him second only to Deng in the crucial military power structure. When Jiang came to power, this was the de facto political leadership that stared him in the face. The only thing that had prevented Li or Qiao from sitting in the position he now occupied was their role in the Beijing massacre.[140] Little wonder that overseas press reports doubted Jiang's staying power.

Jiang was the third major leader of the Chinese Communist Party to come to power in a coup, broadly defined. Mao had seized power at a meeting in remote Guizhou province in 1935 by lambasting the military tactics adopted by the party leadership of that time. Deng had used arcane debates on Cultural Revolution history to discredit remnant Mao supporters and seize power in 1978. Now Jiang had been brought to power following the purge of Zhao Ziyang.

Jiang's accession was bloodier than those of Mao and Deng, if the Tiananmen massacre is interpreted as an action necessary to purge Zhao and his associates from the party. But inside the party, it was less disruptive. Jiang was chosen by Deng and endorsed by broad factional support within the party to be the "core" of a "third generation" of party leadership. The window of opportunity for a radical left-wing coup, say, had closed by the time Jiang was introduced to the Chinese people as their next senior leader. The fall of Zhao Ziyang in mid May may have afforded such left-wing conservatives a rare chance to assert their influence. But without overturning Deng's reform policies, that could not be achieved. Despite problems of corruption and inflation, the reforms were too popular and the memories of Maoism gone awry too vivid to permit that. Deng retained overall control, and he chose Jiang. For party policy, it meant there would be no sharp change in direction. Jiang was hired to ensure that the Dengist legacy was protected.

"Some intellectuals welcomed Jiang's elevation to the top party post in Beijing, considering him an attractive alternative to Premier Li Peng, a hard-line, Soviet-trained technocrat," the *Washington Post* wrote shortly after his appointment. "Jiang is more cosmopolitan and open-minded and is associated with Deng's trade and diplomatic overtures to the West."[141]

Even Deng, though, could not be sure that his third party general secretary in just over a decade would last. Deng had done all he could to ensure that Jiang was not brought down by factional battles or party elders. As with any transplant, however, Deng could not guarantee that the new organ would be accepted by the body politic. Healing the wounds of the massacre and fighting corruption would help Jiang win acceptance, Deng believed. But in the end, his position would depend on ensuring that economic growth continued apace. Only this could keep his rivals within the party at bay and the would-be demonstrators off the streets. "If the economy is not well run," he warned. "Jiang will not last long."[142]

Deng gave Jiang just three to six months to win the trust of a skeptical Chinese nation. If all went well, Deng promised to withdraw into the background for good. If not, he might be forced to remove his third successor.[143]

It is no wonder, given this array of doubts inside the party, in the country, and around the world, that Jiang felt uneasy as he took the reins as Communist China's third-ever party general secretary. Wang Yeping's tears weighed more heavily on him than Wang Daohan's appeals to national heroism. "I felt as if I were standing on the brink of a deep ravine," he would recall, "or walking on thin ice."[144]

Figure 1. Deng Xiaoping and Jiang Zemin at the fifth plenum of the thirteenth central committee in November 1989. Premier Li Peng stands behind them, to Jiang's right. Taking formal leave of the political stage, Deng urged delegates to support Jiang in his new role as chairman of the Central Military Commission. (Xinhua News Agency)

Figure 2. Jiang at a party plenum with Li Peng in June 1989, shortly after his appointment as general secretary of the Chinese Communist Party. Both men wear the gray tunic that signified a return to orthodoxy in the aftermath of the Tiananmen massacre only weeks before. (Xinhua News Agency)

Figure 3. A frail Deng Xiaoping emerges at the close of the fourteenth national party congress in 1992 to show his continued support for Jiang. Deng's daughter and biographer Deng Rong (right) acts as her father's assistant. Li Peng is visible just over Jiang's shoulder. (Xinhua News Agency)

Figure 4. Wearing an unadorned green tunic that belies his lack of military experience, Jiang addresses military delegates to China's national parliament in early 1996. (Xinhua News Agency)

Figure 5. Settling into her role as China's First Lady, Wang Yeping (left) chats with King Juan Carlos of Spain at a state dinner in Madrid in 1996. (Agence France-Presse)

Figure 6. Making a poor impression on the international stage, Jiang falls victim to his own image-conscious habit of combing his hair in public during an official welcoming in Spain hosted by King Juan Carlos. Advisors had failed to warn Jiang about the habit in preceding years. (Agence France-Presse)

Figure 7. Animated after securing an agreement with President Bill Clinton to exchange official state visits in 1997 and 1998, Jiang gestures after their meeting in Manila in November 1996. (Reuters / Gary Hershorn / Archive Photos)

Figure 8.   Jiang surrounded by children sporting the red neckties of the Communist Youth League in Guangxi province in late 1996, mimicking Mao Zedong's pose nearly four decades earlier, which came to symbolize the party's concern for the poor. (Xinhua News Agency)

Figure 9.   Displaying his musical exhibitionism, Jiang enjoys a round of karaoke with Philippine President Fidel Ramos at a party following the APEC summit in Manila, November 1996. (Associated Press Photo)

Figure 10. Alone, but watched by the world, Jiang weeps as he delivers the eulogy for Deng Xiaoping in February 1997. (Agence France-Presse)

Figure 11. In his last glimpse of the man who had brought him to power, Jiang leads Li Peng, Qiao Shi, and Li Ruihuan past Deng Xiaoping's bier. (Xinhua News Agency)

Figure 12.   Before his retirement as chairman of China's national parliament, Qiao Shi stands next to Jiang at the opening of the fifteenth party congress in October 1997 in a show of solidarity. From left: Hu Jintao, Zhu Rongji, Qiao, Jiang, Li Peng, Li Ruihuan, Liu Huaqing. (Xinhua News Agency)

Figure 13.   In a speech to the fifteenth party congress in 1997, Jiang announces plans to divest state assets, cut the number of military personnel, and incorporate Deng Theory into the party constitution. (Xinhua News Agency)

CHAPTER 6

The Great Reconciliation

I

The Middle and South Seas Garden, or Zhongnanhai, lying to the west of the Forbidden City in Beijing, has served as the administrative center of Communist China since 1949. Behind the imposing, camera-strewn walls and the gold-inscribed red screen at the entrance to the complex can be found the offices and meeting halls of the top organs of the party, the government, and the army. The lakes ("seas") that give the garden its name occupy most of the area inside. On the western edge lies a clutter of buildings where senior leaders meet, informally for the most part, but formally on occasion.

Built under the Song dynasty (A.D. 960–1279), the gardens originally served as the playground of the emperor and his retinue, but went through a sort of dynastic cycle of their own, repeatedly falling into disrepair and then being rebuilt. The tall wild grass that is allowed to snake and slither around the stone paths and structures in the present version is a particularly un-Chinese innovation, introduced by the invading Manchus of the Qing dynasty (A.D. 1644–1911).

Mao Zedong resided in the Garden of Abundance, situated between the lakes, where emperors had carried out planting rites to ensure a good harvest. Deng, keen to disassociate himself from Mao's regal intimations, decamped altogether for a two-story house north of the Forbidden City. Party business was still conducted within the walls of

Zhongnanhai, though. Its continuing relevance was symbolized during the 1989 Tiananmen Square movement when students scuffled with soldiers in an attempt to break through the southern "New China" gate in mid April.

On 28 June, as befitted a new emperor, Jiang Zemin undertook his first official duties at a meeting inside Zhongnanhai. The first time the Chinese public saw him in action as party secretary, he was seated next to Li Peng at an oval table (a symbol of discussion) at a televised gathering with officially sponsored noncommunist political groups.[1] Li Peng spoke first, introducing the new six-member Politburo standing committee. Then he gestured to the eager-faced man in the gray Mao tunic and thick black glasses. "Jiang Zemin is the core of our leading body. Henceforth all of us in the leading body will follow his guidance—of course, with the help of the . . . older generation." The last clause was crucial. Although acknowledging Jiang as the core, Li immediately made fealty to the new emperor conditional on continued support for Jiang from party elders. If that dissipated, Li seemed to be saying, the arrangements might not last long.

Jiang then leaned forward and adjusted his microphone. In the hour that he spoke, he evinced none of the easygoing manner he had so carefully cultivated in Shanghai. His words were harsh and strictly in line with party policy, a sign that the speech was probably a group effort. "We must be determined to ferret out and promptly and harshly punish all plotters, organizers, and behind-the-scenes manipulators of the rebellion and unrest," he began. "For these cruel enemies of the people, we must not have the slightest leniency."

Jiang assured the world that the opening and reform policies would "never change," despite the events of June 4th. He then quoted Deng word for word (without acknowledgment) by saying that the reforms would be carried out "better, steadier, and even faster." His comments on the "great number of problems" confronting the leadership were left out of the evening television broadcast but carried in the *People's Daily* the next day. "The jobs of stabilizing the situation, developing the economy, punishing corrupt officials, and unifying people's thinking are especially formidable," he said.

The inauguration complete, Deng Xiaoping left Beijing and repaired to the beach resort of Beidaihe on the nearby Bohai Sea, where the days were passed swimming, playing card games, and in incessant political chat in airy hillside villas. Jiang would visit Deng on occasion at Beidaihe during the summer, always enjoying the privilege of sitting on the patriarch's immediate right in a large, comfortable chair.[2] But Deng was sincere in his wish to retire, and he would not reemerge for three months, the minimum time he had allotted Jiang to establish his image as a credible new leader. Overseas reports worried that Deng was seriously ill, but we now know that he had sent himself on vacation on purpose. "Deng is deliberately keeping away from the top policy-making body in order to give Jiang a free hand," one report stated. "His main concern is to maintain stability and perfect the system that will allow power to be handed over to Jiang."[3]

Cleaning up the political and economic mess left over from Tiananmen would dominate Jiang's first half year as party general secretary. Like the floods that had heralded his arrival in Shanghai four years earlier, the killings in Beijing confronted him with the immediate and pressing need for a disaster relief effort. In the first few weeks after protests were suppressed, officials concentrated on arresting leaders of the movement. By 26 June, 1,800 arrests and 27 executions had been recorded by Western news agencies.[4] After two years, the government confirmed nearly 2,600 arrests related to the disturbances.[5] Many more thousands, however, were given administrative sentences in labor camps; more than 40,000 "criminals" turned themselves in during the five months after the massacre.[6]

Jiang's standing instructions on the witch-hunts sought to limit outright punishment to the hard core of organizers, many of whom had already fled abroad. "The issue of handling those people—especially those students—who did not know the truth, took part in marches, shouted slogans, and participated in hunger strikes is primarily an issue of education," he said in late June.[7] Jiang felt that the party was being indulgent toward those involved in the protests. "Back in the 1940s, if you got caught by the Nationalists, all you could do was wait to be executed. The family was not even informed," he told a visitor from Taiwan, Shen Chun-shan. "Now we're being very lenient."[8]

More controversial was the issue of who or what to blame for the Tiananmen movement. On one side were party elders like Wang Zhen and Peng Zhen who wanted a thorough purge of all those in the party associated with Zhao Ziyang and a sharp repudiation of the liberalizing policies he had followed. "Some party statesmen still consider their present major concern to be that of framing the backers of the riots, namely, Zhao Ziyang and his advisers," an official report said. Others, like Wan Li and Song Ping, expressed sympathy for Zhao and declared that his "contributions to reform" should be reaffirmed.[9]

In essence, the debate boiled down to whether blame for the Tiananmen movement should be laid squarely and narrowly on Zhao and a small group of foreign-backed radical students, or whether broader explanations should be sought in the party and its policies. Jiang stood firmly in the latter camp, as shown by his remarks on the "great number of problems" facing the leadership. The gulf between the two sides came into the open after the formal report on the Tiananmen massacre by Beijing's mayor, Chen Xitong, was delivered on 30 June. In it, Chen blamed the movement on "a tiny bunch of people in the party and society who ganged up and engaged in a lot of extremely inappropriate activities."[10] The very next day, Jiang riposted that the demonstrations "revealed many problems in party organizations and among party members. And some of them are serious."[11] An investigation was needed into the origins of the movement and the lessons to be learned, he said. It was the first act of a two-year reconciliation effort led by Jiang.

Jiang's desire to shelter Zhao and seek broader explanations for Tiananmen is unsurprising. On a personal level, he recognized Zhao's contributions and sympathized with his economically liberal policies. More significant, Jiang had been installed precisely to protect the legacy of economic reform that Zhao had left behind. "Comrade Zhao will be treated in a totally pragmatic manner," Jiang promised shortly after taking office. "His merits will not be erased, but his faults should also be clarified."[12] Ensuring that Zhao's official repute was not thoroughly demolished also served the arguably more difficult task of making amends to China's embattled intellectuals. Moreover, having belonged to a similar student movement half a century before, Jiang felt uncomfortable about being on the side of repression. "We can understand the feelings of the overwhelming majority of students. Our policy is to unite and educate them," he said in one of his first of many peace offerings.[13] "Under no circumstances should we push students toward the enemy."[14]

Jiang, in comparison with Li Peng, was accustomed to meeting with students and answering their questions. His local government experience came in handy in this respect when he took his by now well-rehearsed "meet the students" show to Beijing's prestigious Qinghua University in late August.[15] For four hours, Jiang was pounded with difficult questions about the political witch-hunts being carried out on campuses. "I am 'a rioter.' That's what they call me here," one of the fifteen invited students complained. Jiang turned to university and city officials on hand, who denied labeling the student a rioter. "Who has stuck that label on you?

The university and the city have not. Neither have I," Jiang said at last. "I am also an intellectual, and I understand intellectuals well. We have this weakness. When things are going well, we lose our heads. But when things go badly, we consider ourselves useless and lose all our motivation. This is not a good habit. You should brace up again."[16]

Jiang was only slightly less accommodating toward intellectuals in the party who had taken part in the demonstrations. "There were a lot of party members demonstrating on the streets, and that was a serious problem," he said in August.[17] "If such people leave the party, it will have no effect. They shouldn't have joined in the first place." His aim in showing some party members the door, however, was less to punish them than to rid the ranks of cadres whom he suspected of disloyalty to his new regime. "The fence-sitters are the most dangerous," he said. "Some members are still taking a wait-and-see attitude. They wonder if there will be more [political] changes. We cannot tolerate this."

A screening campaign of party membership launched in the wake of Tiananmen was intended to weed out all the fence-sitters in the ranks. But, as the sinologist Richard Baum has noted, "when the final results of the campaign were announced . . . the numbers were surprisingly small." Just over 13,000 cadres were disciplined for various political offenses, of whom just 1,179 were specifically charged with taking part in the protests.[18] The numbers seem to show that despite Jiang's assertion that "a lot" of the 50 million party members took part in the demonstrations, only a tiny minority were being formally disciplined. The new leadership was trying to be as conciliatory to wayward party members as it was to students.

The one identifiable group that Jiang made no attempt to conciliate was the media. This should not be surprising given his penchant for berating the press while in Shanghai. But the vitriol he poured on the tens of thousands of mainland journalists who had taken to the streets during the Tiananmen protests, carrying banners representing their organizations and calling for genuine press freedom, suggested that insecurity about his own position rather than retribution was his main concern. In a speech to national media heads in November, Jiang blasted "certain media organizations" that, instead of denouncing the protests, "provided a forum for the instigators of the turmoil, thus adding fuel to the flames."[19] While a few newspapers, like the PLA's *Jiefangjun bao* and the *Beijing ribao* (Beijing Daily), had stuck to the party line, many others, like the *World Economic Herald*, "went against the central authorities' correct principles and openly sang a different tune," he said. "Some were totally devastated." Quoting Mao twice and borrowing liberally from Lenin's critique of the privately owned Western press, Jiang insisted that only party-led journalism could truly represent the interests of everyone in China. "From now on," he said, "our media should never be a forum for bourgeois liberalization."

A subsequent shakeout of media leaders was conducted by Xu Weicheng, the former Beijing municipal propaganda director, who was appointed executive deputy director of the central party's Propaganda Department in February 1990. Among the changes was the appointment of Xu Guangchun, who had headed the Shanghai branch of Xinhua while Jiang was in the city, as executive deputy of the intellectual *Guangming ribao,* whose staff had given wide and frank coverage to the protests. Many more journals were shut down altogether. By the end of 1990, the number of newspapers had fallen by 38 percent, to 1,445, compared to 1988, the high point of the liberal era, while the number of magazines had dipped by 10 percent, to 5,300.[20] Jiang might have sensed the irony of his own role in this crackdown, given that the Nationalists had shut down one title after another launched by his own uncles in the 1920s and 1930s. But he also shared his uncles' vision of the press as a buttress for the party and a fount of edifying reports. "Newspapers can criticize, but they should also suggest improvements," he told a Hong Kong media delegation shortly after Tiananmen. "If they just expose and criticize the dark side of society, everyone will be depressed."[21]

2

After his few glorious years on the Shanghai diplomatic cocktail circuit, Jiang was dismayed by the sanctions and pull-outs by Western countries in the wake of the Tiananmen massacre. For a local mayor, foreign relations had been the stuff of economics and goodwill. Now, at the national level, he was discovering there were more serious issues of sovereignty and national prestige at stake.

The U.S. president, George Bush, had suspended all military and high-level contacts between the two governments in June and said pressure would be put on the World Bank to suspend new loans to China. The 50,000 mainland students studying in the United States were allowed to extend their visas indefinitely. Paris said it would "freeze" diplomatic contacts with Beijing, and Japan—China's largest foreign-aid supplier—

suspended consideration of a five-year, U.S.$5.6 billion aid program beginning in 1990.[22] Reaction from other Western countries was similar.

The results were plain to see in the rows of suddenly empty hotels throughout the country. Tourism receipts—even on the arguably inflated official count—fell 10 percent, to U.S.$1.9 billion, in 1989, while the growth of foreign investment slowed to 11 percent, and then to 2 percent in 1990, both well below the rates of the preceding years.[23] GNP growth for 1989 was to plummet to just 3.9 percent, after two years at over 10 percent.[24]

On the surface, Jiang was defiant. "Some Western countries want to stifle socialism. They want to crush us. But they will not scare us," he told the general secretary of India's ruling Congress Party, the first foreign dignitary he met as general secretary, in early July.[25] In imagining a proud nation "carefree and immutable" to foreign economic sanctions, Jiang drew heavily on his admiration for the Yangzhou poet Zhu Ziqing. "The young people of China," Jiang said, "should take him as a model and not bow, act obsequiously to, and blindly envy the West."[26] Chinese dissidents in the United States had done quite the opposite in his view, teaming up with members of Congress to advocate sanctions against China and green cards for themselves: "I wonder whether those people still carry the blood of the Chinese nation in their veins?" he wondered aloud.[27]

The posturing was important for Jiang's early assertion of authority, but in private he admitted to colleagues that the Western sanctions were making China's diplomacy more difficult.[28] It was his good fortune that he at first bore little responsibility for breaking China out of diplomatic isolation. As party general secretary, Jiang was not the lead player in China's foreign affairs, either in theory or in practice. The president, who in theory is the top representative of the state in foreign dealings, was still Yang Shangkun. The party's leading group on foreign affairs, meanwhile, the real center of power in diplomacy, was headed by Li Peng. Jiang had the luxury of standing on the high ground of principle, leaving others to seek practical ways out.

The Bush administration had made secret attempts, despite its public rhetoric, to maintain close contacts with Beijing in the wake of June 4th. Bush had even tried to telephone the Chinese leadership shortly after the massacre, failing to patch through, he explained, because "the line was busy."[29] In July and then again in December, Bush dispatched his national security advisor, Brent Scowcroft, on secret missions to China.[30] Scowcroft met Deng, Jiang, Li, and Foreign Minister Qian

Qichen, sometimes together, sometimes individually. In this way, the groundwork was laid for a resumption of normal ties once public outrage in the West had subsided. In the meantime, intimate consultations took place via various emissaries. Among the go-betweens were former president Richard Nixon and former secretary of state Henry Kissinger. Jiang met both men when they visited in late October and early November respectively and in his characteristic manner took the opportunity to deliver impolite lectures. "They came over and said June 4th was so and so," he recalled. "I told them I knew more about the United States than they knew about China."[31]

Despite the prickly start, Jiang eventually did his bit to improve ties with Washington through a series of media appearances in the United States in the first half of 1990, just as relations were being mended. His interviews with *U.S. News & World Report* and on ABC TV conveyed a moderate and friendly image that was a welcome respite from the stiff and curt Li Peng. ABC correspondent Barbara Walters described Jiang as having "a lovely smile and eyes that go cold."[32] Jiang made his points in an amicable way. He joked about his weight, painting himself as a Japanese sumo wrestler, whom foreigners should be wary of tangling with: "As someone educated as a scientist and engineer, I always talk about China as a very big mass," he said. "Myself, I am also a very big mass at 209 pounds. It is difficult for you to push away such a big mass. You might sometimes have to retreat or even fall down yourself as a result."[33]

Jiang also scored a minor coup by answering a letter from nine students at California State Polytechnic University in early June. Point by point, for ten pages, he carefully explained China's line on the differences between the two countries.[34] Underlying his view of Sino–U.S. relations, and the West in general, was an intellectual's persnickety attention to differences that were only to be bridged for strategic reasons. "The restoration and development of Sino–U.S. relations are due to the major interests shared by the two sides and not an identity of their values," he wrote to the California students.

The end of the Sino–U.S. freeze, and with it China's post-Tiananmen diplomatic isolation, would finally come in June 1990, when the astrophysicist Fang Lizhi and his wife were allowed to leave the U.S. embassy in Beijing for asylum abroad, after holding out inside for three weeks. The man whose orations in Shanghai had set off the 1986 protests was the butt of one last spiteful outburst by Jiang. Fang represented the very obsequiousness that Jiang abhorred in China's relations with the West. "His English is worse than mine but he still goes around talking about politics and cursing [Chinese] leaders abroad," he declaimed. "I really have no respect for people like him."[35]

3

Amid the red and white banners fluttering in the breezes of Tiananmen Square in April and May had been appeals for a "clean" Chinese Communist Party. The fight against corruption was as old as the party itself. But in the wake of Tiananmen, it changed from being a defensive response to public opinion to a means by which the party might actively seek to heal the wounds of the June 4th massacre. Deng told Jiang that fighting corruption was one of "several good things for the people" he should do to win popular appeal.[36] It appears that Jiang was aware as early as May that he would be expected to tackle the issue. That month, he had committed his ideas to paper in an article that appeared in the journal *Dang jian* (Party Building) in July 1989:

> There is indeed the danger of corruption. It is growing in the soil, in the air, in nooks and in crannies. If we fail to get a grip on these problems or if we permit negative phenomena like corruption to go on for a long time, they certainly will prevent our party from displaying its fighting power. Our party and state might even perish. . . . If all our party and government organs use their power to seek material benefits, then isn't this just like fleecing the people in broad daylight? And if that's the case, wouldn't it be strange if our country did not collapse?[37]

They were strong words. Even Deng had never gone so far as to predict the collapse of Communist rule in China if graft were not reined in. Jiang made the connection explicit both in the article and in a later stock formula, which he first used at a meeting in late July: "The problem of promoting a clean and honest administration and opposing corruption concerns the life and death of the ruling party."[38]

Jiang's first opportunity to put on display his corruption-fighting image came in dealing with torrential floods that swept the country in mid and late July, inundating large areas of Hubei and Anhui provinces. The floods were the fifth worst since 1949 and killed close to 6,000 people.

Everywhere he went, Jiang insisted on traveling in a minivan rather than in one of the black sedans with tinted-glass windows that usually convey high Communist functionaries. Box lunches rather than banquets were the rule for meals, and money or grain coupons were handed over for the simple victuals.[39] Jiang would take his "new style" from one end of the country to the other in the following months, insisting on traveling by regular train service in northeastern Heilongjiang province and declining offers of "sweet and glistening" mangoes in a steamy orchard in southern Hainan province. He did not appear to shed many pounds for all his reputed abstemiousness. But whatever the reality of his travel style, China's new emperor was sending a clear signal to officials to keep their noses clean. "From General Secretary Jiang, we can see that there is hope for the party style to take a turn for the better," *Hainan ribao* commented.[40]

The higher priority accorded to stamping out official corruption was reflected in the courts. There were 25,000 people charged in lower courts with bribery and corruption in 1990, a 44 percent increase over 1989.[41] As far as the party itself was concerned, 79,000 members were expelled for corruption in 1990 and another 260,000 were disciplined.[42] Numbers were less important for the credibility of the campaign than the entrapment of senior officials, rather than just petty bureaucrats: "tigers" as well as "flies," as they were described in a Chinese expression. A few notable tigers were indeed bagged by the anti-corruption campaign early on; the Hainan governor, Liang Xiang, was sacked in September 1989 for his role in an illegal car import racket, as well as the shady property dealings of his wife and son, and the vice-minister of railroads, Luo Yunguang, was fired in March 1990 for accepting bribes.[43]

Most prized, though, and most dangerous to hunt, were the children of senior cadres and the companies they ran. The problem of companies run by these so-called red princes had first surfaced over the issue of *guandao,* or official profiteering, in 1988. A seven-point program issued after the first Politburo meeting Jiang chaired, in late July 1989, for the first time formally banned the children and spouses of senior cadres from operating companies. The seven-point program, Jiang said, should be carried out "starting with the members of the Politburo," so that lower-level officials did not think it was merely "a gust of wind" that would soon pass.[44] A few red princes were tripped up. Most spectacular was Deng Pufang, the crippled son of Deng Xiaoping. He was exposed in the *People's Daily* in late August 1989 for official profiteering involving the Kang Hua Development Corporation of the China Federation for the Disabled, which he headed, and was fined U.S.$3 million.[45] It was less than the fines slapped on two other red prince-linked companies at the same time. But leveling charges of tax evasion and *guandao* against members of the Deng family clearly showed that no tiger would be allowed to roam freely under the new regime. Jiang and his colleagues had a mandate to go after big game, and that was what they were doing.

Jiang's anti-graft fervor seems to have been born of two factors. Most immediate, corruption was a key grievance that had fueled the Tiananmen movement, bringing the party closer to overthrow than at any time since 1949. Jiang was charged with pulling the party back from that giddy brink. "He considered the Tiananmen protests to be a 'terrifying wave,' not just a 'gentle ripple,'" one official report explained, referring to the nonchalant description of the movement used by Deng.[46]

More subtle was Jiang's barely concealed disdain for the unfettered proto-capitalism that Deng's reforms had unleashed in many sectors and regions. Corruption was not just bribes for favors, Jiang believed. It was a more deeply rooted flaw in the system of exchange that was causing income disparities across the nation: "The problem now is that a small number of people rely on illegal means—such as tax avoidance, cheating, monopolizing markets, jacking up prices, abusing power for personal gain, corruption, bribe-taking, smuggling, and profiteering—to gain ill-gotten wealth. . . . If this matter is not handled well, social stability can be affected."[47]

Jiang's point was that some regions were rich and some state enterprise managers were well paid, not because they were more productive, but rather because of corrupt, illicit practices. The haves and have-nots were distinguished, not by how hard they worked, as Deng might have hoped, but by whether they had the right connections. Appealing for remedies was bold, because it took direct aim at Deng's near-sacred promise to "let some people get rich first," a slogan that ended up becoming a sort of political guarantee throughout the 1980s for moonlighters, private businessmen, and other entrepreneurs, whose activities often took place on the margins of the law. Jiang rephrased Deng's slogan in a cheeky but revealing way in a speech on the eve of the party's 1 October anniversary that was broadcast live around the nation: "We believe in letting some people get rich first *through their honest labor and legal business operations*," he said (emphasis added).[48]

Given his enthusiasm for the anti-corruption campaign, it is not surprising that Jiang took special care in the months after he became general secretary to ensure that his own family affairs were in order. "When I call upon others to be honest, I should do so myself," Jiang told *U.S. News & World Report*. "We are in the Forbidden City, walled in by a crimson wall. I just hope that we are not completely isolated from the masses outside."[49]

Immediate interest focused on his two sons, Jiang Mianheng, now 37, and Jiang Miankang, 35. Given the high-profile attacks on other red

princes by the Tiananmen protesters, Jiang was lucky that neither son
was involved in business or politics at the time. Mianheng was studying
in the United States, and Miankang was a researcher in Shanghai.

Still, Jiang's treatment of his sons was not entirely aboveboard. In the
wake of the Cultural Revolution, Mianheng had belatedly obtained an
undergraduate degree from Shanghai's Fudan University. When his father became mayor of Shanghai in 1985, Mianheng applied to Drexel
University in Philadelphia to pursue postgraduate studies in electrical engineering. One of his father's former classmates from Jiaotong University, Sun Hun, and one of his former Jiaotong teachers, Gu Yuxiu, were
both teaching at Drexel. Mianheng may have wanted to use these connections to win a chance to study abroad. Never having heard of Fudan
University, however, Drexel initially rejected his application.[50] In response, Jiang Zemin sent another former Jiaotong classmate who
had worked under him at the Ministry of Electronics to Drexel to resolve the problem. After meeting Gu and Sun, and following a return
trip to Shanghai by Drexel officials, Mianheng was given a place in the
school. He arrived in the United States in 1986 and was joined a year
later by his wife, Wang Xiaolin.[51]

Short like his father and sporting the same thick, square glasses, Mianheng lived in a three-story redbrick row house in west Philadelphia.
When away from his studies and his wife's community college courses
in English, the couple traveled extensively around the United States,
friends said.[52] Their daughter, known as "fuzzy head" (*maotou*) among
the Jiang family, was born in the United States in 1989. Jiang, evidently
a contented grandfather, kept her picture tucked in his breast pocket.[53]

During the Tiananmen protests, Drexel students, including most of
its 300 mainland Chinese students, protested in sympathy with those in
the square in Beijing. Two days after the massacre, the university re-
scinded a planned honorary degree for Tian Jiyun, a vice-premier. Mianheng was careful not to take part in the protests, which won him his
father's commendation as "a good boy."[54] After his father came to
power, Mianheng tried to keep a low profile and declined offers of a personal bodyguard. "I don't want to be popular. I hope you understand,"
he told a local reporter.[55]

Back home, though, Mianheng was a red prince of the highest order. A Hong Kong magazine said that on a trip to China in 1990, he
angrily refused to submit to a blood test to check for HIV at the Shanghai airport.[56]

Mianheng was eligible to stay in the United States under the post-Tiananmen amnesty granted to all Chinese students by the Bush administration. But when he graduated in June 1991, he returned to China with his family, becoming director of the Shanghai Metallurgical Research Institute under the Chinese Academy of Sciences.[57]

Miankang, meanwhile, had remained in Shanghai after the Cultural Revolution. He won a degree there in the mid 1980s and took a job in the Shanghai Electrical Equipment Research Institute, where both of his parents had worked. At the time of the Tiananmen protests, Miankang was in Germany training with the giant engineering corporation Siemens AG, and there is no evidence that he took part in sympathy protests there. He returned to Shanghai and now works as a software researcher at the Shanghai Underground Pipeline Information System. He and his wife had a son in 1987.[58]

Although Jiang rarely mentioned his sons, he knew they provided excellent political capital for him. For one thing, their return to China from abroad gave Jiang a moral advantage over other senior leaders whose children remained abroad after Tiananmen. While Bo Yibo's daughter lived in the United States and Zhu Rongji's son worked in Hong Kong, no one could claim that Jiang's sons were privileged or indifferent to their nation's needs. "I take great satisfaction that both of them behave very well and both have come back to work here in China," he would boast to *Time* magazine.[59]

Their deliberate avoidance of business and politics also ensured that Jiang's sons were never suspected of corruption. "The two sons have made a good showing. They work and study hard," *Wen Wei Po* remarked. "They are neither 'spoiled sons of senior cadres' nor involved in any official profiteering."[60] Jiang and his wife seemed to take special care to ensure that this remained the case, forbidding their sons to enter politics or business. "The politician in our family has reached the top, so the involvement of our family in politics is at an end," Wang Yeping lectured them shortly after Tiananmen. "You should rely on yourselves by making an honest living as professionals. No getting involved in politics!"[61]

The Jiang family maintained a house in Shanghai after 1989, where the two sons and their families lived, and to which Wang Yeping frequently returned. The maintenance of the traditional Chinese household—"many generations under one roof"—bolstered Jiang's claims to represent a return to traditional values. "We treat our daughters-in-law like daughters," he told one Japanese reporter.[62] The family was also law-abiding, he added: "We have one grandson and one granddaughter, and that is in line with the requirements of family planning."

More difficult to keep uncorrupted were Jiang's relatives. "When a man gains power, even his chickens and dogs get promoted," an old Chinese proverb declares, and Jiang's relatives were keenly aware of it. His determination to make a solo ascent required a resolution that bordered on the menacing. When he bade his final farewell to Shanghai friends in August 1989, Jiang made an unreported trip home to Yangzhou to warn off relatives who might fancy themselves as high-flying chickens or dogs. "He told us to abide by the law and not engage in abusing our privileges," his sister Jiang Zefen recalled. "Anyone who got themselves into trouble would not get a helping hand from brother Jiang," she said.[63]

Jiang Zefen and her family, it will be recalled, had lived with Jiang Zemin in Beijing in the late 1970s before returning to their life of poverty in Jiangsu's northern town of Gu. When he detoured to the town on his trip home, Jiang was astonished by the wretched life they led. Their cramped three-bedroom apartment was atrocious. The rear wall had nearly collapsed, and one could barely turn around for all the clutter. "This place is a mess. How about we fix it up?" Jiang suggested. Jiang Zefen was not in a position to refuse offers of help. She had been living on a monthly stipend of just Rmb30 since being branded a rightist in the 1950s. Within a few weeks of the offer, Jiang had sent her a worn-out old sofa, a small table, and a kitchen cupboard.[64] The furniture probably came from his old family apartment in Shanghai, which his family had held onto even after he moved into better quarters as the city's mayor. It was not much of a sacrifice on Jiang's part to send his sister these disused chattels. Indeed, that may have been the point. The worn-out furniture made it clear to his relatives that they should not expect special favors from their successful brother.

Perhaps the most cruel expression of this dictate was Jiang's failure in 1989 to attend the funeral of his elder brother, Jiang Zhijun, who had taken responsibility for family affairs after their father died in 1973 and had helped pay Jiang Zemin's way through university. Jiang Zhijun had worked at the Nanjing Museum, but he had retired in the 1980s and had been bedridden for several years before his death in the city. When he received the news of his brother's passing, Jiang insisted that he could not attend the funeral "because of work."[65] Instead, he sent along a simple silk banner inscribed with his name, costing about Rmb45.

He was equally insistent on frugality when the fiftieth anniversary of the death of his foster father, the martyred Jiang Shangqing, rolled around on 29 August 1989.[66] Relatives planned an elaborate memorial celebration. Ideas were floated for a "Jiang Shangqing opera" to be performed in Yangzhou, and for a grand ceremony at the grave in northern Jiangsu. Jiang's foster sister Jiang Zehui traveled to Beijing to seek her newly powerful brother's support.[67] But he demurred. "This is exactly the kind of thing that students complained about during the turmoil," he told her. "We are trying to cut down on all these official celebrations." The insistent stepsister was told that the graveside service must be kept simple. A lone basket of flowers "that you prepare yourselves" would suffice as a show of respect, Jiang suggested. Offers from Jiangsu's Sihong county government to rebuild the gravesite itself were rejected out of hand, along with the opera idea. "Members of our family absolutely must not bother local officials with this, and neither should they accept invitations to banquets from them," he insisted. "They cannot be seen to enjoy a special status, and neither should they harbor any extravagant hopes."[68]

These strictures succeeded for the most part in keeping the Jiang family from developing into a corrupt dynasty, which could only have reflected badly on his image as a stickler for honesty among officials. There were only two occasions when the strong Chinese sense of family promotion successfully reared its ugly head among Jiang's relatives.

Jiang's eldest foster sister, Jiang Zeling, had retired in Yangzhou after teaching middle school there. In contrast to Jiang Zehui, her brainy sister, Zeling was unambitious, a typical poor country cousin. Her one and only son, Tai Zhan, remained in Yangzhou, where in 1988 he was made general manager of a ten-story office complex in the city called the Yangzhou Tower.[69] The enterprising Tai asked his uncle Jiang, then still Shanghai party boss, to inscribe the Chinese characters of the building name as a personal souvenir. The scrawled characters suddenly became more valuable once Jiang was elevated to party general secretary. Tai fished the calligraphy out of his desk drawer in 1990 and had a local sign maker blow the four characters up into 10-foot size, which he fastened on the second-floor balcony of the building, overlooking one of the city's busiest intersections.

Jiang was not informed of the fact that his calligraphy was being used to attract shoppers to his nephew's department store. According to sources in the city, he made the discovery, much to his chagrin, in October 1991, while showing off his hometown to North Korea's president,

Kim Il Sung. As their motorcade sped toward an eastern suburb, Jiang saw the letters from the car window and swore under his breath. "It wasn't a cultural or a historical site. It was just a shopping center," recalled a Yangzhou official who was in the car with the two leaders. "Jiang blushed when the calligraphy was pointed out to him." Back in Beijing, he telephoned the Jiangsu province party office and told them to take the swirling characters down at once.

The second instance of Jiang's relatives throwing their influence around related to his foster sister Jiang Zehui, the self-appointed family busybody. In 1993, Jiang Zehui was made a vice-chairman of the Anhui Provincial People's Congress, even though she held the relatively undistinguished post of vice-president and party secretary of the Anhui Agricultural College. According to provincial officials in Anhui, Jiang Zehui threatened to return to her native Jiangsu province, which was offering her the same position in its congress, unless a matching offer were made. She would later succeed in being appointed a member of the national body, the CPPCC, in 1998. She became the lone red princess of the Jiang family.[70]

Even for someone as determined to fight corruption as Jiang Zemin, it seemed, Chinese tradition died hard. But these were mild infractions, unlikely to be held against him. Jiang was clean himself, and his relatives were for the most part kept in check.

4

Although Jiang had been elevated to the highest position of power in the party at the plenum right after the Tiananmen Square events, he was not given even an ordinary membership in the Central Military Commission, which oversees the army. Deng remained the commission chairman, his last formal post, and the post of first vice-chairman, which had been held by Zhao Ziyang, was taken over by President Yang Shangkun. The reasons were obvious: Jiang had never served in the army, and his experience in handling military affairs while in Shanghai had been brief and mostly ceremonial. Deng had maneuvered deftly to install Jiang as number one in the party at a crucial moment. Giving him a say over the army was more difficult. In any case, it was not self-evident that the party chief needed to be personally involved with the military. Hu Yaobang had never held a seat on the Central Military Commission and was not noticeably weaker for it. By contrast, Hua Guofeng *had* held the post of Central Military Commission chairman but was not saved by it.

After 1989, most observers expected that Yang would succeed Deng as chairman of the Central Military Commission. But as early as September 1989, Deng was laying the groundwork for his own full retirement and for Jiang's assumption of the military commission chairmanship. The two moves, although separate, were intimately related. Deng had postponed his planned retirement after Tiananmen because of the political uncertainty that surrounded Jiang's ascent to party general secretary. Much of that uncertainty, of course, concerned factions within the party itself that might conspire to undermine or even destroy Jiang's authority. But another equally large question mark hung over the issue of army loyalty. While he could be reasonably confident that party leaders would respect Jiang, Deng was understandably doubtful of army loyalty to this nonveteran of the Long March, who had never fired a gun. As he warned army leaders in September: "It has been our tradition that the army obeys the party. . . . The army must not do anything under its own banner."[71]

With the immediate threats to Jiang's position in temporary abeyance within the party, the obvious way to ensure army fealty was to give Jiang control of the Central Military Commission. Deng summed up his reductionist logic thus: "Jiang is well qualified to be chairman of the military commission *because* he is well qualified to be general secretary of the party."[72] Never before had the paramountcy of political over military credentials for the post been made so explicit. Deng obviously felt, although he never said as much, that absolute army loyalty to the party would be in doubt if Yang were to take over. In effect, it would consolidate the role of army elders even as elders were being pushed out of party posts and from their roosting perch on the Central Advisory Commission. "If Yang had taken over then, Deng's retirement would not have had much significance," the Hong Kong magazine *Jing bao* noted later.[73]

Throughout September and October, Deng was, by his own admission, "working to obtain" permission to retire from the Central Military Commission in favor of Jiang.[74] Besides the political logic of the reshuffle, Deng could make more personal appeals to his growing age to pressure the Politburo and Central Military Commission into accepting his proposed deal before it was too late. "When a man gets old, he becomes stubborn and fragile. . . . I am old now, and although my mind is fine, I am likely to lose my senses in the future," he said.[75] The change was eventually agreed to, but not without the opposition of Yang Shangkun. Yang's objection stemmed from the dangers of having a civilian party politician in charge of the military. If Zhao Ziyang had been military commission chairman during the Tiananmen debacle, Yang noted, the use of martial law would have been constitutionally more difficult, if not impossible.[76] Deng could, however, point to Jiang's track record in dealing with the 1986 and 1989 protests to show that he could be relied upon in times of crisis. "And if there *are* disturbances," Deng added. "*I* will get [back] involved."[77]

Jiang's elevation to chairman of the Central Military Commission was the main item on the agenda of the party plenum held in early November 1989.[78] Deng's daughter describes the scene of her father arriving at the Great Hall of the People at around four o'clock on 9 November, shortly after the vote was taken to allow him to stand down in favor of Jiang:

> As Father entered the reception area, senior comrades of the central committee came out of the meeting hall. One comrade after another approached him to shake hands. Jiang Zemin, the new military commission chairman, stepped forward and grasped Father's hand. Jiang proposed taking a group photo of party leaders with Father. . . . As Father was about to leave the Great Hall of the People, Jiang Zemin went with him to the door. With a fervent handshake, Jiang pledged to dedicate his life to the cause.[79]

The attempt to portray Jiang as the sole successor to Deng on the military front was betrayed by the other changes announced at the plenum, however. Yang Shangkun remained first vice-chairman, while his half-brother, Yang Baibing, director of the army's General Political Department, took over the post of commission secretary-general, in charge of day-to-day affairs. To balance the Yang family interests, Liu Huaqing, a former navy commander, was brought out of retirement, at age 73, to serve as Deng's eyes and ears on the commission as second vice-chairman. "He will listen to the party," Deng noted.[80]

Jiang was taking over an army of three million soldiers, which in the wake of a reduction of one million in the mid 1980s was facing a grave challenge to modernize. Mao's concept of "people's war" was hopelessly outdated in the era of integrated, computer-controlled weaponry and satellite communications, and Jiang knew it. "I was not fully prepared when I was elected party general secretary, and I am not fully prepared now," he told the November plenum. "I have no experience in military work and I feel my abilities fall far short of what the position demands." Casting his eyes around the meeting hall full of skeptical officers, Jiang was the first to admit that he was starting from square one. "Since the party has assigned the work to me, I must make every effort to learn about military affairs and familiarize myself as soon as possible with the armed forces," he told the session.

In the coming two years, Jiang would be true to his word, setting off around the country with army officers in tow on tours that would take him to nearly a hundred army units. In place of the typical "sit and talk" meetings with local officers, Jiang preferred to walk through the barracks at various units, patting the cots and jabbing his finger into pots of stew bubbling on open fires. Were there enough vegetables? Was the food shop open late? Finding himself in barracks libraries put him on familiar ground. He would urge local officers to stock more books, everything from Marx to Malraux. For one unschooled in arcane military matters, it was an obvious way to bond with the troops and one he would repeat often.

Wherever he went, Jiang brought a simple message to the troops. Party control over the army was essential and must be strengthened. "The soldiers should never forget it," he said two months after his appointment.[81] He had no intention, however, of getting involved in divisive personnel decisions. Yang Shangkun and Yang Baibing called the shots in the first reshufflings of the top ranks of both the PAP and the PLA in early 1990. The military was rewarded for its fealty with hefty budget increases in the early 1990s, which halted defense spending's slide in the national budget at around 8 to 10 percent.[82]

Addressing PLA delegates at the national parliament in early 1990, Jiang lavished praise on the army as "an important factor behind China's current political situation of stability and unity."[83] Harping on the issue of stability, he called the PLA a "powerful backup" against attempts to overthrow socialism by hostile forces in the West. "I am telling you this," he told the officers, "because I need your help."[84]

With Jiang formally in command of both the party and the military, and the new leadership apparently working in concord, Deng finally retired after sixty-five years of loyal service to the cause of Communist China. "The response to Jiang has been calm. There have been no cynical remarks," he told fellow party elders. "We should let the new Politburo standing committee think and work independently, even let them make their own mistakes."[85]

Deng chose a meeting with Japanese business leaders in the Great Hall of the People in mid November to announce that he would no longer meet foreign guests as an official representative of China. "Next time you come, we may have to meet at a hotel," he told the bemused tycoons.[86]

The *People's Daily* headline drove the point home the next day: "Last Time to Meet Foreign Guests," it read.[87] Deng told his Japanese guests that Jiang was "an intellectual, whose knowledge is greater than mine." Of course, he added, "he is a little less experienced than I am, but experience can be gained. He's only 63." In an unwitting but slightly varied echo of Mao Zedong's remark to his doomed successor, Hua Guofeng ("With you in charge I can relax"), Deng added: "With this leading group in place, I can relax."[88] It is noteworthy that the group, not Jiang alone, was the source of the patriarch's confidence.

Although Jiang was clearly eager to crawl out from under Deng's shadow, he could not display unseemly enthusiasm. He insisted at the November plenum that he had wanted Deng to remain in power, "considering that our country's construction and reform are at a key juncture and that China is facing a complicated international situation." Even after the old man's desire to leave the stage had been accepted, Jiang made it clear that he would be relying on Deng's continued good fettle to ensure his own political survival. "The health and longevity of Comrade Xiaoping are of great significance to the smooth development of the work of the party and state," he said. This "health and longevity" were not to be preferred indefinitely, however. "Of course we hope for Deng's longevity, but we no longer talk about living forever," he said, in an unsubtle reference to the "Long Live Mao" slogans that eventually won the Great Helmsman's corpse a permanent display case in Tiananmen Square.[89]

By his own admission, Jiang had felt as though he were walking on thin ice or standing on the brink of a deep ravine in June 1989. Six months later, having successfully assumed the Central Military Commission chairmanship and waved adieu with mixed feelings to Deng's public persona, his confidence showed no signs of having grown. Jiang's sense of security was heavily braced by appeals for support from the army, the Politburo, and Deng.

The lifting of martial law in Beijing took place in a somber ceremony at midnight on 10 January 1990. It was like a lifting of the curtain on Jiang's rule of Communist China. Significantly, it was soldiers from the PAP rather than the PLA who took the orders to stand down, a seeming admission—in line with Jiang's comments in July—that the paramilitary, not the army, were the proper guardians of social peace. Tiananmen Square was reopened to the public, although surveillance cameras now watched from every light standard and newly posted rules forbade the display of "paintings, writings, carvings, slogans, big or small character posters, or other kinds of propaganda materials."[90]

Jiang celebrated the return to normalcy by mingling with the crowds in Beijing's Dongdan fresh-food market two weeks later. It took a few minutes before any of the busy shoppers even recognized him.[91] For all his titles, it was apparent that Jiang was still a long way from enjoying any recognition in the streets.

5

The slightly accommodating ideological policy that Jiang had sought to implement in the wake of the Tiananmen movement was fundamentally altered by the wave of democratic changes that swept Eastern Europe in late 1989. The fall of communist rulers, first in Poland, then in Hungary, East Germany, Bulgaria, and Czechoslovakia, laid bare the fragility of the elaborate Leninist states that had been constructed to uphold party rule in Europe's communist countries. The grisly scene of the former Romanian president Nicolae Ceaușescu and his wife, Elena, slumped in pools of blood against a pock-marked wall after being executed by firing squad on Christmas Day made Communist leaders in China clutch their throats in horror. Ceaușescu's regime had been the first Jiang had thanked for its support of the crushing of the Tiananmen Square movement. "We cannot say that the situation in Eastern Europe will not have an impact on China," Jiang said when the Romanian uprising began. "We need to pay attention to this."[92]

As democracy spread through Eastern Europe, Jiang, along with the rest of the leadership, maintained a stiff upper lip internationally. "I'll admit that socialism is at a low ebb right now," he told American television. "But I don't think we should jump to the conclusion that it is falling apart."[93] As if to prove the point, Jiang made his first foreign trip as party general secretary to North Korea in March 1990. Clinging to each other for warmth in the frosty international climate, Jiang and his counterpart Kim Il Sung embraced "like relatives," Beijing Radio noted.[94]

Within the party, however, Ceaușescu's sudden and violent death sparked a clear hard-line response. The party leadership now asserted its opposition to even moderate political reform, which was blamed for precipitating the changes in Eastern Europe. The official line was that a withering of Marxist orthodoxy and political discipline within the ruling Communist parties had caused the changes in Eastern Europe, an assessment that clashed with the predominant Western view that slow economic growth and social discontent were responsible. The new hard-line position in Beijing was outlined in depth by Jiang in his new year's address. Revolutionary zeal was needed to carry the party through an "extremely critical time," he said. The banner headline in *People's Daily,* which devoted half its front page to the speech, summed up the response: "The authority of leadership in the party and the country must be held in the hands of people who are loyal to Marxism."[95]

Jiang's apparent new enthusiasm for Marxism reflected his subservience to party ideologues in meeting the challenge of Eastern Europe. It was by no means genuine and would fade as the sudden threat posed by the international changes receded. However, it did give rise to a more subtle and long-lasting theme in post-Tiananmen party policy; this was the idea that maintaining social stability—not economic development, not political reform—was the key task.

In the six months after Jiang's new year's speech—during which Mikhail Gorbachev made electrifying moves to introduce multiparty democracy in the USSR, which were eventually to result in the breakup of the Soviet empire—the theme of maintaining stability in China became a national campaign. By the time of the first anniversary of the Tiananmen massacre, *People's Daily* was prepared to make it official: "Stability Overrides Everything," read an editorial headline on 4 June 1990.[96]

Although lip service had been paid to the idea of stability in the wake of the Tiananmen Square massacre, Jiang's initial task as outlined by Deng was to establish an image as an economic reformer and gain the confidence of the people through good deeds like fighting corruption. Only after the changes in Eastern Europe did Jiang's role shift to the maintenance of stability above all else. Jiang summed up the new guiding policy before PLA deputies at the NPC in March 1990:

> It is of paramount importance to maintain stability no matter what changes occur in the international situation. By stability, we mean preserving the political stability and unity that has not come easily, and maintaining sustained, stable, and coordinated economic development. We mainly have to avoid the kind of policies that caused drastic fluctuations a few years ago. That is not good for the economy. However, we must not go to the other extreme; in other words, we should not try to stay on the safe side at all times and hesitate in taking bold action. That is also not good.[97]

The new emphasis on stability prompted by the changes in Eastern Europe thus gave rise to the twin-track policy of political and ideological consolidation and cautious but steady economic reforms, which was basically to characterize Jiang's rule well into the 1990s.

6

Mirroring the turmoil in Eastern Europe and the Soviet Union, high politics within the crimson walls of Zhongnanhai in the period 1990 to 1991 were both fractious and intense. Deng, of course, had chosen Jiang partly because he lacked a clear factional base. Other senior leaders were warned against taking advantage of this. But it was inevitable that, in practice, it would take time and effort on Jiang's part to assert his position within the party. In particular, this meant overcoming the entrenched influence of Premier Li Peng.

The honeymoon with party factions lasted barely a year. By mid 1990, there were signs that Li Peng was quietly trying to upstage his new "big brother" by taking control of economy policy. In his government work report to the national parliament in March 1990, Li argued that economic growth should be "sustained, steady, and coordinated," proposing this as a slogan to replace the Dengist idea of "opening and reform" as the party's guiding economic principle, which he flatly rejected.[98] Li was working with the conservative vice premier Yao Yilin at this time on draft proposals for the eighth five-year plan (1991 to 1995). Yao retained considerable influence in the bureaucracy, even though he had been eased out of the State Planning Commission ministership at the end of 1989. The pair set growth for 1990 at a sickly 5 percent, and for the entire decade at just 5.8 percent.

Sensing that Li was seeking to set the direction of economic policy in isolation from Jiang, Deng began speaking out again. "Unity between the first and second men in command is particularly important now," the lately retired patriarch said in April. "We should leave no loopholes for others to exploit."[99]

Partly to assert his own supposed preeminence in party decision-making, Jiang announced in early July that in order to save money, the annual summer retreat to Beidaihe—the seaside resort that symbolized both the collective and arcane aspects of high politics in China—would not be held that year.[100] The decision not to frolic in Beidaihe had been made by the Politburo internally in late 1989 to reduce the appearance of extravagance.[101] But Jiang's public announcement of the fact appeared aimed at downplaying the whole collective decision-making system, which he was finding more a threat than a comfort.

Meetings among elders took place nonetheless. Vice-President Wang Zhen shuttled between Beijing and the beach eight times between July and August, since government and party youngsters were not allowed to attend the meetings.[102] Deng, in several meetings with the elders at Beidaihe, warned them against creating "many centers."[103] Wang, for example, was accused of trying to elevate the status of Li Peng by seeking support from fellow conservative elders. The "many centers" debate broke into the open in mid July, when Wang commented to foreign visitors that the second generation of leaders "centered around Deng Xiaoping" had chosen a third generation of leaders "composed of Comrades Jiang Zemin, Li Peng, and others."[104] The startling break with describing Jiang as the sole "core" of the third generation—which appeared on the front page of *People's Daily* the next day—was not unintentional. Wang had been one of the most strident critics of Deng's plan to make Jiang the one-man center of the post-Tiananmen leadership, arguing that he was too inexperienced. This public pronouncement showed how insecure Jiang's position remained.

In mid August, Deng summoned Jiang, along with Yao Yilin and the economist Gu Mu (Jiang's former boss in the investment and foreign trade commissions of the early 1980s), to his villa in Beidaihe to discuss the drafting of the five-year plan. Before the meeting began, he reassured Jiang that he would continue fending off the nosy elders as planning progressed. "I have told them not to act like imperial commissioners, obstructing reforms at every turn. The Central Committee did not give them some magic sword. Everything must be done in line with the policies of the present leadership."[105]

A few weeks later, Deng again took to task several party elders—presumably including Chen Yun and Wang Zhen—for engaging in "secret business" within the party. His admonitions to the clamorous elders, who were proposing a range of new party lines that might be adopted at the upcoming seventh party plenum, are worth quoting at length:

> You should take the lead and consult Jiang Zemin more often, and take care not to make too many appearances or interfere too much. The third generation of leaders are doing well now, reversing the situation much more rapidly than I had imagined. You therefore have just one responsibility: to give your full support and obedience to the Politburo leadership centered on Jiang Zemin. There is no room for bargaining on this issue.[106]

The need for Deng to endorse Jiang's performance and warn off those with their own agendas showed just how important the supposedly retired patriarch remained. He even arranged for Jiang—rather than himself as originally planned—to preside over the opening of the Asian Games in Beijing in late August. The symbolism of Jiang holding the torch aloft in Tiananmen Square to open the games could not have been lost on these rivals.

Deng gave Jiang another fillip during the establishment of a new economic zone at Pudong, on the eastern side of the Huangpu River in Shanghai, which was announced in April 1990.[107] Although Jiang had no direct role in its establishment, Deng made it clear that he was to be in overall charge on behalf of the central government. Li Peng's role would be secondary. "Difficulties will arise, resistance will emerge, and questions will come up," he told Shanghai cadres. "If so, you may go and consult your old secretary [Jiang]. You may also consult the State Council."[108]

While Deng was still needed as a sort of cowcatcher on the front of Jiang's chugging locomotive, Li Peng was eventually swept off the tracks by his own economic policies. The economy had grown by a meager 1.6 percent in the first half of 1990, and no one was in a mood to hear conservative talk. At a drafting session for the five-year plan held in mid September, Li Peng and Yao Yilin argued that the economy had bottomed out. In fact, they were right. A loosening of credit in the spring had brought industrial growth roaring back, and a record harvest was lifting rural incomes. Growth for the full year would rebound to a respectable 5 percent. But at the time, provincial and local leaders feeling the pinch were unconvinced. They argued for greater autonomy during the upcoming plan so as to jump-start their own economies. It was one of the most acrimonious national economic conferences in years. "The conference failed to reach consensus and broke up on a sour note," one report noted.[109]

Jiang, it seems, got past this period—arguably the greatest threat to his position as core leader he ever faced—by relying on Deng's admonitions to elders and the provincial assault on Li Peng's go-slow policies. Neither of these was his own doing. But he had the political savvy to remain patient and let both take effect. Deng ceased all public appearances after his July inspection of the Asian Games facilities and did not reemerge until December. The extended five-month absence, which outlasted his three-month disappearing act after the Tiananmen Square massacre, was an obvious signal that he retained confidence in Jiang. But for all his attempts to retire, Deng remained China's paramount political leader.

When the party convened its annual plenum in December 1990, debates were raging about the direction of both short-term and long-term economic policy. The meeting was supposed to last ten days, but it broke up in disagreement after just six. It was described by the Hong Kong magazine *Guangjiaojing* (Wide Angle) as "the most heated plenum since Jiang took office."[110] At immediate issue was the slow growth at home, which, although already picking up, had damaged Li Peng's credibility. In the longer term, the plenum was to discuss the upcoming five-year plan along with a ten-year economic blueprint. Deng had vetoed earlier drafts of the plans for failing even to mention adherence to the policy of opening and reform and for laying too much emphasis on rebuilding state planning.[111]

In all cases, the economic debates pitted liberal economists against ideological hard-liners.[112] The night before the plenum, Deng met Jiang to convey his views on the brewing debate.[113] It was important, Deng told his acolyte, to make clear to the plenum the distinction between capitalism and socialism. "It is not the same as the difference between a market economy and a planned economy," he ventured. "Socialism has some regulation by market forces, and capitalism has some control through planning."[114] Getting away from the old planning-based definition of socialism was crucial if Deng was to dodge criticisms of taking the capitalist road. The new definition he proposed to Jiang described socialism as distinguished by public ownership and the goal of common prosperity, not by whether or not there was state planning. Market forces could play a useful role in China's socialist system, Deng said. "If we did not have a market economy, . . . we would have to reconcile ourselves to lagging behind." Deng asked Jiang to convey his "new cat theory," as he coined it, to the plenum. The nickname referred to Deng's use in the early 1960s of an old Sichuan proverb that encapsulated his pragmatic approach: "It doesn't matter whether a cat is black or white as long as it catches mice."[115]

In the end, the new cat theory fell flat. The communiqué that emerged after the plenum stressed the "tremendous achievements" of the Deng reforms in the 1980s. But it committed the party to better "macro-level regulation and control." Economic growth in the 1990s was set at a mere 6 percent, substantially reduced from the 9 percent rate registered in the 1980s. Growth was to proceed in a "sustained, steady, and coordinated" manner—Li Peng's phrase. The fact that actual growth would probably eclipse the planned rate (between 1990 and 1996, it would average 10 percent) did not matter as much in the occult world of Chinese high politics: the low rate showed that planners maintained significant influence over government decisions.

Frustrated by the lack of support for unhindered growth, Deng decamped to Shanghai in early February 1991. There he made an exuberant television appearance on the eve of the lunar new year, along with Yang Shangkun and Li Xiannian. "Firm steps alone will not do," Deng told his audience in remarks aimed directly at Li Peng, broadcast around the nation. "You also have to move forward."[116]

While in Shanghai, Deng arranged with members of the Shanghai municipal propaganda department to pen a series of editorials for the local daily paper, *Jiefang ribao,* advocating faster reforms. "No one is listening to me [in Beijing] now. I have no choice but to have my articles published in Shanghai," he explained.[117] The so-called Huang Puping (a pen name that sounded like "commentary from Shanghai") editorials, which were written by the *Jiefang ribao* party chief and deputy editor Zhou Ruijin (later to take over as head of the *People's Daily's* Shanghai bureau), ran in *Jiefang ribao* in three installments in March and April. They castigated old-timers who insisted that planning and markets were mutually exclusive and appealed for fewer controls on foreign investment.

The use of Shanghai newspapers to attack party obstinacy in Beijing had, of course, been the tactic used by Mao to launch the Cultural Revolution. "Their tricks are outdated as well as disgusting," complained Xu Weicheng, executive deputy propaganda chief.[118] In retort, Xu had *People's Daily* reprint a hard-line magazine article on "why it is necessary to oppose bourgeois liberalization," which appeared in the newspaper in late April.[119] The spectacle of high-level party infighting in the pages of the country's daily newspapers aroused concern among party academics. "These [things] should not be made public," the academic He Xin wrote to the Central Committee about the polemics. "After all, they are just disputes over fast and slow growth, not life and death struggles against liberalization."[120]

The open disputes brought about an important change, however. Deng finally gained the upper hand. His appeal through the Shanghai press for a more expansive economic policy attracted the support of many local leaders. Among them was Zhu Rongji, Jiang's erstwhile aide in Shanghai, who openly admitted to supporting the Huang Puping commentaries when the hard-line *People's Daily* director Gao Di was sent to Shanghai on two secret trips to investigate the polemics.[121] In April 1991, Deng managed to promote Zhu to the post of vice-premier.

It was a happy reunion for Jiang to have Zhu working in Beijing again. Although the two evinced no expressions of intimacy, having Zhu as a counterweight to Li on the State Council could only strengthen Jiang's hand in trying to assert his supremacy as "core leader." Zhu's promotion also made it easier for Jiang to continue to advocate faster economic growth. "If we do not boost our economy, we shall have no say in the world," he told troops in Sichuan province. "As the saying goes: 'A wealthy person speaks louder than others.'" [122] The pickup in economic growth in 1991—to 8 percent from 5 percent in 1990—appeared to show that the game had been won.

Throughout 1991, almost imperceptibly, amid the apparent "two-line struggle" taking place over economic policy, there emerged a new school of thought that combined the pro–economic reform thinking of Deng with the hard-line anti-Western ideological political views of Marxists like Chen Yun. It was this middle way, a third approach, that Jiang helped to pioneer. While staunchly defending Deng's economic views, Jiang was careful to make an equally conspicuous show of his opposition to Westernization and Zhao Ziyang–style political reforms. At a party gathering in April, he provided this early summation of what would later become his guiding philosophy for ruling China: "Economic development and ideological integrity must not be set against each other. We must persevere in reform and opening up, and at the same time we must also resolutely resist the corrosive influence of decadent capitalist ideology. These are two sides of the same coin." [123]

The debate over political reform, already rumbling in the wake of the collapse of communism in Eastern Europe, was stirred by the failed coup by Communist Party conservatives in the Soviet Union in August 1991. Although President Mikhail Gorbachev returned to power within days, the vulnerability of the Soviet communist state that the coup demonstrated shocked leaders in Beijing, who ruled under an identical system. Jiang cut short a tour of Qinghai province to return to Beijing on the day of the coup.

In internal talks, Deng immediately downplayed the importance of the changes in the USSR. The Chinese Communists had overreacted in 1956 when the Hungarian uprising aroused fears of the toppling of communism the world over, Deng said. The same danger of overreaction now existed in the case of the Soviet changes. [124]

But in this, Deng was alone. Even Jiang rejected Deng's cool attitude to the attempted coup in Moscow. "There are many factors that caused the Soviet failure, but it would be wrong to assume that socialism was one of them," Jiang told the *Washington Times* in October. The Soviet Union had failed, Jiang asserted, because it had "mishandled its different nationalities and ethnic groups." It also should have given a higher priority to economic reform than to political reform, he said.[125]

This philosophy of combining political control with economic freedom that Jiang helped articulate in the latter half of 1991 would be described by some as "neoauthoritarian." Drawing from the experience of other rapidly developing Asian states, this theory argued that a strong state and limits on personal freedoms were necessary to ensure rapid and sustained economic growth. Freedoms were curtailed in a sophisticated way, however. State controls over the media and over political activities, and a ruthlessly efficient internal security force, were the tools of the neoauthoritarian state. It would simultaneously allow citizens to be unfettered, atomistic economic agents and require them to be politically docile: captains of industry but cabin boys of the state. The articulation of this new political philosophy by Jiang and others was a departure from Deng's single minded attention to economic growth. But by now Jiang was convinced that any loosening of the reins of control risked disaster. While he stood firmly on Deng's side throughout the 1990 and 1991 debates on economic policy, debates that Deng would ultimately win, Jiang was more concerned than the patriarch to stymie any threats to Communist power in China. He would not be China's Gorbachev.

7

Whereas the election trail affords state leaders in democratic countries the opportunity to see every corner of their countries, imperial-style "inspection tours" are the accepted method of getting out and about in Communist China. Jiang had remained close to Beijing for most of the latter half of 1989, but beginning in 1990, he took to the road with relish.

The theme of his early visits was frontiers. These, after all, symbolized the Chinese state's tradition of walled independence; the right to wall in those over whom it claimed sovereignty and to wall out those whom it wanted to keep at bay. "China liked its wall and liked looking over it as well," the British sinologist W. J. F. Jenner has noted.[126] In the latter half of 1990, Jiang made a dizzying series of visits in turn to Tibet, Xinjiang, Inner Mongolia, Liaoning, Guangxi, and Jilin. Taking into account his earlier visits to Heilongjiang and Yunnan, he had circled virtually the entire national ramparts by early 1991. Huge swathes of the populous inland had not been graced by his presence, but at least he had surveyed China's land borders.

The timing of Jiang's borderland trips was crucial. Tibet had been under martial law for fourteen months since March 1989, following a violent crackdown on anti-Chinese demonstrations in the capital, Lhasa. Xinjiang and Inner Mongolia, meanwhile, were being affected by the breakup of the Soviet Union and the resultant rebirth of Uighur and Mongolian nationalism across their borders. By this pacing around the perimeter, Jiang was making a clear show of his imperial authority to peoples on both sides of the Chinese wall.

"While posing a challenge to us, the current situation at home and abroad also provides us with a good opportunity," he blustered while in Inner Mongolia in late September. "It is a rare opportunity to build the Chinese nation."[127]

His trip to Tibet in July came just ten weeks after martial law was lifted there. Chinese troops had invaded Tibet in 1950 and had suppressed an armed independence movement there in 1959. The "Tibet autonomous region" (TAR) was established in 1965. But a quarter century later, Tibet remained poor and unstable. Protests and bombings became frequent in the late 1980s.

Jiang was the first party general secretary since Hu Yaobang in 1980 to visit Tibet, and the first chairman of the Central Military Commission to do so. It was a rare show of Beijing's authority. The infrequency of appearances there by Chinese bigwigs was not mainly because of the risks of assassination, although these were not to be ignored. More important, few Beijing paper-pushers could bear up in the thin atmosphere on the Tibetan plateau, over 13,000 feet above sea level. Doctors advised Jiang's delegation to enter Tibet by car rather than fly directly to Lhasa. The 24-member group first flew to Golmud in adjoining Qinghai province and then drove the 718 miles (1,155 km) to Lhasa in buses over the next three days, snaking their lonely way along the long road through the valley separating Qinghai and Tibet. "Let's try to do something that will really help the Tibetans out, rather than just offering cheap words of support," Jiang reportedly advised his companions on the trip, who included a party secretariat member, Ding Guangen; the PLA's chief of staff, Chi Haotian; and the now ubiquitous Zeng Qinghong.[128]

Sporting embroidered Tibetan hats and scarves, Jiang seemed to enjoy his first visit to Tibet. In Lhasa, he made the usual rounds of rug factories, Tibetan Buddhist temples, and military bases. Accompanying doctors warned him to keep his activities to a minimum and gave him a checkup each evening. Canisters of oxygen were toted everywhere.[129] Most of the time, Jiang seemed to bear up better than his companions, but on one occasion, near the end of the trip, he was briefly overcome. When the group paid its respects to the embalmed remains of a pro-Beijing monk, Bainqen Ordini Qoigyi Gyaincain, in Xigaze on 26 July, the combination of pungent incense and oil lamps burning at the altar was too much. Standing at his side during the lengthy ceremony, the recently appointed governor of Tibet, Gyaincain Norbu, noticed that Jiang was having trouble breathing. "There were thousands of oil lamps burning, so the already thin air became even more stifling," he recalled.[130] Soon Jiang broke into a sweat. "The memorial hall was not well ventilated and the oil lamps were burning and giving off a lot of thick black smoke," Jiang admitted later. "I felt really dizzy."[131] Bursting out of the hall coughing and swaying at the end of the service, he sat down to rest on a stone; he accepted an oxygen mask but waved away a stretcher.

As to his promise to do some real good, the most Jiang could show for the trip was the approval of a new airport for the eastern city of Qamdo and a vague promise to assign more technically minded cadres to the TAR. He also pledged "special policies and flexible measures to speed up Tibet's economic development."[132] The offers were modest and fell far short of the initiatives launched by Hu Yaobang during his 1980 visit. Hu had irked party hard-liners by recommending government concessions allowing Tibet to reject any central policies "not suited to Tibetan conditions" and had initiated a bold new policy of allowing a modest revival of religious activity and the breakup of agricultural collectives in the TAR. It was a hard act for Jiang to follow. In any case, he had neither the courage nor the political backing to suggest radical solutions to unrest in Tibet that might have gone to the root of the problem. Before leaving, he told TAR leaders to "take resolute and effective measures to rebuff the disturbances caused by separatists" and called for a better-equipped armed police force to deal with unrest.[133]

Emphasizing the greater fears of instability in the Muslim-dominated region of Xinjiang, Jiang was accompanied there by Yang Baibing, secretary of the Central Military Commission, and by the commander of the local military region, Fu Quanyou. During the ten-day trip in late August, Jiang made a point of visiting the border patrol garrison at Korgas, as well as three other military facilities and the regional headquarters of the armed police. "Xinjiang's position is important because it is China's door in the northwest region," he told the frontier guardians. "It is very important to maintain stability. We should launch a campaign to bring about a good social mood in which everyone stresses national unity and struggles against words and acts harmful to national unity."[134]

Jiang's visits to Tibet, Xinjiang, and Inner Mongolia doubtless left mixed impressions. The scarved women and capped men huddling around the mosque he visited in the Xinjiang capital, Urumqi, for example, are said to have been incensed by the dust kicked up by the cars in his motorcade.[135] Jiang did not, however, exhibit the marks of a Han nationalist during his imperial progress around perimeters of the People's Republic. He was proud of the Han Chinese cultural tradition, but he also adhered to the idea that communism could unite disparate ethnic groups, and his worldly intellect inhibited a narrow, Han-based outlook on the minorities as inferior, tributary nations. A man who praised Western Christian oratory to Buddhist monks and recommended Balzac to young female soldiers in Guangzhou was unlikely to assert the innate superiority of one ethnic group in the PRC over another.[136]

Indeed, Jiang censured Han behavior in the frontier regions on several occasions. Slash-and-burn agriculture in the lush tropical forests of southern Yunnan was mainly practiced by Han settlers, he pointed out while visiting the province. "Hans should learn to be more prudent about tree cutting, like the Dai people," he said.[137] In a silk factory in Xinjiang, he even accused the Hans of looking down on other ethnic groups. "The Uighur nationality needs the support and assistance of the Han nationality, but the Han nationality must not be arrogant," he told Han masters and Uighur apprentices in the factory. "The Han peoples should modestly learn from the minorities too."[138]

Jiang has never subsequently inspected the frontiers so completely. His inspections of the national sentry posts in 1990 were meant to establish his authority, not bring about change. Minority affairs would always be low on his agenda and would be handled by other Politburo members in line with the repressive party policy that Mao had instituted. In later years, Jiang would launch new guidelines on "religious work," which called for stricter party management. For the Tibetans, the Uighurs, and many other groups, Jiang was little more than a distant ruler from a foreign land.

8

Yitao township is located in northern Jiangsu province. With a per capita income of just Rmb290 in 1990, it was one of the poorest parts

of a province better known for its rural prosperity. That had done little
to prevent local officials from levying various fines and charges on the
penniless peasants, however, often to support their drinking habits. In
one village, called Wandui, peasants totted up twenty-nine different "illegal" fees levied against them in that year. Such was their rage that when
the Xinhua news agency's senior reporter in Jiangsu, Zhou Zhenfeng,
visited in early 1991, they performed a song and dance, to the beat of
traditional drums, that they had specially composed to warn the cadres
of their growing resentment. It sounded like the makings of a peasant
revolt, and Zhou wrote as much in a confidential report to the Politburo
in April 1991.

The sorry tale of grinding poverty and petty corruption in Yitao township was passed on to Jiang. The report made him seethe. "If this is true,
it will really make me boil with anger," Jiang wrote to the provincial
party in June 1991. "Even feudal officials looked after the people better
than this."[139]

Besides ordering the sacking of most of the Yitao township party committee, Jiang dispatched investigation teams from the party's general office to report on the situation of peasants in ten other major breadbas-
ket provinces. They returned with armfuls of evidence that Yitao was
not alone. It seemed as if the rural sea over which the Chinese Communists had sailed to power in 1949 was now in danger of overturning the
ship. "All that's needed now is a few peasant leaders like they had in the
Qing dynasty to lead an uprising," an old peasant told one of the groups.
Jiang was alarmed by the findings. "This is a warning to us," he told the
Politburo. "We must be very careful."

The long-term decline of state industries was the reason for the worsening condition of China's workers, but the more recent malaise in the
rural sector had set in only in the mid 1980s, after spectacular leaps in
production and income had been registered in the first half of the decade.
After average growth of 18 percent in net incomes in the first five years
of the decade, mainly based on an expansion of rural industry, growth
slowed to just 2 percent in 1985–88, and to 0.7 percent in the three years
of economic retrenchment (1989–91) that followed.[140] Central government investment in agriculture, meanwhile, fell from over 10 percent of
the budget in the early 1980s to around 8 percent in the early 1990s.[141]
The number of people living in poverty in the country, which had fallen
dramatically from 250 million in 1978 to 125 million by 1985, thereafter inched downward only slowly, reaching 80 million by 1992.[142] Virtually all were in rural areas.

The agricultural theme had, of course, been raised by Jiang early on as part of his concern about regional income disparities. Peasants left in the dust were a big constituency that he hoped to make his own. On a trip to the Guangxi region of southwest China in November 1990, Jiang first put on display his concern for the rural poor. Ironically, the place he chose, intentionally or not, was a village in Bose prefecture that had been the site of a legendary 1929 peasant uprising led by a Communist army to which Deng had been a party envoy. Jiang was led into the house of a family surnamed Fu, belonging to the Zhuang minority, who populate the region. "The wind blew in from all sides. There were no clothes in the drawer, and there was only half a pail of grain," local radio reported.[143]

Local cadres may have led him to the wretched household intentionally; nine of the twelve counties in Bose prefecture were listed as poor areas by the State Council, and keeping that listing would ensure a steady flow of aid from Beijing. Nonetheless, it was a pathetic scene. Father Fu told Jiang that he was too poor to raise pigs because all the sugar and maize he grew went to feed his wife and two children. Even then, he said, it lasted only two or three months. The rest of the time they begged, stole, or relied on government handouts.

Jiang trudged out of the shack visibly glum. "I feel sad after visiting the Fus," he told village cadres afterward. "And they're not even the poorest people here!"

Given also the sad stories brought back by his investigators in the wake of the Yitao township affair, Jiang was sufficiently convinced of the need for a renewed emphasis on agriculture. Agriculture was the focus of the party plenum held in late November 1991. The resolution pledged to uphold the rural reforms of the past decade—in particular the system of making households responsible for their own production and profits—but promised new central investment in rural social services, irrigation, and other facilities. Levies were also to be held to a maximum of 5 percent of net rural incomes. Perhaps recalling the near rebellion in Yitao, Jiang told officials in Guizhou to publicize the plenum decision among the peasantry: "We want it to be well understood by every household," he said.[144]

The rural issue would reappear regularly on Jiang's agenda in the coming years as the sorry plight of the country's vast rural unwashed became apparent to those in Beijing. More policies would be promulgated to guarantee annual income growth for rural areas and the rights of the semi-private township enterprises that absorbed much surplus labor. Jiang's concern for the farmers was mainly political; he had no peasant roots and had never been rusticated for ideological purification. But he staked out the issue early and made it his own. For that he would be commended.

9

In his first two and a half years as party general secretary, Jiang was perhaps most notable for what he did *not* do. Unlike Hua Guofeng, with whom he was compared incessantly in the foreign media, Jiang did not try to assert his power over rivals in the Politburo or State Council in a way that would jeopardize his own position. In many ways, he was not in control at all; the propaganda apparatus, as we have seen, was firmly in the hands of the likes of Deng Liqun and Gao Di; the military was being run by the Yang brothers; and Li Peng, despite being embattled, continued to have a big say in economic policy.

Jiang *was* making inroads in all areas, though, gently injecting his authority into each field so far as he could without threatening those who controlled it. Touring the provinces also helped him win support within the Central Committee, whose members include most provincial governors and party chiefs. But to the extent that Jiang's authority grew, Deng's ferocious attacks on party conservatives were chiefly responsible. At this rate, it might have taken several years more for Jiang to wield any kind of decisive authority over the economy, the army, and the propaganda apparatus. But 1992 was to see Deng make a final assault on party conservatism that accelerated the process beyond all expectations.

In the early morning of 17 January 1992, an unmarked train pulled out from among the soot-encrusted platform billboards of Beijing's main train station. The green, eight-carriage train headed immediately south, along the line that cuts through the heart of the country and ends in the bustling city of Guangzhou at the head of the Pearl River Delta. Inside was the diminutive figure of Deng Xiaoping, peeking out from the lace curtains with a cup of green tea wobbling on the table in front of him. Along for the ride were two of his three daughters, Deng Rong and Deng Lin, as well as his wife, Zhuo Lin.[145] Other family members would join them later.

Roused by his successful crossing of swords with party conservatives throughout most of 1991, Deng had made an extraordinary decision in the depths of winter. Prior to his trip to Shanghai for the lunar new year in 1992, the 87-year-old retiree had decided to visit the booming south.

His last glimpse of Guangdong province had been in 1984, just as the economic reforms he had engineered were switching into high gear. "I don't even recognize the place now," he would comment.

Although Deng's subsequent "southern tour" has been characterized as a desperate move by the patriarch to save his economic reforms from an onslaught of party conservatism, as we have seen, he was probably already winning that battle by the time he journeyed south. At the party plenum in November 1991, he had succeeded in overruling a proposal to give greater prominence to the struggle against Western influences. The reassertion of the paramountcy of economic development over all other concerns in the plenum communiqué was the concrete expression of Deng's assertion that the party should not overreact to events in the Soviet Union. "Deng has once again successfully foiled an attempt by conservative forces inside the party to change the basic line," *Jing bao* commented afterward. "People in Beijing believe that the political weather in China may warm up in 1992, and that there will be a strong atmosphere of reform and opening up."[146] It did not take long for the magazine to be proven right.

The southern tour was to be the culmination of Deng's assault on those afraid to release the controls on economic growth and change. His pent-up anger was obvious. He had the train make an unscheduled stop at Wuchang, half way to Guangzhou, on the morning of 18 January, and summoned the Hubei province governor and party chief to the station to hear him out. "I'll tell you what the problem is right now," he said. "Everyone is going through the motions, but nobody's doing any real good. Every time I turn on the TV, half the news is filled with meetings and ceremonies. A lot of our leaders have become television stars."[147]

Deng was in a feisty mood. Those on board the train knew they could expect more of this in the south, and when the train pulled into Shenzhen at 9 A.M. on 19 January, they were not disappointed. "Some people have been fretting that using more foreign investment will mean more capitalism in China," Deng commented bumping along in a minivan with the Guangdong party chief, Xie Fei, after visiting the Huanggang border crossing with Hong Kong. "These people have no common sense. These firms make profits in accordance with our laws. And besides, we levy taxes, our workers are paid, and we learn new technology and management. What's wrong with that?"

Deng's message in various sermons delivered over the following ten days in Shenzhen and the other two SEZs in the province, Shekou and Zhuhai, was clearly aimed at setting off a new wave of economic growth. Stock markets in Shenzhen and Shanghai were good ideas, he said. The SEZs should continue to enjoy special policies. Guangdong should try to join the ranks of the "Asian tigers" by the year 2010. Deng even reiterated his "new cat theory" about the acceptability of market forces in a socialist system.

As for his critics in Beijing, Deng had a simple message: "China should maintain vigilance against the right, but we should mainly guard against the left," he said. "The view that reform and opening will bring capitalism and that peaceful evolution stems from economic development are leftist tendencies." Even Li Peng's "steady and coordinated" growth slogan came in for attack: "Steadiness and coordination are only relative, not absolute," Deng said. "Like a boat sailing against the current, we must forge ahead or be swept downstream."

Jiang had almost certainly been informed about Deng's trip before the patriarch's train chugged out of Beijing station. One official account says "key organs" knew about the trip, a phrase that would almost certainly have included Jiang, since he was mostly on Deng's side in the 1991 debates over economic reforms.[148] A few days *before* Deng left, Jiang called on officials in Shanghai to "accelerate reform and opening to the outside world" and "take new steps in deepening reforms," phrases that Deng himself would use on his tour.[149]

Once Deng left Beijing, and despite himself being on the road touring Shanghai and Jiangsu, Jiang was in constant touch with his mentor's entourage. Two days after Deng's outburst in Wuchang on 18 January against meetings and ceremonies, for example, Jiang parroted to cadres in Jiangsu that they must "vigorously cut back nonessential meetings and reduce excessive routine public functions."[150] Jiang then had the party office prepare a document on reducing the "routine public functions" of state leaders so that they could concentrate more on making and implementing new economic policies.[151]

While he was in the south, Deng's anger was mostly vented on Li Peng. Jiang, by contrast, won mild praise. "The present central leadership has done a good job," Deng said. "Of course, there are still many problems, but problems exist at any time." Since it was already "a little advanced in years," Deng said, the current leadership should retire after another ten years in power. That would give Jiang the right to rule China until the party's sixteenth congress in 2002.

When Jiang got back to Beijing in late January, the southern tour had just concluded. Deng was in Shanghai to usher in the year of the monkey, and Jiang made a publicized telephone call to the patriarch to wish him well.[152] By then, Deng's southern tour, also known as the "spring-time story," was an open secret in China. But no official reports had been carried in the domestic press. Jiang suddenly found himself faced with the tricky task of overcoming conservatives in the propaganda appara-tus to have Deng's speeches reported in the national press. It would take forty days before the official Xinhua News Agency reported the tour.

Certainly, the delay had nothing to do with Deng's desire to keep a low profile. Xie Fei asked Deng several times during the tour to allow him to reveal the trip, which was being reported in Hong Kong within days of Deng's arrival in Shenzhen.[153] The official line was that Deng re-fused.[154] But although he may modestly have declined widespread me-dia coverage while in Guangdong, Deng certainly intended that his words should echo farther than the precincts of the amusement parks and joint venture factories he visited in the province. Instead, reliable re-ports put the blame squarely on the conservatives in charge of the pro-paganda system, one of the areas, as we have seen, where Jiang had lit-tle control as yet.[155] *People's Daily* and Xinhua remained under the firm control of Xu Weicheng at the party's Propaganda Department.

Jiang obviously decided that his best hope of getting at the belly of the prickly propaganda system was, so to speak, to tickle its nose. In a new year's address, Jiang surprised those gathered by quoting from Deng, without reference, in calling on cadres to "make bold explorations" and "accelerate reforms."[156] A week later, at an enlarged Politburo meeting, Jiang circulated a compilation of Deng's speeches.[157] Within days, the speeches were sent down the line to the army and local party branches. By the end of February, anyone with a friend of even modest rank in a local party cell had access to the new gospel. "We passed on the contents of Deng's speeches to the whole party and to the whole country at an early stage," Jiang would later admit, chuffed by the success of his arti-fice.[158] Television stations and newspapers duly began to shift their em-phasis toward the new "wave" of economic reform, but stopped short of linking this to Deng's still unreported tour. Pressure for a full public disclosure of the trip grew.

The break finally came at a Politburo meeting in early March. Jiang began the meeting by summing up Deng's speeches.[159] He then took a remarkable step by offering a self-criticism. "He admitted a lack of sen-sitivity in seizing opportunities to promote reform and opening as well as a lack of forcefulness in opposing leftist tendencies," *Jing bao* re-ported.[160] Jiang's action was canny. If he had bragged at the meeting about how he had supported Deng from the start—which he could justifiably have claimed—it might have alienated many. But by offering himself as the chief leftist, a label no one would seriously consider accepting, Jiang encouraged others to join in admitting the error of suppressing the speeches. A beaten Li Peng, just back from a trip to Europe dogged by protests, offered no objection to the resolution to endorse Deng's speeches wholeheartedly. In a symbolic act, Yao Yilin, the 74-year-old conservative economic planner who had helped Li Peng draft his slow-growth five-year plan, submitted his retirement from all posts at the Politburo meeting.[161] It was accepted and made official later in the year.

When the belated Xinhua report was issued on 11 March, it was the end of the long propaganda struggle. Millions of Chinese woke up to a single sentence that began the next morning's radio broadcast: "We should be more daring in opening and reform."[162] Deng's springtime story was official.

10

Under the influence of Deng's southern tour, China's economy erupted in a spasm of growth. Economic growth and foreign investment inflow had picked up modestly in 1991 after a painful three-year retrenchment. Growth was already above Li Peng's conservative target of 6 percent, a target given a symbolic upward revision to 6.5 percent at the annual parliament gathering in late March 1992. But by midyear, Chinese economists estimated it was in double digits. The final numbers surprised everyone: growth was 13 percent for all of 1992, while foreign investment rose by 66 percent, to U.S.$19 billion. Most of the growth was initiated by local governments. Deng's talks and the symbolic upward revision of the growth rate gave them a green light for new projects. Pleased with himself, Deng even reemerged in late May to pay a visit to the Capital Iron and Steel Company in Beijing. State enterprises took the cue and invested heavily.

In speech after speech throughout 1992, Jiang reiterated Deng's points. At the end of May, he wrote to the entire Politburo asking them to be more enthusiastic about Deng's speeches. Local governments, meanwhile, should strive for "relatively high economic growth."[163] Most conspicuously, in early June, Jiang marched right into the heart of party conservatism—the Central Party School in Beijing—and told graduates that any cadre tinkering with Deng's policies "could be sacked at any time."[164]

Jiang's speech at Central Party School was ultrareformist. Anything
went, as far as the economy was concerned. Old warnings about decadent Western influences were thrown in for political balance, but such
campaigns would be "mutually coordinated" with faster reforms. So excited was Jiang that he inadvertently leaked the fact that he wanted the
party to adopt the rubric "socialist market economy" at its fall congress
as the constitutional description of the country's economic structure, replacing "socialist economic system."[165] The debate on the name change
was still raging internally, and the term "socialist market economy"
would not formally be included in the constitution until the next year.
But Jiang was obviously confident that the conservatives would lose
again. "The venue and audience of the general secretary's speech indi-
cates that the party's top leadership is launching an . . . unprecedented
new phase of China's reform and opening," *China Daily* gushed in an
editorial.[166]

An external manifestation of this "new phase" came on 24 August:
China was establishing diplomatic relations with South Korea, arch-
enemy of one of Beijing's few remaining socialist allies in the world,
North Korea. Seoul promised to invest more in China, which would
speed up the creation of the "several Hong Kongs" along the Chinese
coast that Deng had appealed for while in the south. Old dogmas of all
sorts were shattering as the patriarch's rallying cry continued to sound.

In retrospect, the splurge of growth caused by Deng's southern tour
and the subsequent beating of the drum by Jiang and allies of his such
as Zhu Rongji should have been controlled. Inflation would skyrocket
in the next two years as the effects filtered through the economy, necessitating drastic credit restrictions, which would throw millions of workers in state enterprises out of their jobs. Zhu would later regret his cheer-
leading, calling the 1992 spurt of growth "crazy."[167] But as a newly
elected vice-premier at the time, he could hardly afford to be the lone
Cassandra. Nor could Jiang and others like him. They had fought hard
to publicize Deng's speeches and were not going to lose the chance to be
their natural advocates.

Not until a riot erupted over new share certificates in Shenzhen in
early August—where twelve people were arrested after two nights of
looting, burning, and attacks on government offices—were there inklings
of second thoughts in Beijing. The official reaction was to downplay the
events. After all, Deng had said on his southern tour that the two stock-
markets in Shenzhen and Shanghai, opened in late 1990, should be given
at least one or two more years before they were judged worthwhile or

not. More to the point, while touring Capital Iron, he had frankly said that even if some reforms caused social unrest, it should not be an excuse for wavering: "We must still brace up. Those who support reforms and development have to stand firm even if there is disorder [*luanzi*]," Deng had told the steelworkers.[168]

Dissenting in a carefully worded statement while in Gansu province a few days after the Shenzhen share riots, Jiang said: "Some places are now vying to develop stock markets, real estate projects, and processing industries without reference to their capabilities. I do not mean they cannot develop these things. But it's not good if they just jump on the bandwagon without thinking. If we continue to allow them to do this, the consequences will be serious."[169]

Jiang's unwillingness to countenance "disorder" is instructive, but not surprising. It will be recalled that his overriding aim in the wake of the changes in Eastern Europe had been to preserve stability. For Deng in 1992, stability was only one of several equally pressing goals, others being faster economic growth and trouncing party conservatives. More recently, Jiang had begun to articulate a distinct governing philosophy, a third way, in which economic growth was complemented, rather than constrained, by political controls. There was no optimal amount of disorder, as Deng seemed to suggest. It was simply not desirable.

Still, the southern tour and the subsequent growth boom were mainly significant as the culmination of Deng's assault on party conservatism in economic matters. Concerns about a possible slippery descent toward capitalism were henceforth abandoned once and for all. This was confirmed by the proposal to insert the term "socialist market economy" in the state constitution at the October party congress (approved a year later). Deng had shown a simple truth about post-Tiananmen China: the best way to give everyone a feeling of having a stake in the country's present stability and future prosperity was to offer economic opportunities that had been undreamed of even a decade earlier.

Jiang's handling of the tour was masterful. The indications from Deng throughout 1991 had been that he was frustrated by the slow growth of the previous three years. By the time the patriarch was ready to go south, Jiang was already well aware of the importance of being on the side of the renewed reform drive at an early stage. He conveyed Deng's remarks with alacrity, issuing new directives and circulating the patriarch's pithy speeches at a critical time. By offering himself up as the scapegoat for the slow reform and opening, Jiang ensured that most senior leaders could move toward the spirit of the southern tour talks in unison.

Indeed, so successful was Jiang in capturing the spirit of Deng's southern tour that his June speech at the Central Party School became the basis for the political report he delivered at the party's fourteenth congress in October. Deng read the speech that summer at Beidaihe while recuperating from his exertions and literally retitled it "The Fourteenth Congress Political Report" in red ink.[170]

"Jiang Zemin has consolidated his position as the core leader by his extraordinary knowledge and outstanding abilities in leading China's opening and reforms and promoting its socialist modernization," one mainland commentator wrote just after the 1992 congress.[171] The tone was hyperbolic, but there is little doubt that Jiang had used Deng's southern tour to strengthen his own hand in Beijing.

More generally, the southern tour marked the end of the post-Tiananmen healing process, "the great reconciliation" of the general populace. Stability had been assured through a combination of repression of perceived threats to the state and an economic boom that distracted most from the cause of rebellion. Jiang played an important role in this process and was rewarded for his efforts with a second term in office as party general secretary and military commission chairman, announced at the party congress. "In the past three years," the official biography stated, "Jiang has made universally acknowledged contributions to the stability and development of the country."[172]

If Jiang had felt as though he were walking on thin ice or standing on the brink of a deep ravine when he took over in 1989, he could at least now claim with some confidence that the ice underfoot was white and hard, the lip of the ravine comfortably distant.

PART 4

Taking Command, 1993–1994

CHAPTER 7

The President's Men

I

The all-consuming economic twister that swept across the Chinese
political landscape in the wake of Deng Xiaoping's southern tour did
much to alter that landscape in 1992 and 1993. Factional disputes died
down considerably, and when they surfaced, it was often in a competition to voice the loudest support for Deng's speeches. Jiang saw his influence expand noticeably within the party and government. It was not
so much that Jiang was an individual whose own notions attracted growing support within the senior leadership. Rather, his good instincts in
promoting Deng's new reform drive at an early stage made him seem a
more reliable ally to the ambitious.

It was an important time for Jiang to be gaining respect. Deng, whose
long retirement before death might be said to have really begun when he
repaired to Beidaihe in the summer of 1992, would not be able to muster
the energy to tame all the demons of high politics forever. He had offered Jiang a cause and been his protector in the three years since 1989.
But once he retired from the giddiness of his triumphant tour of the
south, Jiang was left truly and wholly alone.

The most prominent threat to Jiang's assumption of supreme power
was the determined military empire-building of Yang Baibing, secretary
general (in charge of day-to-day affairs) of the Central Military Commission and half-brother of Yang Shangkun, the state president. Since

winning a post on the commission in late 1989, Yang Baibing had alienated many senior and influential retired officers by installing friends and cronies in top posts in the PLA headquarters and in the seven military regions.[1] For Jiang, such empire-building represented a clear challenge to his political authority over the army.

The blatant politicization of the promotion process also grated on the consciences of the many officers for whom a restoration of professionalism after the military junta–like use of the army during the Cultural Revolution was a cherished goal. The officers knew that the rapid modernization of the PLA, in the early 1990s still essentially a 1940s army, required that more of a meritocracy be in place at the top. The importance of rapid modernization had been underlined during the Gulf War of early 1991. The display of American technological superiority in the war had conclusively shown China's generals the impossibility of successfully prosecuting a 1940s-style "people's war" in the new era. Even from this purely military perspective, Jiang shared the concerns of those in the army who hated Yang Baibing. Jiang, of course, was something of a high-tech buff because of his engineering and electronics background. The sight of American missiles pummeling their targets during the 1991 Gulf War seems to have disturbed him more than most. "Previous regional wars, especially the recent one [in the Gulf] have all pointed to the fact that modern warfare has become a high-technology affair," Jiang told researchers at the National Defense University just after the war ended. "If we lag behind in technological development, it will land us in a passive position, vulnerable to attack."[2]

Jiang, as we have seen, was content in his early years as military commission chairman to visit the barracks and familiarize himself with army life. As the months passed, he began to emphasize party control over the army, but without much conviction. Not until Yang Baibing emerged as a threat, both to Jiang's political authority and to his strategic priorities in the PLA, did this change.

For most of 1991 and 1992, Jiang and Yang Baibing had played something of a cat-and-mouse game in seeking to win more support from senior PLA officers. If one of them pounced on the opening of a TV series on the PLA, within days the other would scurry to a revolutionary base for a photo opportunity. Jiang, of course, could rely on the wise counsel and support of Liu Huaqing, Deng's eyes and ears on the Central Military Commission. But the Yang brothers had more support in the lower ranks.

Fortunately for Jiang, it was Yang Baibing who overplayed his hand first. At the annual meeting of the national parliament in March 1992,

Yang, voicing his support for Deng's southern speeches, said that the PLA should act as the "protective escort" (*baojia huhang*) of the reforms.[3] He later expanded on the term in a July *People's Daily* editorial.[4] On the surface, it was not a particularly unusual slogan. For one, both the Yang brothers had joined Deng on parts of his southern tour, giving them an apparent role as protectors of its legacy. What's more, Jiang himself had called on the army in a late 1990 speech to provide the country with "a powerful guarantee" (*baozhang youli*), which many interpreted as meaning "a powerful political guarantee." Yet Yang Baibing's new slogan caused consternation. It may simply have been because it was Yang Baibing, already suspected of wanting to repoliticize the army, who said it. The statement confirmed to many both within and outside the PLA that his support for reforms was out of ulterior motives. And while it was all right for Jiang to ask the army for political support, it was quite another thing for a senior serving officer (Yang was also director of the PLA's General Political Department) to be laying claim to such an outwardly political role for the army.

With his political capital devaluing at an alarming rate because of the remark, Yang convened a series of secret meetings with senior officers throughout the summer of 1992. Most of his appointees in the military regions attended, but at the higher levels of the Politburo, this tactic only elicited growing disgust. Jiang's once unimpassioned appeals for party control over the army now became more strident. Backed by Liu Huaqing, Jiang asked Deng in September to sanction the removal of Yang from all his party posts for "usurping power and leadership over the army."[5] As Jiang was to explain: "We should regard merit, fame and personal interests as unimportant, and regard the cause of the party as like a heavy mountain."[6]

It is not clear who, besides Liu, was aligned on the side of Jiang in seeking to oust Yang Baibing. Liu was due to be elevated to the Politburo standing committee at the congress, but his support alone could not have been enough. Yang Shangkun, whose term as state president was nearing an end, was almost certainly opposed. In any case, Jiang's determination to purge an officer traditionally seen as a Deng loyalist finally won the day. Yang was stripped of all his military posts at the October congress, still talking about the PLA's "special mission" right to the end.[7] As a face-saving gesture, he was elevated to the Politburo, but he would not be given any practical responsibilities on the body and would gradually fade from sight. Yang Shangkun, meanwhile, was also stripped of his post as first vice-chairman of the military commission.

"It is critical to form a good leadership at all levels, particularly the top level," Jiang would stress in the wake of the purge of the so-called "Yang family clan." "This will ensure that the army is firmly in control of those loyal to the cause of the party and the people."[8]

In the months after the purge, more than 300 senior officers and 1,000 regional commanders were reassigned or retired throughout the country. One leading Communist newspaper described it as "the biggest, widest and most extensive high-level military reshuffle since the founding of the People's Republic."[9] Lieutenant-General Yu Yongbo, who had been political commissar of the Nanjing military region (which includes Shanghai) when Jiang was in Shanghai, replaced Yang Baibing as director of the PLA's General Political Department and was added to the military commission. Another Deng loyalist, General Zhang Zhen, was made a vice-chairman of the military commission.

Back at the National Defense University in December, Jiang seemed to make explicit the link between the reshuffle and army modernization. "Army officers, particularly senior ones, must grasp a full understanding of the current international situation," Jiang said. "We must move with the times, study new changes in the army's modernization drive, and strengthen the army's quality."[10]

The purge of the Yang family clan would reverberate through the PLA for months, if not years, to come. At the most general level, the move was significant as Jiang's first outwardly aggressive act to establish his authority as Deng faded from the political scene. Losing control over the army might have been a prelude to losing further control over other areas. The purge of Yang Shangkun from the military commission, although less electrifying because of his age, 85, also showed that Jiang did not want another party elder to fill in where Deng had left off. As Jiang noted, "with the establishment of the new military commission, the quality of the whole leadership has been improved."[11]

One respected writer in Singapore, Jiang An, has commented that the 1992 congress "marked the beginning of Jiang's actual control over the military."[12] From what we know of his gentle early years as party chief, and of the wider implications of the Yang family purge, this may even be an understatement. As the first sign that Jiang would indeed be more than a transitional figure after Tiananmen, the congress may have marked the onset of his control over China itself. For like a sea breeze dispelling layer upon layer of accumulated cloud, the dismissal of Yang Baibing brought about wide-ranging changes in the senior leadership and cleared away any remaining doubts that Jiang was, at least on paper, the holder of supreme power. At the same party congress, Jiang took control of the party's three leading groups (policy-formulating bodies) on Taiwan, legal, and economic affairs, leaving Li Peng with only foreign affairs in his ambit.[13] The Central Advisory Commission, the old men's club created by Deng in 1982 to ease party elders out of power, was abolished. And a raft of young technocratic leaders, like Foreign Minister Qian Qichen and Wu Bangguo, the wiry new Shanghai party chief, were appointed to the Politburo. They were exactly the kind of ambitious younger men who would obey Jiang as long as his instincts kept him on the right side of the economic reform movement.

Zhu Rongji, whom Deng had wanted put to better use because of his economic acumen, was added to the Politburo's standing committee, further indicating that he would assume more influence in the cabinet at the expense of Li Peng. Zhu was joined by Liu Huaqing and the outgoing Tibet party secretary Hu Jintao, replacing the conservative elders Song Ping and Yao Yilin. In all, more than half of the 300-odd members of the new party Central Committee were new. The average age of the committee actually rose slightly, to 56 years, but this was still well below the mid-sixties average that had been the rule in the 1970s and early 1980s.

When Deng finally made a cameo appearance on TV at the end of the congress as a "specially invited delegate," his verbal and body language made it clear that Jiang was now being treated as his equal. While Li Peng trailed behind, Jiang walked side by side with Deng and spoke to the patriarch "on behalf of the newly elected central leading collective." Just before he left, Deng turned to Jiang and took his hands: "The congress was a success. I hope all of you will continue to work hard."[14]

The final piece fell into place for Jiang by early 1993. Yang Shangkun had left the Politburo and military commission at the congress in preparation for his retirement as state president. But his replacement in this largely ceremonial position as head of state was the subject of debate. Party elders, including Wang Zhen, argued that to avoid undue concentration of power in one person, the presidency should not be given to Jiang. Not since the ill-fated Hua Guofeng had the top posts in the party, army, and state been held concurrently. "If any troubles occur, political wavering will increase a lot because of the [dependence on] this single person," the elders argued in a letter of protest.[15] Wang Zhen even expressed his displeasure openly by repeating his earlier devious aside that "Jiang *and* Li are the third-generation leadership successors."[16]

Fortunately, Wang's opposition went to the grave with him when he died three days before the parliamentary session began. When voting was

held, only 60 of the nearly 3,000 delegates did not approve of Jiang's assumption of the presidency. By contrast, 340 failed to vote for Li Peng's
second term as premier.

So flushed with success was Jiang that the night before the vote for
the presidency, he worked feverishly to compose a lengthy slogan written in classical four-character sentences that, he hoped, would be the
hallmark of his reign. But the slogan was neither memorable nor concise and would be politely forgotten within a few years. Fortunately,
dainty poems were not his source of strength. Jiang held all the top titles now because he was a competent, even brilliant, manager of political factions and a clear voice for the economic reforms and political self-
strengthening that most Chinese leaders reckoned were needed. President
Jiang, as the foreign press would now refer to him, did not need to inspire. He only needed to lead.

2

Jiang quickly made use of his new powers to install friends in the propaganda and security apparatus, which had hitherto been beyond his
reach. A close associate and fellow Jiangsu native, Ding Guangen, was
appointed head of the party's Propaganda Department and took over the
party's leading group on propaganda and ideology from the hopelessly
liberal, and thus powerless, Li Ruihuan. Being, like Jiang, more of a traditional than an ideological conservative, Ding would finally succeed in
wresting control of party propaganda from the Marxist ideologues who
had frustrated the early publication of Deng's southern tour speeches.

Other key propaganda appointments at this time included those of
Zhou Ruijin, the author of several of the Huang Puping commentaries,
who was sent from Shanghai's *Jiefang ribao* to be a deputy chief editor
of the *People's Daily,* and Gong Xinhan, who vaulted from number two
in the Shanghai propaganda department to number two in the central
party propaganda department. Jiang gave his new troops their marching orders at the first national propaganda conference, chaired by Ding
Guangen, in January 1993. Publicizing Deng's recent speeches, Jiang
said, was "the fundamental task and the central link of our propaganda
and ideological work in the new period."[17] It could scarcely have been
made plainer than that.

In early 1993, Jiang also brought out of retirement the former commander of the Shanghai army garrison, Major General (later Lieutenant

General) Ba Zhongtan, and put him in charge of the paramilitary People's Armed Police (PAP). Part of the reason for dragging Ba, then aged
63, out of retirement was to replace Yang Baibing's appointee as PAP
commander, Zhou Yushu, with someone more loyal. Jiang had indicated
very soon after taking over in 1989 that he wanted the PAP to be a sort
of private army for use in strengthening his hand over other security areas, especially the PLA itself. It was while touring a PAP unit in Sichuan
in early 1991, for example, where Jiang first dared to put on the green
tunic usually reserved only for those who had seen active duty in the military.[18] "This will be a boost for Jiang's leadership over defense, public
security and political and legal affairs work," the Hong Kong magazine
Guangjiaojing commented on Ba's appointment.[19]

Besides factional considerations, though, Jiang was obviously keen to
continue building up the PAP as an effective internal security organ. He
had mentioned the need to equip the PAP with nonlethal anti-riot equipment shortly after the Tiananmen massacre. Within months, the PAP was
being equipped with rubber bullets and water cannons.[20] The armory
would soon expand to include stun guns, tear-gas canisters and launch-
ers, and heavily armored police vehicles.[21] "If large-scale disturbances
break out, the military will not be called out again. The PAP will be expected to deal with the problems on its own," an official magazine
noted.[22] In the wake of Tiananmen, the PAP was also expanded by about
100,000 troops, to 700,000, by transferring dozens of military units to
its control.[23] Ba Zhongtan would ensure that this new "fourth force" in
the security apparatus (after the police, state security, and army) was
firmly under Jiang's control.

While the appointments to the propaganda and security apparatus
served to strengthen Jiang's influence in an immediate and direct way, he
also made moves to secure more lasting influence by taking tentative
steps toward the creation of a personal think tank. In his early years as
party general secretary, as we have seen, Jiang made departures from
Deng's position on issues such as rural poverty, income distribution, and
the importance of stability and political control. But to meld these disparate thoughts into a full-fledged "set of ideas" required thinkers of
greater stature than himself.

Most prominently, Zeng Qinghong, his personal secretary and sometime confidant, was promoted at the March 1993 parliament to director of the party's General Office, the de facto "Jiang office" that handles
day-to-day affairs and fills in the details of new party policies. Another

new appointee at this time was Liu Ji, who was made a vice-president of the Chinese Academy of Social Sciences in early 1993. Small, with wire-rimmed glasses and a red button nose, Liu, 58, had headed the team that took over the *World Economic Herald* in 1989, helping Jiang to weather a storm in a way that would later win him plaudits in Beijing. Liu shared with Jiang the desire to avoid the trendy Western academic prescriptions for China's economic and political ills that Zhao Ziyang had been ac-cused of favoring. "One of Comrade Zhao's biggest mistakes," Liu wrote after Tiananmen, "was to listen to every word of those think-tank mem-bers who got their doctorates in the West but didn't have the faintest idea about the realities of China."[24]

It escaped no one's notice that the raft of appointments Jiang made in late 1992 and early 1993 contained a large number of Shanghai cadres. Many, such as Zhu Rongji and Lieutenant General Yu Yongbo, were sim-ply being taken from the Shanghai incubator for up-and-comers where they had been sent in the first place, a system explained earlier. But oth-ers, like Zeng Qinghong, Liu Ji, Ba Zhongtan, Gong Xinhan, and Zhou Ruijin, seemed to constitute a kind of "Shanghai faction." They were promoted primarily because of their affiliations with Jiang. This did not prove that Beijing was being taken over by Jiang's cronies. Many others with no apparent link to Jiang or Shanghai were being transferred to top posts in Beijing at the same time. The new vice-premier, Li Lanqing, and the four new members of the party secretariat, Wei Jianxing, Wen Jiabao, Hu Jintao, and Ren Jianxin, were all examples. Rather, the significance of the promotions lay in the fact that they showed how Jiang had come of age. After three years, he was finally able to promote his own quota of friends and associates to Beijing, a prerogative of every senior leader. The "Shanghai faction" was neither unique nor dominant in Beijing; it was a mere adjunct of Jiang's coming of age.

3

When a scruffy, chain-smoking peasant leader named Zhang Zhongjian was called to an important meeting with a "central leader" one day in December 1992, the first thing he did was prepare a written statement. Arriving at the local guesthouse in Hubei province's central Xiaogan district, where he was party secretary, Zhang entered the empty meeting room, doffed his heavy farmer's overcoat, and began rehearsing his speech. Half an hour later, a minibus and a black Audi car pulled into the guesthouse parking lot. Within minutes, the travelers had dropped their bags in their rooms and were assembling to hear what Zhang had to say. At the head of the table sat Jiang Zemin.

Zhang cleared his throat and began his speech. "We are very honored to . . ." He never got past the first line. "Forget the speech, Comrade Zhang. We can read it later," Jiang interrupted. "We want to hear about peasant problems in Xiaogan. That's why we're here."[25]

Of all the negative consequences of the 1992–93 economic boom, perhaps nowhere was the damage as great as in the countryside. The scramble for resources caused by Deng's boom had sent the prices of agricultural inputs skyrocketing, while state-controlled output prices rose only slightly. Local governments, meanwhile, confiscated agricultural land to build grandiose economic development zones and real estate projects, and imposed heavier taxes on the peasantry to finance new infrastructure. While the problems besetting farmers were not the only ones—the financial system, for example, was in a mess as well—they had the most apparent potential to cause social unrest. Jiang, it will be recalled, had barely averted riots in Jiangsu's Yitao township in 1991. Now the problem was back, in spades.

"I can sum up the situation in one phrase," Zhang said after putting down his speech. "In the midst of happiness, we have become really worried."

Prior to a national agricultural work conference at the end of December 1992, Jiang had set off unannounced for Hubei with only his agricultural czars, Wen Jiabao and Chen Junsheng, in tow. The trio plied the back roads of the province's fertile Jianghan plain in a minibus, with only one security car, in order to be better informed when they met provincial leaders at the conference. It was a sorry scene they found. In Xiaogan, Zhang reported, farmers were being sliced up so badly by the "scissors" of rising input prices and fixed output prices that their 1992 average net income, Rmb636, would actually be *lower* than in 1990. That was quite an achievement in a country where rising rural incomes had come effortlessly in the 1980s, mainly on the back of rural industry. While rural industry continued to make gains, farming was becoming less and less remunerative. In the cotton-producing district of Tianmen, officials had issued an astounding Rmb223 million worth of IOUs to local farmers for the cotton they produced. Either the government did not have the money to pay or it had diverted it to other uses. In Jingzhou district, IOUs had been issued for 80 percent of the value of all agricultural output; many farmers could not afford even to see a doctor. Corruption and illegal levies on farmers were also rampant. "There are so many levies I can't count them all," complained a mason, Liu Keju. "And our village has to spend at least Rmb10,000 on entertainment every time cadres come here for meetings."

The four days of rustication paid off. By the time Jiang convened the three-day rural work conference in the provincial capital Wuhan on 24 December, attended by the governors and party chiefs of six central provinces, he could claim to know the situation as well as the local leaders. "Look at these ditties," Jiang said as he passed around his notebook from the trip, on which were scribbled several anti-government slogans he had heard from peasants during the inspection. "They are extreme and not totally accurate, but they reflect the feelings of the peasants," he said. Two simple orders came out of the meeting: IOUs were forbidden and all outstanding ones must be paid within months. Levies, meanwhile, must be limited to 5 percent of the average net income in each district, a restatement of a 1991 decree that had never been implemented. The governors retired from the meeting suitably chastened.

A few months later, at the national parliament meeting, Zhu Rongji drove the point home about limiting IOUs. "I'll cut off the head of anyone who issues more IOUs to farmers," he declared to delegates from Hunan province.[26] The hard-pressed delegates rose to their feet in applause. "Long Live Zhu Rongji! Long Live Zhu Rongji!" they chanted.

The new orders came too late to avert an uprising in Sichuan's Renshou county in late May by 10,000 peasants protesting the heavy taxes being imposed by the local government to build highways and factories. "If the cadres don't help solve our problems, we will never pay these fees," one of the peasant leaders detained in the revolt, Li Haichi, chanted as the crowds overturned and torched police vehicles.[27] The Renshou riot was one of twenty-three violent mass protests against taxes in the countryside officially admitted to during 1993, compared to just sixteen the year before.[28] "If problems in the countryside continue to worsen," Jiang warned at a second rural work conference in October 1993, "they may seriously affect social stability, as well as the government's hold on power."[29]

By the end of the year, such dire warnings were finally having the intended effects. The problem of the IOUs would be cleared up and excess levies brought under control. Central government investment in farming (mainly irrigation), meanwhile, would register large increases in the following two years. The "rural problem," as it came to be called, would disappear from the headlines in coming years as input prices fell and financial order was restored nationwide. Jiang's attention to the problems in the countryside was, of course, a reaction to events. But as an example of his fire-fighting abilities, it came off well. The rebellious instincts of this massive constituency he had marked out as his own remained in check.

The two closely related issues of regional power and financial order, which had also worsened as a result of the Dengist boom, were less amenable to solution. Zhu's threat to decapitate unruly local leaders, besides its specific application to rural problems, also reflected concerns in Beijing about growing regional autonomy. Deng's emphasis on each locality going its own way had given rise to regional disobedience to central dictates that threatened Beijing's ability to control the national economy. "In passing on the gist of the congress, certain localities have relayed only those policies they like," Jiang complained in late 1992. "This is a problem and an extremely incorrect practice."[30]

Likewise, institutions in the financial system had taken their cue from Deng and began flaunting the rules to earn higher income by lending their money to the highest bidder. The money in such so-called "external circulation" reached an estimated Rmb100 billion in April 1993, or the equivalent of 10 percent of the national deposit base. Citizens also withdrew their money to pile into high-interest fund raising schemes, most of them illegal. Zhu Rongji was "buried in an avalanche of urgent cables" from banks that were dangerously close to defaulting on deposits.[31] A lot of the money went into investment in fixed assets, which leapt 61 percent in the first half of 1993. Imports leapt 23 percent over the same period, and foreign exchange reserves plummeted. Growth remained high, and inflation in cities was now over 20 percent.

Zhu called an urgent national economic meeting on 1 April 1993, where he first dared to speak against Deng's boom. "Certainly, we should 'grasp the opportunity,'" he said, repeating Deng's slogan, "But things will go wrong if we grasp and find that we haven't got a firm grip."[32] Jiang added his support: "We have to solve the economic problems that are arising promptly," he said. "If we don't, they will lead to disaster."[33]

Zhu's desire to take control of economic policy-making put him in direct conflict with Li Peng, who wanted nothing to do with the peppy vice-premier. Among the changes Zhu wanted to make, for example, was to sack Li Guixian, the ineffective head of the central bank, who was a classmate and protégé of the premier's. Li Peng demurred at first, but soon fate intervened. On 19 April, after a vigorous game of tennis with Singapore's prime minister, Goh Chok Tong, Li Peng suffered a heart attack.

It was mild, but serious enough to put Li out of action for the next four months. Zhu moved quickly to fill his place in economic policy-making.

There was a sense of déjà vu in the economic policy duet between Zhu and Jiang. In Shanghai, they had teamed up to reduce the paperwork required of foreign investors. Now the task was bringing regional governments and the financial system into line. Their solution was to impose national macroeconomic controls. In early June, they visited Deng to seek his approval.[34] Open-minded and practical as ever, the patriarch expressed support for the plans. His only request was that the measures should not "dampen the enthusiasm" of local governments. "You two are on the front line now. Do what you must," Deng said with resignation.

Zhu announced his sixteen-point austerity package weeks later. Eleven of the measures involved a clampdown on financial excesses, while others covered imports and fixed investment. To make it clear who was in charge, Zhu installed himself as central bank governor, replacing Li Guixian. The austerity package was euphemistically called "macroeconomic adjustment." The new orthodoxy—"sustainable, fast, and healthy" (*chixu, kuaisu, jiankang*) growth—also understated the force with which the brakes were being applied. Local leaders continued to stream to places like Hong Kong to sign up foreign investors, whose contracted foreign investment of U.S.$110 billion for the year would not be reached again that decade. But the monetary squeeze Zhu engineered was felt nonetheless. Regions began to squeal with displeasure as their showcase projects came grinding to a halt, and state firms began withholding workers' pay because their bankers were being squeezed.

When the austerity measures were being planned, Jiang had told the provinces that they should "speak Beijing dialect more often and support central authorities."[35] Some poor inland provinces, like Jiangxi, were commended by Jiang for responding obediently to central directives on the economy. But far more provinces, especially in the south, continued to balk at the new controls. "Some economists and theorists had different ideas about the macroeconomic adjustment," a mainland magazine wrote. "They thought it was an administrative method of a planned economy. Some newspapers even printed articles calling for a rethinking of the policy."[36] Jiang was eventually forced to act. In September, he convened a meeting of the governors and party chiefs of ten southern provinces in Guangzhou. The official report said that the local leaders "spoke their minds freely," but none of their no doubt colorful testimony was recorded.[37] Jiang's tone was conciliatory. He repeated

Deng's creed that local areas should grow according to their abilities. And his appeal for cooperation was couched in reciprocal terms: "National interests must take precedence over local interests at all times, but consideration should be given to local interests as well." Jiang also called out the big guns in the editorial department of the *People's Daily* to beat back the critics. After long talks with Jiang and Zhu, who ran the central financial and economic leading group, the newspaper in early November declared the "correctness and timeliness" of the measures in a front-page editorial.[38]

The regional complaints were not totally ignored; the austerity program would be loosened on at least two occasions in the three years it took to bring the economy down with a "soft landing." But the program continued until it achieved its objectives and the regional governments stopped complaining. Jiang and Zhu had won the day again.

Looking back, the mid 1993 austerity campaign changed the relationship between Jiang and Li Peng forever. Not only did Zhu Rongji emerge as Jiang's "economic czar" in place of Li, but the lame premier was pushed permanently into the background of coming debates on further economic reforms. The ailing Li obviously felt his growing irrelevance. In a Maoist trick of old, Li had *People's Daily* publish a photograph of him frolicking on the shores of Beidaihe in mid August 1993, as if to prove his robust condition.[39] But the photo served mainly to underline his literally "beached" status. Li would not be swept away by the undercurrent, such was the strength of his position within the Chinese bureaucracy, but after 1993, his role in crucial economic decisions would diminish greatly.

By the same token, Jiang had again proven his uncanny ability to support the man of the moment, in this case, Zhu Rongji. By backing Zhu's tough implementation of economic controls, Jiang again demonstrated his well-developed sense of backing winners. In so doing, he not only achieved his first victory against regionalism but also showed that Deng's policies *could* be tampered with if they were patently failing. All that thanks to Li Peng's weak heart.

4

Rich and audacious, the village of Daqiuzhuang in the southern reaches of the Tianjin municipality came to prominence in the mid 1980s as a sort of model for the new era. Its village chieftain, Yu Zuomin, was concurrently party chief, mayor, president of the village holding company and dispenser of wisdom on how to follow Deng Xiaoping's policies to glory. Over several glasses of bourbon and multiple packages of cigarettes, the gaunt Yu could be found on any given evening entertaining visiting officials from Beijing or from other provinces in his own walled-off version of the Zhongnanhai leaders compound which sat on the western edge of the village.

The story was heartening.[40] After borrowing some money to build a cold-strip steel mill in 1978, the village committee went from success to success by expanding the steel complex and branching out into plywood and industrial machines. Operating outside state planning, the village of 4,300 could hire and fire migrant workers at will and sell to the highest bidder. By 1992, its annual per capita income was U.S.$4,700, five times that of Shenzhen. It was a far cry from the days when only two of the village's 260 bachelors could afford to get married.

Yu Zuomin was the subject of countless paeans in the official media. In 1992, his creation was paid the ultimate tribute: the leaders of Mao Zedong's model commune in the 1960s, Dazhai, went cap in hand to Daqiuzhuang seeking donations and advice on how to escape from poverty.[41] Deng's formula for success was clearly the preferred alternative to Mao's approach.

The only problem was that the leadership of Daqiuzhuang, like the leadership of Dazhai before it, was notoriously corrupt. Lording it over his kingdom like the tyrants of the "old society" the Chinese communists had overthrown, Yu Zuomin was well known for beating workers and getting away with it, and for stashing away millions of renminbi in communal funds for the purchase of his fleet of Mercedes cars. In 1990, the Tianjin bureau chief of the *Fazhi ribao* (Legal Daily) newspaper, Liu Linshan, wrote his first "internal reference" report to the Beijing leadership describing Yu's involvement in the beating to death of a local worker that April.[42] Despite the tip-off, however, Yu escaped punishment.

A similar incident occurred two years later, in December 1992, when a local worker was beaten to death after being suspected of embezzling money from one of the village companies. Four Tianjin police sent to investigate the murder were detained. Days later, an armed standoff involving a reported 1,000 police officers and villagers armed with rifles and bats ensued. Both sides retreated. In the wake of the incident, Liu wrote another internal report to the central leadership describing the lawless behavior of the villagers, and how Yu had paid several million renminbi in bribes to get details of the Tianjin police investigation into the murder. It was widely believed that he had also escaped implication in the earlier murder through bribery.

This second report was seen by Jiang. He sent it back to the Tianjin police with the scribbled comment: "This is in defiance of all human and divine laws." Over the next several months, Liu kept Jiang informed about the progress of the case. This time, however, Jiang was not help-less against this model worker of the Dengist rural miracle. For along with the economic austerity program being planned in Beijing at this time, Jiang was designing a renewed and highly public campaign against official corruption. The reasoning, on which Jiang and Zhu concurred, was that there was a close interrelationship between the runaway econ-omy and abuses of power in many localities. "If we want to overcome financial chaos and cool down the feverish economy, we must combat corruption and encourage honesty in politics," Jiang said privately as the plans were being made.[43] The three key party elders, Deng, Chen Yun, and Peng Zhen, all agreed.[44]

Throughout the summer, Jiang was meeting resistance from some lo-cal leaders, who warned that a high-profile anti-corruption struggle now would be dangerous to the squeezed economy. Jiang rejected the argu-ments. "Those who hold the view that opposition to corruption will af-fect reform and opening and economic development are completely wrong, and their views are extremely dangerous," he told a party an-niversary gathering in late June. "Negative and corrupt phenomena have seriously interfered with the work of reform and opening, and the peo-ple are rather dissatisfied. If we do not take resolute measures to over-come them, they will bury the effort of reform and opening and will jeop-ardize our party's rule."[45] The scales were tipped in mid July, when the Politburo heard two reports on corruption around the country from party anti-graft bodies.[46] Among the reports circulated at the meeting was one on Daqiuzhuang. It was decided that the new campaign would be "large-scale" and would involve the arrest of a number of officials, "no matter how senior."

Sitting in detention in a Tianjin courthouse, Yu Zuomin was a sitting duck as the anti-corruption drive's first victim.[47] Jiang had managed to have him arrested in April. Once the Politburo standing committee agreed to launch the anti-corruption campaign, the Tianjin court was told to begin preparing its guilty verdict. The anti-corruption campaign was formally launched on 21 August and carried on national television three weeks later. Jiang promised that the new campaign would not be "a mass movement where everyone has to pass a test." But "major, high-profile" cases of corruption and abuses of power, especially in local areas, would be investigated and prosecuted. The results of past campaigns had been "insignificant," he said. This time, significant results were expected in a year by using "radical and stopgap measures."

The sentence against Yu Zuomin was announced six days later: twenty years' imprisonment on charges of offering bribes, harboring criminals, obstructing justice, and unlawfully detaining others. The biggest single term, ten years, was on the bribery charge. Yu was a big tiger to catch, not because of his wealth but because of his association with Deng. The renewed anti-corruption campaign was off to a flying start.

Although Jiang had made fighting corruption a personal priority as soon as he took over in 1989, the campaign had seemed to trail off in the early 1990s. Maintaining political stability in the face of the changes in Eastern Europe and then restarting the economy after Deng's southern tour took precedence over it. Jiang did not have the personal authority to wage such a campaign with any greater industry than the party elders or the locally dominated Central Committee allowed. His personal desires mattered little when his power was so attenuated.

By mid 1993, however, the political calculus had changed. For one thing, there was a more widespread belief that Deng's economic boom had indeed encouraged greater official corruption and profiteering. In addition, Jiang's own growing authority, specifically his leadership of the party's leading group on legal affairs, gave him the power to see this argument through to the launch of the campaign. A wily former minister of supervision, Wei Jianxing, had taken over the party's Disciplinary Commission in late 1992 with the grim determination needed to implement the campaign, given the political backing. He brought along his former deputy minister, Xu Qing, a former classmate of Jiang's at Jiao-tong University, to serve as his deputy on the commission.

In the coming year, the party and government anti-corruption bodies would duly announce large increases in the number of cadres and officials prosecuted for corruption. Half a year into the campaign, Jiang reported that some local governments were guilty of "gross protectionism" in blocking the investigation of major cases, while others had "not displayed adequate initiative."[48] But the campaign would continue, he said; otherwise, Communist rule in China would "collapse."

The anti-corruption safari moved haltingly across the savanna throughout late 1993 and 1994. Bigger and nastier tigers would be caught. Among them would be Yan Jianhong, the former head of the

Guizhou International Trust and Investment Corporation and vice-director of the provincial planning commission, who was arrested in late 1993 and finally executed over a year later for taking bribes and embezzling nearly Rmb3 million. Yan's case was a watershed attack on local interests; her husband, Liu Zhengwei, was the Guizhou party secretary at the time and was transferred to a post in Beijing so that investigators could probe his wife's dirty deeds. "Those that must be tried, will be tried, those that must be sentenced to death, will be sentenced to death," the *People's Daily* commented on the case.[49]

Popular perceptions would still assert that many tiger lairs were never disturbed. But one certain result of the campaign was Jiang's enhanced image as a stickler for honest government. Jiang could claim the post-1993 anti-corruption campaign as his own. When major cases were prosecuted, he could take the credit. In a period when Deng's influence was now seriously declining, this fillip to his authority could not have come at a better time.

5

U.S. policy toward China in the four years after the Tiananmen massacre was both hostile and distant. Ongoing human rights abuses in China in the wake of the 1989 tragedy and a growing Chinese trade surplus with the United States prevented Washington from developing the closer ties with Beijing that President George Bush desired. Beijing had its gripes too: the Bush administration sold fighter planes to Taiwan, and the U.S. Congress had passed a law to "monitor" Hong Kong's autonomy from Beijing after its return to Chinese sovereignty in 1997.

When Bill Clinton came to power as president in early 1993, prospects appeared bleak for any improvement in the bilateral relationship. Clinton had pilloried Bush during the election campaign for "coddling dictators in Beijing," while the new secretary of state, Warren Christopher, declared at his confirmation hearing that Washington wanted to "facilitate a peaceful evolution of China from communism to democracy." In interviews with the U.S. media in early 1993, Jiang made it clear that the statements had raised hackles in Beijing. "We favor dialogue and oppose the use of pressure in resolving bilateral differences over things like human rights," he told *U.S. News & World Report* in February. "We disapprove of exploiting the human rights issue to interfere in the internal affairs of other countries."[50]

Jiang was no hard-liner in dealings with the United States. Since his days in Shanghai, he had developed close friends in the United States, especially within the Chinese community in San Francisco and among business leaders. Although his tastes in Western music and literature were overwhelmingly European, Jiang made a point of playing up his proficiency in English and his nodding acquaintance with speeches by Lincoln and Jefferson and songs like "One Day When We Were Young" from *The Great Waltz,* a 1938 American movie about the composer Johann Strauss the Younger. As with many Chinese intellectuals, however, the obverse of his fascination with America was the Chinese nationalist sensitivity expressed in the writings of Zhu Ziqing and Lu Xun. China was China and the United States was the United States, Jiang believed, and the two would forever be at odds. "The differences between China and the United States are a reflection of the diversity of the world we live in," he told foreign reporters that year. "It would be impossible to make all countries of the world identical. That kind of world would be too monolithic."[51]

Still, Jiang had no personal stake in allowing the Tiananmen-induced freeze in bilateral ties to continue. He was not one of the "butchers of Beijing" in U.S. eyes, and he knew it. "Our differences can be settled through dialogue," he told CNN in May 1993. "If we can't resolve the differences, we should set them aside and seek common ground elsewhere."[52] As was his wont, Jiang soon came up with a 16-character slogan to describe his new approach to relations with the United States: "Increase mutual confidence, reduce troubles, develop cooperation, and don't engage in confrontation." It was a little snappier than his earlier efforts at sloganeering and, above all, expressed his desire to improve ties.

Those ties would have to weather two more storms before Jiang got his chance to break the post-Tiananmen estrangement. In August 1993, the Chinese cargo ship *Yinhe hao* (Silver River) was forcibly searched for chemical weapons at a Saudi Arabian port after being kept at sea for three weeks by U.S. Navy surveillance vessels. Nothing illicit turned up amid the cargo of machinery and paper bound for Iran, just as Jiang had calmly informed visiting U.S. congressmen weeks before. Beijing immediately demanded compensation, and state media lambasted the United States for acting like a "self-appointed global policeman." But the incident, although a blatant violation by the United States of international norms of conduct, was not allowed to escalate. Hong Kong shippers demanding a more strident response to the U.S. actions were told by Beijing that "Jiang does not want this to ruin the improvement in bilateral ties."[53]

Months later, Beijing's failed bid to win the Olympic Games in 2000 was widely blamed in China on American opposition. The U.S. Congress had passed a resolution opposing the bid, and there was evidence of behind-the-scenes vote swapping by Western countries to ensure that Sydney, Australia, won if the British city of Manchester did not. Still, Beijing lost by only two votes after five rounds of voting. Cooler heads prevailed in the top leadership.

The biding of time finally paid off. In early November, Assistant Secretary of State Winston Lord announced that following a policy review, Washington would seek to "restore momentum" to the Sino–U.S. relationship.[54] Jiang would get his first chance to encourage the new U.S. attitude during a private meeting with Clinton when he attended the summit of fifteen government leaders of the Asia-Pacific Economic Cooperation (APEC) forum in Seattle in late November. It would be the first meeting between top leaders from the two countries since President George Bush had visited Beijing in February 1989.

Although portrayed in the U.S. media as a concession to China, Jiang's acceptance of the offer of a meeting with Clinton was by no means assured. Unnamed "old generals" in the Chinese military wrote to the Central Committee in October requesting that Jiang not attend the meeting "because the United States has created a series of incidents to oppose China and intervene in its internal affairs."[55] The *Yinhe hao* and Olympics issues topped the list. The debate was finally broken by Deng, now rarely consulted, who said that Jiang should be allowed to go "to express our position and thus increase understanding."

That was exactly what Jiang did. According to sources in attendance, the face-to-face meeting between Clinton and Jiang on 19 November turned into something of a farce.[56] Clinton, Christopher, and the rest of the U.S. delegation entered the club where the meeting was to be held just after 1 o'clock, followed by the Chinese. Clinton began with some introductory welcoming remarks. Jiang responded curtly and pulled from his jacket a prepared statement, which he began to read. It criticized the United States for its attitude on China's human rights record and said that the two countries should respect each other's differences. Twenty minutes into the lecture, a surprised Clinton began to shift uneasily in his chair, looking at his aides with disbelief.

"Mr. Jiang," the president ventured. "We should be talking, not lecturing."

Jiang looked up briefly, but was determined to read his speech. It was as if all the "old generals" were perched on his shoulder.

Ten minutes later, an exasperated Clinton finally gave up. "I should have brought my saxophone along to get some practice in," he joked out loud to his aides.

Jiang's interpreter overheard the remark, but missed the meaning. "Mr. Clinton says he would like to play his saxophone for you," the earnest interpreter whispered to Jiang, careful not to interrupt his president's oratory.

Jiang's eyes lit up with glee. "Really!" he said, finally putting down his speech, "That's great. I play the erhu. I should invite you to my home in Beijing and you could play your saxophone while I play my erhu!"

The laughter on the Clinton side was graciously concealed as expressions of joy at Jiang's generous offer. If their briefing papers hadn't mentioned that Jiang was prone to making silly off-the-cuff remarks, they knew it now.

The meeting broke up with nothing gained in substance. Clinton restated American policy on Taiwan and human rights issues and reiterated the desire for better ties. The Chinese called the encounter "positive and constructive"; the Americans, "a good start." Clinton would henceforth hold Jiang in low esteem. Jiang, for his part, left the meeting with no particular affection for Clinton.

But back home, where it counted, Jiang's trip was a roaring success. "Jiang was able to obtain guarantees from President Clinton to improve Sino–U.S. relations without making any concessions on human rights and other controversial issues," the China News Service proclaimed.[57] Defense Minister Chi Haotian reported to army brass that Jiang had "frankly set out the Chinese government's principled stand and views on a number of controversial issues." Zhang Zhen, the military commission's vice-chairman, added: "He was neither haughty nor humble . . . the whole Chinese army is proud of and inspired by Comrade Jiang Zemin."[58]

Despite his dismal performance with Clinton, Jiang did loosen up considerably during the rest of his U.S. trip. It was the more natural and unburdened Jiang, for example, who visited the cozy home of Cary Qualls, an assembly worker at the huge Boeing aircraft factory outside Seattle, and came away with a bag of chocolate chip cookies for the road.[59]

Before leaving Seattle, Jiang also faced the international press corps, which variously described him at the hour-long session as "supremely confident" and "stiff but confident."[60] After parrying tough questions on Tiananmen, human rights, defense, and Taiwan, Jiang delighted the hardened scribes by wishing them all a happy Thanksgiving. Although only a minority of the reporters present were American, the gesture won him applause. "Thanks everyone!" he called out in English, clapping in reply.

Jiang had achieved in Seattle what he set out to do. He made no concessions in his meeting with Clinton, calculating correctly that the shift in American policy was motivated mainly by potential lost economic opportunities in China and would continue despite the unfriendly lecture he had delivered. His performance was enough to reassure critics in China that despite his conciliatory tone, he could still be relied upon to hold firm in dealings with the United States. Outside the meeting with Clinton, Jiang had enjoyed more scope for maneuvering. He showed the world a friendly face, one not associated with the Tiananmen mess. His naturally folksy ways, although a disaster in his meeting with Clinton, were a hit with the press. Here was a Chinese leader more akin to the Deng Xiaoping who had sported a 10-gallon hat while attending a rodeo in the United States in 1979 than the gray-garbed cadres who had presided over the June 4th massacre.

Little wonder that when Jiang and his delegation climbed back into their Boeing 747 for the return journey after brief visits to Cuba, Brazil, and Portugal, they were in a celebratory mood—so much so that national television was allowed to broadcast excerpts from their high-altitude festivities.[61] For three minutes on evening television on 1 December, the Chinese nation was treated to the spectacle of their president and foreign minister making merry as elegant air hostesses passed around drinks. Dressed casually, with no tie and his collar unbuttoned, Jiang giggled as he asked Qian Qichen over the plane's loudspeaker system to join him in a Xinjiang folk song. Qian declined, so Jiang plunged right into the opening strains of "Rose," his voice resounding through the cabin. A rather stiff-looking Qian was up next. "I'll tell a joke," he began. "Once there was an official who went to a village to make a speech, not knowing . . ." Before the Chinese people could find out whether their foreign minister had a sense of humor, a television announcer drowned out the rest of the joke, assuring viewers that Qian had "brought rounds of laughter from the cabin."

Jiang had just presided over the official end of the post-Tiananmen freeze in Sino–U.S. relations. As the airborne karaoke session continued in the background, Liu Huaqiu, the vice–foreign minister, stepped into the camera's field to bid the nation adieu: "Good-bye from the happiest group of people in the world!" he called out.

6

Jiang's televised airborne sing-along after his meeting with Clinton was the first sign that he was developing his own "presidential style." There he was in China's version of Air Force One, surrounded by his aides and confident in his growing international stature.

As the undisputed official head of the party, state, and army, it was not unreasonable for Jiang to start behaving in a more presidential way. But the extent to which that status was used, or abused, showed much about the individual. Mao, with his private trains, clutch of nubile peasant women, and imperial food testers, had displayed a megalomania that Jiang could not hope to approach. Jiang's immediate predecessor, though, was Deng, whose simple travel habits and assiduous downplaying of his own importance were the new standard.

Several little things added up to a new Jiang style. His suits were better tailored, even if he could not shake the habit of hoisting his trousers halfway up his belly. He finally parted with the four-inch Russian-style men's elevator shoes he had worn in Shanghai because of his modest height and switched to unremarkable brown and black Oxfords. Likewise, his thick-rimmed, V-shaped black glasses of old, which made him look ready for a game of squash, were replaced by two pairs with dignified level frames and thinner rims, one for normal use and one for reading. Even his Audi V-6 car was outfitted with tinted windows. About the only trapping of presidential power that Jiang failed to enjoy now was a better salary; his income as party general secretary was Rmb1,240 per month (Rmb100 more than Li Peng) and as military commission chairman about Rmb1,400 per month, rising to Rmb2,900 per month a few years later.[62] Added up, it was probably not enough to pay for the fuel in his Audi, much less support a retired wife and buy his fine suits.

On the road—often the best indicator of presidential style—Jiang's new sense of self-importance was no less evident. While he had relied on different Boeing 737 planes in his early years as party general secretary, there was soon a dedicated 737 at his disposal for domestic trips. It would take off from the unmarked Nanyuan airstrip south of the Summer Palace in Beijing and land at heavily guarded military airports

around the country. Different Air China jumbos were still called out for
foreign trips, but technicians spent up to a month tuning them up for
each sortie.[63]

Inside the planes could be found a new stable of aides, amounting to
no less than a complete presidential office. In his early years traveling
around China, Jiang had invariably been accompanied only by the officials whose industries or sectors were relevant to the trip; the coal minister when in Shanxi, the minorities minister when in Xinjiang, and so
on. The only permanent aide seen with him was Zeng Qinghong. With
faint reminders of Don Quixote and Sancho Panza, the pair had criss-
crossed the country in the years after Tiananmen with lofty sentiments
but little authority to show for them. "Zeng is his only lieutenant," one
commentator noted.[64]

This traveling in isolation was a reflection of Jiang's isolation in
Zhongnanhai. So few lieutenants did he have, that Jiang became famous
in his early years for telephoning direct to various departments to seek
answers. Once when he telephoned the head of the State Statistical Bureau, Zhang Sai, seeking information on the economy, the director was
caught off guard, thinking it was a namesake in the bureau also from
Jiangsu province. "Jiang Zemin? You mean the Jiang Zemin of Zhongnanhai?" the embarrassed Zhang asked on realizing his mistake.[65]

This was now changing. In addition to Zeng, who might best be described as Jiang's "political minder," three new permanent aides appeared handling security, speech writing, and economic matters. These
aides, although often holding official titles in the party or government,
were all under the main control of the party General Office, which Zeng
headed from early 1993. They were part of the new "Jiang office," which
soon had a life of its own.

First and foremost was Jiang's selection of a new personal bodyguard,
You Xigui. Major-General You first appeared at Jiang's side when he visited Jakarta in November 1994, but the actual change was probably
made earlier in the year. He replaced the longtime bodyguard chief, Yang
Dezhong, who was promoted to full general shortly before his retirement. Yang, by then 71, had served a remarkable stint as chief of guards
for Chinese leaders since 1953. Choosing a successor had been a long
process.[66] The Central Guards Bureau and its associated 8,000-man reg-
iment, the actual group of soldiers guarding top leaders, were directly
under the party General Office, essentially the Jiang office after 1993.
But lines of command were shared with the army, which provided

technical support, and the paramilitary, which provided the men. The complicated structure meant that any personnel change had to be approved by all three groups.

Major-General You was a career soldier who had worked in Shanghai while Jiang was mayor and party chief. He left the local garrison to take over the party organization's management department as director in 1985. There he coordinated personal security arrangements for Shanghai leaders, including Jiang. Some say he shielded Jiang from stones thrown at him by angry students along the Bund when he visited protesters there in mid May 1989. When Jiang went to Beijing, he brought along You, who was made deputy commander of the Central Guards Bureau. Yang Dezhong continued to accompany Jiang on trips, but You gradually took over security for Jiang's apartment and office. In 1991 he was made a major general. The Jakarta trip in 1994 would be his first international trip as guards chief. After that, You's presence at Jiang's side became a common sight.

There was another less well known security guard at Jiang's side, Jia Tingan, who watched for snipers and pre-inspected venues. Less known because Jiang seems to have imposed a blanket ban on mentions of his name whenever he followed his boss on his travels. Jia may have been at Jiang's side as early as his stint as electronics minister in the early 1980s.[67] Little is known of him except that he is a Shanghai native. The administrative necessity of his having an official post would eventually see him appointed deputy director of the military commission general office in 1994.

Only one or two steps behind the security guards was Teng Wensheng, who was to Jiang what the intellectual Bao Tong had been to Zhao Ziyang; speechwriter and walking think tank. With his thick thatch of hair combed across the top of his head and his permanent frown, Teng became an unmistakable part of Jiang's entourage. He joined Jiang first on his trip to Xinjiang in August 1990 and was increasingly seen in the following two years. He would not, however, join foreign trips until 1995, when he joined Jiang's entourages to Moscow and later New York. On domestic trips, Teng's title as deputy director of the party's research office would be given. On foreign visits, he would be called, along with the other aides, a "special assistant to the president."

A graduate in party history of People's University, Teng was an editor of the party's *Hong qi* (Red Flag) magazine before being brought into the party secretariat's research office by the hard-line ideologue Deng Liqun, its director, in 1980.[68] After Deng Liqun fell from grace in 1987,

Teng was transferred in disgrace to the old man's club, the Central Advisory Commission, to serve as deputy secretary. In the wake of the Tiananmen massacre, Teng was first brought back to help build the party case against Zhao Ziyang's "mistakes." At age 50 in 1990, he was fully rehabilitated as deputy director of the party's research office, a think tank more closely linked to the party general secretary.

It is not clear how Teng was chosen by Jiang as his speechwriter. Teng was known for his florid prose, which no doubt appealed to the pretentious intellectual in Jiang. But there was a more obvious political reason. For Jiang, a person like Teng represented a guarantee that he would not make the same mistakes as Zhao and Hu Yaobang. With Teng along at every step—ready to answer a difficult theoretical question that might have wider implications or prepare a speech with the right tone when a particular issue remained contentious and thus dangerous—Jiang could do no wrong. Of course, most of Teng's work was done behind the scenes in Beijing, where he handled political, ideological, and some military speeches. But on the road, he gave Jiang the presidential air that became increasingly conspicuous.

Another unmistakable face in the expanding Jiang entourage was Zeng Peiyan. Always in a Western suit, with his hair parted on the side and top-rimmed glasses, Zeng was like a walking version of the economic or management pocketbooks that many executives lug around in their briefcases. Everywhere Jiang traveled in China to deal with pressing economic concerns like state enterprises, SEZs, and inland investment, Zeng went along with a folder full of briefing papers and charts. Sometimes Jiang would simply give Zeng the floor, although the official report always put the words in Jiang's mouth. The heavily domestic portfolio meant that Zeng rarely traveled abroad with Jiang and thus did not enjoy the same status in the presidential entourage as Zeng Qinghong or Teng Wensheng.

Born in 1938, Zeng Peiyan had a long association with Jiang. One of his first jobs after graduation was working under Jiang in the Shanghai Electrical Equipment Research Institute in the early 1960s. He would remain in the First Machine-Building Ministry until a stint in the Chinese embassy in Washington in the early 1980s. He then served for another year under Jiang as a vice-minister of the Electronics Ministry when Jiang was minister. When Jiang took over the central leading group on finance and economics in 1993, Zeng was put in charge of the leading group's office, which handles day-to-day affairs. Zeng retained his post as planning commission vice-minister, and later minister, but his key post was with the leading group.

With this presidential entourage of five men—Zeng Qinghong, You Xigui, Jia Tingan, Teng Wensheng, and Zeng Peiyan—Jiang was now fully outfitted as China's president. His entourage gave him the presidential air that was important to his image and an intellectual armory to bolster his governance. When Jiang later gave interviews to the foreign media, some or all of these five were always on hand. In at least one case, in an interview with the *Washington Post*, they were the ones who decided which off-the-record comments could be published.[69] Moreover, the loyalty of his entourage to Jiang was purely personal and thus absolute. "There's not a single successful Chinese leader who has not been molded by his counselors," the respected China-watcher Gao Xin wrote. "When people are surprised by the recent political behavior of Jiang, which is more astute than we expect from him, there's this secret [of his counselors] waiting to be revealed."[70]

7

One final member of "Team Jiang" appeared when an Air China jumbo jet rolled to a halt on the tarmac of Moscow's Vnukovo-2 airport in early September 1994. The occasion was a grand one indeed. Jiang was about to become the first Chinese head of state to visit Russia since Mao had come in 1957 to thank the USSR for agreeing to pass on a copy of an atomic bomb, a gift that was never sent. Inside the plane, Jiang could feel in a very personal way the extent to which Beijing's relations with Moscow had now come full circle. His stint in the Stalin autoworks in Moscow in the early 1950s mirrored the onset of comradely relations between the two communist powers. But as a power engineer at the Changchun car plant, Jiang had been left twisting in the wind along with the rest of the country when the Soviet advisors suddenly broke camp in 1959. Now a new warmth was in the air. President Boris Yeltsin was seeking a new "constructive partnership" between the two countries that would entail everything from reducing troops along their joint border to selling Russian military technology to China and joining forces to oppose what they saw as excessive American influence in the inchoate "new world order" that many were predicting.[71]

As the scream of the jet engines died away, the world's media waited breathlessly in a roped-off area about fifty meters from the front of the plane. But for several suspicious minutes after the chocks were thrown under the parked jumbo and its forward door opened, no one emerged onto the staircase wheeled up in greeting. Jiang was never one to spurn attention and it was not that he had stage fright. Instead, the delay was because he had for the first time brought along his wife.

Ever since Jiang had come to power, the identity of Wang Yeping had remained a closely guarded secret in China and abroad. The clever woman with the small, darting eyes had often been seen at her husband's side on the cocktail party circuit while in Shanghai. But she had disappeared from sight after he went to Beijing. Partly it was her long-standing reluctance to live in the capital, which had kept them apart before. But by this time Wang was also suffering from an affliction of the cervical vertebrae, which left her weak and frequently ill.[72] Only in 1991 did she move to the capital to join Jiang, bringing along a clutch of doctors from Shanghai's East China Hospital.[73] Jiang admitted in 1992 that his wife had "not been feeling too well" since joining him in Beijing.[74] It was little surprise that she chafed at suggestions that she accompany her husband abroad. "It would be too much of a burden," she explained. "My health is not good, and I am not suited for the limelight."

The result was that China's would-be "new face" to the world, President Jiang Zemin, traveled the globe like a lonely bachelor. Protocol was awkward when foreign heads of state and government met Jiang with their spouses. The Chinese Foreign Ministry was also keenly aware that traveling with spouses helped to soften the image of Chinese leaders as harsh dictators.

These considerations would have been only a minor concern to Jiang were it not for the domestic political implications of the solo routine. Owing to his disassociation from the Tiananmen massacre, Jiang had already begun to eclipse Li Peng as a diplomat by the early 1990s. Li, though, could always count on the company of his spouse, Zhu Lin, when he went abroad. It was an edge over Jiang in their diplomatic competition that the declining Li apparently hoped to press to his advantage. "Li Peng feels that opportunities for him to appear with his wife exceed those of other leaders and that this is not very appropriate," *Jing bao* reported, quoting an official from Jiang's office. "He has suggested to other leaders that they should also turn up with their wives on proper occasions."[75] As head of the party's foreign affairs leading group, Li still had a say in who traveled abroad. Jiang would not have been prevented from visiting Moscow merely for lack of a spouse, but the pressure on him to "act more presidential" was clear. Fortunately, Wang Yeping rose to the challenge and boarded the plane for Moscow.

Inside the Air China 747 on that bright day at the Moscow airport, she was slow to get ready to face the unsuspecting world outside. The arrival protocol had been discussed several times during the flight with her two female secretaries. But it was still a big step for the self-styled lover of "peaceful and quiet days" to march into the world of international diplomacy. After some delay, during which several jokes were cracked among the waiting press about Jiang's stagefright, the couple finally emerged onto the nonskid landing at the top of the stairs. Camera lenses flickered and sound poles reached toward the disembarking delegation to catch Jiang's opening words. Wang walked slightly behind, wearing a simple suit jacket with Chinese-style buttons and a broach over a white blouse. The favorable impression she left was somewhat lessened by a hideous pair of sunglasses. But for Jiang, it was a triumph over Li Peng's petty criticisms at home. Over the next four days, he would revel in the success of his Moscow visit.

Wang would subsequently join Jiang for trips to South Korea, Europe, again to Russia, and to the United States, in the coming three years. When he went to more rugged regions, like Africa, she would pass. The awful sunglasses would be ditched. Her outfits would soon be better coordinated with the suits Jiang wore. Few in the press corps, or on the Russian side, that day in Moscow knew that Jiang's smiles were only partly because of his role in resuming closer ties with Russia. The glow belied the fact that he had just scored an important political victory in the arcane machinations of Zhongnanhai; his wife, and China's First Lady, was now official.

CHAPTER 8

Glad and at Ease

I

The year 1994 was billed in China as the "year of reforms," when wide-ranging changes in the tax, banking, price-setting, and state industry systems would be introduced that would once and for all put markets rather than bureaucrats in charge of the economy. Public ownership would remain "the mainstay" of the economy, but the government's role would be indirect, exercised by the same tools of fiscal and monetary policy used in capitalist countries.

The premise of this "shock therapy" was that the root of the problems that Zhu Rongji's mid-1993 austerity package had sought to ameliorate could be found in the remnants of the old planning system. If these were swept away in one stroke, the logic went, low inflation and financial order would prevail even as growth continued. "The basic way to deal with current and future economic problems lies in deepening reforms," Jiang had declared in September 1993.[1]

The shock therapy was also crucial if Jiang and Zhu were to retain the initiative in making economic policy. The austerity program had held the provinces upside down by their ankles in an attempt to shake all the loose change from their pockets. The predictable squeals of protest were soon finding sympathy in the central leadership. "Despite its initial success the readjustment package was too indiscriminate," *China Daily* wrote in October 1993. "Enterprises which should have been encouraged to develop were squeezed by the tight bank credits which targeted real-estate and stock-market speculators."[2]

The shock therapy was to be prescribed in the November 1993 plenum, and Jiang and Zhu lobbied hard for support. Zhu toured coastal provinces handing out loans in exchange for allegiance to a 50-point list of changes. Jiang, meanwhile, invoked the authority of Deng to win support. In early November, the long-awaited third volume of Deng's speeches, covering the period 1982 to 1992, was suddenly issued after being delayed since the Tiananmen ordeal. A huge publicity campaign was launched to study the book, which many compared to the exhortations to study Mao's works during the Cultural Revolution. Deng, wary as ever of the creation of a Mao-like personality cult around himself, had agreed to publication in the interests of building support for the proposed changes.[3]

By the time the final plenum document was ready, more than 400 revisions had been made by provincial governments, central ministries, party elders, mass organizations, and the plenum itself.[4] Predictably, it was a less radical document than expected, stressing gradualism rather than shock therapy. The year 2000 was set as the date by which the new market-based economic system should be in place. Nonetheless, Jiang proposed right after the plenum that the year 1994 be designated "the year of reforms." Growth remained high despite the austerity measures, Jiang argued, and since everyone was on board politically, it was a rare chance to forge ahead with the radical reforms; "spurring on the flying horse" was the analogy he used.[5]

The plenum's announcement of a renewed push for price reforms picked up where Zhao Ziyang had left off in mid 1988. Within a week, the prices of certain grains and oils were freed in major cities, including Beijing. The results, as before, were a disaster. In some areas, food-buying panics erupted. Consumers rampaged through shopping malls buying en masse in hopes of beating a planned 17 percent value-added tax and a 33 percent devaluation of the renminbi. Price controls were immediately reimposed on twenty-seven commodities in Beijing in late December, while emergency grain shipments were rushed across the country to cities where the panics were worst.[6] Local officials called out paramilitary troops in some markets to keep order. It seemed like a replay of the sudden price rises that had brought students into the streets three times in the 1980s. The flying horse was bucking wildly.

Beijing's response was paralysis. Jiang made no public statements as the crisis evolved. Indeed, only semi-official news agencies reported the

crisis at all. Not until mid January did Jiang visit a Beijing fresh-food
market to survey the situation. With all too characteristic party and personal arrogance, he blamed the panics on ignorance and opportunism
among the people. The party leadership shared only part of the blame:
"We did not sufficiently understand some reform measures that had been
put into effect," he said.

More important, Jiang's tone was suddenly conservative and risk-
averse: "Neither reform nor development can be separated from stability," he said.[7] Soon he was cautioning that price reforms should be advanced "in due course," while "ample preparations" would be needed
before the reforms to the banking, fiscal, and public investment systems
were made.[8] Other leaders, now circling the wagons, voiced similar fears.
Led by Li Peng, they now warned that the people's "ability to absorb the
shocks" caused by reforms had to be taken into account. Shock therapy
was out. Stability was back in again.

As sporadic buying panics and soaring inflation continued apace,
leaders began to contemplate the potential use of force to quell any large-
scale social unrest. Not since 1989 had this been contemplated at such
high levels. The People's Daily warned that "persuasion, education, mediation and consultation" were to be preferred in defusing tensions. "We
must absolutely avoid being rigid, rough, and brutal," it declared.[9] But
Jiang left no doubt that he would send in force at a moment's notice. "In
case there are emergencies, we can immediately send in the armed police
to nip them in the bud, especially in large cities," he declared after watching a PAP anti-riot exercise in Tianjin in early 1994.[10]

More eerie was Jiang's appeal to the lethal weaponry of the PLA for
support. "This year, the reforms will deal with some of the most difficult issues and will thus be rather risky," he told army leaders in early
1994. "Under these circumstances, the army will have to provide effective security guarantees for the advances of reforms."[11] It was an odd
appeal, given that Jiang had staked his post-Tiananmen credibility on
avoiding use of the PLA in favor of the PAP in handling domestic unrest.
Obviously, despite years of building up the PAP, the PLA was still what
stood between the Communist regime and party-threatening economic
riots and demonstrations.

Jiang made as much clear in a strong and vocal justification of the
Tiananmen massacre on the eve of the fifth anniversary of the tragedy.
The issue might not have been raised had it not been for the threat of
similar unrest that summer. "Looking back at the political disturbance
of the spring and summer of 1989, if resolute measures had not been

taken then, China would not enjoy today's stability," he told the Malaysian prime minister. Then he added a cruel addendum: "A bad thing has been turned into a good thing. As a result, our reform and opening program has forged ahead with steadier, better and even quicker steps." Although this was portrayed at the time as an example of his heartlessness, Jiang was in fact merely reaching into his bursting mental trove of Maoist aphorisms. The idea of "turning good things into bad things" was a direct quotation from Mao's 1957 admonitions on the lessons to be learned from anti-government protest.[12] Every good Chinese Communist knew it by heart.

The "quicker steps" of reform Jiang asserted were, however, noticeably slow for the rest of 1994. Reeling from the panics at the beginning of the year, the party gave every city mayor the responsibility for keeping prices in a selected "shopping basket" of foodstuffs stable and low. Provincial governors, meanwhile, were charged with meeting quotas on a "rice bag" of grain production. "Without the peasants' enthusiasm to grow food," Jiang told farmers in Sichuan later in the year, "we will not be able to maintain social stability, especially in cities."[13]

The great expectations dashed, 1994 in effect became the "year of the shopping basket" rather than the "year of reforms." Tax and banking changes were introduced, but only piecemeal. Not until the following year did the tax reforms begin to have the intended effect of strengthening Beijing's hold on government revenues at the expense of local governments. Growth would slow slightly in 1994 to 12 percent, but consumer prices—feeling the effects of the new taxes and the buying panics—surged to 22 percent for the year, the highest rise since the Communist takeover of 1949. All local leaders were urged by Jiang to study market economics "to make up for their missed lessons."[14]

If the revisions to the plenum document had partly derailed the planned "year of reforms," the early 1994 buying panics threw it off track for good. The plenum's call for a careful balance to be struck between necessary reforms and faster growth—"reform and development," as they were termed—was now supplemented by a third term: stability. Henceforth, the key slogan would be "handling the relations between reform, development, and stability well." If Deng's southern tour had briefly distracted the leadership from the paramount issue of stability—which had been asserted after the collapse of communism in Eastern Europe and the Soviet Union between 1989 and 1991—that period was now over. Stability was again paramount.

For Jiang, it was a setback, although not a lasting one, which showed that he was not infallible in backing winners on economic policy. He alone had unleashed Zhu Rongji on the provinces to get their support for the tax and public investment reforms. He had then ignored the cautious revisions made to the plenum document of late 1993 and, in his own words, "spurred the flying horse." He was a victim of his own enthusiasm. He was miraculously to escape blame for the economic problems of 1994, however. It would be Li Peng who would make a rare admission that the government had made mistakes in 1994 by unleashing market reforms on an unsuspecting public.[15] Jiang would even take a friendly swipe at Li for allowing inflation to rise well above his own target of 10 percent: "Premier Li Peng had to make a self-criticism," he told the U.S. magazine *Business Week* with glee in May 1996.[16]

Jiang had made a mistake, but he recovered quickly, backing off from shock therapy and preparing to quell social unrest by force if necessary. It showed the buffer his political status now enjoyed, a buffer thick enough to cushion his fall from a flying horse.

2

If 1992–93 was the period when Jiang cracked the whip in the senior ranks of the PLA, 1993–94 was when he established his authority further down the line. Jiang, as we have seen, had made his mark in the wake of the purge of Yang Baibing through a high-level reshuffle in the military regions and the PLA headquarters. Three of the new appointees to the headquarters, Zhang Wannian, Yu Yongbo, and Fu Quanyou, were soon made full generals in the first batch of six promotions announced by Jiang as chairman of the Central Military Commission.

The completion of this high-level shakeup came through a second major personnel reshuffle in January 1994 aimed at rooting out remaining Yang Baibing loyalists.[17] Only five of the twenty-two senior officers in the PLA headquarters prior to 1992 and only four of the commanders and political commissars in the military regions remained in place.[18] Among those demoted was Lieutenant General Zhang Gong, the officer who had commanded the Tiananmen massacre.[19]

But while Jiang was able to clean out the senior ranks, his ability to win the loyalty of the rank and file remained in question. In May 1993, the army newspaper, *Jiefangjun bao,* typified the aloof stance of the military by relegating the Xinhua version of Jiang's interview with CNN to page 4.[20] Jiang's immediate reaction to the slight was to sack the newspaper's director, Zhu Tingxun, and the editor-in-chief, Yang Zicai (both major generals). A new director, Major General Xu Caihou, was brought over from the PLA's General Political Department, and within days, *Jiefangjun bao* began dutifully chirping about Jiang's heartfelt concern for the common soldiery.[21] "Following the reshuffle, *Jiefangjun bao* has stressed the need to implement Jiang's slogans on army development assiduously in the new era," *Jing bao* noted.[22]

The real solution to Jiang's lack of prestige in the army, though, was for him to ingratiate himself more with the foot soldiers and junior officers whose interests had been overlooked in all the court politics of the Yang Baibing purge. "After a series of moves to bring the senior ranks under control, the next step for Jiang is to stabilize the rank and file," *Guangjiaojing* commented in mid 1994.[23] Jiang announced a series of measures, beginning in 1994, aimed at improving the living conditions of army units and reversing the continuing decline in logistical support capabilities that belt-tightening in the 1980s had necessitated. In this way, he began what would henceforth dominate his approach to army control: it was to be bottom-up rather than top-down. Jiang's so-called "army morale project" was aimed mainly at the cannon fodder. "In improving the life of the military, common soldiers should take precedence over officers," he said in early 1994. "First come the soldiers, then the officers. This should be our standard practice in future."[24] To pay for higher salaries, new food subsidies and better housing, the defense budget rose by 20 percent in 1994, the biggest jump since 1979, and it would continue to increase at an average of just under 15 percent a year for the next three years.

Jiang continued to visit army units, almost as if his main aim was to cover the map rather than learn about the troops. "Yours is the only unit in the Beijing military region I have not visited," he boasted sitting in a field on a campstool at one camp north of the capital in late 1994.[25]

Boosting army morale also meant striking out at the invidious business interests that had caused an alarming deterioration in discipline in the lower ranks. From 1985 to 1992, the PLA had expanded quickly into business sectors as diverse as property, health, and telecommunications to compensate for falling budgets. By 1993, the 20,000 PLA firms made total profits estimated at between U.S.$2–3 billion, adding as much as a third to the official defense budget.[26] Soldiers who should have been training were busy handing out business cards and answering faxes; corruption and crime spread; an unfair type of competition was introduced into the Chinese business environment; and the army's autonomy from the purse, and thus the control, of the party grew. Cutting away the businesses in the lower ranks became a critical aspect of Jiang's "bottom-up" army control strategy. "We must resolutely resist and oppose money worship, pleasure-seeking, and extreme individualism in the army," Jiang had told troops in Qinghai province in mid 1993. "Only through hard struggle can we resist corruption and stand the test of power, money, and beautiful women."[27]

Under a "rectification" campaign launched in early 1994, all army firms were put under the direct control of the military regions. In many ways, the restructuring of the PLA business empire was Jiang's most difficult job in building loyalty among the lower ranks. The undisciplined business executives were also often the most powerful junior commanders. But by the end of the year, the number of firms had fallen from 20,000 to about 15,000. Close to a thousand of those closed were in Shenzhen alone, many of which had clearly been planning a "leap" into Hong Kong after the colony reverted to Chinese rule in 1997.

With that complete, Jiang could for the first time claim to be the true commander in chief of the PLA—from the top brass down to the most remotely stationed private. "After five years of getting to know the army," *Jing bao* declared, "Jiang has finally succeeded in gaining control."[28] As with his support in the party, Jiang's support in the army derived from the fact that his policies largely jibed with the interests and desires of those with the potential to oppose his authority. Depoliticizing the senior ranks and improving discipline and living conditions in the lower ranks were the common aspiration of PLA professionals determined to bring the army into the twenty-first century. As with the party, Jiang could depend on the support of the army so long as he did not veer from this mainstream opinion.

3

Since the triumphant conclusion of Deng's 1992 southern tour and the close it brought to the post-Tiananmen healing process, Jiang had moved in several areas—in particular economic policy and the military, as discussed above—to take control of the country that had been forced into his reluctant hands in 1989. There is a good argument to be made that the final transfer of power from Deng Xiaoping to Jiang Zemin, the heads of the second and third generations of the communist leadership respectively, took place in 1994.

Although no one event can be singled out as having first suggested it, a smattering of official indications confirmed that this momentous change had occurred. The standoffish Li Peng admitted at the beginning of the year that the third-generation leadership had "started to mature."[29] Then the sprightly party elder Wan Li, who would always bear a grudge against Jiang for detaining him at the Shanghai airport at the height of the 1989 student demonstrations, finally agreed to bury the hatchet as best he could and support Jiang.[30] And when the North Korean leader Kim Il Sung died in July, the wreath Jiang sent to the North Korean embassy in Beijing took center stage, while Deng's was at the side.

Deng had bidden what turned out to be his final farewell to the world in February, his first appearance in a year. It was a sickly sight. Standing with the support of his daughter Deng Rong on the newly opened Yangpu bridge in Shanghai, Deng's eyes wandered and his mouth hung open. Deng Rong said afterward that her father would appear again only "when necessary," an ironic statement, given that it ended up meaning never.[31] A final photograph of Deng watching the National Day fireworks display on 1 October made it clear that he was nearing death. His cheeks were sunken, and he stared vacantly off into the distance, his crippled legs covered by a blanket. For those unable to read the tea leaves, the change was put in writing at the party plenum in September. "The party has already completed the transfer from the second generation of central leadership collective to the third," the plenum communiqué read. The next day, in a rare example of getting it right, the People's Daily called the statement "imbued with deep and far-reaching meaning."[32]

The question was, what "meaning"? Jiang had been the ostensible leader of the party and military for five years. But Deng had continued to set the boundaries for major decisions, and in some instances, like the southern tour, to set the agenda as well. If power had indeed been transferred, it meant not only that Jiang could make major decisions by himself without consulting Deng, but also that those decisions would be accepted by other party leaders and elders.

With his characteristically historical turn of mind, the party elder Bo Yibo compared the handover to events in the years 1948 and 1978. In those two years respectively, the first-generation leadership led by Mao and the second generation under Deng had won support from the party and people at a "critical time," Bo wrote in the People's Daily in November.[33] That had allowed them to exercise real power and carry out much-needed reforms, he said. Now was such a time again. With Deng ailing, Bo hinted, there was a danger that Jiang's assumption of supreme authority might be challenged. "We must uphold Jiang Zemin as the *only* core," he wrote.

Jiang's emergence as "the only core" was the significance of the completion of the transition. It was no longer the prerogative of Deng and his generation even to be consulted. Since Deng's southern tour, Jiang had emerged as a supreme commander both in style and in substance, and it seemed appropriate that this change be acknowledged. The new generation was now in complete control. As he explained, using an old proverb from his native Jiangsu: "The back waves of the Yangtze River will always catch up with the front waves."[34]

In the coming year, the "fact" of the transition would be continually pounded into the national psyche through subtle and less than subtle means. The lunar new year newspapers would feature nothing but Jiang photos on the front page, whereas Deng and Li had shared the front page with him a year before.[35] A more subtle attempt would be the appearance of an officially sponsored poster entitled "Glad and at Ease" (*xin wei*), in which Jiang gazed down on Deng, standing with a cane before him. The poster, which Xinhua would describe as "both political and artistic," recalled a mural produced in late 1976 in which the lately departed Mao Zedong sat with his hand resting on the sleeve of the ill-fated Hua Guofeng; "With you in charge," Mao said, "I can rest at ease."[36] Even at his moment of triumph, the haunting comparison with Hua would still cast frightening shadows on the wall of Jiang's authority.

China had entered the post-Deng era. No one used the words "Jiang Zemin era" to describe the new beginning, but that was the implication. The new emperor compared starkly to his predecessors, and it is worth noting the differences. Jiang was neither a peasant nor a soldier. He was an urban intellectual whose speeches were peppered with high-sounding literary references to Song dynasty poetry and Shakespeare rather than the crude earthy analogies favored by Mao and Deng. Both of his predecessors smoked and drank, probably more than was good for them. Jiang got flushed after a single glass of *maotai* liquor and abhorred smoking.

Jiang also had a worldliness that distinguished him from Mao and Deng. He could discuss the aperture between the circuits in a semiconductor with one researcher and chaos theory and its possible applications to history with another.[37] He would engage Buddhist monks on topics of religion. And, within months of its appearance, Jiang was even quoting from the American professor Samuel Huntington's influential book *The Clash of Civilizations and the Remaking of World Order*.[38]

Jiang was self-effacing in a way that Deng, let alone Mao, had never been. During floods, he joked that his name could mean "inundate the people." He joked about his weight (209 pounds, or 95 kilograms), telling both foreign and Chinese guests that given his bulk, it would be hard to move (i.e., depose) him.[39] When he fell off a folding stool while visiting a military camp in Guangdong, because, as the army newspaper said charitably, "the general secretary is of stalwart build," Jiang joked that he would be safer sitting on the ground, which could at least support him. "Everyone broke into laughter," the newspaper reported. "His easygoing and humorous manner immediately dispelled the awkwardness and nervousness of the officers and soldiers."[40]

Few first-time encounters with Jiang ended in anything but hearty handshakes and friendly small talk. Jiang made others like him. Deng and Mao had been liable to sink back into deep armchairs and emit cool statements of state policy along with hot streams of cigarette smoke when they met foreign guests. Jiang, by contrast, would lean forward attentively and bob his head as he gesticulated and made jokes, not necessarily funny ones. "He's relaxed, even self-effacing. He also has a confident manner that goes against the outside perception that his grip on power is shaky," the U.S. magazine *Business Week* wrote after meeting him.[41]

It was not only for foreign guests that Jiang put on the happy face. Anecdotes abounded in which he would chat up people for no apparent reason other than his boundless gregariousness. "How's your camera? Have you got a lighter one yet?" he called out to a Chinese TV crew one gray afternoon in early 1994 standing on the steps of the Great Hall of the People waiting for the visiting president of Estonia to arrive for a photo opportunity. "We've switched. It weighs only ten kilograms," the cameraman replied. Jiang seized the apparatus and weighed it up and down. "Nope. Too heavy. Your 'burdens' are too heavy," he declared at length, playing on the Chinese word *fudan,* which often refers to excessive taxation of farmers. "Ha! Ha! Ha! 'Burdens' too heavy. Get it? Ha! Ha! Ha!" he cackled as he broke away to greet the arriving limousine.[42]

The fact that Jiang did not take himself too seriously helped balance the less attractive aspects of his character. His intellectual arrogance, for example, which went on display every time he lectured students about the meaning of life or dropped the names of books he'd read, could be overlooked given his good nature. Unlike Li Peng, who was not only arrogant but also took himself seriously, Jiang was not a man to hate, either at home or abroad.

There are good reasons why Jiang did not share the tough, almost embittered, personality of Deng and Mao. He had never fought in the anti-Japanese or civil wars. He had escaped punishment during the 1950s anti-rightist campaign and got off lightly during the Cultural Revolution. In short, his refined Yangzhou upbringing had never succumbed to any adversity. Jiang's nature remained just as it had been when he began happily singing songs and playing musical instruments at Yangzhou Primary School.

Jiang could also count on an outstanding trait that Mao and Deng had lacked: a mesmerizing ability as a public speaker, which he mastered as his time in office lengthened. Mao and Deng had spoken in the almost unintelligible accents of their native inland provinces and in squeaky and high-pitched tones. Jiang, by contrast, spoke the national *putonghua* (or "common") language with only soft accenting from his native Yangzhou and adopted Shanghai. His deep, sonorous voice could make the most banal speech resonate with meaning and novelty. He would add emphasis by gurgling the word *hen* (meaning "very"), digging deeply into the syllable, before jabbing sharply and quickly into whatever adjective or adverb followed. The words came out slowly, in a measured rhythm that belied his musical background. In a country where the art of the two-, three- or even four-hour speech lived on, Jiang was well served by his voice.

Jiang was not and could not afford to be as authoritarian as Mao, or even as Deng. His leadership style has been described by one overseas Chinese scholar as "consensual."[43] On several occasions in meetings of the Politburo standing committee, he would declare: "We are a working collective. As a leader of this working committee I have only one vote, with no special powers."[44] A piece of Beijing doggerel summed up the differences:

> Mao's word could command thousands of people,
> Deng's word could command dozens of people,
> But Jiang's word can command just one person.[45]

This was partly owing to his personal disposition to conciliation; as we have seen from his days in Shanghai, Jiang preferred to play politics by backing winners rather than attacking losers. It was also out of necessity; Jiang had neither the authority nor the charisma to purge those who threatened him without a lengthy process of building support. In addition, by the time he came to power, China's political structure was too far advanced down the road of moderate checks on authority exercised by the national parliament and by government ministries to allow any leader to rule absolutely. As Jiang told U.S. reporters: "It's impossible for another Mao Zedong or Deng Xiaoping to appear in China."[46]

Jiang also shared some affinities with his predecessors, although more so with Mao than with Deng. He shared Deng's inclination for straight talk and his dislike of any suggestions of a personality cult, such as Mao had built around himself. He also roughly shared Deng's ideological makeup, although he was a somewhat less reckless economic reformer and somewhat more cautious on political and ideological issues. This philosophical consanguinity was, of course, no coincidence; it had been exactly why Deng chose Jiang in 1989.

More complex and interesting was Jiang's kinship with Mao. Even on the surface, there was physical resemblance: the protruding forehead, the prominent facial mole, the back-combed hair, the barely visible double chin, and the concomitant belly. Jiang shared several psychological features with Mao as well, the most obvious being his egotism and his intellect. Mao's egotism, his love of being at the center of attention, had been self-evident in the adoring crowds that he insisted greet his arrival in every town he visited and in the personality cult he had built around himself. Jiang's egotism was more sincere, if that is possible. He wanted to work for the attention lavished on him. Most obvious among his efforts to win praise were his frequent fits of musical exhibitionism. Jiang, of course, had excelled at music from a young age and had groomed his public performance skills while sawing on his erhu as a student in Shanghai. Many other Chinese leaders were also dab hands at music, but were reluctant to flaunt their skills. Not so Jiang. Starting from the day he seized the conductor's baton at the 1987 National Day soirée in Shanghai, Jiang's love of showing off his musical skills would develop into a more polished and audacious routine. After his initial foreign visit as party general secretary to North Korea in 1990, he had sat down at the piano in the Pyongyang departure lounge and pounded out a rendition of the "Yellow Water" ballad from the well-known Yellow River chorus, forcing everyone to sing along.[47] In Fujian province in mid 1994, he seized a flute from a member of an opera orchestra after a performance and "entertained" the audience with his prowess.[48] After that, he would lose all scruples and let it rip abroad too. In Finland in mid 1995, he surprised his hosts with an impromptu organ recital while visiting the popular Temppeliaukio church. "He really seemed to enjoy himself," the church guide would comment.[49]

Jiang's egotism was mostly harmless, unlike Mao's. In politics, Jiang was tactful enough not to dominate discussions among senior leaders, as was his wont with subordinates. He was also sensitive enough about the national revulsion at Mao's personality cult to avoid suggestions of doing likewise. Yet inside was the mind of a man who loved center stage.

The intellectual affinities Jiang shared with Mao were less obvious. Although not an intellectual by class, Mao had been one by nature. The beauty of his poetry and his erudition in classic Chinese novels and histories were among the few virtues on which most Chinese could agree. Jiang was no poet, but he was well read in the classics—perhaps better acquainted with classical poetry than Mao himself. Mao famously sat in a wicker chair surveying the overlapping peaks of Mount Lu in 1959 and wrote: "I have leapt over four hundred peaks to reach this verdant crest. Now, impassively, I survey the world beyond the sea."[50] Jiang, in a faint reenactment of the scene on Mount Lu, bounded up the ninety steps of the newly opened reconstruction of the Tang dynasty Tengwang pavilion in Jiangxi province in late 1989 and recited a poem dedicated to the pavilion when it was first built. "Painting the cloud moving southward, I see rain, like pearl curtains, enshrouding Mount Xi." Journalists could only remark on his ostentatious display. "Judging from the tone, rhythm, and fluency of the recitation, it is obvious that he has recited it since childhood," an accompanying journalist noted.[51]

Jiang's sprightly ascent of the Tengwang pavilion and recitation of the poem suggests that he was intentionally seeking to impersonate Mao, almost like a form of hero worship. The conscious and unconscious affinities he shared with Mao were hard to disentangle. Jiang would rarely be drawn away from the official party verdict on Mao—that he had done mostly good but had committed "major mistakes" in his dying years. But as early as 1990, Jiang seemed to be seeing himself as a Mao-like figure. Asked in that year if his new job was difficult, Jiang had directly compared himself to Mao by recounting a traditional fable called "The Foolish Old Man Who Removed Mountains" (*Yugong yi shan*). The story recounts how God takes pity on an endearing but muddle-headed old man who is trying to level two large mountains blocking the road in front of his house and sends two angels to cart the hills away on their backs. God, in the Communist interpretation, was the Chinese people. Mao had famously appealed to the fable in 1945, when U.S. support for the Nationalists in the wake of the war against Japan made Communist victory seemingly impossible. The same could be applied now, Jiang said, when "the Chinese people are trying to modernize but face many difficulties." "It *is* difficult to be party general secretary, but with God's help the difficulties can be overcome," he said.[52]

Besides identifying with Mao psychologically, there were also obvious political reasons why Jiang would liken himself to the Great Helmsman. When the Chinese people spoke of "the era of Mao Zedong," they meant the period of the 1950s, when optimism was in the air and the streets were safe. Jiang, who had shared in the élan of that pre–Cultural Revolution decade, found its recollection an appropriate device for defending the party after Tiananmen. Deng, who had suffered twice at Mao's hands, had advised Jiang to rebuild the party's image on other grounds, but Jiang seemed to wish to refurbish the Maoist tradition as well.

Jiang's first trips outside Beijing as party general secretary in 1989 had been to the old revolutionary bases of Yanan and Jinggangshan. Like a priest making a pilgrimage to a sacred religious site after being elected bishop, Jiang seemed to be seeking inspiration and enlightenment from the old fortress areas so closely associated with Mao's takeover of the party. Yanan in northwestern Shaanxi province had served as the party headquarters from 1936 to 1947 and was where Mao had set the tone for the party's ruling style, which has continued down to the present. The town was the highlight of Jiang's five-day tour of the province in mid September 1989.[53] While there, he liberally quoted from Mao on issues like grain self-sufficiency and media controls. "We cannot do without the spirit of Yanan," he explained.[54] At Jinggangshan, where the Fourth Red Army was formed by Mao and Zhu De in 1928, and where early Communist land reform was carried out, Jiang laid a similar emphasis on revolutionary tradition. He ate red rice and pumpkin soup, the simple victuals of the old base area.[55] "With the spirit of Jinggangshan, are there any difficulties we cannot overcome today?" he asked.[56] When he left the area and passed by a statue of Mao erected on the mountain slope, Jiang stopped, doffed his summer hat and stood silent, "lost in thought."[57]

The gingerly revival of the Maoist tradition after more than a decade of execration jibed nicely with a popular upsurge of nostalgia for the Great Helmsman, which would peak as the centenary of his birth approached in 1993. Jiang's donning of revolutionary clothing, as mentioned, would later see the date of his joining the Communist Party moved back by three years to 1943 in order to align him more closely with Mao's generation, which had fought against the Japanese as well as the Nationalists. As we shall see, as China emerged after 1994 into the era of Jiang Zemin, this Maoist heritage would be relied on for more than just symbolism.

PART 5

Breaking with Deng, 1995–1998

CHAPTER 9

Independent Kingdoms

1

Scattered throughout the ancient records of past Chinese dynasties are examples of prime ministers who came to power in the wake of great visionaries. For a time, these second-rate successors would tend the imperial system left to them, seeming even to be accumulating some measure of authority. Soon, however, new problems would arise that these mandarins, with little more than an ability to manage factions, could not resolve. Flooding along the Yellow or Yangtze rivers, invasion from the nomadic tribes living outside the Great Wall, or agrarian tax revolts in the south and central plains were frequent challenges. Frozen in the face of such external threats, these prime ministers would soon be deposed by nervous emperors. "Prime Minister Cao Can just followed the pattern laid down by his predecessor, Xiao He" (*Xiao gui Cao sui*) went the Han dynasty proverb based on one such ill-fated official.

Poised on the edge of his own "era" in the wake of a great visionary, Jiang Zemin was clearly aware of the danger of *Deng gui Jiang sui*. While he had remained a consensus-builder in his rise to ultimate authority by the end of 1994, he was also seeking to identify items that together could make up his own "pattern" of rule. While still required to stay within the boundaries of the post-1978 opening and reform policy Deng had marked out, Jiang was staking out his own sizable plot at an early stage. He was determined not to suffer the fate of the ancient prime minister Cao Can, or his more recent incarnation, Mao's successor Hua Guofeng. At the same time, Jiang was also being forced by the tide of history to outline, or at least guide, the emergence of a new vision of China's future.

Thus, both immediate political necessity and pressing historical exigency called on Jiang to articulate a vision of China's future. By 1995, he had the political authority to do so. Five issues in particular—patriotism, anti-corruption, party rebuilding, social rejuvenation, and redefining the state's role in the economy—would come to dominate Jiang's agenda beginning in 1995. Many observers would see in these issues the seeds of imperial disintegration. Jiang, the argument went, was merely reacting by stuffing his fingers into the fissures appearing along the dam of Communist rule, but would be unable to prevent its inevitable collapse. To be sure, he left no doubt that he addressed these issues in order to bolster Communist rule in China. But, more important, they were key components in building the sort of new China that he imagined, and that the tide of history was forcing him and China's other leaders to define.

As mentioned at the outset, by the mid 1990s, China seemed to be heading in the direction of a sort of "developmental dictatorship" of the kind that exists in Singapore and Malaysia, and had existed in South Korea and Taiwan, coupling economic and social freedoms with strict political and media controls. That meant a state that was both powerful and efficient and a society and economy that were flourishing. Even the 1997–98 economic crises in several Asian "developmental dictatorships," including Malaysia, South Korea, and Indonesia, would not tarnish this model in the eyes of China's leaders.

From what we have seen of Jiang throughout his life, certain themes of his character help explain his choice of this model: his attention to Chinese tradition; his economically liberal instincts; his willingness to adapt (some would say betray) Marxism in the face of new circumstances; his insistence on strict political and media controls.

Jiang's vision was not radical, and it was not imposed on China all at once. As the opportunities arose beginning in 1995, he jumped to assert his views and make the issues his own. Other leaders were often his allies, or he theirs; Zhu Rongji's re-engineering of the national economy and Qiao Shi's insistence on allowing more supervisory powers for the standing committees of the national parliament were both ideas backed by Jiang. It was a process that would take several years. Through it, Jiang was able to make himself significant in the annals of Chinese history as a leader who ushered in a truly modern Chinese state.

Fighting corruption and bolstering patriotism were two of the earliest issues to be tackled.

2

When it first opened in 1990, the McDonald's fast-food restaurant on the corner of the Wangfujing avenue shopping district in central Beijing was a symbol of the post-Tiananmen recovery in foreign investor confidence in China. The fact that it was just a stone's throw away from Tiananmen Square, and across from the Beijing Hotel, where many foreign reporters had watched the massacre of June 4th, added to the sense of renewal. McDonald's signed a twenty-year lease on the site and watched the outlet, the biggest in the world, turn into one of its busiest.

The welcome symbolism of the outlet made it doubly unusual when, in late 1994, McDonald's was suddenly told to quit the site to make way for a huge new U.S.$2 billion Hong Kong–financed real estate development. No warning was given, no talks were offered. McDonald's was to be turfed out, no questions asked. It seemed that the restoration in foreign investor confidence carefully cultivated by the country's senior leadership could be seriously impaired by a single unruly commercial incident. Senior leaders began questioning the proposed Oriental Plaza project, which was backed by mavericks in the Beijing municipal leadership.

Mao Zedong had once described Beijing as "an independent kingdom, impenetrable and watertight."[1] The centrally administered capital had been virtually ruled by one man, Peng Zhen, in the first decade of the People's Republic before coming under Mao's control during the Cultural Revolution. In the early 1980s, a former Beijing rural official took over as mayor and then party secretary: Chen Xitong would rule the city with such utter control that people would call it the "Chen System," a play on his given name, Xitong, a homonym of the Chinese word for system.

Chen was best known in the West for asserting that only a few hundred people had been killed in the Tiananmen massacre. But in the capital, he was better known for his mistresses, private secretaries, and luxury villas. His private secretary, Chen Jian, took huge bribes for access to the boss. He had a mistress, a slender, coy woman named He Ping, who worked as a deputy general manager at the Holiday Inn Downtown in the city. The sprawling villa complex where they cavorted in Beijing's northwest suburbs was outfitted with satellite TV, swimming pools, and German shepherd guard dogs.[2] One son, Chen Xiaoxi, ran a real estate company using city money. The other, Chen Xiaotong, squandered huge sums on trips to Hawaii and held fancy dinners where pornographic videos were shown to invited guests.[3]

The spoils system of Beijing under Chen Xitong was as great as the famously corrupt Tammany Hall system of New York City's dominant Democratic establishment in the late nineteenth and early twentieth centuries. The cronyism and interlocking web of favors was so deeply embedded that few corruption investigations could proceed. When party investigators had sought in 1991 to look into the personal affairs of Zhou Beifang, the head of the Hong Kong operations of Beijing's Dengist model enterprise, Capital Iron and Steel, they had been blocked at every turn.[4] His father, the company chairman, Zhou Guanwu, and his friend, Chen Xitong's son, Chen Xiaotong, had both appealed to city leaders to head off the probe, which was subsequently dropped. The Chen System, as with those before it in the capital, was both impenetrable and watertight.

For Jiang Zemin, the Chen System represented a double challenge. For one thing, it made a mockery of his anti-corruption campaign. This, of course, was one of his trademark issues, and one in which netting "tigers" as well as "flies" was a key plank. The corruption in Beijing was all the more galling because it was happening right under Jiang's nose. "Some leading cadres, including some high-ranking ones . . . stand high above the masses and act like overlords," he warned at a January 1995 meeting, sheathed in a gray, collarless tunic, or Mao jacket, for added gravitas. "They abuse their power to seek private gain, trade power for money, and embezzle state assets."[5]

Just as significant was the political threat posed by Chen Xitong and his system. Jiang and Chen had never got along well. On at least three occasions since Jiang had become party general secretary, Chen had openly challenged his authority.[6] In 1992, for example, Chen had made a glaring attempt to paint Jiang unfairly as a conservative by allowing the local daily *Beijing ribao* to report on Deng's southern tour the day before Jiang overcame propaganda conservatives in the central party to have a national report issued. He then personally arranged for Deng's tour in May of that year of the Capital Iron and Steel plant, styling himself as the mouthpiece for Deng's reforms. Most enraging, however, was Chen's unwillingness to submit to Jiang's unquestioned political authority, even after it had been put in writing by the September 1994 plenum. "The core is not bestowed," Chen told Beijing colleagues shortly after the plenum. "The core is something you have to live up to, you have to rely on everyone to support you."[7]

Chen's impertinent attitude reflected a certain complacency. He and his friends were so closely linked with Deng that nothing could touch them, or so it seemed. That was exactly the kind of local protectionism and cockiness that was perhaps the greatest challenge to Jiang's hold on power and to the emergence of a strong central state that would usher in China's new age as a "developmental dictatorship." Jiang's anti-corruption drive had been first launched in 1989 and then again in 1993. Several "tigers" had been caught. But none as big as Chen Xitong and none in such seemingly unassailable lairs as the Beijing municipality.

By early 1995, McDonald's was still selling hamburgers on Wangfujing. This suggested to many that something else was afoot. They were right. Since the initial evacuation order had been given to McDonald's, party anti-corruption investigators had finally begun to penetrate the Chen System.

One of the ironies of the wide ranging purge of the Beijing leadership that took place was that the incontrovertible evidence needed to begin the cleanup was obtained quite close to Jiang's hometown. Since 1992, investigators in the sleepy southern Jiangsu province city of Wuxi had been watching an illegal fund-raising scheme run by a local company ultimately owned by the Beijing municipality's State Security Bureau. When they finally moved in to break up the U.S.$380 million scam in mid 1994, they found a trail of bribery and embezzlement that went right to the highest levels in Beijing.[8]

With that evidence firmly in hand, there began a carefully orchestrated tightening of the noose on the Chen System. The key figure was a deputy chief of the Beijing State Security Bureau, Li Min, who doubled as private secretary to Mayor Li Qiyan. He was the first to be arrested in late 1994 for his role as the Beijing director of the fund-raising scam. Once in custody and with promises of leniency, Li Min spilled the beans. He admitted to bribing senior officials of the Beijing municipality, including a vice-mayor, Wang Baosen, to invest in the fund-raising scheme. He also owned up about taking bribes from Capital Iron and Steel's Hong Kong manager, Zhou Beifang, to arrange for the resettlement of Zhou's wife and daughter in the British colony.

That set off new investigations in both directions. Capital Iron and Steel, Deng's model enterprise, was the easiest target. In mid February 1995, Zhou Beifang's father, Zhou Guanwu, was forced to step down as company chairman. The next day, Zhou Beifang was detained while relaxing by the pool at his suburban villa during a brief visit back to the capital from Hong Kong. It signified that those whom Deng had favored were no longer off limits. Perhaps to avoid alarming the Beijing leadership, Jiang lied outright and said that the resignation of Zhou Guanwu was "very natural" and had "nothing to do" with the alleged crimes of his son.[9]

Tackling high-level graft in the Beijing leadership had to be conducted carefully. While following up leads on bribes paid to Beijing officials to invest in the fund-raising scheme, investigators found evidence that Vice-Mayor Wang Baosen and Chen had also accepted bribes to overlook Oriental Plaza approval problems.[10] The project's planned height of 70 meters (almost 230 ft.) was more than twice that allowed by regulations. There were also suspicions (later confirmed) that the building site contained precious Stone Age relics. The sudden scrutiny of the Oriental Plaza project by anti-corruption investigators explained why McDonald's was able to keep selling burgers on the proposed site. The Chen System was under pressure on many fronts, and its once confident barking at the fast-food chain had now been replaced by silence.

The McDonald's controversy, it turned out, was just a canary in a coalmine already badly poisoned by corruption. Besides the bribes paid over the Oriental Plaza, Wang and Chen were also found to be in possession of several large villas each and to have diverted countless millions of dollars of city money into the pockets of friends and relatives. As the noose tightened, Wang, who had diverted U.S.$37 million in city money into the Wuxi fund-raising scheme, was the first to crack. In early April, with questions being asked about his villas, his jewelry, and his mistresses, he asked his driver to take him to a sparsely populated part of Beijing's northern Huairou county. After climbing halfway up the peat brown stubble of a remote hillside, he took out a handgun and shot himself in the head.

The suicide probably made the house of cards collapse faster than it otherwise might have. The "miserable end" to Wang's life, as Wei Jianxing, the party's chief anti-corruption investigator, would call it, dislodged most of the remaining supports holding up the crumbling Chen System.[11] In an almost comical attempt to save his skin, Chen Xitong showed up at a party conference on morality a week later and made seven references to Jiang's leadership in a ten-minute address.[12] After watching him wriggle and squirm for another two weeks, Jiang ordered Chen detained and taken to the seaside resort of Beidaihe on 26 April.[13]

The Politburo standing committee member with special responsibility for the capital, Hu Jintao, was "entrusted" with explaining the reasons for the purge to Beijing cadres the next day. On one side of him sat Wei Jianxing, the party discipline inspector who would take over as the city's acting party secretary. On the other sat Zeng Qinghong, Jiang's chief political advisor. If there had been any doubt that Jiang was behind the move, it was dispelled by the prominent and unexplained appearance of Zeng, who was called a "responsible person from a relevant central department."[14]

The official explanation at first was that Chen had resigned to atone for Wang's crimes. But by July, Chen had been placed under investigation for corruption, and in September he became the first Politburo member in Communist China's history to be expelled for corruption—in his case, totaling U.S.$24 million. After sitting in detention in Inner Mongolia for two more years, Chen was expelled from the party and handed over for criminal prosecution on charges of embezzlement and dereliction of duty. He was the highest party official to stand trial since the Gang of Four in 1980. His mistress, He Ping, fled the country. His playboy son, Chen Xiaotong, was given a 12-year jail term for taking bribes and misusing public funds.

Each of the pieces of wreckage from the collapsed Chen System was separately dragged off and examined in detail. Zhou Beifang drew a suspended death sentence. Li Min got a life term. And Chen Jian got fifteen years. A few were executed, including Deng Bin, the hapless woman who had run the Wuxi fund-raising scam, and Guan Zhicheng, the former party chief at Capital Iron and Steel, who had tried to protect Zhou Beifang. Dozens more middle and senior-ranking cadres in Beijing were sacked, disciplined, and even charged for living high off the Chen System. Although attempts were made to separate these officials from the work of the city in general, the impression given was that the place was rotten to the core.

Jiang's stature gained markedly from the expulsion of Chen and his cronies from Beijing, the nation's showcase to the world. Like Mao before him, Jiang had taken radical action to disabuse the capital of its independent kingdom mentality. "This amply demonstrates that the third-generation collective leadership under Jiang Zemin is strong and powerful," the official China News Service wrote.[15]

The success of the purge could be attributed to two factors. In the first place, Jiang was not alone in wanting to crack the Chen System. Wei Jianxing, for one, had clearly been trying to get at the top leadership for several years. The immediate expressions of support from the army, the State Council, and the National People's Congress for once were probably genuine.[16] Secondly, there was widespread public support for the removal of Chen. Although the party reiterated his "contributions" to suppressing the Tiananmen movement, popular opinion detested Chen for this same reason and many others, including his broken pledge to jump from one of Beijing's highest buildings if the city failed to win the 2000 Olympics.

There is a small irony here; Jiang partly owed his job to Chen, who, along with Li Peng, had succeeded in labeling the 1989 protests as "counterrevolutionary." The result had been that Deng was compelled to dump Zhao Ziyang and install Jiang as his successor. But that was the past, and Jiang was not a sentimental man. "The Central Committee took charge of the cases of Wang and Chen, receiving a positive response both inside and outside the party," Jiang boasted in his first public statement on the purge. "As a result, the anti-corruption effort is now being carried out more extensively."[17]

The removal of Chen Xitong and friends was also significant in that there is no evidence that Jiang sought Deng's advice or approval. Unlike in the purge of Yang Baibing in late 1992, in this case Jiang acted independently of the second generation of party elders. He sought and received support from the current leadership and that was enough.

The almost plodding nature of the purge, which took three years by the time everyone had been charged or let go, also suggested a political maturity not common in the early years of the People's Republic. To have allowed Chen Xitong and Zhou Beifang to sit accused for so long before their cases were concluded suggested a placid confidence that contrasted greatly with the dog-eat-dog infighting under Mao. Jiang never allowed the purge to seem like a personal vendetta against Chen. Official statements talked of the "dissolute lives" of Wang and Chen, but neither Jiang nor any other senior leader descended to adding personal insults. When a novel appeared based on the case, which vividly described the corruption in Beijing, it was banned.[18] It was exactly the kind of dull, bureaucratic politics that Jiang excelled at; not a charismatic rout of enemies, but a dispassionate culling of those who had crossed the lines of acceptability.

When Jiang finally made an emperor-like inspection tour of the capital in late 1995, a sign that the palace purge had run its course, he spoke of the "profound lesson" to be learned from the case. "Comrades working in the Beijing municipality should take the initiative in increasing communications with central government departments, giving reports to them, and consulting them more frequently," he said.[19] Several changes were made to prevent the reemergence of another independent kingdom on Jiang's doorstep. A new Capital Planning and Construction Committee was set up to monitor building in the city, headed by State Councilor Luo Gan. Its first act was to scale back the size of the Oriental Plaza. The municipal people's congress was given sweeping new powers to vet the city budget, from which U.S.$2.1 billion had been found to be missing in the wake of the purge. And Jia Qinglin, the governor of Fujian province, was brought in to replace Li Qiyan as mayor, and later party secretary, completing the cleanup of the Chen System.

It remained only for McDonald's to close its 700-seat restaurant and move a little farther up Wangfujing street. After taking a U.S.$12 million payoff for its troubles, the company obliged and vacated in favor of the wrecking balls in December 1996. By that time, the Beijing purge was already passing into history. But Jiang would continue to reap the political rewards of his bold and ultimately successful first strike as the unfettered leader of the third generation.

3

While Jiang could readily chalk up victory over the independent kingdom in the Beijing municipality, it was trickier to romp to victory over the independent kingdom on the lush, mountainous island of Taiwan, about 112 miles off the southeast coast of China. Settled en masse in 1949 by the fleeing remnants of the Nationalist army, the "Republic of China" on Taiwan had long upheld the myth of being the legitimate ruler of all China. But after losing China's United Nations seat to Beijing in 1971, Taiwan's claim rang increasingly hollow, and the number of countries according it diplomatic recognition plummeted to fewer than thirty. As the country moved rapidly toward full democracy and a robust sense of its own identity in the 1980s, the myth also began to crumble within Taiwan. By early 1995, a quarter of the population advocated full independence from the mainland, even though Beijing threatened to go to war to retake the island if it edged closer to an outright declaration of independence.[20]

Reunification with Taiwan was one of the issues where Deng Xiaoping, for all his achievements on domestic and other diplomatic fronts, had made little headway. His elucidation of the "one country, two systems" concept to be implemented in Hong Kong after 1997 as a model for reunification with Taiwan was rejected outright by the government in Taipei. With its strong patriotic overtones, it was an obvious issue for Jiang to make his own.

Jiang also had a personal interest in relations with the rival regime. He had begun his working life in a Nationalist-owned factory in Shanghai and defended it against feared evacuation when the Nationalists fled to Taiwan. During his years in Shanghai, he had also made several friends in Taiwan whose families were originally from the city. One of his middle school classmates had even become the chairman of one of Taiwan's biggest car makers.[21] By 1995, Jiang also had the wherewithal to make policy initiatives on the Taiwan issue. He had taken over the party's leading group on Taiwan affairs and his longtime mentor, Wang Daohan, had been put in charge of Beijing's cross-strait contact group, the Association for Relations Across the Taiwan Strait (ARATS). (The two governments could never agree on conditions for direct talks.)

What were Jiang's views on the Taiwan issue? In a revealing series of three discussions between 1990 and 1992 with Shen Chun-shan (Shen Junshan), a researcher at the official National Unification Council of Taiwan, Jiang revealed a burning desire to see the defiant island return to the fold of mainland China.[22] "My generation and the last generation have suffered a lot," Jiang told Shen, who was always the gentleman in their lengthy conversations despite the sometimes belligerent tone Jiang adopted. "The Chinese people stood up only with great difficulties. Now we should unify the whole people to make things perfect."[23] Jiang had little new to offer in Beijing's negotiating stance. Taiwan must accept Beijing as the central government responsible for all foreign affairs of China. "Only if I am able to occupy exactly the same position that I occupy now could we say that it was one nation, one state, one central government," he said.[24] Military force to achieve reunification could not be ruled out, he added, because of the activities of Taiwan's independence forces and foreign governments in arming the island. "This is not aimed at the people of Taiwan," he said.

Most prominent in Jiang's discourses was a sense of urgency. Partly, he said, this was driven by the rapid social and economic changes in Taiwan, which were flinging it farther from the orbit of China. More immediate was pressure he was getting from unnamed party elders, as he revealed to Shen:

> A lot of our old comrades are anxious. They want to see us sit down and talk a little sooner. . . . A few days ago, a group of comrades about to retire sent me an urgent letter. They said that when they entered the party in their youth,

it was to build socialism and to unite the country. Now they're about to retire and find the Taiwan issue is still not resolved. They said they would not
give it up. We had a lot of discussions about this letter internally. In general,
the consensus was that we could not let the issue drag on. At the very least,
we have to sit down and begin direct talks.[25]

In the years after he met Shen, the Taiwan issue slowly, almost imperceptibly, moved to the top of the Chinese Communists' policy
agenda. Again, both developments in Taiwan and increasing impatience
by old cadres in China were to blame. As part of a wide-ranging military modernization begun in the early 1990s, Taiwan had secured deals
to buy 60 Mirage fighters from France and another 150 F-16 fighters
from the United States. Also on order from the two countries were new
anti-missile defense systems, frigates, and anti-aircraft missiles. The
buildup suggested that Taipei was readying for a possible invasion
should the island's domestic politics continue to advance toward a
recognition of de facto independence from China. There were also
mounting concerns in Beijing that Taiwan's native-born Nationalist
president since 1988, Lee Teng-hui, favored independence, despite an
avowed desire for reunification. This was problematic in itself, but all
the more so because Beijing was pinning its hopes on holding direct
talks with Lee, who might be ousted by an even more independence-ori-
ented Nationalist leader in future. A PLA-run think tank warned of the
loss of the island in a 1994 book entitled *Taiwan neng duli ma?* (Can
Taiwan Achieve Independence?),[26] and the growing tensions created a
ready market in Taiwan for books like Zheng Langping's *Yi jiu jiu wu
run ba yue* (T-Day: Warning of Taiwan Strait War), a blow-by-blow pre-
diction of a mainland invasion in mid 1995, which was a best-seller
throughout 1994.[27] "There are lots of books like this on the market in
Taiwan. I have not read any of them," Jiang sniffed when presented
with a copy of *Yi jiu jiu wu run ba yue* in late 1994. "I am the chairman
of the Central Military Commission, and I am not aware of such plans.
So how could they exist?"[28]

In this already charged atmosphere, Jiang suggested that a new proposal should be put to Taipei for immediate reunification talks. Probably, the pressure of party elders and the army was a critical reason for
the new initiative. Planning for the new proposal was led by Jiang in his
role as head of the party's leading group on Taiwan affairs. But it was
by no means a solo effort. The plan underwent "repeated study, discussion, and revision" in senior party and army ranks before being eventually agreed on.[29] The consensus-based nature of the effort would be

emphasized a year later when Li Peng presided over the first anniversary of its announcement.

The Taiwan issue figured prominently when Jiang held his second meeting with U.S. president Bill Clinton at the November 1994 summit of countries of the Asia-Pacific Economic Cooperation forum in Jakarta. The Chinese insisted on playing host to the meeting, renting the elaborately decorated great hall in the Jakarta International Convention Center and ensuring that their delegation of ten at the meeting was exactly one more than the number on the American side.[30] All the batik shirts and fragrant wood must have had some effect on the atmosphere, which was more cordial than at the previous encounter. The pair agreed to "a new constructive relationship" that would include high-level visits. But Jiang had one stern message: "Any stirring of the grass on the Taiwan issue will directly affect the feelings of the Chinese people," he warned. "In the event of foreign interference that creates a turbulent situation between China and Taiwan, we will by no means just sit and tolerate it."[31] That new tough-guy attitude on the Taiwan issue was obviously part of laying the groundwork for the renewed drive for reunification. Beijing rejected any third-party role in the cross-strait issue, which Taipei favored. That meant keeping the Americans at bay.

Jiang finally announced his "eight views and propositions" on reunification at the end of January 1995.[32] Much of what he said was old and tired, although the tone was mild. Experts in Taiwan carefully picked through the so-called Eight Points looking for implicit meaning in what was said, and in what was not. But the only patently new proposals were an offer of immediate talks to end the official state of war that still existed between the two sides and an invitation to Lee Teng-hui to visit the mainland if he would agree not to be called the "president of the Republic of China."

Even before Lee Teng-hui's belated response to the Eight Points speech, it was clear that Jiang would be snubbed. As the weeks dragged by, Taiwan officials buried their heads in calls for closer economic and cultural exchanges and did not respond directly to the speech. When Lee Teng-hui finally responded in early April, his message was a carefully crafted rejection of the Eight Points. While holding high the banners of nationalism and reunification, he rejected the two new proposals; he would only meet Jiang in a neutral third place, and no peace talks could begin until Beijing renounced the use of force to achieve reunification.

One can understand why Jiang felt angered at the response. The Eight Points had in many ways been his chance to win fame with a breakthrough in the long-stalemated cross-strait relationship. Although the timing probably owed partly to pressure from elders, it was also an opportune moment for him to make a start on one of the unresolved issues from the Deng era. Now he was at risk of shouldering the blame for making the Chinese Communists look silly.

The entire exercise might have been politely forgotten had it not been for a more serious snub to China. Lee Teng-hui, who had earned a Ph.D. in agricultural economics from Cornell University in 1968, had been invited to attend his college reunion at the school in Ithaca, New York, in early June 1995. His disingenuous application for a visa to attend was at first rejected by the United States, in line with an agreement not to have high-level contacts with Taiwan officials or in any way support the separation of China. Secretary of State Warren Christopher even personally informed Qian Qichen, the Chinese foreign minister, in April that a visa would not be granted because it would violate the bilateral agreements. Unfortunately, the U.S. Congress thought differently, voting 396 to 0 in the House of Representatives and 97 to 1 in the Senate to grant Lee the visa. Already stung for having sold human rights down the river by giving China Most Favored Nation trading status a year earlier, Clinton reversed administration policy and issued the visa in May. Jiang was furious, having been informed by Qian and the Chinese embassy in Washington that there would be no visa. China's defense minister, Chi Haotian, called off a planned trip to the United States, while the air force commander, Yu Zhenwu, cut short his American tour and returned home.

The visa and Lee's subsequent high-profile trip to Cornell meant two things: first, it confirmed in Chinese minds the U.S. role in supporting Taiwan's quest for international recognition. Second, it confirmed that Lee was all too insincere in his stated desire to improve cross-strait relations and begin reunification talks. His speech at Cornell, entitled "Always in My Heart," was a plaintive appeal for world recognition of Taiwan's separateness from the mainland.

Jiang was no hard-liner on the Taiwan issue. The tone of his Eight Points speech had been mild. But he had been forced into putting some kind of pressure on Taiwan by elders and possibly the military. Now his goodwill looked naive. Lee had brushed off the advances of one lover and rushed into the arms of another. Among the most angered parties in China was the army.

The PLA had a special interest in Taiwan because of long-standing fears that the island could become a base for U.S. planes in the event of a regional war. The rapid modernization of the Taiwan military had also awakened the slumbering PLA, which was seeing its eight-to-one advantage in ground forces eroded by more and better fighters and an emerging missile defense system in Taiwan. Lee Teng-hui's snubbing of the Eight Points and trip to the United States were more than anything just reminders to the PLA of its deteriorating military position. "The Taiwan government leaders have so far not made a positive response to President Jiang's Eight Points on peaceful reunification, but instead have further enhanced their independence activities," complained Senior Captain Lin Shuangqiao, head of the landing forces in the East Sea Fleet, which would be in charge of invading Taiwan in the event of war. "We must pay sufficient attention to this. The PLA is the loyal protector of the people's interests, unshakably dedicated to guarding the nation's sovereignty and territory."[33] Adding to the pressure were the senior generals in the PLA, many retired but still influential, who brought to this strategic concern an added sense of a historical mission to "liberate" Taiwan. Like the elders who Jiang said were pressuring him to speed up talks on reunification, these old brass would not let the issue drag on forever. Now Lee Teng-hui had too greatly tried their patience.

Once Lee concluded his successful trip to the United States, Jiang was under heavy pressure from a "very angry" senior leadership in the party and army to respond sternly.[34] It was decided to give up hopes of negotiations with Lee Teng-hui. In the meantime, a forceful "political, propaganda, and military" response was to be made to his alleged "separatist" actions. Chinese leaders took different views about which mixture of politics, propaganda, and military force to deploy. Qiao Shi, the chairman of the national parliament, for example, was the man behind a guns-blaring propaganda assault in two sets of scathing personal attacks on Lee issued jointly by Xinhua and the *People's Daily* in late July and early August.[35] Jiang, with his control over political organs, favored a mainly political response, while continuing to advocate a policy of "peaceful means as the norm" in dealing with the new tensions with Taiwan.[36] China's ambassador to the United States was recalled for two months beginning in June, while a planned historic second meeting between Wang Daohan, the head of China's cross-strait contact group, and his Taiwan counterpart, Koo Chen-fu, was canceled in mid June. In his first public statement on the issue in late June, Jiang warned that the United States would "eat its own bitter fruit" for allowing the Lee visit. "The United States has severely damaged the basis of Sino–U.S. relations," he said. "It is just natural that we have had strong reactions."[37]

But this was not enough to satisfy the army, which was demanding a military response. As early as March, two months after his Eight Points speech, Jiang had admitted for the first time that the military would play a role in scaring Taiwan into reunification talks. "The PLA will play an extremely important role in accomplishing reunification," he told restless army delegates at a closed-door meeting. "When the armed forces are further strengthened, there will be a greater possibility for peaceful reunification."[38] The obvious solution now was to allow that strength to be put on display in a show of military force in the Taiwan Strait. Jiang authorized the fireworks in early July. In an unprecedented announcement issued on 18 July, Xinhua, on behalf of the PLA, notified foreign vessels and aircraft that the army would conduct guided missile drills in the Taiwan Strait about 87 miles north of Taiwan at the end of the month. It would be the first time in a decade that the PLA lobbed missiles into the sea around Taiwan. A total of six medium-range M-9 surface-to-surface missiles were fired during the period from a base in inland Jiangxi province. The effects were felt in Taiwan immediately, the stock market plunged and panic rice-buying erupted in coastal towns close to the mainland.

A month later, the PLA was at it again, this time sending both anti-ship missiles and long-range artillery shells splashing into a large zone about 106 miles north of Taiwan. Both sets of missile tests seemed to simulate a blockade of the key northern port of Keelung, an overture to massive beach landings and inland helicopter drops of troops in most war scenarios. The PLA was still not finished. The missile tests were followed by two sets of combined-forces war games in the Taiwan Strait in October and November by the newly named Nanjing War Theater Command of the Nanjing military region. While less threatening in military terms than the missile tests, the circus-like combined-forces drills gave the PLA a chance to showcase its new equipment—such as hovercraft, tank landing craft, and helicopters—that would be used in an invasion of Taiwan.

Most important to Jiang, the October combined-forces drills gave him a perfect opportunity to "go to war" for the first time. As has been noted, Jiang's prestige in the army had always suffered because of his lack of war experience. Slipping on a green tunic every once in a while to attend an army meeting did little to change his image as an outsider. Now was his chance to be seen in a "war zone." Arriving at a military airport in Fujian province on the morning of 16 October, he was told to prepare to inspect a naval unit and an air force unit in the afternoon.[39] Foul weather caused the air force visit to be shortened, but the full regalia naval inspection went ahead as planned. Jiang stood in the back of a jeep while it drove slowly along a kilometer-long stretch of dock where crews stood at attention on frigates and escort vessels. The scene was clearly an attempt to evoke memories of similarly triumphal army inspections by Mao and Deng. In 1949, when Mao was about to enter Beijing to found the People's Republic, he stood in a captured American jeep and reviewed a brigade of Communist troops at a military airport in the city's western suburbs. In 1984, it was the turn of Deng, who reviewed a million PLA troops in Tiananmen Square standing in an open-top black sedan. In both cases, the troop reviews came a few years after their formal ascent to power and at a time when their self-confidence was brimming over. So too with Jiang. After six years as chairman of the military commission, he was finally able to stand with his troops in a warlike situation with little fear of exciting a revolt in the ranks. Their loyalty was now assured, and this caudillo-style review proved it.

The next day, Jiang was on board a command ship to watch a combined-forces operation at sea. Huddled behind a console on an exposed bridge, Jiang's head was distinguished by his flimsy beret amid all the stiff military caps. "The current situation has placed new demands on building the navy," he told military leaders as missiles zoomed overhead and fighters criss-crossed the sky. "We need to speed up modernization to ensure our marine defense and promote reunification with Taiwan."[40]

After the three-hour drill, a procession of planes and ships went past the command ship to take Jiang's salute. Then he was given a microphone to the loudspeakers on the command ship: "Hello, comrades!" he said, his voice trailing into the sea spray. "You're certainly working hard!" It was not exactly the stirring call to arms of an inspirational military commander. But the point was clear—Jiang was in the front line with his troops. "It was the first time in the navy's history that a military commission chairman personally led the military commission leadership to inspect naval troops and watch a maritime exercise," the official magazine *Liaowang* noted.[41]

It was probably just as well that Jiang chose not to repeat the feat by attending the November combined-forces landing drills off Fujian's Dongshan islands. U.S. satellite photos showed that three of the six days of planned drills had to be called off because of foul weather.[42] Taiwan spy planes observing the drills dipped in and out of the clouds with impunity, the hamstrung Chinese air force unable to chase them away.[43]

Despite the clumsy effort, the drills appeared to have paid off, at least insofar as they deterred Taiwan voters from supporting the island's pro-independence opposition in a national parliamentary poll in early December. The lost votes did not go to the pro-unification parties, however, but to the Nationalists, who swept 85 of 164 seats (52 percent) in the chamber.

The four consecutive sets of war games had, of course, been planned long before the tensions with Taiwan erupted.[44] But the uncomfortably close splash zones of the missiles and the unprecedented publicity for the landing and sea drills were decided on later and clearly had a political message. In Taiwan, in the United States, and in China itself, it was clear that the Chinese leadership headed by Jiang was prepared to go to war to prevent Taiwan moving any further toward de facto independence.

For Jiang, it was beginning to look as though yet another bad thing had been turned into a good thing. When his mild overtures to Taiwan were rebuffed, he had found himself besieged by angry party elders and army officers over the apparent setback in recovering Taiwan. The four sets of war games not only vented some of this anger, they had also given him a much-needed opportunity to go to war, in a manner of speaking.

The tensions with Taiwan sent China's ties with the United States into a downward spiral. Jiang accused Washington of running a "confusing and arrogant" policy toward China, saying that the administration could have prevented Lee Teng-hui's trip.[45] The harsh attacks prompted U.S. officials to deny Jiang a full-blown state visit to the United States when he was scheduled to be in New York for the fiftieth anniversary of the United Nations in October. He settled for a humiliating bilateral meeting with President Clinton at Lincoln Center. After the meeting, Jiang noted that the Taiwan issue remained "the most important and the most sensitive issue in Sino–U.S. relations."[46]

In handling relations with the United States, Jiang had to be mindful of the fact that simple bullying and intimidation would not work, as they had been seen to in the case of Taiwan. Not only would the United States respond in kind, but the very fact of poor relations between the United States and China would be viewed in Beijing as an undesirable outcome, no matter what the reason. In the case of Taiwan, poor relations were seen in some circles as a sign of strength, displayed with pride, like Prussian generals comparing fencing scars.

Two more drills were planned in the Taiwan Strait to immediately precede the 23 March 1996 presidential election on the island: a test of four intercontinental missiles, which landed pincer-like around Taiwan's two

main ports, Keelung in the north and Kaohsiung in the south; and another combined-forces war game involving 150,000 troops along the
Chinese coast between Xiamen and Shantou, which put on display new
Russian-built submarines. But at the same time, Jiang and other Chinese
leaders sought to portray an improving Sino–U.S. relationship.[47]

The U.S. reaction to this two-faced policy was bellicose. "They are
miscalculating," Assistant Secretary of State for Asian Affairs Winston
Lord said in mid March 1996, just as Congress passed a nonbinding resolution demanding U.S. intervention in support of Taiwan if China invaded. "They've already suffered damage through their actions" and had
"probably ensured" Lee Teng-hui's re-election as Taiwan president, he
said.[48] The concrete expression of the stern U.S. response was the massing south of the Taiwan Strait of the biggest American naval armada
since the end of the Vietnam War. The group of ships built around the
carrier USS *Independence* was sent to the region in mid March, and it
was joined by the *Nimitz* group later in the month. "America has the
best damned navy in the world, and no one should ever forget that," the
U.S. defense secretary, William Perry, said in Washington as the ships
took up their positions. "Beijing should know—and this [armada] will
remind them—that . . . the premier, the strongest military power in the
Western Pacific is the United States."[49]

Chinese generals leapt to pick up the rhetorical gauntlet, threatening
to deal the carriers "a head-on blow" if they interfered in the cross-strait
crisis.[50] Several official editorials in the mainland press made it clear that
the March exercises and missile drills were aimed at warning off Taiwan
independence forces. "Our troops are keeping a close watch on the
movements on the opposite side of the strait," the *People's Daily* said.
"We should never be indifferent to the increasingly rampant muddy
stream of the Taiwan independence movement or let it move along."[51]

The coming of the presidential election and associated local elections
on 23 March was probably a relief for all three sides. Not since the mutual bombardments of the 1950s had the strait come so apparently close
to war, with the United States right in the middle. Each side could find
solace in the election results. Lee Teng-hui—who had been depicted in a
mural on a Taipei building as a caped crusader, deflecting incoming missiles with his bare hands—swept to victory as president for four more
years, with 54 percent of the popular vote. Beijing's vituperative personal
attacks on him had been fruitless, perhaps even counterproductive. As
they had during the December parliamentary elections, however, voters
also rejected the pro-independence candidate of the main opposition

party, who won only 21 percent of the vote, compared to a combined 25 percent for the two staunchly pro-unification candidates. Beijing hailed this as a rebuff to the advocates of independence. "Taiwan residents share the view that the only way out for Taiwan is to develop relations across the Taiwan Strait," Xinhua said the day after the election.[52]

Beijing's self-consoling reaction to the Taiwan election results elicited comparisons with the wretched young man Ah Q, portrayed by Chinese writer Lu Xun in a 1921 short story of the same name. A symbol of Chinese national failings, Ah Q constantly deluded himself that he had won a brilliant victory each time he was humiliated by others. Humiliation certainly seemed the order of the day for Beijing as Lee Teng-hui gained victory. But for Jiang himself, the results of the year-long dustup with Taiwan were not all bad. He could claim at home to have led his troops into battle against separatist forces in Taiwan, which had had the effect of curtailing the overseas visits of the island's leaders and denying the opposition party electoral gains.

Ties with the United States would remain a perennial bugbear for Beijing after the Taiwan affair died down. Jiang, as much as any other Chinese leader, and the country at large, was torn between love and hatred of the United States. He was also highly suspicious of the motives of the American "engagement" policy toward China; the Taiwan affair had shown it to be a way of dressing up Washington's blatantly imperialist "containment" strategy borne of the Cold War. "Is this not actual containment?" he asked a private meeting in late 1995. "Of course, it is all done in the name of high-sounding objectives, and it is correct to say that the United States does not want to break with China. But the issue is that . . . the two tactics are similarly tough. Is there really any difference between shadowboxing and the real thing?"[53]

While Jiang could claim to have cauterized the Taiwan independence forces and responded with proper indignation to U.S. intervention, the whole affair had also laid bare his lack of control over the military. After cold water was poured on his offer of peace talks in the Eight Points, Jiang appeared to lose the initiative on the Taiwan issue. Months after the Taiwan election, Lee would tell *Newsweek* magazine that while Jiang seemed "quite reasonable compared to the others" in the Chinese leadership, it would be "very difficult" for him to implement his Eight Points "because he has no control over the military."[54]

Jiang would make several attempts to refute the accusation, the most forthright in a meeting with Japanese politicians a month after the Taiwan election. It was he who had thrust the sword skyward to order missile drills to be continued after the U.S. armada moved into the strait in March, he asserted. "The military drills were demonstrations of our position on Taiwan's independence and foreign interference," he huffed. "Why were foreign aircraft carriers dispatched in response to military drills within our own territory?"[55] In the same talk, however, Jiang's nervous tone suggested a feeling of insecurity on the issue. "I am sorry I am speaking excitedly," he told the Japanese delegation, wiping his brow with a washcloth. "I cannot help getting excited. I have experienced the [civil] war and witnessed too many tragedies." As they filed out, he repeated the apology. "I spoke a little loudly today. I did not do so on purpose. Thinking of the past, I unconsciously become emotional." Jiang would also play victorious commander by making a special trip to Shanghai in May 1996 to commend the troops. The drills, he said, "fully demonstrated China's resolve and ability to safeguard national sovereignty and national reunification."[56]

But the overwhelming impression was of Jiang following rather than leading the army into battle against Taiwan. The entire affair elevated the role of the PLA in the Taiwan issue to a level it had not enjoyed since the 1950s. Although he headed the party's leading group on Taiwan, this suddenly seemed less important than his chairmanship of the military commission. Still, if he could hold on tight enough, he could ride the PLA's indignation to gain greater say over the Taiwan issue as military commission chairman. It was a risky and entirely opportunistic way to salvage his hopes of becoming the "reunification president"—of achieving what Deng had not. His initial approach, endorsed by the party, of offering peace had now come full circle to threats of war. The carrot had failed and the stick was brandished.

As tensions subsided in the year after the Taiwan presidential election, it became clear that the stick would not achieve quick results either. Taiwan was one independent kingdom that Jiang could not bring to heel so easily.

4

One of the quaint pleasures of strolling through the old lanes that line the canalways in Jiang's hometown of Yangzhou is coming across barbershops that could have been featured in a Norman Rockwell painting.

Amid the pottery and tea stalls are scattered an astonishing number of Western-style barbershops, complete with large leather and metal swivel chairs made in Shanghai and uniformed male staff trained in the old school of men's hair styling, with warm shaving cream and hot towels.

Partly, this is a legacy spread upriver from the Shanghai of the 1920s and 1930s, where Western-style barbershops were common. But it also harks back to a native tradition in Yangzhou. The city has been known since the Sui dynasty (A.D. 581–618) for its "three blades": the blades used in cooking, in foot care, and in hair cutting, three skills at which the locals excelled. "The skill of Yangzhou barbers is well known," a local tourist pamphlet boasts. "They represent one of the four great branches of the barber profession in China, and in terms of professional skills are perhaps the best of the four."[57]

Growing up in a sophisticated family in the city, Jiang no doubt availed himself of these skills. A Yangzhou male's attention to the state of his hair was as natural as his attention to dress or deportment. Jiang, of course, was particularly sensitive about his personal image. To borrow the description of a character in Proust: "The arrangement of his hair was a matter of anxious deliberation. In his twofold preoccupation with his profile and his reputation, he had always to make sure that it was so brushed as to give him the air at once of a lion and of a philosopher."[58]

Jiang's long hair, it will be recalled, had become a subject of contention during the Cultural Revolution, when he was forced, against the advice of his local barber in Wuhan, to get a brush cut. That was no doubt a cruel fate for one whose upbringing had instilled into him a sense of the importance of a well-oiled, flowing mane. Jiang grew it long again the moment he was rehabilitated. With the aid of black dye, oil and, some say, tonics, Jiang managed to maintain a thinning but still ample head of hair throughout the 1980s and 1990s. "On public occasions, Jiang wears neat, back-combed black hair with a pair of wide-rimmed spectacles," his official biography says.[59]

As a state leader, Jiang thought nothing of combing his hair in public and always took care to ensure that his locks were in order before any photographs were taken. While touring a Beijing middle school in late 1995, for example, he delayed a photograph with the students so that he could attend to his coiffure. "First I shall have to set my hair in good order," he explained to the giggling students.[60] Some saw in Jiang's habit of grooming in public suggestions of ostentation or even dandyism. Others thought it a reflection of his deep-seated nervousness about his appearance. The habit may indeed reflect some sense of inferiority, as psychologists have suggested.[61] But there may be equally important historical reasons for the habit—namely, Jiang's upbringing in a city abounding in skilled barbers, his university days in Shanghai, and the humiliation of having had to part with most of his hair to survive the Cultural Revolution.

At home in China, the habit was of little concern. No one would dare to comment unfavorably. Nor would the heavily controlled media be so bold as to print or broadcast an image of Jiang primping, a sure invitation to shutdown or punishment. But the world outside was different, as Jiang discovered. His habit had first come to international attention at the 1993 national parliament meeting, when the French news agency Agence France-Presse, and much of the Hong Kong media, caught him and his little comb in the act on the huge podium. The photograph was broadcast to the delight of newspapers around the world and to the consternation of the Chinese Foreign Ministry. Then in late 1995, Jiang was caught again, this time by TV cameras while attending the UN's fiftieth anniversary celebrations in New York.

The two incidents should have been ample warning that Jiang's public hair-combing habit, whatever its reasons, had to stop. His image as an aspiring international statesman was at risk. But it failed to draw the attention of his minders and spin doctors, like Zeng Qinghong, or even that of his timid wife, Wang Yeping. Either no one in Jiang's entourage realized that it was unbecoming behavior in a head of state or else no one dared to tell him as much. The oversight eventually came back to haunt Jiang, and China.

In the wake of the Taiwan crisis, China's attempt to project a powerful and credible image abroad took on added importance. Jiang made two major trips in mid 1996, to Africa and to Europe, aimed at countering support for Taiwan in these areas. In Africa, which accounted for a mere 1 percent of China's foreign trade, Jiang could easily win friends by dishing out aid in exchange for pledges to refrain from developing closer ties with Taiwan. But in Europe he faced a more implacable audience. Sympathies for Taiwan ran high, especially in the two Western European countries he would visit, Spain and Norway. Jiang needed to show that he was a sophisticated and dignified statesman, not an unruly terrorist, as the war games near Taiwan had suggested to many.

Spain was his first stop. King Juan Carlos, always the gracious host, turned up for the welcoming ceremony on 24 June. In broad daylight, as the two men chatted prior to the review of an honor guard in Madrid,

Jiang instinctively reached for his comb. Shutters began clicking furiously. Juan Carlos appeared startled. But Jiang did not cotton on, even continuing to talk to the king as he readied himself for the world press. But the press already had its photo. "China's 'Strong Man' in Madrid!" ran the banner headline the next day in the popular *El Pais* newspaper beside a photograph of Jiang smoothing back his hair with one hand as he ran the comb from front to back with the other. Here was the belligerent commander in chief who had threatened Taiwan with invasion showing himself to be both impolite and a bit of a dandy. "The Controversial Image of the Chinese President!" read the headline caption in *El Mundo*.[62] The same photographs appeared in newspapers around the world and would become standard fare in articles on Jiang and the Chinese leadership. The Chinese delegation were furious. Foreign Minister Qian Qichen skipped a promised press briefing the next day. Jiang gave a promised interview to *El Pais*, but he prohibited the accompanying photographer from capturing him sipping tea, presumably to prevent further ridicule.

The Madrid incident caused much hand-wringing among the overseas Chinese intellectual community. "Is modern China so wrought by wars, famines, and internal strife that we don't even have time to behave properly, overlooking politeness in all our troubles?" asked one commentator.[63] Another, Yan Jiaqi, a former political advisor to Zhao Ziyang, called the incident a revelation of Jiang's inferiority complex and his sensitivity to criticism: "Not even Qian Qichen dares tell him to stop," Yan wrote.[64]

Such behavior suggested to the world that China's leaders of the 1990s were little different from the peasant warriors who had founded the People's Republic. Some Chinese intellectuals bemoaned the damage done to their national image abroad by the persistence of such habits as clipping one's nails or spitting in public. They said Jiang's gesture recalled the Chinese military commander and statesman Li Hongzhang, who in the late nineteenth century was known for his habit of ejecting huge gobs of phlegm onto the freshly cleaned carpets of state buildings everywhere from France to Japan.

The Madrid embarrassment *did* seem to get the message across, though. If no one in Jiang's entourage had dared tell him before, the international press had now done so. Jiang's public grooming ceased, although he still carried the comb and would disappear to prepare in private if a photograph was imminent.

It had taken a gross infraction of the norms of statesmanlike behavior for Jiang to be told, or to realize, where he was erring. The episode told a good deal about the isolation of the Chinese leaders, about Jiang's sensitivity about his appearance and to personal ridicule, and about the heightened importance attached to China's international image in the wake of the Taiwan crisis. With Taiwan winning world sympathy for bravely forging ahead with democratization while China's one-party rulers terrorized the island by hurling missiles into the Taiwan Strait, this negative publicity came at a bad time. For all the gains Jiang had made at home over the Taiwan crisis, his image on the world stage still left much to be desired.

CHAPTER 10

Jiang Thought

I

In the late summer of 1996, Jiang called together a group of eight leading historians from Beijing and Tianjin to a seaside seminar on history and development at the Beidaihe retreat.[1] Each was asked to prepare a paper on some aspect of recent Chinese or world history. With echoes of former British Prime Minister Margaret Thatcher's frequent convocation of academic seminars, Jiang held court in the breezy hillside villa where the scholars gathered, interrupting freely, as was his wont. Li Wenhai from People's University of China in Beijing spoke on famines and social stability in recent Chinese history. His colleague, Dai Yi, described tensions in China's minority areas. Gong Shuduo from Beijing Normal University outlined the recent "revolution" in Chinese society. Others covered topics like China's relations with the United States and Russia, and the relationship between capitalism and cultural vitality. After dinner, they all went swimming together to wash away the day's exertions.

Despite his academic leanings, the gathering was not just for Jiang's own edification. A package of the papers, nine in total, was printed by the party central office and distributed to every cadre in the country in charge of a government department or higher, several thousand in all. On the title page was printed "In accordance with Jiang Zemin's instructions"—meaning that the package was to be read. "I know you're all busy," Jiang wrote in a preface, "but we still have to set aside some time to study."

By the mid 1990s, there was a sense among many in China, not just those on the left, that the "stability" of the period since the Tiananmen massacre masked a terrible underlying current. A decline in public morality, in national self-esteem, and in party and state control was felt to be slowly eating away at the corpus of Communist China like a cancer. The official Xinhua news agency, for the first time anyone could remember such a forthright criticism, alleged in a May 1995 report that "even though the market economics propounded by Deng Xiaoping have won the support of the Chinese people, complaints about the fall in moral standards have increased day by day." Some of the most serious problems facing the West had begun to appear in China, it said, including the "disappearance of social norms, the death of morals, and the disintegration of traditional values."[2] A survey of 2,000 households in forty cities by the State Economic Reform Commission seemed to confirm the warning: "The level of people's satisfaction with the reforms has continued to fall year by year," it said, while "demands for a greater sense of security have clearly risen."[3]

It was reformist China's turn to be riven by angst. If the 1980s had been an era when every new foreign soft drink and every stirring tale of a successful entrepreneur had excited general squeals of joy, the 1990s were the onset of a less breathless period, at least in the cities. The *Weltschmerz* that settled on Chinese urbanites found expression in everything from nostalgia for the Maoist era to a religious revival that the party found hard to contain. Jiang's purpose in calling together the scholars at Beidaihe in the summer of 1996 was to address this pervasive feeling of moral and political crisis. Adding some historical perspective to the concerns, he hoped, would help allay fears that China was headed for disaster. "If you don't understand history, especially modern Chinese history, you'll never get a handle on the principles governing the development of our society," he said shortly before the conclave.[4]

As mentioned at the beginning of chapter 9, Jiang was at this time being forced to provide a vision of China's future by both the political necessity of putting a personal stamp on his own reign and the historical necessity of making a successful transition from the Marxist-Leninist state. That future would probably look something like a "developmental dictatorship," a strong, politically authoritarian state, but with a notable degree of social and economic freedom. Jiang's handling of high-level corruption in Beijing and his beating of the patriotic drum over Taiwan were among the earliest instances where his vision was put into practice. Now, a national sense of unease afforded him with the opportunity to further trumpet his vision of China's future.

It was an urgent need. The underlying sense of national despair in the mid 1990s was already feeding an alternative vision on the left that might pose a threat to Jiang if allowed to gain adherents. In mid 1995, leftist writers associated with the former party propaganda chief Deng Liqun had circulated among Politburo members a lengthy tract, written in dark and cataclysmic prose, that warned of several threats to Communist rule, all of them resulting from Deng's opening and reform policies.[5] The laundry list of the so-called Ten Thousand Character Document, formally titled "Certain Factors Affecting China's National Security," was nothing new. It included the declining role of the state sector in the national economy, the rise of a capitalist class, increasing Western as well as Hong Kong and Taiwan cultural influences, and the weakening of the party's role in everyday life. It made no mention of Jiang, aside from an opening sentence to the effect that his policies since 1989, although "correct," had failed to resolve the problems they were supposed to address. The conclusion minced no words: "If these things are not rectified now, the number of people supporting the party and government will probably fall, while the number in opposition or taking a neutral stand will be bound to rise. When a political storm comes, and we find ourselves in an unfavorable position, it may be too late to reverse the situation."

The tract's plea for a return to the pre-reform era, which tapped a general nostalgia for the 1950s in the country, outraged many liberals. The liberal economist Cao Siyuan, for example, who had been detained for a year after the Tiananmen massacre for siding with the protesters, fumed that the document "totally repudiates the political, economic and organizational lines pursued over the past seventeen years, stirring up ideological confusion among people who fear state policy will turn to the left."[6] If the veer to the left came about, Cao warned, "this document will go down in history as the battle cry for the second Cultural Revolution, an 'honor' it would fully deserve."

More interesting was the repudiation of the tract by Deng's eldest son, Deng Pufang. Once a tall, dashing young man, with a Clark Gable–like wisp of a mustache, Pufang had attempted suicide by leaping from a fourth-story chemistry lab window in 1968 after being hounded by Red Guards. The jump left him wheelchair-bound and chubby. His visceral hatred of the left could be taken as read. "Invariably when problems crop up, some people begin to doubt the [party's] basic line," he said in a speech to the China Disabled Persons' Federation in July 1996.[7] Those who "blindly follow the 'leftist' trend of thought," he said, "cannot adapt themselves to the new mode of [income] distribution because they are still deeply influenced by absolute egalitarianism and cannot understand the reforms." He went on: "Some people say the flourishing private sector is a great danger because it may shake the foundations of socialism. In the past, we practiced the large-scale, collective system of people's communes. Did it work? Why can't we develop an economy other than a public ownership system? . . . All enterprises in the former Soviet Union were state-owned enterprises, but they failed in the end!"

The Ten Thousand Character Document, and the indignant liberal reaction it provoked, led to obvious questions about where, if anywhere, Jiang would lead the country.[8] In many ways, he sat squarely between the two camps. He had no interest either in unseating economic development as the party's top priority or in slowing the reforms. But he did sympathize with some of the noneconomic ideas on the left reflected by the Ten Thousand Character Document.

In breaking out from under the shadow of the ailing Deng, Jiang could not reverse the economic or diplomatic policies that the patriarch had set in motion. These were roundly supported and working well. Instead, Jiang set himself the task of addressing some of the things that Deng had left undone, or had let slip. A few of these areas—the fight against corruption and Taiwan reunification—have already been touched upon. They were the simple tasks, where all could agree that "more should be done."

Deng had paid lip service to other issues, such as upholding public morality, promoting Chinese culture and strengthening the organization and discipline of the party. But making long speeches on such issues that could be quoted by posterity was different from actually tackling them. For all his wide-ranging discussions, Deng in the end had worked hardest on rescuing China's economy and its international relations from the abyss into which they had fallen during the Cultural Revolution. The country had been held together by rising standards of living and the occasional sharp crackdown on dissent.

In Jiang's vision, the economy would no longer constitute China's be-all and end-all. "It's not that Jiang has gone off the Deng track, it's just that his focus is a little different," *Jing bao* explained.[9] This realignment of policy priorities was partly intended to head off the gathering leftist forces.[10] But it also reflected Jiang's own vision of the "developmental dictatorship" that China would become. "We should not get immersed in day-to-day work and forget political work," he said in mid 1995. "And at no time and under no circumstances should we try to seek economic development at the expense of ethics."[11]

As early as 1991, when debate raged at the top levels of the party about fears of capitalism, Jiang had marked out a philosophy distinct from Deng's, which encouraged both economic development *and* ideological integrity. These two, he said, were "two sides of the same coin" and "must not be set against each other." That centrist philosophy, dormant for the intervening period of Deng's southern tour and its aftermath, now came together in a more coherent set of proposals by Jiang. From late 1995 through to the end of 1996, Jiang outlined his new vision, in which political and ideological issues would be put on an equal footing with economic issues. Aided by his advisors Zeng Qinghong and Teng Wensheng, Liu Ji, and a new face, Wang Huning, Jiang would articulate a vision to remedy the "complaints" of the Deng era. "Jiang Thought" would be born.

2

The first plank of Jiang Thought was laid down at a party plenum in September 1995. The speech called on cadres to "pay attention to politics" (*jiang zhengzhi*), a moderated but clear echo of Mao's slogan "emphasize politics" (*tuchu zhengzhi*). Jiang's brand of politics was different from Mao's. For Mao, politics had meant class struggle and rooting out the "feudal" culture of the pre-1949 era. For Jiang, it meant making the party work better: less official corruption, less bickering between the central and local governments, and higher ideological standards for cadres. In short, a less dysfunctional party-led state. "Our central task is economic development, but we must have political guarantees to back that up," he said. "It just won't do if we don't pay attention to politics."[12]

Coming at around the same time as the Ten Thousand Character Document appeared, Jiang's "pay attention to politics" speech sparked fears that he was caving in to the leftists. Partly these were fueled by the applause that Jiang's new battle cry won from the left, which called his remarks "important and timely."[13] But there were also genuine concerns that even the slightest deviation from the preeminence of economic issues would be undesirable. "This has nothing to do with paying attention to economics [*jiang jingji*] and nothing to do with paying attention to raising people's standards of living [*jiang renmin shenghuo zhiliang de tigao*]," the liberal Politburo standing committee member Li Ruihuan remarked caustically of Jiang's new slogan while in Guangdong province in early 1996.[14] "Just because a few flies and mosquitoes have come through the springtime window of reform doesn't mean we should return to the long winter of the past," Li added.

With confusion reigning about exactly what "paying attention to politics" would entail, Jiang was forced to make several clarifications, some would say climbdowns, throughout 1996. "The requirement to pay attention to politics will absolutely not affect economic development. We do not have any intention of replacing economic work with political work," he assured the nation.[15] Instead, Jiang said, he was taking aim at what he awkwardly termed "economy-ism" (*jingji zhuyi*), namely, completely discarding party and ideological dogma in the pursuit of growth.[16] "We shall closely integrate politics with economic and other work so that they can proceed in a more orderly manner along the right path," he said.[17] No political campaigns, no struggle sessions, but also no forgetting that the party was in charge and that its role would not diminish.

The moderation of the campaign showed the limits to Jiang's ability to tinker with Deng's sacred assertion of economic development above all else. "Paying attention to politics is not meant to correct 'excesses' of the reforms," *Wen Wei Po* assured its readers, "but to help us reform even better."[18]

Within the party, the "pay attention to politics" campaign was an obvious way for Jiang to consolidate his personal authority, just as the Cultural Revolution had been used by Mao. Several mainland commentators spoke of how Jiang was "developing his sources of political capital" through the campaign.[19] As evidence, it emerged that the purge of the Beijing municipal leadership was the first instance in which Jiang had appealed to the slogan in internal speeches to ensure that there was no dissent.[20] It helped ensure that the purge went off without a hitch, despite the entrenched interests involved.

New cadre selection rules that emphasized stricter political and ideological standards were another result. The party's Organization Department had concluded in early 1996 that nearly 40 percent of cadres promoted to department- or bureau-level posts and above in the 1990s suffered from "serious political and economic work-style problems." As a consequence, it said, "they have no base of support among the people."[21] Jiang's response was to impose new criteria on cadres who were to be promoted into positions that would see them into the next century.[22] These included the requirement that promoted cadres be popular, honest, and obedient to the party. Clearly, the economic superstars of the

Deng era, many of whom were corrupt or closet capitalists, or who trampled over the common people in their zeal to build new projects, had no
place in Jiang's house. "Jiang is extremely concerned that the next generation of young leaders are evolving into pragmatic bureaucrats with
no education, political sense, or ideals," *Jing bao* commented.[23]

For the man on the street, Jiang's "pay attention to politics" campaign
would show up in the spray of new social and ideological policies announced in 1995 and 1996. Jiang was, of course, a genuine Chinese intellectual: he harbored a deep desire to promote Chinese culture and to
restrict the inflow of foreign cultures. He was also a profound social conservative: he believed in the state's promotion of public morality and its
duty to suppress radical views. He had evinced signs of wanting to impose his vision on Chinese society very soon after taking office in 1989.
But not until the mid 1990s was public concern about the decline in the
country's moral and social fabric great enough, and Jiang's own political authority strong enough, to furnish the opportunity he needed. "If
they are not able to offer convincing solutions to these problems,"
Guangjiaojing commented in mid 1996, "the third-generation leaders
will find it very hard to shoulder the heavy historic responsibility of leading the post-Deng era."[24]

Jiang's injunction to the Chinese citizenry to "pay attention to politics" envisioned a vast attempt to rebuild social ethics, what the party
called "spiritual culture." Like the "pay attention to politics" campaign,
the "spiritual culture" campaign at times seemed to be little more than
a big basket into which anything and everything could be thrown. There
was one thing, however, that bound together the diverse strands of Jiang's
new society; many of the tenets and the symbols of the "spiritual culture" campaign drew on, or blatantly copied from, Mao. These affinities were no surprise, given Jiang's admiration for the Great Helmsman
and his apparent psychological intimations of being a chip off the Maoist
block, discussed earlier.

At least two of the bundles to be found inside the bulging hamper of
"spiritual culture" were directly linked to Mao: artistic guidelines and
media controls. In May 1995, Jiang delivered a lengthy speech in which
he called for a revitalization of China's traditional arts. In a clear attempt
to associate himself with the Maoist tradition of literature and art, Jiang
had the speech made public on the anniversary of Mao's 1942 "Yanan
talks" on art and literature, which had served as political guidelines for
artists in China ever since. As an aspiring intellectual himself, Jiang took
obvious pleasure in the field of national art and literature. "Literature

and art are not my specialties, but I like them a lot," he once said.[25] His
preference was for "mainstream" works that would shore up the Communist Party's hold on power, just as Mao had instructed.[26] In line with
the new spirit, Jiang authorized a loan of nearly Rmb100 million to build
a library of modern literature in Beijing, following several appeals from
his Shanghai friend Ba Jin, the doyen of the official literature establishment. "Jiang has written an important chapter in the country's literary
heritage," Xinhua said after the foundation-laying in late 1996.[27]

In the case of renewed media controls, Jiang's reenactments of Mao
bordered on the farcical. They began when he visited *Jiefangjun bao* (the
PLA daily) in January 1996 and revived Mao's 1957 slogan that "newspapers must be run by politicians [*zhengzhi jia*]" rather than intellectuals.[28] This meant that consistency with the party line, rather than liveli-
ness or interest of coverage, was the most important task of the media.
Then, in September 1996, he visited the *People's Daily,* as Mao had done
in 1959. The occasion was used to warn the media that party control
would not relax. "Just one article, one erroneous remark, or one mistake in the press may lead to political instability," he warned journalists
at the newspaper. "In view of this, we should act in an extraordinarily
careful and prudent way, and maintain a high degree of consistency with
the party."[29]

At the same time, spiritual culture embraced several bundles that were
not to be found in Mao's social vision. Some of these, like the revival of
traditional values, were clearly at odds with Mao. An official revival of
Confucian teachings was begun in 1994, and within a few years, the
state media also began to tout virtues traditionally attributed to Chinese
society, such as practicing thrift, and respecting teachers and the aged.
A new law went into effect in September 1996 under which every ad-
vertising agency had to launch at least one advertisement a year promoting the "traditional virtues of the Chinese nation."[30] Mao had, of
course, bewailed the hold of Confucian thought on Chinese society and
espoused a "new socialist" system of virtues. But Jiang could safely revive "traditional virtues" as consistent with the need to rebuild the country's moral fabric.

Another bundle missing from the Maoist hamper, the attempt to check
the perceived foreign cultural invasion, had been less of an issue in the
autarkic Maoist era. In the era of reform, however, Jiang felt that the
party should control the inflow of ubiquitous Western, mainly American, culture. That inflow was wiping out *baozi* (Chinese steamed stuffed
buns) with its *hanbaobao* (hamburgers), and the paternal Chinese state

needed to offer a defense. In several speeches in 1995 and 1996, Jiang enjoined the nation to filter out "decadent" influences from the outside world, while making extra efforts to draw in "distinguished" influences.[31] "Where will our people end up if advertisements and product names with Western-sounding names flutter before their eyes everywhere they go?" he wondered aloud at a national propaganda meeting in early 1996.[32] He also penned his first *People's Daily* commentary railing against "cultural colonialism" (*zhimin wenhua*) in September 1995.[33] The results of all this hand-wringing could be seen in many areas. In 1996, nearly 4,000 company and product names were banned for having allegedly Western-sounding names, such as "professional killer," "emperor," "rich wife," "mafia," and "queen."[34] The use of English was even dropped from the weekly Foreign Ministry press briefing for a year, before being brought back in response to journalists' protests.

Most symbolic, perhaps, was the assault on Mickey Mouse, whose inexplicable popularity among adults in China (as well as Hong Kong and Taiwan) left Communist cadres seething. In April 1996, Jiang met Michael Ovitz, president and chief executive officer of Disney/ABC in Beijing, and expressed the hope that the company would "make additional valuable contributions" to Sino–U.S. understanding.[35] But just three months later, he turned around and began a campaign to drive Mickey out of the minds of China's children. "I hope that Chinese children can soon have their very own cartoon heroes," he wrote in a letter to the Shanghai Animation Film Studio, one of five state media companies charged with coming up with rivals to the likes of Mickey Mouse and Donald Duck.[36] The rivals that appeared included "Soccer Boy" a young boy who excels through teamwork and obedience, and cartoon fables about famous figures in Chinese history such as Confucius and the poet Li Bai.[37] Jiang was not blindly anti-Hollywood though; he would later praise the blockbuster film *Titanic* for its educational moral value.

A final bundle in the spiritual culture campaign, patriotism, has already been seen at work in Jiang's dealings with Taiwan. It would also figure prominently in the return of Hong Kong to mainland sovereignty in 1997. The new patriotism drive had echoes of the Maoist era. But in many ways it was also at odds with the internationalism of the old socialist outlook. Jiang first mooted the idea of a nationwide patriotism campaign when he stood before the tomb of Lin Zexu in Guangzhou in June 1990. It was the memory of this opium-spoiling hero of the Qing dynasty, it will be recalled, whom Wang Daohan had invoked to steel

Jiang's nerves before the latter took up the party general secretary's post in 1989. "A nation must have national self-esteem, self-confidence, and integrity. Otherwise it will be spurned," Jiang said. "Patriotic education should begin in primary and secondary school and should be conducted among children as well."[38] Seeking support for the campaign, Jiang wrote to the education minister, Li Tieying, and the education vice-minister, He Dongchang, in early 1991 suggesting a patriotic education project in schools. New educational materials should be produced, he wrote, that imbued young people with a renewed belief in socialism and anti-imperialism. "They would be meant to heighten the national self-respect and confidence of the Chinese people, especially the young and to help them guard against worshipping and blindly trusting all things foreign."[39] The patriotism campaign would gather steam in 1994, when all karaoke bars and dance halls were obliged to buy an officially sponsored compact disc full of old-time revolutionary favorites. In 1996, state-sponsored patriotic video games for children went on sale.

These various bundles inside the "spiritual culture" basket were brought together in a heavily publicized "spiritual culture" guiding policy announced at the party plenum of October 1996.[40] The communiqué drafters were led by the party propaganda chief Ding Guangen and by Shao Huaze, a director of the *People's Daily*. Under Jiang's direction to ensure that economic development was still billed as the central task, they came up with a document that deflated criticisms both from the left that they were not doing enough and from the right that they were doing too much.[41] It was a perfect example of Jiang steering the steady middle course. The final communiqué essentially summed up much of what is discussed above. But for Jiang, the elevation of these strands to the level of a plenum communiqué, requiring national study sessions and implementation reports, was crucial. In May 1997, a newly formed "central spiritual culture guiding committee" headed by Ding Guangen would hold its first meeting in Beijing charged with "supervising and inspecting" the implementation of the program nationwide.[42] Later, Jiang would coin a slogan that consciously sought to better Deng's oft-repeated statement "socialism does not mean being poor" by adding this cultural dimension: "Socialism does not mean being poor, nor does it mean being culturally deprived [*jingshen kuifa*]."

Those who needed to see in order to believe could troop to the "spiritual culture" model community of Zhangjiagang in Jiang's native Jiangsu province. This was the Jiangist successor to Deng's corrupt and capitalist rich village, Daqiuzhuang, and to Mao's paragon of collectivist virtue, Dazhai. Here everything seemed to work right: there was little crime or corruption, the public toilets were clean, and people even deposited their orange peels in waste bins. Jiang visited this "town" of close to a million in May 1995 and decided on the spot that it would be the showroom for his "spiritual culture" campaign.

Perhaps the most interesting aspect of the promotion of the "spiritual culture" and "pay attention to politics" campaigns was Jiang's use of the PLA. Jiang had inherited from Mao a vision of the PLA as a huge experimental social machine, like a greenhouse of policy changes. The army, Jiang hoped, could be used to nurture the seedlings of every aspect of the "pay attention to politics" and "spiritual culture" trees before transplanting them to the nation at large. "The military should lead the entire society in promoting socialist spiritual culture," Jiang told PLA delegates at the 1996 parliament.[43] With three million soldiers, its own government, schools, companies, and towns, the PLA was a big greenhouse indeed. Jiang's employment of the PLA in this way was ironic; his purge of Yang Baibing in 1992 had been prompted by the Yang family's attempted repoliticization of the army. Now he was doing the same thing himself. "Using the military to 'take the first step' is a long tradition in China, used by Mao, Zhou [Enlai], and Deng," *Guangjiaojing* explained. "Using it to make clear the political line that will lead China into the next century is the latest example of the wisdom of Jiang Zemin and his Politburo."[44]

Jiang's chief gardeners were the PLA's chief of staff, Zhang Wannian, and the defense minister, Chi Haotian, both of whom were elevated to vice-chairmen of the Central Military Commission in September 1995. Under their leadership, Jiang used the PLA countless times to sprout his new policies. His new cadre promotion criteria and the idea of strengthening central authority, for example, were both stressed first in military policies.[45] Even the Taiwan missile drills and the army's newly elevated status in the reunification drive were held out as part of the effort: "Our army has conducted a series of successful military exercises in the Taiwan Strait that greatly boosted the prestige of the state and enhanced the army's might," *Jiefangjun bao* said a few months after Lee Teng-hui swept to victory. "Who can deny that these are not the fruits of paying more attention to politics?"[46] Most helpful was the use of "pay attention to politics" to bolster allegiance to Jiang and place him on par with Mao and Deng. In July 1996, it was announced that the inscriptions of slogans on army development by Mao, Deng, and Jiang would be pasted on the walls of every barracks in the country.[47] More starkly, at a national soirée by army entertainment troupes to celebrate the sixtieth anniversary of the Long March in October 1996, the backdrop of the stage featured photographs of equal size of Mao, Deng, and Jiang. The comparison of Jiang with the two Long Marchers would have been unthinkable in the past.

The PLA would also take the first tentative steps toward displacing Deng's theories with those of Jiang. The National Defense University, site of most major military study sessions, used Deng's theories as "guidance" but gave Jiang's speeches top billing as "the key discussion point" at one seminar in early 1996.[48] On another occasion, the NDU would gather officers for a seminar on Jiang's "expositions" (*lunshu*).[49] This was the closest he had ever come to being put on a theoretical par with Deng, whose talks were called "theory" (*lilun*), a term implying slightly higher rank. It was still a big step away from the wisdom of Mao, which was still worshipped as "thought" (*sixiang*), but Jiang was at least closing in on his predecessor as party patriarch.

In many ways, the "pay attention to politics" and "spiritual culture" campaigns were a profile of Jiang Zemin himself. With their attention to patriotism, tradition, and party indoctrination, they brought together many aspects of his character that were emerging long before 1989. While borrowing heavily from Mao, and confined by the broad policy directions set by Deng, they were distinct enough to be called Jiang's own. It would be many years before historians could decide whether they had changed China. But they distinguished Jiang's rule and that perhaps was more important.

3

Like many of the young soldiers who guard the homes and offices of senior officials in Beijing, 18-year-old Zhang Jinlong was from a poor part of China. Recruited from his home village in northwestern Shanxi province in late 1994, Zhang had been assigned to a People's Armed Police (PAP) detachment in Beijing. A few months later, he was rotated onto guard duty outside the home of Li Peiyao, a vice-chairman of the NPC.

Standing guard during the wintertime in Beijing is pure misery. Many have sympathized while hastening past the poor young men standing motionless in their PLA-issue full-length coats in front of embassies and official Chinese buildings, the bitter Siberian winds blowing dust and snow into the air. For a fresh-faced private from the inland, the thought of protecting the homes of the rich and powerful must have made the suffering all the more unbearable.

In the small hours of 2 February 1996, Zhang Jinlong quietly stepped down from his sentry post and broke into the house he was supposed to be guarding. After confirming that Li Peiyao was away, he searched for valuables. Rummaging around, he found a leather coat, a camera, a watch, jewelry worth about U.S.$3,000 and another U.S.$100 in cash. Unfortunately for Zhang, however, Li came home late and accosted the young guard in the kitchen. A struggle ensued. Li was a big man, but too old to overpower Zhang, who seized two kitchen knives and stabbed Li several times in the head and body. The 62-year-old parliamentarian fell dead in a pool of blood.

As if reenacting the gruesome tales that fill the magazines and novels sold at popular street stalls in China, Zhang lost no time in chopping up his victim into fifty-seven more or less equally sized bits. These he stuffed one by one into a central heating duct surrounding the kitchen. After mopping up the blood from the floor and laying a carpet over some stubborn stains, he proceeded on his way, taking the valuables.

There is little doubt that Zhang would have been caught eventually, but in his haste to escape, he walked straight out of the front door and into the suspicious arms of two fellow guards. Shaking visibly, he threw off their clasp and tried to climb the compound wall, but lost his grip and fell back. He was immediately detained for the murder.

At a time when public concern about crime was on the rise, the murder might have played perfectly into Jiang's attempt to build support for his "spiritual culture" campaign. Unfortunately, these modest political benefits were far outweighed by the ruinous consequences of the murder for his attempt to build the PAP into a private army. Had the murderer been attached to either one of the other three security forces, the police, state security, or the army, the incident might have passed with little uproar. After all, when a lieutenant from the Beijing military garrison ran amok with a submachine gun in rush-hour traffic in September 1994—killing more than thirty people, including an Iranian diplomat and his son—the incident had essentially been swept under the carpet. But the paramilitary PAP was Jiang Zemin's praetorian guard. Its evolution as a nonlethal anti-riot force had been Jiang's way of distancing himself from the 1989 Tiananmen massacre. The PAP also served as an effective counterbalance to the overarching influence of the military in security affairs. Although loyal to Jiang in every other way, the army top brass had fought doggedly against the creation of a Jiang-led

PAP; they had constantly rebuffed Jiang's attempt to install the PAP's commander, Ba Zhongtan, his friend from Shanghai days, on the Central Military Commission.[50] By 1996, both sides were waiting for something to break the standoff.

The Li Peiyao murder played right into the hands of the opponents of Jiang's paramilitary corps. It offered the perfect opportunity to rid the corps of its Jiang loyalists and place it firmly and finally back under the control of the army. It was ironic that it took place in the same compound of drab gray dormitories on Cuiwei Road in western Beijing where Jiang had lived when he served as minister in the nearby Electronics Ministry. In an unprecedented move, Xinhua announced on 13 February that several senior PAP officers had been sacked for "dereliction of duty" over the murder. They included the commander of the Beijing PAP garrison, Major General Meng Zhende, and several others. Days later, Ba Zhongtan and his political commissar Zhang Shutian were also sacked, depriving the PAP of its number one and number two. "Li's relatives," Xinhua noted, "expressed their satisfaction with the handling of the case."[51]

Most of the replacements for those ousted—including Ba's successor, Lieutenant General Yang Guoping (later a full general), and Meng's successor, Major General Zhu Shuguang—were from the PLA. Indeed, the incident would set off a year-long period of change in which the PLA was given greater control over the PAP. All PAP appointments at the garrison level and above were henceforth passed through the Central Military Commission, and the PAP's command structure was rearranged to mirror that of the PLA, making it easier to rotate PLA officers in and out of the paramilitary corps.

For Jiang, it was the biggest setback in security affairs since he had taken over as head of the military commission in 1989. "The occurrence of this case has sounded the alarm," he humbly told the national parliament in March. "It has exposed problems in our work of security, maintaining social order, and other areas."[52] The commander of the PAP's Fujian command, Lieutenant General Hong Shaohu, was more blunt: "This has shocked people at home and abroad and tarnished the image of the PAP."[53]

The changes showed the limits on Jiang's ability to create a private army to counter PLA influence. They also showed the carefully nuanced nature of the PLA's support for him. The PLA might welcome him as one of its own, obey every one of his reasonable commands, and even take the lead in promoting his "pay attention to politics" and "spiritual culture" campaigns. These things were all within his purview and enjoyed broad support. But the PLA was loathe to allow a second force to challenge it for supremacy in the security apparatus. This was outside Jiang's authority and had clearly selfish motives.

The reverberations of the Li Peiyao murder would continue for several years. A "strike hard" swoop on crime was launched shortly after the murder that resulted in the arrest of an astounding 358,000 people by the end of the year.[54] Thousands of executions were carried out in the process, a blood-letting that seemed to symbolize Jiang's frustration at how the incident had lost him an army. Among those given a bullet in the back of the head was Zhang Jinlong, whose sorry image sitting in the dock losing a final appeal on grounds of being "young and ignorant" was splashed across TV screens nationwide. "Strike hard" meshed nicely with the "spiritual culture" campaign in any case and would be continued right through 1997. Jiang had lost an important internal political battle; the least he could do was try to win a fight against crime.

4

The "pay attention to politics" and "spiritual culture" campaigns were essentially concerned with ideology. Through them, Jiang was gently but firmly able to shift the guiding ideology away from the economy-led approach to policy to one that might best be described as economy-centered. That is, while economic concerns remained at the heart of party goals, they no longer set the pace for achieving those goals. Under these twin campaigns, political and ideological concerns were gently brought back to life in late-twentieth-century China.

A lot of the ideas for this new political economy came from the thinking of two men: Liu Ji, whom we have met, and Wang Huning, a prodigy with a wavy thatch of hair and wire rimmed glasses. Wang's wide ranging articles and books on China's political economy caught the attention of officials in the early 1980s, and in 1986, aged 31, he became the youngest-ever associate professor at Shanghai's Fudan University. The next year he was the youngest member on the team drafting the report to the party's thirteenth congress.[55] Many called Wang one of the fathers of China's "new authoritarianism." This was a governing philosophy that justified one-party rule in China by the need for efficient and strict governance to attain economic goals. It was a modern term for the "developmental dictatorship." Gone were Marxism's historical justifications for Communist rule. In the new era described by Wang, it was the drive for economic development that necessitated one-party rule and a strong central government. "There is enormous political and economic pressure from acute international competition to develop our state power and capabilities," he wrote.[56]

It was while Jiang was mayor of Shanghai that he first noticed Wang. When formally taking leave of the city in August 1989, Jiang had carried in his leather briefcase a paper Wang had written on fighting corruption.[57] By 1994, Wang was close enough to the senior leadership to join the summer deliberations at Beidaihe. Partly, this was a reward for the numerous papers he had already submitted to Jiang. Besides splashing around in the waters in front of the Western-style villa he was allocated, Wang spent his time watching Western movies such as Martin Scorsese's *The Last Temptation of Christ* (1988) and Steven Spielberg's *Schindler's List* (1993). He also held serious discussions with Jiang on economic and political issues.[58] By early 1995, as Jiang was mulling the major speeches to be delivered at that fall's plenum, he brought Wang to Beijing for good as a deputy director of the party's Central Policy Research Center.[59] While traveling with Jiang abroad, he would be described as a department head of the State Council's foreign affairs office.

Putting into practice the political economy of Liu Ji and Wang Huning, Jiang at the September 1995 party plenum had delivered another talk on what he called "the twelve great relationships" of modern economic policy. The symbolism was important. In 1956, Mao had outlined "ten great relationships" in building Chinese socialism, most of which concerned the economy. Jiang borrowed heavily from Mao, rephrasing most of the old relationships and adding some that reflected the new challenges of the market economy. In plain language, they were as follows:

1. Reform, development, and stability
2. Economic growth and efficiency
3. Economic development, population, resources, and environment
4. Primary, secondary, and tertiary sectors
5. Coastal and inland regions
6. The market system and macroeconomic control
7. Public ownership and nonpublic ownership
8. Public, corporate, and personal income distribution
9. Economic opening and national industry
10. Central and local governments

11. National defense and economic development

12. Material and spiritual culture

The only brand-new relationships Jiang introduced were numbers two, three, and six, all of which clearly reflected the desire to contain the negative fallout from Deng's fast growth policies. He left out Mao's "Han Chinese and ethnic minorities" relationship, apparently because he wanted his list to be essentially concerned with economic policy. But the rest of Mao's relationships were all there, suitably updated in terminology.

It is obvious why Jiang would have harkened back to Mao now that the economy was no longer to dominate all other policy objectives. Mao had ruled in the heyday of state planning. There were no suggestions that the market reforms be rolled back. But if economic objectives were to be subsumed under other goals, some lessons from the Mao era might nevertheless be relearned. The "neoauthoritarian" state that people like Wang Huning envisaged would still wield significant influence over how resources were allocated in the economy. It was the kind of "developmental dictatorship" approach that had already worked in other states in Asia, such as South Korea and Singapore, Japan and Taiwan.

"We should realize that the market can be spontaneous, blind, and lag behind," Jiang explained in his "twelve relationships" speech. "Therefore the state must give correct guidance to and exercise control over market activities . . . to curb inflation, to realize overall economic balance, and to optimize the economic structure."[60] Jiang would even admit later that he had been feverishly reading a biography of the American president Franklin D. Roosevelt at this time. Roosevelt's interventions to moderate the worst effects of unbridled capitalism were said to have "deeply impressed" him.[61]

The new role of the state in the economy could be seen in many areas, all of them covered by Jiang's "twelve great relationships." Most of his attention was given to areas he best understood, like state enterprises, science and technology, foreign investment, and income disparities. In brief, major new policy initiatives were launched in the following areas:

Income Redistribution. This, of course, had been a favorite theme of Jiang's from the day he took office. In 1996, Jiang revived the policy of paying attention to the interests of the Maoist triptych of "workers, farmers, and intellectuals." "In wealth distribution, emphasis must be placed on ensuring they get actual benefits and that their living standards keep improving. Only when there is a general improvement in their living standards can our reform and economic development have popular support," he told the parliament.[62] Among the attempts to engineer this change was the introduction of a new personal income tax, which brought in Rmb13 billion in 1995, Rmb19 billion in 1996, and an estimated Rmb27 billion in 1997.[63] New taxes on land appreciation, inheritance, and gifts were also introduced.

Central Power. Tax reforms launched in 1994 had helped raise the central government's share of total public revenue to around 55 percent in the first three years of the change, compared to an average of 38 percent in the previous decade.[64] This was critical to the "neoauthoritarian" state's exercise of effective power. It also brought about a significant change in the balance of power in favor of the central government, a fact that explained why Jiang and Zhu Rongji, as well as the finance minister, Liu Zhongli, had to spend so much time persuading the provinces to accept the changes. Prior to the reforms, Beijing had had absolute control over only agricultural taxes, which were falling as a percentage of the economy as industrialization continued. After the reforms, Beijing won control of luxury goods taxes, customs duties, and income taxes from centrally run state enterprises. It also won control of 75 percent of the revenues from a new, streamlined value-added tax. Beijing set up its own national tax collection system to ensure that its lawful revenues were duly collected. Many provinces responded to the loss of tax powers by introducing dozens of new fees and levies. Such "off budget" taxes may have accounted for up to a third of total government (central and local) revenues in the first year of the reforms.[65]

Inland Regions. The five-year and ten-year plans announced at the September 1995 plenum had made development in inland regions a priority. Jiang pledged outright to "bring prosperity to central and western China."[66] It was an ironic reversal for a man who had been one of the keenest advocates of Zhao Ziyang's coastal-based development strategy as Shanghai party chief in 1988 and a founder of the special economic zones. A symbolic gesture was the elevation in early 1997 of the city of Chongqing in Sichuan province to the status of a municipality answering directly to the central government, the first inland city to enjoy this status.

Rural Policies. Jiang reasserted the Maoist slogan that "agriculture is the base" of the economy.[67] This, as we have seen, was an area that he had made his own ever since taking over as party general secretary. National rural work meetings were convened in every year beginning in 1993. Governors were put in charge of grain self-sufficiency in their provinces. "In recent years, the central authorities have repeatedly stressed the need to make agriculture the top priority in all of economic work. I have also repeatedly addressed this issue in recent years," Jiang said after inspecting Henan province in June 1996. "I'm not saying we can't launch industrial projects. I only hope that the major agricultural provinces will . . . explore a successful path for maintaining stable agricultural development amid rapid economic growth."[68]

Poverty Relief. Those officially in poverty had fallen from 250 million in 1978 to 65 million by 1995. But the World Bank, using the higher poverty line common worldwide, put the figure at closer to 300 million.[69] The official figure reflected those living quite literally on the brink of survival, whereas the World Bank figure included all those who, while not in immediate danger of death, did not enjoy adequate food, clothing, or shelter as defined in the world context. Either way, it was an enormous problem, which had remained unresolved despite Deng's economic boom. Jiang used the September 1996 opening of the Beijing to Hong Kong railway, which cut through poor inland areas, to tout a new awareness of poverty relief. "We urge leading cadres to pay attention to politics. For poverty-stricken areas, the greatest political issue is none other than ensuring that people are properly fed and clothed," he said.[70] Then during his visit to Guangxi province the next month, he pledged to "never let people live in poverty-stricken mountain areas with no one to care for them."[71] While in Guangxi, he even arranged a photograph of himself wearing the red scarf of the Communist Youth League and surrounded by children from poor areas, an almost perfect replay of a stunt pulled by Mao on his return to his poor hometown in Hunan province in 1959. Jiang's stated goal was to ensure sufficient food and clothing for all those in poverty by the year 2000. Government spending on this would rise by Rmb1.5 billion a year from 1997 until the year 2000. "This," he said, "will mean finally settling the right to subsistence of the Chinese people, the biggest and most basic human rights issue ever . . . and also a feat of great daring in the course of human history."[72]

State Enterprises. Jiang was an ardent believer in state enterprises, not because of Marxism but because of his own personal background in state firms. "We can work miracles!" he exclaimed while visiting state firms in his old haunt of Changchun in mid 1995.[73] In any case, the constitution demanded that public ownership, which included collectively owned firms, should remain the "mainstay" of the economy. State-owned firms meanwhile were to play a "leading role" in key sectors like transport, telecommunications, oil and gas, and power supply. For Jiang, caution was the byword in reforming state enterprises at first, despite their huge drag on the national economy. The result of his caution, however, was that the plight of the firms worsened. The percentage of state firms losing money rose from 45 percent in 1995 to 60 percent in 1996, and for the first time, total losses exceeded total taxes and profits; in simple terms, it meant that shutting down every state firm, with their 100 million workers, would actually result in a gain.[74] The sorry results even forced Liu Ji to defend Jiang in the official *Jingji ribao* (Economic Daily): "The slow pace of state enterprise reform," he wrote, "is in no way related to the personal qualities of the leadership or their lack of understanding of the problems."[75] As will be seen, Jiang later endorsed a shareholding system that would effectively allow state enterprises to be privatized. Jiang's model state enterprise was the Shanghai-based Three Guns (*san qiang*) textiles group, whose gun-emblazoned underwear could be purchased nationwide. Three Guns' chairman, Su Shounan, was a friend of Jiang's from his Shanghai days. Jiang authorized timely loans to the group—in one case worth Rmb60 million[76]—in return for its takeover of seven money-losing state firms with Rmb1.2 billion in bad debts. The group's profits and sales doubled annually during the 1990s, thanks to Jiang's top-level support, reaching Rmb69 million on sales of Rmb1.2 billion in 1996.[77]

In all these areas, Jiang was outlining a new framework for the government's role in China's economic life in the twenty-first century. His "twelve relationships" echoed Mao not only in content but also in substance. The brief Dengist era of rolling back the frontiers of the state was at an end, or at least it was to be followed by the rolling out of a less intrusive but more effective state. In the Jiang era, the state would better manage the burgeoning quasi-capitalist economy.

5

In April 1996, a state publisher in Moscow issued a Russian-language book called *The Selected Works of Jiang Zemin*.[78] It came on the eve of a visit to China by Boris Yeltsin, the Russian president, which was to cement the "strategic partnership" he and Jiang had announced a year and a half earlier.

Jiang had been China's party chief for nearly seven years. His hundreds of speeches and pronouncements over that period provided ample materials for such a book. In 1995 and 1996, as he outlined a more systematic theory of rule, it seemed sensible to gather together some key speeches into a book. But the day when Jiang's collected speeches could be published at home in China was still far off. In a country where the written word is sacred, the issuance of books summing up the policies and philosophy of a given leader requires more than just a few years at the top. It also requires the right political timing; Jiang, it will be recalled, had accelerated the issuance of Deng's third volume of speeches when he was having problems pushing through new reforms in late 1993.

There were reports that as early as 1994, a drafting team had been set up under the party secretariat to gather together some of Jiang's speeches in book form.[79] But the road from there to actual publication was a long and highly politicized one. Jiang's contribution to national literature thus far was one translated book on power generation, and possibly another on the sacred Mount Tai.[80] The comical official fanfare that marked the reissuance in November 1996 of a speech he had made while mayor of Shanghai on the weighty issue of fire prevention confirmed to many Chinese that their jolly party chief was an intellectual lightweight.[81] Publication of his selected works was certainly not warranted.

Still, the deluge of new theories, slogans, and campaigns from Jiang in 1995 and 1996 eventually inspired a group of twenty-two youthful scholars at the cabinet-level Chinese Academy of Social Sciences (CASS) to try to make some sense of it all. How could one sum up the apparently disparate strands of "pay attention to politics," "spiritual culture," and the "twelve great relationships"? To make an attempt, the CASS scholars organized a so-called Youth Social Sciences Forum to discuss and write about Jiang's visions. It was overseen by Liu Ji, a clear indication that it had official support.

After several seminars and article revisions, a book entitled *Yu zongshuji tanxin* (Talking Heart-to-Heart with the General Secretary) was issued in October 1996, its cover graced by a picture of Jiang Zemin in the throes of a hearty laugh. It was the first book in China that dealt solely with Jiang. In the preface, Liu Ji wrote that the articles, taken together, were a "sparkling elucidation" of Jiang's speeches.[82] Although there was no official fanfare, no one doubted the book's authority. "From the book's contents and its timing, it would be hard to say that it is not officially backed," *Guangjiaojing* commented.[83] Distribution was handled by the Xinhua bookstore chain. The first 100,000 copies sold out immediately.[84] After that, pirate editions began to appear, the highest form of flattery in the lawless Chinese intellectual property market.

A few months later, in early 1997, another "Jiang Thought" book was issued. The title, *Guanjian shike* (Critical Moment), came from Jiang's own assertion in 1996 that China was at a "critical stage, a critical moment" in its reform drive. Again, Liu Ji wrote the preface, and the authors of the twenty-seven topical chapters—on issues that, the subtitle explained, "must urgently be resolved"—were mostly CASS scholars. "While there have been brilliant achievements of the reform and modernization drive, problems have also accumulated whose resolution is now at a critical moment," Liu observed. "If these problems are not resolved, they will become a yoke on the further advance of China's socialist modernization."[85]

If there was one theme that stood out clearly in the babble of chapters in *Yu zongshuji tanxin* and *Guanjian shike,* it was that Jiang was a pragmatist, a middle-of-the-roader, and no committed Marxist. That was probably why the books were not accorded any official fanfare, except for a few scattered articles in the provincial press. The authors made clear that they reckoned Jiang's philosophy was more worldly and flexible than orthodox Marxism. "We make no attempt to conceal the fact that we are in the reformist faction of socialism," the editors of *Guanjian shike* declared. "We are opposed to every kind of extreme position. . . . Extremism of the left and right will both bring disaster on China."[86]

The self-styled moderates were mainly an annoyance to the left. The authors argued, for example, that the decline of the state sector was not a matter for concern because stockholding companies and collectives were a form of public ownership, a direct contradiction of an assertion in the Ten Thousand Character Document. They also argued that Western culture, "individualism," and even traditional Chinese culture could all be absorbed into a "new socialist outlook," notions that made Marxist hard-liners seethe. "This book [*Yu zongshuji tanxin*] is an attempt to advocate individualism in the name of 'talking heart-to-heart with the general secretary' under the guidance of a deputy president of CASS [Liu Ji]," *Zhenli de zhuiqiu* (The Search for Truth) fumed. "It's an attempt to hoodwink the people."[87]

Jiang's lack of conviction about Marxism had been commented on before by overseas scholars, who characterized him as a "working Marxist" or a "pragmatic Marxist." "Coming from a family of traditional intellectuals and having received his early education in schools under the Nationalists, but later joining the Communist Party, Jiang's ideology is quite complex," a Taiwan scholar wrote. "Although he is a loyal Communist, he is by no means a theoretician or a dogmatist. His speeches characterize him as a pragmatic Marxist."[88] That may have been all right so long as it was read into Jiang's speeches and policies. But *Yu zongshuji tanxin* and *Guanjian shike* spelled things out in black and white. It was too much for the diehards on the left to stomach. "*Yu zongshuji tanxin* contains egregious errors and puts forward a theoretical framework at odds with the resolution of the [1996] sixth plenum," the Marxist historian Feng Baoxing wrote in a review in early 1997.[89] Feng even directly criticized Liu Ji for writing in a preface that the book was a "sparkling elucidation" of Jiang's speeches. "I fail to understand why this leading comrade has such high praise for a work that contains viewpoints at odds with the party's consistent position, with the resolution of the sixth plenum, and with the general secretary's proposals about building the socialist spiritual culture," Feng wrote. The review was first carried in the February issue of the influential left wing theoretical journal *Zhongliu* (Mainstream). The issue was banned after only a week in print, and the magazine was criticized for "sabotaging stability and solidarity."[90] That did not prevent another left-wing magazine, the Communist Youth League's monthly *Zhongguo qingnian* (China Youth), from printing the review, though.

The veiled attacks on Jiang's theories of governance in magazines like *Zhongliu* and *Zhenli de zhuiqiu*, which would continue through 1997, were serious indeed. The examples of Hu Yaobang and Zhao Ziyang provided ample evidence that while a modern Chinese leader could make mistakes on any number of government policies and emerge unscathed, when it came to ideology, there was no room for compromise. Jiang had apparently come close to committing an ideological fault by offering tacit support for *Yu zongshuji tanxin* and *Guanjian shike*. Now he was paying the price.

The controversy also had disturbing echoes of the last days of Mao's shrill wife, Jiang Qing. In 1972 as her power was crumbling, Jiang Qing had invited an American scholar, Roxana Witke, to China to write her life story. The result of their thirty hours of interviews was the book *Comrade Chiang Ch'ing,* an initial copy of which appeared in 1976 as Mao lay dying and knives were being sharpened against the Gang of Four, led by Jiang Qing.[91] The blatant attempt to bolster her image through a self-serving work by an academic, even as her patron lay dying, ended up sealing her fate.

Was Jiang Zemin now in the same position? On the surface, the attacks on *Yu zongshuji tanxin* and *Guanjian shike,* books written by
scholars while Deng was living out his final months, strongly suggested
a repetition of the fall of Jiang Qing. But there were important differences. Jiang Zemin had not directly overseen the books. And there were
no immediate threats to his position as China's supreme leader. He could
easily dodge the blame for the scribblings of a clutch of youthful scholars; more evidence than this would be needed by orthodox Marxists to
prove his ideological wavering. Still, the controversy over the books
served as a further reminder of the narrow confines in which Jiang sought
to steer his middle course. Knives were being sharpened as the post-Deng
era neared.

6

Although it never won the accolade of "Jiang Thought," the series of
policy initiatives Jiang launched in 1995 and 1996 was as close as he
would ever come to outlining a governing philosophy. The revenants of
Maoism in the images and slogans he used told much about the man.
Like Mao, Jiang was obsessed with political control; Mao more than
anything had laid down a system—in the media, in political economy,
in the party—designed to uphold his position as core leader, and Jiang
naturally took his cue from this. Unlike Mao's, however, Jiang's allegiance to Marxism was in doubt, and he did not harbor radical social
ideas; quite the contrary, he was a social conservative.

In the process of outlining "Jiang Thought," there were modest but
important departures from Deng's policies. The official press would
stress the consanguinity of the two: "Jiang has defined a set of political
and economic principles that are the concrete application and continuation of Deng Xiaoping's major principle of building socialism with Chinese characteristics," *Wen Wei Po* said.[92] Certainly, there were no major
departures, and ample backing for the new policies could be found in
Deng's dusty old speeches. But the stress was entirely different. No longer
would the economy rule the commanding heights of policy, as it had under Deng. And Jiang also found fertile soil in areas that Deng had neglected or failed to tackle; patriotism, anti-corruption, poverty, crime,
party-building, moral strengthening, and much more became issues that
Jiang could call his own. In articulating this vision, Jiang was able to address pressing concerns of the day, as well as put his own stamp of authority on his reign. The ancient nightmare of Prime Minister Cao Can, and

the more recent one of Party General Secretary Hua Guofeng, could at least temporarily be forgotten. At the same time, Jiang was helping to guide China toward a future as a sort of "developmental dictatorship" in which the state had a significant role despite growing economic and social freedoms.

There were also signs, however, that Jiang had hit a sort of glass ceiling in his hitherto steady rise to a position of unrivaled authority. He was forced into a significant climbdown on the "pay attention to politics" campaign under pressure from the right. He lost his key ally in the PAP, and thus his control of that force itself, over a relatively minor affair. And he came closer perhaps than he had ever come to being associated with ideological mistakes with the books *Yu zongshuji tanxin* and *Guanjian shike*.

This was the paradoxical political status of Jiang Zemin on the eve of lunar new year 1997. On the outside, all the trappings of supreme authority were his. His theory of ruling was being discussed, his image in the army was being put on par with those of Deng and Mao, and two books devoted to him alone had finally appeared. But inside the finely balanced high politics of Zhongnanhai, signs indicated that detractors were gaining influence. For the first seven years of his rule, potential rivals and plain critics had been kept at bay because Jiang represented a consensus opinion that was in the ascendant. Now they showed signs of coming out of the woodwork to declare that his power had reached its zenith.

Perhaps it was no surprise. As Jiang himself had noted, there were limits on the power one leader could amass in modern-day China. He had always been gentle in testing those limits. If he remained so, the occasional rebuff might serve as a useful reminder of the modesty and consensus on which his authority was based. If not, the closing years of the century might see his position fatally challenged.

CHAPTER 11

The Emperor's Mandate

1

By early 1997, a photograph made public of a shriveled and crippled Deng Xiaoping watching the National Day fireworks on 1 October 1994 in Beijing remained the most recent image of the architect of reforms seen by the Chinese people. Not that the whole nation cared. Deng had long withdrawn from the public eye, and most Chinese people, when asked, concurred with the official line that his passing would not bring much change. Even internally, Deng had stopped commenting on policies by the end of 1995, after which his personal office was closed and its former head, General Wang Ruilin, compensated with elevation to the Central Military Commission.[1] The five Deng children handled all affairs relating to their father.

At 92, even the hearty Deng was weakening. Parkinson's disease had rendered him increasingly stiff, tremulous, and weak for the previous eight years, and it was now aggravated by failing kidneys, a weak heart, and lungs that were frequently infected.[2] His left hand quivered uncontrollably, and his hearing was virtually gone. Two minor brain embolisms since 1994 had made movements increasingly difficult.

Deng was given the best medical care available. A group of doctors from around the country was assembled to keep him alive as long as possible. He was also a good patient. "Deng and his family were always very deferent to the views of doctors about his health. They respected science and cooperated fully," Zhong Nanshan, president of the Guangzhou Medical College, a specialist in internal medicine, and a member of the Deng medical team, would recall.[3] Although his two-story residence behind the Forbidden City was equipped with an emergency resuscitation room, Deng spent an increasing amount of time on the top floor of the so-called "elders building" in the drab 301 Hospital of the PLA in Beijing's western suburbs. The hospital, whose public name, the PLA General Hospital, was inscribed in huge letters on the roof of the new wing by Jiang Zemin, along with his signed name, was the best equipped in the country. Doctors there performed several blood transfusions on Deng beginning in 1995, the effects of which were said to be "pretty good."[4] But when he caught a cold in early 1996, it took the medical team a month of frantic efforts to save him. From then on, the little man from Sichuan drifted in and out of consciousness. Kept under an isolation tent to avoid further infections, Deng was simply biding time on the edge of death. A picture obtained by a Hong Kong newspaper from December 1996 showed his eyes bruised and his facial skin covered in burst blood vessels. It was time.

For Jiang, Deng's protracted last gasp was a gift from heaven. In the previous two years, as Jiang had outlined the ways in which he would distinguish his rule, the abiding presence of Deng had seemed to lend a sort of imprimatur to his efforts. To have attacked corruption in the Beijing municipality, lobbed missiles at Taiwan, or articulated a range of new theories *after* Deng's death would have been seen as a brazen attempt to fiddle with the patriarch's legacy and heartlessly take advantage of his departure. With the old man still around, Jiang's claim to be merely marching the next step down the Dengist path was more credible. It was no wonder that he had said back in 1989 that "the health and longevity of Comrade Xiaoping are of great significance to the smooth development of the work of the party and state."

By late 1996, doctors were warning that Deng's life was ending. The patriarch's hope of visiting Hong Kong after its return to Chinese sovereignty on 1 July 1997 looked increasingly forlorn. As a result, a documentary on Deng in preparation for four years by China Central Television, originally intended to have been shown on the eve of the Hong Kong handover, was given a hasty green light. For twelve consecutive evenings beginning on 1 January, an estimated 224 million people—28 percent of the 800 million Chinese with access to a television—watched a carefully crafted version of Deng's life, which emphasized Jiang's position as the patriarch's successor.[5] As Deng walked off the television set, Jiang came into view, smiling and waving.

The first day of the lunar new year, the Year of the Ox, passed on 7 February without the traditional greeting from Deng. Xinhua had reported, rather cruelly in retrospect, that Jiang and Li had visited Deng on New Year's Eve to wish him "good health."[6] Within days of the festival, Deng contracted a viral flu that coursed voraciously through his vulnerable body.[7] Every effort was made to keep him alive, at least until the two weeks of the new year celebrations had passed. If he died before then, it would be inauspicious according to Chinese tradition.

A devoted communist to the end, Deng did not oblige these superstitious hopes. Sometime on Thursday, 13 February, he suffered a stroke.[8] His heart stopped beating. Doctors thought it might be the end, but after a few minutes, a faint pulse reappeared. The next one would be fatal. Jiang, who had remained close to Beijing throughout the past month, rushed back to the capital from Jiangxi province, where, appropriately enough, given his distancing from Deng's legacy, he had been inspecting poverty alleviation work.[9] Over the weekend, Politburo standing committee members took turns keeping watch at Deng's bedside along with family members.[10] Deng Pufang, whose father had nursed him so lovingly in a Beijing courtyard after he was crippled during the Cultural Revolution, refused to leave the bedside. Among senior leaders, only Vice-Premier Li Lanqing and Defense Minister Chi Haotian were out of the country.

When stock trading opened on Monday morning, both the Shanghai and Shenzhen markets plummeted by the maximum 10 percent within minutes before a mandatory floor was imposed. A Foreign Ministry spokesman said on Tuesday only that there was "no big change" in Deng's health, omitting the usual statement about his health being good for a man of his age. But Deng was plucky. Not until 5 P.M. on Wednesday, 19 February, did the doctors step back, remove their gloves and declare that his passing was nigh. Four hours later, at 9:08 P.M. Beijing time, he died.

The moment of Deng's death was something Jiang had anticipated for several years. When Mao died at age 82 in 1976, it had taken the party fifteen hours to announce the fact of his death, several weeks to agree what to do with his corpse, and several years to decide on his legacy. The biggest casualty of the messy Mao death was his chosen successor, Hua Guofeng, whose opponents used the disarray to undermine his authority. This would not happen to Jiang. By the time Deng died, a carefully written script was in place that left nothing to chance.

Jiang would chair the 459-person funeral committee, and, unlike in the case of elder Chen Yun, who had died in April 1995, there would be no vice-chairmen. On the floor below where Deng lay covered by a simple cream-colored sheet on the night of 19 February, Jiang convened an emergency Politburo standing committee meeting shortly after 10 P.M. Everyone present knew of the funeral arrangements. It was simply a matter of filling in the dates for the upcoming memorial ceremonies.

Shortly after midnight, regional party leaders were informed of the death. Then at 2:42 A.M. on February 20, the news was broadcast to the world, five and a half hours late. "Deng Xiaoping passed away because of illness in Beijing at 21:08 on February 19, 1997," the Xinhua News Agency stated baldly in the lead line of its English report. The patriarch, it said, "who had suffered the advanced stage of Parkinson's disease with complications of lung infections, passed away because of the failure of the respiration circulating functions after failing to respond to emergency treatment." President Clinton was informed of the death while having lunch in Boston. The world leaders, including Clinton, who immediately conveyed written condolences to Beijing seemed no less prepared than the Chinese.

In the years after the Tiananmen massacre, Deng's death was considered to be the one event that might tip over the carefully balanced tripod of political discipline, economic expansion, and dissident repression that was the prescribed remedy for the causes of the student led demonstrations. It was a measure of how far China had come since then that the event, when it finally occurred, caused not a tremor. As dawn swept across Tiananmen Square on 20 February and the Chinese flag was raised to half mast, taxi drivers sped past as usual, glancing nonchalantly at the lowered standard as they looked for fares. Police in the square deterred the few attempted expressions of condolence, such as had set off the Tiananmen protests of 1989 and 1976. In Guangdong province, authorities were more tolerant; mourners were permitted to stream to two large billboards of Deng erected in Guangzhou and Shenzhen. The tearful crowds who left their factories and offices to place wreaths before the pictures in Guangdong included a large contingent of migrant workers known affectionately as Deng's Army. They simply gave thanks. No one called for change.

The public calm, even indifference, to Deng's death made Jiang's task much easier. Mourning would last for six days, concluding with the cremation ceremony on 24 February and a memorial meeting the following day. Jiang was to admit later that he was under stress during this somber week and had sought to relax by listening to Mozart and Beethoven.[11]

With the initial announcements successfully made, the care and preparation of Deng's body for the ceremonies began. Jiang convened a Politburo meeting on the morning of 20 February at the 301 Hospital, where all of Deng's children, and his wife, Zhuo Lin, were present. The only key figure missing was a retired pathologist from the Beijing Hospital named Ma Yanlong. Little known except to Deng's medical team, Ma had long been responsible for dressing the corpses of the party elite. Mao Zedong, Zhou Enlai, Zhou's wife, Deng Yingchao, former president Li Xiannian, and even Chen Yun had all been the subjects of Ma's skill.

Ma woke that morning to a dirge on the radio that he knew signified Deng's death. He guessed that the leadership would ask him to dress the body, but he had moved recently and few knew his new phone number. Briefly flustered, Ma hopped on his bicycle and pedaled frantically to the Beijing Hospital, where he thought Deng had died. Realizing he was wrong, he returned home and managed to patch through to the central party office. "We've been looking for you everywhere. The meeting is already in progress. Please hurry to the 301 Hospital," he was told.[12] By the time Ma walked in on the meeting, Jiang had already read out the family bequest that Deng be cremated after his corneas were donated and his organs removed for medical research. "Old Ma," said Jiang as the doctor shuffled into the carpeted room in his black cloth shoes, "You've come just in time."

In the four days after he was entrusted with the task of beautifying the departed patriarch, Ma worked feverishly. It was no easy task. Deng's left hand was clenched tight from the pain of the final moments of his life. His eye sockets were sunken after the removal of his corneas, his mouth was shriveled, and a scar ran across his forehead from an autopsy. It took Ma a final seven-hour burst on the morning of the cremation ceremony to put the final coloration onto Deng's face and lips. Standing back, he then pulled the Chinese flag up to the fourth button of the tunic on the slightly bloated corpse and awaited the arrival of the funeral procession.

Chinese state funerals are complex affairs. Every wreath and potted plant is arranged meticulously to express the proper respect to the departed and the proper positions of those left behind. Deng had requested before he died that there should be no public farewell ceremony, as had been arranged in Tiananmen Square for Mao. But that still left the fairly involved tributes of the cremation ceremony and the memorial meeting. Since both the events would be broadcast on national television, Jiang and other leaders could be excused for having a little stage fright.

Wearing the traditional black suit and a white boutonniere, Jiang was the first to disembark from the procession of black sedans that arrived at the South Wing of the 301 Hospital at 9 A.M. on 24 February for the cremation. Inside the small memorial hall, Ma Yanlong stood waiting. Jiang betrayed no emotion as he gingerly led the opening three bows of respect and then the time-consuming procession to circle the bier and express condolences to the wailing family members. Jiang's fists were clenched and his arms slightly splayed as he paced around the dead figure. It was as if he half expected Deng to spring to life. Other leaders were equally stone-faced as they followed, save for Zhu Rongji, who was a basket case; in tears, he cut short conveying his sympathies to the family and dashed out of sight of the television cameras.

The casket was then carried out to a hearse, which led a mile-and-a-half-long procession to the Babaoshan cemetery for revolutionary martyrs. Xinhua claimed that 100,000 people lined the streets, but most estimates were half that, and most people appeared to have been ordered by their work units to appear for the event. The bowing and circling of the bier were repeated at the cemetery before Deng was turned to ashes. As the casket was about to enter the Japanese-made incinerator, the grief-stricken youngest daughter, Deng Rong, her father's biographer and private secretary, called out in tears: "Daddy's not dead! Daddy's not dead!" Ma Yanlong had done his work well.

Jiang's performance at the memorial meeting the next day was even more important than at the cremation ceremony. After the 10 A.M. start, when factory whistles and train and car horns around the country would sound for three minutes, Jiang's delivery of the eulogy would be telecast live around the nation, and around the world. He had to get the tone right, showing ample grief but not a lack of mettle or resolve. The 10,000 guests crammed into the Great Hall of the People would stand for the duration of the eulogy. Whereas the cremation ceremony had been entirely devoted to mourning and recollections of Deng, the memorial meeting was suffused with more political content. A banner draped from the balcony of the Great Hall of the People urged citizens to "unite more closely around Jiang Zemin." File footage broadcast on national television before the proceedings included Deng's statements that "the choice of Jiang Zemin is correct" and "Jiang Zemin is qualified to be the chairman of the Central Military Commission because he is qualified to be party general secretary." Even in death, it seemed, Deng would support his chosen successor.

After the playing of the national anthem at the beginning of the memorial meeting, and repetition of the three bows, Jiang climbed onto the podium with nothing more than a microphone between him and the world. In a wooden box on the stage behind him lay Deng's ashes, surrounded by flower wreaths, cypress trees, and evergreen clippings, and flanked by six honor guards. Jiang pulled the eulogy from his breast pocket and began. His low and sonorous voice served him well. Dipping and moaning in his accustomed timbres, he made the eulogy sound profound, even though it contained mostly tired propaganda phrases about Deng's life. Five times during the fifty minutes it took him to read the eulogy, he broke into tears and had to stop reading. The emotions were genuine, but no doubt carefully controlled. Reaching for a handkerchief stowed in his right pocket to wipe his eyes and nose, Jiang made prominent displays of his grief, but also displayed his dogged determination, as the slogan went, "to turn grief into strength." If his egomania, his love of attention, had ever come in useful, it was now. The performance was flawless.

The eulogy had been written by consensus. That probably explained why the description of the succession did not mention Jiang: "Comrade Xiaoping created good conditions for the smooth transfer of power to the third-generation collective leadership," it read. While it was mainly an affirmation of Deng's life and a pledge to carry on his policies, several interesting gems were buried in it. On the critical issue of Deng's role in the Tiananmen massacre, the eulogy repeated the verdict contained in the encomium issued along with the death announcement, which spread the responsibility around: "Amid domestic and international political disturbances in the late 1980s and early 1990s, the party and government, with the staunch and powerful support from Comrade Deng Xiaoping and other veterans, and relying on the people as well, maintained a clear-cut stand." If there had been any hopes that Deng's death would occasion a reevaluation of the official verdict on the tragedy, these were quickly dashed.

There was also a surprising appeal to "persist in reform in the political and other fields" for the sake of preserving the economic gains of the past two decades. Political reform had, of course, been a taboo subject since Tiananmen, a codeword for Zhao Ziyang–style weakening of the role of the party. The eulogy did not make clear what was meant by it, but even the mention, at Deng's funeral to boot, suggested that the party leadership under Jiang would revive this long-dormant issue.

A week later, a Chinese-made Yun passenger plane took Deng's ashes out of the capital for good. Circling Beijing once before flying to the nearby Bohai Sea, the plane descended to 1,800 meters so that the handfuls of ash and flower petals could be scooped into a funnel installed in the plane's floor. Family members, former bodyguards, and a Politburo member, Hu Jintao, watched the debris scatter in the wind. "The many ups and downs of [Deng's] political life were just like the sea waves," Xinhua commented. The obvious question now was whether Jiang's immediate future would be any less turbulent.

2

Almost as if a coup had taken place in Beijing, the armed forces and paramilitary commands swore their allegiance to Jiang the day after the memorial meeting. "Before his death, Comrade Deng Xiaoping left an important political instruction urging us to safeguard the authority of the party Central Committee and military commission with Comrade Jiang Zemin as the core," the forces declared in a statement issued by Xinhua. Emphasizing the same point, and in an extreme case of overkill even for the Communist-controlled propaganda machine, the *People's Daily* used the phrase "Jiang Zemin as the core" a total of nine times in the final paragraphs of an editorial that same day on "inheriting the legacy" of Deng's reforms.

The nervous official outbursts were puzzling. On the streets there were certainly no suggestions of social unrest. As Jiang commented later: "Comrade Xiaoping's passing plunged all the party, the army, and the people into deep grief, but the entire mourning activities proceeded in an orderly way."[13] Was there any immediate danger from within the oxblood walls of Zhongnanhai? As we have seen, Jiang had relied on Deng's direct interventions to beat back fractious elders and uphold economic reforms until the end of 1992. In the two years after that, he had drawn on Deng's expressed approval to find his own way as China's top leader. But by early 1997, Jiang had already been ruling without the Dengist training wheels for a year or more. Having successfully completed the funeral ceremonies, there was no reason to expect a sudden challenge. As the China News Service noted: "It is precisely because of the early arrangements made by Deng Xiaoping to minimize his political weight that the third-generation leadership has been able to size up the overall situation effectively and ensure normal operations of the national political situation after the giant's demise."[14]

Indeed, Deng's death probably could not have come at a better time for Jiang. Any earlier and the articulation of "Jiang Thought" would have drawn fire as an attempt to revise the Deng legacy. Any later and Jiang's triumphant presiding over the return of Hong Kong and the fifteenth party congress in 1997 would have been overshadowed by the patriarch's declining health. Deng's exit was incredibly expedient. In death, as in life, Deng was Communist China's greatest pragmatist.

The only signs of faint challenge to Jiang came from the hard left, whose spiritual leader, the former party propaganda chief Deng Liqun, was left out of the memorial meeting at the request of Deng Xiaoping's children.[15] Jiang had already temporarily suspended Deng Liqun's magazine *Zhongliu* (Mainstream) for publishing the book review attacking *Yu zongshuji tanxin* (Talking Heart-to-Heart with the General Secretary). Given the backward-looking views the magazine represented, the suspension had won wide support in the party leadership, as had the barring of the orthodox Marxist from Deng's funeral. By April, Shenzhen magazines were attacking the unfavorable review of *Yu zongshuji tanxin* with a vengeance.[16]

Another absentee from Deng's funeral was the former Beijing mayor Peng Zhen, 95, probably the most senior elder after Deng and a well-known critic of party corruption. Peng had suffered a blood clot in his brain in 1993 that left him wheelchair-bound, with his right side paralyzed. Days before Deng's death he suffered another clot that left him in a coma.[17] For a time, it appeared that the two party giants might die at the same time, which would have presented a logistical nightmare. But Peng held on graciously until 26 April. His death left only three of the party "immortals" alive—Yang Shangkun, Bo Yibo, and Song Renqiong—and none of them appeared to pose even a moderate threat to Jiang.

Proof that Jiang was *not* feeling threatened in the immediate aftermath of Deng's death was provided by the rapid resumption of normal diplomatic activities by all major leaders. Jiang made his first overseas trip, to Russia, as scheduled, at the end of April.[18] While there, he announced to the Russian parliament that the two countries would build a "strategic cooperative partnership" for the coming century.[19] Jiang also took new initiatives on the Taiwan issue. To end a 48-year cross-strait shipping hiatus, Jiang in April compromised on the long-standing prohibition against mainland ships flying the Taiwan flag. This allowed a historic inaugural crossing by a mainland vessel on 19 April. The decision to allow the ship to fly the Taiwan flag briefly when entering the port at Kaohsiung was risky at home; it made Jiang vulnerable to charges of encouraging the island's independence.[20] But Deng's death had clearly given Jiang a boost of self-confidence, even if not of actual power.

Thus the nervous-looking shows of support for Jiang from the military and the party immediately after Deng's death were probably just part of the carefully scripted stage show rather than a response to perceived threats. The whole script had been intended to leave no doubt that Jiang would continue ruling the country; in the event, the reminders proved unnecessary.

3

A more critical issue was *how* Jiang would rule. Days after Deng's death, and before the funeral ceremony, Jiang had boasted to a foreign visitor that he would outperform Deng in running the country. "We shall run China's undertakings still better, and make greater contributions to the cause of peace, development, and the progress of mankind," he said in remarks issued by Xinhua.[21] It was an immediate and blunt declaration that "Jiang Thought," as outlined in chapters 9 and 10, was to be the new guiding policy. Jiang made this clear, and added new dimensions to his vision of China's future, with alacrity.

The convocation of the annual national parliamentary gathering in Beijing in the first week of March provided the perfect forum. Never more than a talking shop at the best of times, the parliament offered Jiang a stage on which to reassure the rank and file of his honorable intentions with respect to the Deng legacy. In his own version of the slavishly imitative approach of Hua Guofeng to Mao's legacy, in which "whatever" the Great Helmsman had said was declared to be sacred, Jiang told army delegates that following Deng's theories was "the most important and fundamental thing." "At no time and under no circumstances should we show the slightest ambiguity or vacillation on this major political issue," he told them at the parliament, wearing his now familiar olive green tunic for the occasion.

At the same time, he could point to the things he would change. The 40 percent of parliamentary deputies who rejected the annual report on fighting crime and corruption, a record protest vote in the body, seemed to add support to the notion of putting emphasis on issues that Deng had failed to solve. It was important that Jiang referred to upholding Deng's theories and not his words or actions. For in those theories could be found ample justification for most of the rearranging that Jiang had initiated. Had not Deng spoken at length about spiritual culture? Had not Deng made several speeches on political indoctrination? The Deng corpus was both broad and accessible. Leafing through the patriarch's legacy when it was needed became the new approach. Hua's "whatever-ism" became Jiang's "whenever-ism."

In the following two months, the new emphasis was made clear. In May, two major internal speeches made by Jiang shortly before Deng's death were dusted off and reissued to the public. They concerned patriotism and corruption, two of the key issues on which, as we have seen, he had staked his authority. Patriotism, he said, "should be turned into a mighty force to push forward the reform, opening up, modernization, and revitalization of the Chinese nation."[22] The speech on corruption was even more strident. The extent of official graft was "startling" (*chumu jingxin*), he said. Officials in areas that could not even pay government salaries were equipping themselves with mobile phones and luxury cars. Many were using their out-of-town offices for gambling, whoring, and drinking to excess. "How much money is wasted in these activities? It's hard to calculate," he said.[23]

Jiang's key speech about where he intended to take China was made at the Central Party School in Beijing on 29 May.[24] All the members of the Politburo, except for Qiao Shi, attended, and the speech was issued to the public the same day. Deng's policies, Jiang said, would remain at the heart of China's development, but "spiritual culture" would be there to "promote" that development, and "political reforms" would be "coordinated" with it. Over the following decade or more, China would experiment with different forms of economic organization, including shareholding, in order to establish a truly advanced market economy. Marxism and socialism, he stated outright, would be applied in light of China's practical conditions, not in a dogmatic way.

Thus in the months after Deng's death, Jiang was able quickly to assert the direction in which he intended to shepherd China. While the late patriarch's economic policies would remain in force, there would be renewed emphasis on fighting corruption, stoking patriotism, permitting shareholding as a form of public ownership, and strengthening the political system. In short, the creation of the "developmental dictatorship" that Jiang had already begun to envision in 1995 and 1996 would be accelerated. The party's fifteenth congress in the fall would provide the forum where these new departures would be carved into stone, as we shall see. As ever, if this process were carried out within the gradual and consensus-based confines in which Jiang had always acted, his position would be consolidated. If not, then there were many risks indeed.

4

Perhaps the shortest flight ever taken by a Chinese head of state on a diplomatic visit was achieved by Jiang Zemin on 30 June 1997. The long-awaited return of Hong Kong to Chinese sovereignty after 156 years as a British colony was due to take place at midnight that day. Jiang would lead the eighteen-member Chinese delegation, including Li Peng and Qian Qichen, to preside over the last rites of British rule and the raising of the Chinese flag in the territory. On that drizzling and humid Monday afternoon, the delegation, plus about 200 other various hangers-on, boarded two Air China 747s at the airport in Shenzhen, where they had arrived from Beijing the night before. The hop across the border to Hong Kong could have been achieved without so much as even retracting the landing gear. It was Jiang's fourth trip to Hong Kong, but he emerged from the plane very hesitantly. Partly this was because of the bulk of a bullet-proof vest, which made him look like Humpty Dumpty. But his careful steps were no doubt also a reflection of the significance of the occasion.

The return of Hong Kong was Jiang's chance to beat the drums of patriotism harder and to further his reputation as China's "reunification president." While he had been frustrated in attempts to achieve progress on the Taiwan issue, he could bask in the triumph of Hong Kong's agreed return to Chinese sovereignty. At a soirée one year before the handover, Jiang's image had been featured along with those of Mao and Deng as a "giant of national reunification."[25] Patriotism was also important for the new China Jiang was building, and the return of Hong Kong was an ideal foundation on which to proceed. "This will be the first stop in the long journey toward the reunification of the motherland," he had said. "A successful resolution of the Hong Kong issue will surely have a splendid impact on prospects for national reunification."[26]

In theory, Jiang had very little to say in the Hong Kong handover. Li Peng and Qian Qichen were in charge of the policies and personnel decisions of the transition itself, while Luo Gan headed the party's working group on the handover ceremony and celebrations.[27] Jiang's only role, in theory, was a ceremonial one as head of the state that was assuming sovereignty. Yet his actual influence on the Hong Kong handover was much more significant, a perfect example of his ability to work around the bureaucratic limitations on his authority.

In the first place, Jiang was instrumental in the critical decision to appoint Tung Chee-hwa (Dong Jianhua), a Hong Kong shipping magnate whose family hailed from Shanghai, as the territory's first chief executive under Chinese rule. Jiang had met Tung for the first time in Shanghai in March 1989, when Jiang was the city's party chief.[28] Tung was showing off his family's charity ship for teaching youngsters about the rigors of the outdoor life, and Jiang took an immediate liking to this avuncular man with a brush cut. A year and a half later, now installed as China's party chief, Jiang was already thinking about who would be chief executive of Hong Kong. He told a Taiwan visitor that Beijing would "send" a Hong Kong patriot to be chief executive, but that a final decision had not been made on whom to choose.[29] In the following six years, until Tung was formally made chief executive by a Beijing-appointed committee in December 1996, the two men maintained close contacts. An intensive search was conducted for a suitable chief executive candidate from among the well-known patriots in Hong Kong. The State Council's Hong Kong and Macao Affairs Office and the Hong Kong branch of the Xinhua News Agency (the de facto Chinese consulate under British rule) drew up two successive shortlists for consideration by Beijing. The best-informed account of the process, by a former journalist for a Beijing-run newspaper in Hong Kong, describes Jiang's role in the chief executive search this way: "He had the right to make very detailed comments and instructions, but he did not make the final decision."[30] The power to "comment and instruct" (*pishi*) was used to its full extent. Almost a year before the formal appointment of Tung, Jiang had committed an enormous but revealing blunder by singling him out from a delegation of 100 Hong Kong advisors for a special handshake in the full glare of the Hong Kong press corps in Beijing. Tung would forever be nicknamed in Hong Kong as "the one whose hand Jiang shook" (*Jiang wo shou*). While he did not have the formal authority to sign Tung's nomination into policy, it was clear that Jiang's "comments and instructions" had favored Tung. In the end, he got his way.

Jiang also took the lead in ensuring that there would be no meddling in Hong Kong affairs by various provincial governments or central ministries and departments. This was revealing. Hong Kong was significant to Jiang mainly because its return played into his greater vision of China's future, in which patriotism was a key element. He had no other interest in Hong Kong, unlike the various departments and local governments of China. Thus his personal desire was to protect the territory from interference, so that its success would forever bestir patriotism in the mainland.

Shortly after Tiananmen, Jiang told three visiting Hong Kong politicians that the classic Chinese proverb "Well water should not be mixed with river water" (*jing shui bu fan he shui*) should guide the relations between the mainland and Hong Kong after 1997.[31] The apparent implication was that Hong Kong people should not interfere in mainland affairs, as evidenced most recently by their sympathy protests and material support for the Tiananmen protesters. This distancing of the two places at a time when they were supposed to be converging toward 1997 provoked criticism within the leadership. "Ninety-eight percent of Hong Kongers are Chinese people. How can you confine them to the status of 'well water,' standing outside the 'river water' of the Chinese people . . . to such a hostile status?" wondered Xu Jiatun, the director of Xinhua Hong Kong at the time.[32] The criticisms were not entirely fair. It is true that Jiang probably intended to warn "subversives" in Hong Kong against bringing their political campaigns to the mainland. But he also quoted the proverb to admonish mainland groups to stay out of Hong Kong affairs; river water also should not be mixed with well water. "The second part of the allegory is taken for granted," he later explained.[33]

Indeed, this implied second meaning would figure much more prominently in Jiang's comments on the Hong Kong issue in coming years. From early 1996 on, he began publicly warning local governments and central ministries and departments against "sticking their hands" into Hong Kong's affairs. He also warned the future PLA garrison in Hong Kong that they were *not* supposed to "liberate" the territory but instead would play a mainly symbolic role. "No one should have the mentality that the handover is like the march south of the PLA in the old days [of the civil war]," he told the Politburo in a closed-door meeting in October 1995. "We have to make sure that we do not cause disorder in Hong Kong."[34] The various warnings were later embodied in a Central Committee document he issued, number nine of April 1997, that forbade any direct contacts between local and central ministry authorities on the mainland and the Hong Kong government after the handover. There were also to be restrictions on the setting up of companies and representative offices in the territory, which would have to be approved and handled by the Hong Kong and Macao Affairs Office.[35] "Even I shall have to obey the 'one country, two systems' formula," Jiang told CNN months before the handover.[36]

In justifying a hands-off policy toward Hong Kong, Jiang could, of course, appeal to the lofty goals of providing the promised "high degree of autonomy" for the territory, making a success of the "one country, two systems" formula, which would later be applied to Taiwan, and ensuring that corruption and red tape from the mainland did not creep across the border and ruin the territory's valuable economy. This would ensure that the patriotic harvest of Hong Kong's return continued to be reaped by Beijing. At the same time, it also meshed nicely with Jiang's own internal political interests in controlling local authorities and the central bureaucracy. Through the Hong Kong issue, Jiang was ensuring that the grudging fealty he had won from the provinces in 1993–94, and over the central bureaucracy through a longer and slower process since 1989, was reemphasized. Just as he had used the Taiwan issue to win greater scope in the diplomatic field, he used the Hong Kong issue to assert his influence over government and party networks at home.

When Jiang stepped off the plane in Hong Kong on 30 June, there were fewer than ten hours left of British sovereignty. He held hasty meetings with the British prime minister, Tony Blair, and then with his counterpart for the handover ceremony, Prince Charles, before retiring to prepare for it. Nothing could go wrong. An estimated 2 billion people would be watching live around the world. Fortunately for Jiang, nothing did go wrong. Both sides had scripted everything, right down to when the reverberations of the cymbals from the British ceremonial band would die out as the British flag was lowered at midnight. "The eyes of the world are on us at this moment," Jiang said with both literal and figurative accuracy shortly after the Chinese flag was raised in the convention center hall and began to flutter in air piped through the base of the flagpole. "This is both a great event for the Chinese nation as well as a victory for the universal cause of peace and justice."[37]

The handover achieved, 4,000 PLA troops moved into the territory by land, air, and sea in the early hours of 1 July. Shortly before arriving in Hong Kong, Jiang had issued the command for the garrison to "enter" Hong Kong. It was the first time that he had ordered a troop mobilization other than for exercises as military commission chairman. While he had been at pains to distinguish the garrison's entry from the "liberation" of cities during the civil war, there was little doubt that the army and many others in the leadership took it as such. The twenty-one armored anti-riot vehicles that rumbled through the streets of Hong

Kong at dawn, their turret men standing erect with leather communications helmets wrapped around their heads, could have been from any scene of the parade of Allied forces through western European cities at the close of World War II.

In late morning on 1 July, at a gathering to mark the establishment of the Hong Kong "special administrative region" of China, Jiang was positively glowing. "This is a glorious page in the annals of the Chinese nation," he told the meeting, looking much more relaxed than at the handover ceremony. Halfway through Tung Chee-hwa's inaugural address, at the mention of the "one country, two systems" formula, Jiang turned to Deng's widow, Zhuo Lin, who was sitting beside him in the front row and raised her to her feet to loud applause. It was Deng, after all, who had borrowed this phrase from a researcher on Taiwan affairs in Beijing in the early 1980s to solve the Hong Kong issue, and Deng who had insisted that China would take back Hong Kong when negotiations with Britain began in 1982. Jiang was now basking in the glory of Deng's work; the least he could do was show some thanks.

Emphasizing the important patriotic capital to be gained from the Hong Kong handover, Jiang rushed back to Beijing after less than twenty-four hours in Hong Kong to take part in celebrations there. The jingoistic language of his speech before 8,000 people crammed into the Workers' Stadium was entirely different from the magnanimity of his utterances in Hong Kong. The 156 years of colonial history had represented "vicissitudes" (*cangsang*) in Hong Kong, but were "a national disgrace" (*guochi*) once he was before the home audience. The peaceful resolution of the Hong Kong issue was a tribute to "people in both China and Britain" when he was in Hong Kong, but to "the leadership of the Chinese Communist Party" in Beijing.[38] Clearly, the return of Hong Kong was being squeezed for every ounce of propaganda value at home.

At the end of the day, Hong Kong was significant to Jiang for several reasons, none of them having to do with Hong Kong itself. Its successful takeover smoothed the way, at least in the minds of mainland officials, for the return of Taiwan. The nationalist surge that it set off played nicely into Jiang's patriotism campaign. And the efforts he made to prevent meddling in Hong Kong affairs helped maintain his leverage with the central bureaucracy and local governments.

Jiang had little experience and no friends among the Cantonese Chinese who mostly peopled the territory. More to the point, he appeared to have little interest in Hong Kong. When someone mentioned the territory's "four kings" of pop music to him on one occasion, he admitted to thinking they were referring to characters in the Chinese classical novel *Journey to the West* and bragged of his ignorance.[39] Another time, after meeting Hong Kong's financial secretary, Donald Tsang, he immediately forgot Tsang's name and title and was disdainful enough to ask another Chinese official to jog his memory when describing the meeting to the press.[40] His clumsy attempts at mimicking the Cantonese dialect of Chinese elicited only laughter.

In many ways, Jiang's attitude to Hong Kong was similar to that of Lin Zexu, the opium-spoiling hero of the late Qing Dynasty whose actions had led to the British takeover of the island. Lin's spirit, it will be recalled, had been invoked by Wang Daohan to encourage Jiang to take up office in Beijing in 1989. Now, like Lin, Jiang saw his role primarily as eliminating a "national disgrace" rather than improving the lives of those being disgraced. Like Lin, he also stood to gain prestige at court in Beijing for his bravery. It was fitting therefore that the southern Chinese soon had a wry sobriquet for the handover of Hong Kong that embodied the true meaning of the change of sovereignty for Jiang: "The revenge of Lin Zexu."

5

When a dozen American academics trooped into a hall at the mock Qing dynasty Diaoyutai state guesthouse in June 1996 for a meeting with Jiang Zemin, they expected little more than stock answers to the four questions on China's future they had submitted in advance. Jiang's black Audi swept up to the entrance promptly at the appointed hour and the party chief marched in with his usual clatter of English travel phrases and hearty chuckles. To their surprise, Jiang sat down, put aside his prepared answers, and launched into a half-hour monologue that might have been entitled: "Why I am not a dictator." As the astounded scholars bent their ears in fascination, he went on about China's third-generation collective leadership, the limits on political power in late-twentieth-century China, and his own consensual style. "By the time you leave this room," Jiang promised, "not one of you will say to yourselves: 'That Jiang fellow is a real dictator.'"[41]

The Chinese Communist Party was approaching its fifteenth congress in September 1997, and it was clear that Jiang was laying the groundwork for securing his own position into the next century. Minutes of the Diaoyutai meeting, as always, would be transcribed by the Jiang Office and circulated to the Politburo, as well as to others specified by Jiang. It was those colleagues, not the American scholars, who were the intended audience for the outburst that day.

Recall that during his southern tour of early 1992, shortly before the fourteenth party congress, Deng Xiaoping had endorsed Jiang's continued rule into the next century. Most took this to mean that Jiang could rule until the sixteenth party congress, which would be held in 2002. In the years since Deng's endorsement, Jiang had achieved much, taming the Dengist growth boom, maintaining political stability, and carefully moving to address areas that Deng had neglected. "Jiang's seven years in power give him a convincing basis on which to hold power into the next century," *Jing bao* commented.[42]

The question was, in what capacity? A whole matrix of personnel issues had to be solved at the fifteenth congress, and Jiang sat at the center. Among the objectives was to clear the way for a "fourth generation" of leaders who would eventually succeed Jiang and his cohorts. One way to ensure a stable succession would be to identify a sort of party chief in waiting at the fifteenth congress, an arrangement favored by Jiang. To achieve this, he suggested reestablishing the position of party chairman, which had been abolished in 1982. He would become party chairman and the future leader would take over as party general secretary.[43] The plan also had the merit that Li Peng could be made a vice-chairman of the party, easing his transition out of power in early 1998 after two terms as premier.

Jiang's impassioned defense of his nondictatorial style before the startled American scholars in mid 1996 appeared aimed at building support for his assuming the magisterial position of party chairman. As part of the same effort, Xing Bensi penned a *People's Daily* commentary in May 1997 arguing that Jiang should become the "principal violinist" in the collective leadership. "A collective leadership should have a representative person. . . . This person should be an individual assuming overall responsibilities and enjoying higher prestige, greater influence, and more experience in the collective leadership," Xing wrote.[44]

Qiao Shi, the chairman of the National People's Congress, raised an early note of constitutional opposition to the plan when it was first floated in early 1996. Qiao told a German newspaper that the country's political system should not change "because of the changing opinions and interests of leaders," a phrase later included in the congress communiqué.[45] But the main opposition to the plan came from the four party

elders who had been "invited" to help make preparations for the fifteenth congress, former Politburo member Bo Yibo, former president
Yang Shangkun, former NPC chairman Wan Li, and former party organization chief Song Ping. None of the four was particularly beholden to
Jiang in the first place.[46] Moreover, they feared that making Jiang party
chairman would risk creating a dictatorial party leader—precisely the
reason Deng had abolished the post—and weaken the collective nature
of the leadership.[47]

In the end, Jiang was forced to back down when final personnel decisions were made at the Beidaihe resort in August 1997. After "contin-
uous consultations" with the four elders, he thought better of the idea
and agreed to remain party general secretary.[48] It was a stark reminder,
especially in the wake of Deng's death, that there were still real limits on
his authority that could not be transgressed.

The dispensation agreed upon at Beidaihe was a well-kept secret. The
party congress opened in Beijing on 12 September. But not until it closed
a week later did the 2,048 delegates, and the rest of the world, find out
what had been decided on the summer beaches.

The biggest surprise was the resignation of Qiao Shi, who was dropped
from the Central Committee (and thus also from the Politburo) on the
grounds that he was too old at 72.[49] To justify this, it had been decided
in Beidaihe that those over 70 by the end of June 1997 should retire.[50]
The age limit itself was not controversial, since it had been the guideline
since the twelfth congress of 1982. But the cutoff date was entirely arbi-
trary and came just two months shy of Jiang's seventy-first birthday. He
later sheepishly admitted the sleight of hand to Japanese visitors: "I
gained some petty advantages [zhan pianyi] in this way," he told them.[51]

Attempts were made to portray Qiao's retirement as a cordial part-
ing of ways rather than as a purge; the goggle-eyed NPC chairman
walked into the opening of the congress shoulder-to-shoulder with Jiang,
and the closing session of the congress was extended by two hours to
heap praise on his achievements. Qiao also sat next to Jiang at the National Day soirée two weeks after the congress closed. "This is a very
natural generational change," Jiang explained of Qiao's departure.[52]

The age argument was plausible enough. But it was clear that Qiao's
departure also reflected his political differences with Jiang and the new
elite. The ten-year veteran of the Politburo standing committee remained
keener on political reforms and on healing the wounds of the Tiananmen
massacre than his colleagues.[53] In May, he had used his evaporating
power to release two dissidents convicted during the 1989 protests.[54] In

internal speeches, he frequently complained about the undue concentration of senior cadres from coastal areas, the lack of power granted to the NPC, and—most courageously—the dangers of Jiang holding the top posts of the party, state and military.[55] His studied absence from Jiang's critical Central Party School speech perfectly reflected his differences with the new elite on all these issues.[56] Stepping down was clearly preferable to the humiliating prospect of becoming a neutered party senior. Qiao would henceforth rank as the number three party elder, after Yang Shangkun and Wan Li, but ahead of Song Ping and Bo Yibo.

For Jiang, the presence of this fellow veteran of the underground Shanghai Communist movement of the 1940s had never been a real threat, as we have seen. Indeed, the ease of Qiao's removal is evidence of this. Yet outside China, rightly or wrongly, Qiao had always been seen as a great democratic hope. His resignation would help dispel doubts abroad that Jiang was fully in charge.

The same message was clear from the entire new lineup announced at the congress. Zhu Rongji was formally made "executive" vice-premier, showing he would replace Li Peng the following spring as premier. Zhu, of course, was being rewarded for his Herculean efforts in reforming China's economic system. He had introduced financial reforms to bring the country out of an inflationary orbit in 1993 and 1994 while maintaining steady economic growth. And he had foisted a new tax system on the provinces, shedding five and a half pounds of weight as a result of his exertions. As premier, he would remain in charge of economic policy-making, enhancing his effectiveness in this area.

His promotion also had implications outside the economic sphere; as premier, Zhu would help strengthen Jiang's hand over the bureaucratic systems that had once balked at his authority. In particular, since Zhu would now replace Li as head of the party's leading group on foreign affairs, Jiang would be in a better position to influence the nation's diplomacy. This might give him more scope for bettering relations with the United States, as well as reducing military influence in foreign policy.[57] At a more general level, Jiang would also bask in the reflected glory of the amiable and effective Zhu Rongji, just as he had in Shanghai. The confident and straight-talking fellow native of Jiangsu province was a vast improvement on the stiff and insecure Li Peng.[58]

There were two new members of the Politburo standing committee. Wei Jianxing was Jiang's aide-de-camp in the war on corruption. Vice-premier Li Lanqing, who would assist in handling economic affairs, was Jiang's former colleague from the Changchun Number One Vehicle Plant in the 1950s. "Team Jiang" also made its presence felt at the congress. Most prominent was the totally shameless elevation of Jiang's spin doctor, Zeng Qinghong, to alternate Politburo member status and membership in the party secretariat, even though he was not even a member of the previous Central Committee. Speechwriter Teng Wensheng also leapt into the Central Committee. Normal promotion rules had clearly been waived for Jiang's closest acolyte. A more stately pace was set by his chief economic advisor, Zeng Peiyan, the man with the charts, who stepped up from being an alternate member to full membership on the Central Committee and was also made minister of the new State Development and Planning Commission.[59] Another Jiang ally joining the Central Committee was the "iron lady" Chen Zhili, also made minister of the new Ministry of Education. As Shanghai's propaganda chief in 1989, Chen had assisted Jiang in closing down the World Economic Herald.

Since Jiang's attempt to reestablish the position of party chairman had been thwarted, the identification of the head of the "fourth generation" who would eventually succeed him as party general secretary was not clear. Some names were clearly in the running, however. Hu Jintao, still just 54 at the time of the congress, not only retained his position on the Politburo standing committee and the party secretariat but would be made vice-president at the following spring's NPC meeting.

Hu had long been marked for greatness within the "fourth generation." Like Jiang, Hu had been brought up in Jiangsu province and in Shanghai. He had only just joined the party when the Cultural Revolution erupted and was sent to do light work in remote Gansu province. There he caught the attention of Song Ping, then Gansu party chief and one of the elders involved in the fifteenth congress personnel debates. After a stint as head of the Communist Youth League in the 1980s, Hu served as party secretary of Tibet from 1988 to 1992. He was recalled to Beijing suffering from altitude sickness and joined the Politburo standing committee in 1992. The following year, he began grooming young cadres as head of the Central Party School and as deputy to Jiang of a leading group on new cadres.[60]

There is little doubt that Hu shares Jiang's concern for whipping the party into shape by means of more thoroughgoing ideological indoctrination and political discipline. Jiang's choice of the Central Party School as the venue for his crucial May 1997 speech reflected the affinities between the two men. Hu, however, has little experience in handling economic affairs. Were he to succeed Jiang as party general secretary, the country's economic reform program might slow. Likewise, Hu has little experience of diplomacy, one apparent reason he was made vice-president, and none of the interest in Western culture of Jiang and Deng. As China's next leader, he might find it difficult to establish a personal rapport with Western, or even Asian, leaders.

Other claimants to fourth-generation leadership positions had also been emerging before the congress. The Shanghai party secretary Huang Ju, 59 at the time of the congress, had been added to the Politburo three years earlier. His immediate predecessor as Shanghai party chief, Wu Bangguo, 56, had been made vice-premier in charge of state industry in early 1995.[61] Both retained their Politburo seats. Meanwhile, two gnomes of the powerful internal party committees that control major decision-making, Luo Gan (aged 62 at the congress) and Wen Jiabao (55), both joined the Politburo. Wen would be made a vice-premier the following spring.

Together, these five men (the only women who appeared to have outside shots were Chen Zhili and state councillor, Wu Yi) would be seen as key members of the "fourth generation" leadership. As legitimately appointed successors, they now had the right to flex their muscles without being accused of engaging in the factional struggles that Deng had excoriated. Jiang's task now was not so much to accumulate authority as to preserve it. Still, while the exact personnel lineup at the sixteenth party congress would depend on events in the interim, it was clear that those in the running for the succession shared Jiang's vision of China's future. Like Jiang, they were all enthusiastic economic reformers, as well as diligent party cadres who "paid attention to politics." It was the dawn of what one Communist newspaper called "the era of government by professionals," dominated by university-educated cadres with experience in specialized areas.[62]

The congress also witnessed the long-expected retirement of the two Dengist representatives on the military commission, Liu Huaqing and Zhang Zhen. While they had not for the most part opposed Jiang on the commission, the two hoary generals were a reminder of the long shadow of the patriarch from which Jiang was now emerging. In the same symbolic vein, General Yang Baibing, whose purge from the military commission in 1992 had heralded the beginning of Jiang's control over the army, was finally dropped from the Politburo and Central Committee.

Liu Huaqing's automatic removal from the Politburo standing committee left that body without a military representative for the first time in the history of Communist China. Military representation on the Central Committee doubled from 15 to 31, but the new appointees were all young soldiers promoted to regional posts under the professional, rules-based criteria favored by Jiang. Their loyalty could be taken as read. The same message of a more professional and less political army was carried in Jiang's announcement at the congress that the PLA would shed 500,000 of its three million soldiers by the year 2000.[63] As when Deng had declared a reduction in the PLA soldiery of one million in 1985, the announcement symbolized Jiang's confidence in his control over the army.

At the end of the congress, Jiang marched his new Politburo standing committee onto a stage before journalists, like a mother duck swimming before her new brood. (See Table 1.) The austere face of Chinese politics since Tiananmen prevailed, and no questions were entertained, partly to avoid prickly queries about Qiao Shi's retirement.[64] Each member was introduced, Zhu being the only one to smile and wave in greeting. Jiang had lobbied hard and accepted some compromises in the new dispensation announced at the fifteenth congress. In the end, though, the new elite that emerged tallied almost perfectly with his goals. His only putative rival, Qiao Shi, was retired; the military commission was purged of its past; and many Jiang acolytes and supporters rose another notch in the hierarchy. It would likely be enough to secure Jiang's leadership into the next century.

6

Sipping tea from a white enamel mug, his live image emblazoned on a giant state-of-the-art video screen, Jiang opened the fifteenth party congress in the Great Hall of the People on 12 September with a two-and-a-half-hour speech that contained several important changes in economic policy and party ideology. Given the limits placed on his power in the personnel debates preceding the congress, it was little surprise that Jiang insisted on having his way in the congress communiqué. If his formal tenure was going to end in 2002, giving him perhaps another five to ten years of significant influence on party decisions after that, the time to put his ideas—"Jiang Thought"—into action was now. "'Jiang Thought' has already taken form in the military," the Hong Kong periodical *Guangjiaojing* (Wide Angle) noted. "At the fifteenth congress, it will be extended to the whole country, having a new influence on twenty-first century China."[65]

Jiang made it clear that he intended to exert a dominant influence on the congress communiqué. At the 1996 party plenum, he took the unusual step of declaring that the congress would be held the following year.[66] He promised that the congress would deliver "a comprehensive

General Secretary
    Jiang Zemin

Political Bureau (Politburo)

Standing Committee Members (7)
    Party general secretary: Jiang Zemin
    NPC chairman: Li Peng
    Premier: Zhu Rongji
    Vice-president, head of party secretariat: Hu Jintao
    CPPCC chairman: Li Ruihuan
    CDIC secretary: Wei Jianxing*
    Vice-premier: Li Lanqing*
    (Qiao Shi)
    (Liu Huaqing)

Regular Members (15)
    Head of party propaganda: Ding Guangen
    NPC executive vice-chairman: Tian Jiyun
    President of Chinese Academy of Social Sciences: Li Tieying
    Vice-premier: Wu Bangguo
    NPC vice-chairman: Jiang Chunyun
    Vice-premier: Qian Qichen
    Shanghai party secretary: Huang Ju
    NPC vice-chairman: Xie Fei
    Guangdong party secretary: Li Changchun*
    Shandong party secretary: Wu Guanzheng*
    State councillor, CMC vice-chairman, defense minister: Chi Haotian*
    CMC vice-chairman: Zhang Wannian*
    State councillor: Luo Gan*
    Beijing party secretary: Jia Qinglin*
    Vice-premier: Wen Jiabao*
    (Yang Baibing)
    (Zou Jiahua)

Alternate Members (2)
    Head of party General Office (Jiang Office): Zeng Qinghong*
    State councillor: Wu Yi*
    (Wang Hanbin)

Party Secretariat (7)
    Hu Jintao
    Wei Jianxing
    Ding Guangen
    Wen Jiabao
    Zeng Qinghong*
    Luo Gan*
    Zhang Wannian*
    (Wu Bangguo)

TABLE 1 *(continued)*

Party Secretariat (continued)
    (Jiang Chunyun)
    (Ren Jianxin)

Central Military Commission

Chairman
    Jiang Zemin

Vice-Chairmen (2)
    Zhang Wannian
    Chi Haotian
    (Liu Huaqing)
    (Zhang Zhen)

Regular Members (4)
    PLA chief of staff: Fu Quanyou
    PLA political department director: Yu Yongbo
    PLA logistics department director: Wang Ke
    PLA political department deputy director: Wang Ruilin

Notes: Members newly elected are marked with an asterisk. Members removed are enclosed in parentheses.

strategic plan for reform, development, stability and other major issues" and later told Korean reporters that this would "provide a strong political and organizational guarantee for smoothly realizing the great blueprint of China for facing the next century."[67]

In October 1996, a team was established led by Ding Guangen to begin drafting the communiqué. Xinhua later claimed that Jiang was virtually writing the document himself.[68] But the fact that it took eight drafts before a final version was agreed to informally at the Beidaihe conclave suggests a process of consensus-building and compromise more typical of Jiang's style.[69] As with the whole thrust of "Jiang Thought", the communiqué consciously laid stress on issues that Deng had neglected or left unresolved.[70]

Most prominent was the decision to allow partial divestment of state-owned enterprises in order to improve their performance. The endorsement of "diversified forms of ownership," the communiqué said, would allow a "strategic adjustment of the role of the state-owned sector in the national economy."

Jiang accepted the popular notion that shareholding enterprises could be considered a form of "public ownership" as long as the state retained a controlling share. This was considered by many economists to be the best solution to the loss of state enterprises that would preserve the myth of China as a socialist state. Gao Shangquan, vice-minister of the state economic reform commission, argued passionately that the shareholding system was the only way to prevent the 240,000 state enterprises from being pushed to the wall. "Otherwise, they will rebel," he said.[71]

Jiang had voiced support for wider shareholding as early as mid 1993.[72] By early 1997, he was lobbying for a formal endorsement of a policy under which the state would divest itself of a significant portion of its productive assets, spreading ownership around collective, foreign, and private entities. The constitutional guarantee of public ownership as the mainstay of the economy would be upheld by the state's retaining a controlling stake in key industries and by widening the definition of "public" to include collectively owned assets as well.

In February 1997, Jiang had first told the national business federation that although government ownership could still be useful in some cases, it was "more important to explore new methods, measures, and practices" of ownership.[73] That meant the shareholding system, he said, "which should not be seen in an oversimplified way as a form of privatization."[74] The message was broadcast loud and clear in the Central Party School speech of May 1997: "We should make every effort to seek new forms of public ownership," he said.

Any endorsement of shareholding as a substitute for state ownership—privatization in most people's eyes—would, of course, be a radical departure for China. A torrid article in the hard-left *Zhenlide zhuiqiu* (Search for Truth) magazine in April 1997 had warned that the plan would virtually bring an end to socialism. "Calling for the implementation of a shareholding system in state-owned enterprises can only have a destructive effect on development," it said. "In essence, this is no more than a cover for weakening the state-owned economy and achieving private ownership."[75]

But Jiang was not acting in isolation in advocating wider use of the shareholding system. He had the support not only of economists like Gao Shangquan, but also of the entire Politburo standing committee, including Li Peng and Zhu Rongji. The outspoken Tian Jiyun even stated that to deny this form of ownership to the struggling state firms "would be a crime against the people and the country."[76]

Perhaps more important, Jiang had the enthusiastic support of local leaders in provinces that were laden with loss-making state enterprises.

"We have to overcome our worries and make shareholding a big part of the state enterprise reforms," said the Shandong party chief Wu Guanzheng.[77] Not that local leaders needed convincing. By 1996, the state-owned sector accounted for just 35 percent of China's GDP, while the collective sector (mainly village- and town-owned firms) accounted for 37 percent. The "non-public" sector (mainly private and foreign firms) accounted for the other 28 percent.[78] More significant, perhaps, was that private and foreign firms had absorbed three-quarters of the 11 million new entrants to the labor force in 1996.[79] With perhaps a third of the 100 million staff in state firms needing to be sacked, the importance of encouraging participation from the "nonpublic" sector was clear. "For us in the poor inland areas, there is an especially great imperative to develop the collective and the nonpublic sectors," the governor of Jiangxi province, Shu Shengyou, said shortly before the congress. "We must not get bogged down in the old question of the proportion [of state ownership] and thereby constrain ourselves."[80]

Less publicly, but equally important, the World Bank was at this time also urging the Chinese government to divest itself of assets and retain controlling stakes only in strategic sectors. "China's future lies with vibrant, competitive and private firms," a World Bank report released during the congress observed.[81]

The diversification of ownership was in any case already in full swing on the ground. By the time of the congress, there were 9,200 medium- and large-scale state enterprises—a quarter of the total—that had turned themselves into limited liability shareholding companies.[82] Some had listed shares on Chinese stock markets, while others had sold shares to employees. In all, the state held just 43 percent of their assets. For shareholding companies as a whole (including those without limited liability and large-sized state firms), the state's average share was 58 percent.[83] As in so many of China's successful economic reforms, the leadership was following in the path of others rather than blazing the trail itself. The party's imprimatur was still important though. Without it, the scale and durability of the changes could not be assured.

In the following years, the new policy would lead to most of the small and medium-sized state firms being spun off or allowed to go under. Zhu Rongji, as usual, would ensure that Jiang looked good by managing the changes. He warned local governments at the congress against launching a "storm" of divestitures.[84] He also cautioned investors in the newly divested firms not to complain to the government if they lost all their money. "Investors these days can't deal with risk. In the old days, shareholders who were ruined simply threw themselves into the Huangpu River [in Shanghai]. Wasn't that better?" he said in a typically blunt aside.[85]

As for the 3,000-odd largest state firms, a third of which lost money, the central government would make a one-time payment of Rmb150 billion to clear up the worst of their debts (which totaled between Rmb300 billion and Rmb400 billion at the end of 1996).[86] After that, even they would be expected to turn a profit. "It will cause temporary difficulties for some workers. But fundamentally speaking it is conducive to economic development," Jiang said at the congress.

At the most general level, the decisive move to solve the state-enterprise quagmire offered hope that China's double-digit growth could be sustained well into the next century. By releasing the pent-up capital of the firms (especially their land) and reducing their drag on the banking system, the reforms would benefit the entire economy. Nonstate firms would have better access to loans and less unfair competition from subsidized state monopolies. The World Bank, which estimated that China's economy had grown at an annual clip of 9.5 percent from 1978 to 1996, predicted that with these and other necessary economic reforms, an average rate of 6.6 percent could be maintained through the year 2020.[87]

The endorsement of wider shareholding was also another chapter in the "gradualist" approach to economic reform, in stark contrast to the "shock therapy" prescribed in the former Soviet Union and Eastern Europe. Jiang himself had by this time mastered gradualist lore. Experiments on the ground were first studied and commended if successful. Then a careful lobbying effort was begun behind closed doors to endorse the changes nationwide, followed by a more public propaganda campaign. Once everyone was in agreement, the reform was put into writing. *Jing bao* was effusive in comparing this to the watershed 1978 rural reforms launched by Deng. "This will become a new milestone in China's economic development and a great event of historical significance to the third generation of the party leadership," it said.[88]

Jiang's second major achievement at the congress was to firmly implant a policy framework that would allow for more such proto-capitalist reforms in the future. At the Central Party School speech in May, Jiang had resurrected the idea that the "socialist" economy of China was still at the stage when it should be strengthened through both public and private ownership. Only later should the issue of "public" ownership be raised. This was the so-called "primary stage" theory, which the *People's Daily* referred to shortly before the congress as "the most basic national condition of China." "This is a golden key to unlocking the courage and wisdom of the Chinese people, as well as their ability to make miracles," the newspaper effused.[89]

The "primary stage" theory was actually a mere reiteration of party policy. In the wake of the Cultural Revolution, Deng had first articulated the theory to prevent a return of radical leftism in economic policy. Zhao Ziyang later wrote it into the thirteenth party congress document in 1987. But because it was tainted by Zhao's hand, and because of the subsequent collapse of communism in Eastern Europe, the theory had been avoided in public speeches since then. Jiang's ability to resurrect it now reflected his own enhanced personal stature as well as a new confidence within the Chinese Communist Party that reducing state ownership would not in itself fatally weaken the party's hold on power.

The thirteenth congress had asserted that the "primary stage" would last for about 100 years from the nationalization of key assets in 1956. That meant that until at least 2056, the state should be satisfied with holding control of key sectors, like transport and telecommunications, oil and gas, grain, banking, iron and steel, and power generation. Everything else could be opened to private control. In theory, the promised socialist Arcadia, where the entire economy was in public hands, would arrive eventually, but that day was now officially deferred until well past the lifetimes of China's current and prospective leaders. Li Ruihuan suggested at the congress that it might take "several generations, a dozen generations or even dozens of generations."[90]

The "primary stage" assertion was written into the congress communiqué as a preface to the section on wider ownership. Besides its far-reaching implications for economic reform, it was also symbolic of Jiang himself. Not only did it reflect his liberal economic instincts and his dislike for orthodox Marxism, but it also fitted his political program at the time. It could form a key element of the distinct philosophy of governance, "Jiang Thought", that he was forging, even if it was borrowed from the past. "By outlining the 'primary stage' situation, Jiang has provided theoretical support for ongoing government work and reform policies," *Jing bao* noted.[91]

A more symbolic part of the policy framework Jiang erected at the fifteenth congress was the incorporation of Deng's theories into the party constitution. This was an unassailable gesture. For not only had Deng articulated the "primary stage" idea, but the whole gamut of the late patriarch's economic policies was the basis on which Jiang and his colleagues continued to push China out of its Stalinist economic past. The

point of Deng's sacred legacy was reinforced when his disabled son, Deng
Pufang, was made an alternate member of the Central Committee. "In
China today, only Deng Xiaoping Theory can solve the future of social-
ism," Jiang said. "It is the new Marxism of China."

7

In stark contrast to the ambitious economic reforms that the fifteenth
congress set in motion, the promise of political reforms was dashed. A
year before Deng's death, *Jing bao* had noted that popular calls for political reforms to be restarted were growing.[92] Political reforms were necessary to ensure that the third generation did not become more dictatorial in the wake of Deng's death, it said. They could also provide new
avenues for popular political participation to prevent a repeat of 1989.

In the run-up to the congress, genuine hopes for such changes had
been raised. The mention of the once taboo phrase "political reforms"
in the Deng eulogy was thought at first to have been a harmless aside.
But in a preface to a new book on Deng's theories issued in mid March,
Jiang broached the issue again. "While deepening economic reforms,
we should also continue to push ahead with political reforms," he
wrote.[93] The *People's Daily*, in the first of a series of editorials in late
March, also echoed the view that political reforms were necessary to
consolidate the gains of the Deng era.[94] At the Central Party School in
May, Jiang made the point again: while seeking breakthroughs in economic reforms, he said, "we should push ahead with political structure
reforms."

As with the economic reforms, the prospect of political reforms was
seized upon with alacrity by scholars and newspapers in the lead-up to
the fifteenth congress. Scholars like Du Guang of the Central Cadres
School and Shang Dewen of Beijing University came out of the wood
work to appeal for faster political reforms, which, Du noted, "have seriously stagnated."[95] Even Liu Ji, one of Jiang's closest theoretical advisors, admitted in a candid interview with the official China News Service
before the congress that political reform was "lagging behind." "When
the people have enough to eat and wear and when they are better educated, they will want to express their views," Liu said. "If the Communist Party is to truly serve the people and wants to be a political party
that stands at the forefront of the times, it should adopt new measures
to satisfy this demand of the people."[96]

Though a full section of Jiang's congress speech was devoted to political reform, it delivered little that was new. Supervision and controls
on party leadership were to be "improved." The direct multi-candidate
elections by universal suffrage already used to choose leaders in most of
the country's 930,000 villages would be expanded to cities. The bureaucracy would be downsized. Fifteen ministries would later be abolished and plans would be set in motion to lay off half of the country's
eight million civil servants. A complete legal system would be established
by the year 2010. But none of the suggestions mooted by scholars in the
elation of the previous months, like veto powers for the NPC standing
committees or direct elections for senior government positions, were
mentioned.

So what did Jiang mean by political reforms? Jiang, like Deng before
him, was a staunch opponent of multiparty democracy. "We should not
mimic Western political systems," he told the congress. In the "developmental dictatorship" he was moving toward, there was no room for
political plurality. Instead, political reform meant increasing the supervision over the ruling Communist Party and allowing a modicum of popular participation in other political decisions. "Political reform must be
beneficial to the strengthening and improvement of the leadership of the
Communist Party," declared the Qinghua University professor Li Li, one
of Jiang's key advisors on political reform.[97] "The starting point and focal point of political reform must be the strengthening and improvement,
not the weakening or abandonment, of the party's leading role," *Jing
bao* added.[98]

Li Li argued in favor of essentially administrative reforms—like more
"sunshine laws" for the reporting of cadre assets, more regulations to
govern cadre promotions, and "closer cooperation" with supervisory
bodies such as the standing committees of the NPC—that would "perfect" the prevailing Leninist system. Elements of popular democracy—
like referendums and elections to the highest government posts (i.e.,
premier)—might be introduced in future, he said, but they were "inappropriate" at present.[99]

Liu Junning of the China Academy of Social Sciences (CASS) argued
that the political reforms of the fifteenth congress were "implicit" rather
than "explicit."[100] The expansion of the shareholding structure, for example, would significantly roll back the frontiers of government, just as
the adoption of the market economy had after the fourteenth congress.

But it was hard to escape the conclusion that Jiang was simply not in-
terested in suggesting the sorts of pluralistic political reforms that had

swallowed up his predecessor, Zhao Ziyang. Of all Chinese leaders, Jiang was the most wary of following in the footsteps of his predecessor as party general secretary. Many Zhaoist ideas were now dismissed out of hand. The withdrawal of party cells from government and enterprises, for example, was rejected, since this weakening of the party's structure was partly blamed for the collapse of communism in Eastern Europe.[101] Nor did Jiang again advocate the open forums with citizens that he had tried out at Zhao's urging while Shanghai mayor. "It's good to have more contacts with the people," he said, "but there's no need to turn them into something like international negotiations."[102]

The only question was, would it work? Was Jiang's idea of strengthening the one-party state likely to succeed in a country that had seen wave after wave of student political movements calling for greater popular democracy? Some said yes. Several studies that appeared from 1995 to 1997 indicated growing popular participation in voicing political concerns through avenues such as the media, local people's congresses, professional organizations, and plain old visits to government and party offices.[103] The dignified New China Gate of Zhongnanhai near Tiananmen Square was the scene of at least two sit-down protests in early 1997 alone, both by local residents involved in property disputes. These new channels for political activity might confine more violent and confrontational political movements, the argument went. As a result, political reform would continue to be slow and cosmetic; the benevolent dictatorship of the Chinese Communist Party would continue well into the twenty-first century before fundamental pluralistic changes were introduced.[104]

Still, despite the reasonable arguments that could be marshaled to prove the security of China's ruling regime, they would always have echoes of the same arguments that were made about Eastern Europe and the former Soviet Union in the 1980s. Stressing the institutional differences between the communist system in China and its erstwhile counterparts in other places obscured the popular similarities. Common people in China complained loud and long about the party.

As with Eastern Europe, China could always fall into popular uprising, as it had in 1989. While this might be less likely given evidence of expanded new outlets for political participation, it remained a distinct possibility. The students of the 1980s who had supposedly buried their heads in studying English and playing mahjong were the same ones who had taken to the streets in 1986 and 1989. Political uprising was always latent in Communist-ruled China.

Jiang and his comrades were aware of this danger. In addition to providing new outlets for pent-up political demands, they also made efforts to improve the image of the party. In mid 1997, a group of political scientists began formulating an "image strategy" aimed at enhancing the prestige of government and party alike.[105] At the same time, Jiang continued to press hard on the issue of corruption, his favorite image-management tool.

In these ways, Jiang set the tone for China's political scene in the coming years. Reforms would be modest and aimed at strengthening the one-party system. At the same time, the party would strive to keep its image out of the mud with slick campaigns and a continued war on corruption. In contrast to the imagination and courage evidenced by economic reforms, the political outlook that Jiang sketched at the fifteenth party congress was decidedly bleak. The "developmental dictatorship" of Jiang's China was not about ceding power.

8

The fifteenth congress was Jiang Zemin's coronation as China's new emperor, even if he had assumed the role in actuality three years earlier. Befitting the occasion, the investiture ceremony was suitably elaborate and filled with symbols of the long and prosperous reign to come. A special team ensured that Jiang's appearance at the congress—his clothes, his hairstyle, his shoes, his wristwatch—conveyed the right message of dignity and authority.[106] Everywhere he walked, his actions were carefully scripted to indicate his preeminence.

It is worth considering the new image of Jiang that the congress unveiled. In the past, his pedestal had stood below those of Deng and Mao in official propaganda. After the congress, this modesty came to an end; Jiang was now exalted as their equal, as an emperor in his own right. In the lead-up to the congress, Ding Guangen engineered a modest loosening of the normal strictures against lavishing praise on individual senior leaders.[107] Several articles immediately appeared about Jiang's achievements on various policy fronts.[108] The People's Publishing House issued a book entitled *Mao Zedong, Deng Xiaoping and Jiang Zemin on the World, Life and Values*.[109] Most revealing, work on the *Selected Works of Jiang Zemin*, a book that, as we saw earlier, may have been in progress since 1994, was accelerated. The first volume was expected to be issued before the end of the century.[110] If so, it would mark the elevation of

"Jiang Thought" to the status of a guiding ideology, along with the thought of Deng and Mao. That would be no small achievement for a man who had few pretensions to theoretical greatness.

The congress also marked the unveiling of Jiang's self-chosen nickname as China's "chief engineer" (*zong gongchengshi*). Mao had been known as the "great helmsman" and Deng as the "chief architect," both of which laid stress on the setting of policy directions. Jiang's title, by contrast, stressed implementation. If he could not dream beyond the imaginations of his predecessors, at least he could achieve more. Xinhua, in a starkly pro-Jiangist editorial before the congress, picked up this theme, suggesting that Jiang was more result-oriented than Mao or Deng had been. "The third generation leadership has boldly dealt with three major issues since the fourteenth party congress—namely tax reform, macroeconomic control and reducing income disparities," the agency quoted the CASS scholar Hu Angang as saying. "These are things that the first two generations of leaders wanted to do but were unable to."[111]

The official biography issued at the end of the congress continued the image makeover. "Since Jiang became party leader, China has seen the most stable political situation, the strongest national strength, the most active diplomatic activities, and the most remarkable improvement in people's lives ever," it effused.[112] The revised life story inflated Jiang's modest role in the creation of the SEZs into a leading role (as had been done already to his subsidiary role in the Shanghai underground communist movement of the 1940s); the rapid development of the SEZs, it said, was "a testament to Jiang's foresight and sagacity." His mastery of "gradualism" in economic reforms was also praised, making a not too subtle contrast with the roller-coaster reforms of Deng's 1980s: "Thorny [*lashou*] reforms in public finance, taxation, and monetary and investment systems have been implemented smoothly without any big ups and downs [*bodong*]," it read.

The new biography also went to great lengths to portray Jiang as an intellectual and a man of the world. He was a person who "loves to make friends with intellectuals" and could be described as a "scholar statesman," it said. He was "highly accomplished" in classical Chinese literature. He was a nationalist, but he was also worldly. Chinese and Western cultures were "able to speak to each other" (*xiangtongde*), he believed. To this supposed polyglot's English and Romanian language skills were now added "a little French and Japanese." His oratorical repertoire of Lincoln's Gettysburg Address was expanded to include

Hamlet's soliloquy (which runs to 35 lines) and Shelley's "Ode to the West Wind" (70 lines).

As with Mao, such hagiographic image-making always bordered on the farcical. Mendacious claims grew by the day. This faint echo of the Mao personality cult was no surprise, of course, since Jiang, as discussed, appeared to have psychological intimations of being a Mao-like figure. But the dangers of building his own personality cult were considerable. He had already tried to have himself appointed Chairman Jiang and failed. That alone should have been warning enough. If he now encouraged party propagandists to make him into a Mao-like figure by other means, it would be certain to incite opposition from the party elders and other senior members.

With that caveat, the fifteenth congress was a triumph for Jiang. The only modest challenger to his authority, Qiao Shi, was politely pushed aside. Young cadres who had worked with him and for him since 1989 finally came into positions of power. And his patient cultivation of the military was rewarded with the graceful exit of Deng's two generals. In policy matters, his governing philosophy—a combination of economic progressivism and political steadfastness—was prominently endorsed by the congress communiqué. It was another testament to the success of his governing style, "racking up small victories to achieve a big victory" (*ji xiao sheng wei da sheng*). Party propagandists began unabashedly proclaiming the superiority of the new emperor.

At the same time, the congress also betrayed the limits to Jiang's power. Party elders prevented his authority from expanding beyond what Deng had intended, forcing him to remain party general secretary. He also made progress only in policy areas where there was already a consensus, such as wider shareholding. His advisors admonished him without respite against pursuing overly ambitious "super targets" (*chaoqian mubiao*) for political and economic reforms.[113] This was, after all, the key to his remaining in power.

In a paradoxical way, the fifteenth congress could also be seen as the beginning of the end for Jiang, if only because it was a high point from which descent was the only retreat. The "fourth generation" of leaders who would formally assume power in 2002 came into view as Jiang's final term as party general secretary began. His ability to make the transition to a powerful party elder thereafter would depend on his ability to prevent these youngsters from upstaging him in the interim. "I have leapt over four hundred peaks to reach this verdant crest; now impassively, I survey the world beyond the sea," Mao had written. Jiang, the new emperor of China, was now enjoying this serene period on the summit. The only question was, how long could he linger there.

9

At the end of the November 1996 APEC meeting in Manila, Fidel Ramos, president of the Philippines, arranged a two-hour pleasure cruise aboard his personal yacht with Jiang, where the Chinese president was positively bumptious. Jiang danced the cha-cha and sang Elvis Presley's "Love Me Tender." "That's the favorite song of [U.S. President] Bill Clinton," Ramos, who had brought along a string quartet because of Jiang's known love of song, remarked after joining him in the romantic hit. "When he visits you, you will surprise him."[114]

Jiang's bubbly mood was understandable. On the sidelines of the Manila meeting, he had met the recently reelected Clinton, their fourth encounter, and secured a promise that the two would swap official state visits in late 1997 and 1998.

The summit was perfectly timed for Jiang. It meant that he would stride manfully abroad in the wake of the Hong Kong handover and the fifteenth congress to be heralded as China's new emperor by the leaders of the world's other celestial empire. Jiang had been denied a full regalia welcome in the United States in 1995 because of the Taiwan crisis and before that because of uncertainty in the West about his hold on power. With these issues fading into the background, his state visit would be a photo opportunity unsullied by doubts about who should be in the frame.

The summit would also be important diplomatically on two levels. Most immediately, it would show that China—and by implication Jiang—had come out on top of the Taiwan crisis. China's ties with Asia and the West were on the upswing as the crisis receded, while Taiwan business leaders continued to invest in mainland China in droves. South Africa, the last major country to recognize Taipei as the seat of the government of China, switched to Beijing in November 1996 after a 36-year hiatus.

More deeply, the U.S. summit would symbolize the end of the post-Tiananmen isolation of Beijing by the West. There had been six Sino–U.S. summits since former U.S. president Richard Nixon's first visit to Beijing in 1972, but none since Tiananmen. The American love affair with China in the 1980s, set off by Deng's trip to the United States in 1979, had given way to disgust and suspicion in the 1990s. Jiang, who was not personally associated with the Tiananmen massacre, was an acceptable figure for renewed cooperation, if not reconciliation, with China.

The summit was scheduled for late October 1997 so that it would be separate from Jiang's attendance at the APEC meeting that took place in Vancouver, Canada, the following month. Nothing would be allowed to overshadow the importance to the Chinese of the full honors accorded their president in the United States.[115] Accordingly, nothing was left to chance. A flurry of high-level visits between Washington and Beijing took place to set the stage for the summit. U.S. Secretary of State Madeleine Albright went to Beijing in the midst of the Deng funeral in February. A month later, it was the turn of Vice President Al Gore, the highest U.S. official to visit China since President George Bush in February 1989. The national security advisers and several top military officials on both sides also swapped visits.

The planning was a fraught affair, however. For one thing, there were concerns about the protests likely to dog Jiang's entourage. Although there was no visceral hatred of Jiang in the United States, as there was for Li Peng, he still represented a state that trampled on freedoms with impunity, and for this he would be taken to task. The Chinese insistence that Jiang visit several prominent sites, like Harvard University and Philadelphia's Independence Hall, would only make matters worse. "He will not have a totally fuzzy time," Albright noted with resignation shortly beforehand.[116]

China also was being stung over allegations that its embassy had given money to friendly congressional leaders and businessmen in the run-up to the 1996 U.S. presidential election. Jiang, whose benighted view of the U.S. political process was shared by most Chinese leaders, said in private that he found the allegations to be evidence of an "erratic and mysterious" American policy toward China.[117] He denied the allegations in an interview with CNN in May, part of a public relations offensive in the run-up to the summit, which also included interviews with *Time* and the *Washington Post*.[118]

The summit itself took place on Wednesday, 29 October, the fourth day of a nine-day visit to the United States. Jiang and his entourage in an Air China 747 arrived in Washington, D.C., the night before. All of Team Jiang was on board: his bodyguard You Xigui, his spin doctor Zeng Qinghong, his speechwriters Zeng Peiyan and Teng Wensheng, and, perhaps most important, given the friendly image Jiang wanted to portray, his wife, Wang Yeping. Clinton and Jiang met informally that evening to go over the next day's agenda. For the Chinese, every detail of the summit and the state banquet to follow had been considered at length.

An American suggestion that the banquet be held in a 400-person tent erected on the White House lawn was rejected by Jiang's team as unbecoming. Deng had been fêted in the East Room of the White House during his triumphant 1979 summit, and the Chinese insisted on the same for Jiang, even though the room could seat only 230.[119] Tents to the Chinese were barbarian, and Jiang was not to be treated like a tribute-bearer.

Jiang had only to show up for the summit for it to be a personal triumph, a crowning achievement to his eventful 1997. The Chinese media coverage was dominated by images of the pomp and circumstance of the visit and by images of Jiang standing shoulder-to-shoulder with Clinton.

In return for this invaluable service to his stature at home, Jiang gave very little in return. The Chinese made two gestures to improve human rights before the summit: China became the one hundred and thirty-seventh signatory to the United Nations covenant on economic, social, and cultural rights (and later the covenant on civil and political rights); and the Chinese invited three religious leaders from the United States, a Protestant, a Catholic, and a Jew, to visit China for talks on religious freedom (even though Muslims and Buddhists constitute the major religious groups in the country). Jiang also agreed during the summit to resume a human rights dialogue with Washington, and he invited the Speaker of the U.S. House of Representatives, Newt Gingrich, to visit Tibet. But at the press conference that followed their 90-minute meeting, and in an evening news broadcast, he defended the Tiananmen massacre as a "necessary measure" and repeated the line that human rights were an "internal affair." His adumbration at Harvard University that the use of force in Tiananmen might some day be declared a mistake was too veiled to win him much applause in the United States. Clinton charged that China was "on the wrong side of history" in trying to bottle up political dissent. Not until after the summit, in mid November, did Beijing release the country's best-known political dissident, Wei Jingsheng, from prison and put him on a plane for the United States. By delaying the move until after the summit, Jiang ensured that the effective exile of Wei was not seen as a sign that he would stoop to anything to ensure a warm welcome in Washington.

Alongside the mainly symbolic gestures on human rights were three economic offerings: a U.S.$3 billion nonbinding order for 50 Boeing passenger aircraft, mostly puny 737s; a promise to reduce tariffs on U.S.$1.4 billion in U.S. computer exports to China to zero by the year 2000; and an almost certain order for U.S.-made nuclear power generation equipment in return for Clinton's lifting of a post-Tiananmen ban on such exports. All three offerings were for much-needed capital equipment, and the computers and planes likely would have been bought from the United States in any case.

With so little to show for inviting Jiang into the White House (despite China's obstinate stand on issues like Taiwan and Tiananmen), it surprised many that Clinton had been able to muster the political support to hold the summit at all. From the U.S. perspective, however, the Jiang-Clinton summit was viewed as a form of Cold War détente. That is, while there was no love for Jiang or the Chinese Communists, China's emergence as a major power in the world begged a U.S. response. Jiang was not being welcomed to Washington as an ally, but as an enemy. As much was clear from the American insistence on setting up a hot line between the two presidents, which was agreed at the summit. The Chinese were puzzled by this request. They thought hot lines, like the one they connected to Moscow in 1996, were for friends. For the Clinton administration, however, the establishment of a hot line similar to the one set up between Washington and Moscow in 1963, would symbolize its successful grappling with the enemy. Better the one you can call than the one you cannot.

The same détente-style reasoning was evident from Clinton's 25-minute address on relations with China delivered at the offices of the Voice of America radio station shortly before the summit. Three of the six reasons he gave for strengthening ties with China concerned international security.[120] The others concerned business, cross-border crime and the environment. He even quoted Nixon from 1967 on the need to ensure that China did not live in "angry isolation." These were the sober calculations of the Cold War era, not the enthusiastic outward-looking initiatives of the global era.

For Clinton, the summit was the culmination of his attempts to steer this middle course of détente with China; on one side, he faced hundreds of lobbyists, movie stars, and members of Congress who sought to isolate China; on the other, he faced the strategic counsel of his national security advisors, as well as the self-interested appeals of business leaders and dozens of paid consultants to Beijing among U.S. academics and former officials all urging friendly ties. In the end, Jiang was allowed into the White House, but his visit was brief and businesslike. Clinton's middle course—embracing China, but as an enemy rather than as a friend—would likely set the pattern for U.S. policy toward China for some time to come.

Jiang did nothing to change the American view that he was a Cold War adversary. He arrived at the state banquet sporting a jaunty new dark blue Mao jacket, a collarless tunic with four pockets and five buttons. The Mao jacket had been designed by the founder of the Republic of China, Sun Yat-sen, after he overthrew the Qing dynasty in 1911, as a practical alternative to traditional costume. Since then, however, it had been more associated with Mao and Communist China. For Jiang, standing alongside Clinton in a tuxedo on the lawn of the White House that night, it symbolized the separateness of China from the United States, which had long been a theme of his personal views of Sino–U.S. ties. It was the outward sign of the proud and indignant nationalism that he had harbored since his youth. Jiang ate the pepper-crusted Oregon beef and drank the California Chardonnay, but in spirit he was rejecting American relief grain along with his hometown hero, Zhu Ziqing.

Against the backdrop of high-level political calculations and symbolism on both sides, Jiang still was able to inject some of his normally irrepressible personality into the visit. He strummed a steel guitar and danced the hula in Hawaii. He donned a colonial-style tricorn hat in Williamsburg, Virginia. And at the end of a performance by the National Symphony Orchestra on the White House lawn after the summit, he repeated his goofy offer to Clinton from their first meeting in 1993 to join the U.S. president in a duet some day. "Sometimes I play the flute. I know you play very good sax. Someday we can play a duet!" After the summit, he rang the bell to open trading on the New York Stock Exchange with the words "I wish a good luck for you." At a banquet in Los Angeles prior to leaving, he sang an excerpt from the Chinese opera *Zhuofangcao* and conducted the 1,000 Chinese-American guests in a rendition of the patriotic song "The Great Motherland." "Gales of Laughter as Jovial Jiang Goes into Entertainment Overdrive" ran the banner headline on the front page of the *South China Morning Post* in Hong Kong.[121]

Wang Yeping also won many hearts with her unaffected demeanor. She was clearly overwhelmed by the summit itself and gripped Hillary Clinton's arm closely as they walked through the White House. For the state banquet, she wore a dark blue traditional *qipao* (cheongsam) dress, the female counterpart to her husband's symbolic garb. After years of flinching at the demands of being China's First Lady, the U.S. trip was like Wang's coming-out party.

All the friendliness did nothing to deflate Jiang's critics, of course. Protests in Philadelphia forced the abandonment of a visit to the Liberty Bell. The governor of New York state, George Pataki, and the mayor of

New York city, Rudolph Giuliani, both refused to greet him on arrival there. At Harvard, protesters using loudspeakers could be heard inside the hall where Jiang spoke. "I may be 71, but my ears still work well," he said. "The only thing I could do was speak louder."122

Fortunately for Jiang, the mere holding of the summit and the jovial persona he conveyed during the six-state visit was all that was required to make the trip a success. After an eight-year hiatus, the world's two principal powers put aside their differences and shook hands stiffly, pledging to build a "constructive strategic partnership for the twenty-first century." With blanket media coverage at home, Jiang finally basked in the glory of being received as China's top leader in the world's most powerful country. Having established his credibility with the Chinese military via the Taiwan missile drills of 1995–96, he was able to visit Washington with more confidence than when he went to Seattle in 1993. This was perfectly reflected by his aside at Harvard that Tiananmen might have been a mistake. Freed from the constraining influence of hard-liners at home, Jiang was able to relax and mingle with even his harshest critics. His personal stature and his diplomatic role were enhanced.123

When he returned to North America the following month for the APEC summit in Vancouver, Jiang was finally greeted as a world statesman and as China's unrivaled leader. "Sporting a leather bomber jacket and a proud smile, Jiang confirmed he was finally a man at ease in the international spotlight," Reuters News Agency wrote.124 The throwaway lines in news agency stories about his grip on power being "shaky" began to disappear. In a brief state visit to Canada following the summit, Jiang was at last photographed wearing a white Stetson, as Deng had been in the United States in 1979. To the audience in China and in much of Asia, transfixed by the romance and ruggedness of the North American cowboy image, this photo call was of particular importance.

The swagger of the Chinese delegation, which had been somewhat subdued in the United States, was evident in Canada when a Foreign Ministry spokesman, Shen Guofang, commented that they "couldn't care less" about the handful of protesters trailing Jiang's delegation across the country. In another brief visit to Mexico that followed, Jiang commented approvingly that the country seemed more "calm" compared to the "noise" (*zayin*) of protesters which had offended his senses in Canada and the United States. By this time, Jiang knew that Western countries were too concerned about security and economic ties with China to jeopardize them over human rights issues.

Jiang would round out the end-of-year diplomatic flurry by attending the first-ever summit of all East and Southeast Asian nations in Malaysia in December, where his ability to chart the course of China's diplomacy was recognized by regional leaders. Along with the Clinton summit, this event confirmed Jiang's status to outsiders as China's new emperor.

The following year, 1998, would bring Clinton to China for the first time as U.S. president, while Jiang would make the first visit by China's head of state to Japan. Jiang would also be formally reconfirmed as state president and military commission chairman by the national parliament with 98 percent approval for both posts. Though reconfirmation was a foregone conclusion, the high percentages—which compared to just 89 percent for Li Peng's NPC chairmanship and 83 percent for outgoing vice-premier Jiang Chunyun's NPC vice chairmanship—reflected the broad support Jiang continued to enjoy. After beginning 1997 in the frigid confines of Deng's death chamber, Jiang was ringing out the year in style. He had indeed "turned grief into strength."

Conclusion

I

The Shaobo boat locks sit peaceably amid pine trees and sandy river islands just east of Yangzhou, Jiang Zemin's hometown. Built in the 1960s, when their name was inscribed by Mao Zedong in his flowing calligraphy, the locks today guide long, slender boats, laden with canvas-covered cargoes, between the Yangtze River and the Grand Canal. The upriver boats move patiently from one lock to the next, gaining a few yards each time before emerging into the open canal heading north beside Shaobo Lake. The passage takes over an hour, during which the boatsmen hop from one craft to the next as the artificial flood tide raises the whole scene skyward.

Jiang Zemin has come a long way since the days when he played along the shores of Shaobo Lake as a boy. There were locks along the canal in those days too, although they were not as big. The progress of Jiang's own life and career before he broke into the open waters of the post-Deng era in 1997 was in many ways like the movement of the boats through the locks. He began life laden with a heavy cargo of intellectual rigor and activism, as well as with personal experience of the Japanese invasion and the Chinese civil war. From there, he moved patiently through each stage of his career as a Communist Party member and his life as a self-professed intellectual. Each time he gained a little stature and was guided to the next stage. There were no major mishaps and only the occasional burst of speed. By the time he emerged into the open waters, his direction was clear, even if his destination was not. His life progressed, not by scuttling rivals and throwing up a huge wake, but by joining the pack and emerging in the lead.

What kind of man is Jiang Zemin? Biography has the implicit purpose of answering this question, and I hope that some clues have been provided here. As an individual, Jiang is arrogant, but at the same time self-effacing. He has committed minor sins, but he is not a man to hate.

A rich vein of egoism has moved him to musical performance on several occasions. Although not exactly obsessed with his public image, he has been concerned enough about it on occasion to comb his hair assiduously before photographs and to react violently to newspapers that presented him in a bad light. He can also be incredibly cordial and easygoing with visitors, especially those from the West.

Jiang's upbringing made him a pragmatic, nondoctrinaire member of the Communist Party, more schooled in traditional Chinese and Western culture than in modern Marxism. His later emphasis on a rather narrowly defined patriotism (especially vis-à-vis the West), and on promoting traditional Chinese values, owes much to this upbringing. In addition, his odd experience of having been handed from one family to another at the tender age of 13 left him with a detached sense of his relatives. This unsentimental view of family life allowed him to act swiftly and harshly against corruption involving the children of senior leaders and nepotism when he came to power after 1989.

Jiang is not a charismatic leader. Indeed, his earliest years in the party as a student activist at Jiaotong University showed him to be more a worthy disciple than a sensational messiah. If such wartime conditions had continued, Jiang might never have stood a chance of emerging on top in the Chinese Communist Party. But with the victory of the Communists in 1949, the game changed. Jiang's ability to motivate and get along with others in the humdrum life of factories and research institutes brought him steady promotions. This same leadership style, based on consensus and friendly persuasion, would characterize his leadership even after his own era began in 1997. Jiang was the first to admit that it was not possible for a Mao or Deng to rule China like an emperor again. By the time he came to power, the political system, although by no means democratic, was nonetheless characterized by modest checks on the authority of even the "core leader."

It was not until he was well into his career, and aged 28, that Jiang left China for the first time. Unlike Deng Xiaoping, Jiang is not enamored of the West, despite his partiality to Western classical music and literature. In his later diplomacy, he has continually stressed the differences rather than the universalities of human experience. There are "useful" and "quintessential" elements of foreign cultures that are worthy of introduction to China. But the Great Wall of Chinese separateness stands firm.

The political campaigns of Mao Zedong's China brought Jiang hardship, but not persecution. During the anti-rightist campaign of the 1950s, he dished out punishment, albeit grudgingly, rather than suffering it. In the Cultural Revolution of the 1960s, he was sidelined with little more to complain of than a short haircut and a missed opportunity to see Premier Zhou Enlai. Accordingly, Jiang is neither an extreme political conservative, like those who benefited from, or at least did not suffer during, these Maoist movements, nor a political liberal, like those who suffered greatly. During the 1989 Tiananmen movement, he steered cautiously between the swelling tide of conservative opinion in Beijing and the demands of the protesters in Shanghai. After Deng's death, he began to suggest in public, as he had in private, that the use of force in Tiananmen had been a mistake.

Jiang has been a lasting beneficiary of the economic reforms launched by Deng in 1978. He owed his first job outside the First Machine-Building Ministry to the new emphasis on expanding China's foreign investment and trade, and his later jumps to electronics minister and then mayor and party chief of Shanghai were also owing to the central government's new attention to economic development. It is thus no surprise that Jiang was a keen economic reformer after he came to power in 1989. He got behind Deng's southern tour at an early stage and left little doubt after Deng's death that economic reforms would continue apace.

In these respects, Jiang is representative of the new Chinese elite whose members emerged into positions of power in the 1980s and 1990s. Although they experienced invasion, civil war, famine, and political persecution, they were slightly too young to suffer greatly as a result. By rising through the ranks in Mao's China, they learned political caution and consensual leadership. Under Deng, they were immediate beneficiaries of economic reforms. The China they seek to usher into the twenty-first century is one in which they can imagine enjoying both the fruits of economic reform and the certainties of authoritarian rule.

Jiang was by no means "plucked out of nowhere" in 1989, as foreign commentaries at the time suggested. He had joined the Central Committee in 1982 and the Politburo in 1987. His assignment to Shanghai in 1985 showed that he was *already* in line for a top posting at the party center, although not necessarily that of party general secretary. Being a well-known economic reformer was one of several factors that won Jiang the mantle of "core" of China's third-generation leadership after 1989. Also, his political views were less conservative and autocratic than those of other potential candidates for that role, but nonetheless firm enough to allay fears that he would repeat the mistakes of his two predecessors, Hu Yaobang and Zhao Ziyang.

His factional base was narrow, consisting of just a few people, among them Wang Daohan, General Zhang Aiping, and the former president Li Xiannian. His relations with others, like Li Peng and Qiao Shi, were cordial but not trouble-free. Elders like Chen Yun, Wang Zhen, and Wan Li grudgingly accepted Jiang's promotion in 1989, but did not refrain from voicing their dissent in later years. It was Deng's support above all that proved crucial in beating back the critics, especially in the first five years after Tiananmen. This very lack of strong factional allies was at once Jiang's greatest strength and his greatest weakness. Potential opponents could never claim that he led a faction that was ganging up on them. Unless they made egregious errors, as had General Yang Baibing and the Beijing party chief Chen Xitong, he did not seem like a threat to anyone.

For the most part, in fact, Jiang is not a threatening leader. His rise suggests that the "informal politics" that dominate the "formal politics" of high-level decision-making in China have changed. Factions are now more like case-by-case lobby groups; if you have the right ideas on each issue, you can be assured of an issue-specific faction to back you. Jiang has needed only to have a keen sense of which policies to follow to ensure support within the leadership. This he has done, with great success.

Jiang's overriding task in the wake of the Tiananmen massacre was to reestablish political stability, while at the same time maintaining the momentum of economic reform. The collapse of communism in Eastern Europe had the unfortunate consequence of elevating stability, now including political and ideological stability, far above economic concerns. It took Deng's southern tour to bring the economy back to center stage. In all this, Jiang played his role admirably. He was the right man at the right time to shoulder these tasks; economic reform and political caution were in his blood.

Through a series of moves between 1993 and 1996, Jiang was able to establish his authority as the unrivaled top leader, and one now free from the buttressing once provided by Deng. A few Shanghai colleagues were brought to Beijing, authority in the army was established by purges and new policies, diplomatic affairs were wrested from the domination of

Li Peng, and a sort of presidential entourage was created. By 1997, these moves had put paid to the idea that Jiang had somehow blundered his way to authority. A saying often leveled at him, "A fool has fool's luck" (*sharen you sha fuqi*), simply does not hold up in light of these quite deliberate maneuvers.

Jiang made his mark by focusing clearly on areas that Deng had left unresolved: patriotism, anti-corruption, party rebuilding, social rejuvenation, and redefining the state's role in the economy were the major themes. Other issues—like poverty and income disparities—were addressed as well. In these themes could be found the seeds of the full-blown governing philosophy, "Jiang Thought," that would be put into writing at the fifteenth party congress in 1997. It was a vision of China that Jiang needed in order to maintain the authority he had worked so hard to amass. But it was also a critical contribution to China's historical transition from a Marxist-Leninist state into something more akin to a "developmental dictatorship." In seeking to bolster the political controls of the state while at the same time promoting the economic and social freedoms necessary for China to modernize, Jiang was prodding the country along a path that had led to success elsewhere in Asia. His significance as a leader is thus not only that he helped pull China back from the brink in 1989, but that he set it off in a new direction offering better prospects for a stable future.

Deng's death came at an ideal juncture for Jiang. The seeds of his vision of the new China had been planted beforehand, which meant that they could be more easily cultivated after Deng's passing. It also meant that Jiang could bask in the sunlight of Hong Kong's return to Chinese sovereignty, the fifteenth party congress, and his state visit to the United States without the clouds of Deng's declining health casting any shadows. *Asiaweek* magazine's characterization of Jiang as "the most powerful man in Asia" in a mid-1997 regional power ranking would not have been possible if the patriarch had still been around. As it was, Deng's passing was a fading memory and the Jiang era had begun.

2

The questions remain, however, about the future. Jiang is scheduled to relinquish the presidency and then the party general secretary post in the lead-up to the sixteenth congress of 2002. His last position, CMC chairman, will be handed over at the congress. Jiang will then become China's patriarch.

The possibility of Jiang being ousted from power in a coup before then appears small, but is not remote. As we have seen, there have been real limits on Jiang's authority since 1989. His success owes much to his recognition of those limits. Three possible scenarios can be suggested for how he might fall. One would be a simple attempt to amass greater authority than he has at present; the lessons of the sacking of the PAP commander Ba Zhongtan and of Jiang's failure to win approval to become party chairman are evidence enough that the military and party respectively are determined to maintain some limits on his rule. If he were to seek with unseemly vigor to breach those limits, he might go the way of Hua Guofeng, whose effective fall in 1978 was owing partly to his attempt to put himself above all limitations.

Another possibility, always looming in the high politics of Communist China, might be an ideological mistake. Since his days in Shanghai, Jiang has sought to encourage more open discussion to ensure progress on ideological issues. To some extent, this has succeeded in widening the scope for ideological debate since the end of the post-Tiananmen freeze. Given the liberties they take with classical Marxism, *Guanjian shike* and *Yu zongshuji tanxin* would have been unthinkable in, say, 1991, and they were reviled in the left-wing press even in 1996–97. Jiang's experimentation with shareholding, his ambivalence as to the "correctness" of the Tiananmen massacre, or any one of an array of other issues, could easily land him in ideological hot water. Ideology is always a jungle to be stepped through with care by Chinese leaders. Finally, there is the danger of Jiang seeking to build a personality cult around himself. Even if he had Mao's charisma, memories of Maoism run wild are too fresh for such a Jiang cult to be tolerated. Fortunately, Jiang appears to be aware of this danger. As a Xinhua biography noted in late 1997, and again in 1998, seemingly with vague reference to Mao, "Jiang has never been intoxicated with his success."[1]

The greatest threats to Jiang thus come from Jiang himself. There are no apparent rivals seeking to grab power from him merely for the sake of power. If Jiang wants to remain active politically after 2002, *Jingbao* has noted, "not only will he have to be politically powerful, but he will also have to remain physically healthy and strong."[2] He will be 74 in the year 2000, not old by Chinese standards. At the same age, Deng made his political comeback after the Cultural Revolution and launched China into the reform era. Former president Yang Shangkun, meanwhile, has done much to secure influence as an elder since his retirement as president in 1993 at the age of 86. Both Deng and Yang had good health on their side. Yang, for example, has criss-crossed the country on inspection tours and has a penchant for inviting friends for swimming parties in the southern city of Zhuhai.

There have been reports in the Hong Kong press that since the mid 1990s, Jiang has suffered from heart flutters, digestive problems, and high blood pressure as a result of overwork. Doctors have reportedly issued "five don'ts" for his work schedule, including limiting his work hours and avoiding inspections at high altitudes and in hot parts of the country.[3] He says his wife frequently admonishes him to go to bed rather than work late into the night.[4] And there is the problem of his weight, which at 210 pounds is about 22 pounds above the ideal. Jiang's fondness for Russian bread, Taiwan-style beef noodles, and 12-course banquets for visiting VIPs has taken its toll. Family members say he has another bad habit of finishing off meals by eating dollops of white rice soaked in the leftover oil of dishes of stir-fried vegetables.[5]

Still, Jiang's heart is probably in good shape. He continues a habit of swimming 600 meters a day in a pool in Zhongnanhai, an ongoing legacy of his Cultural Revolution sidelining.[6] When he went for an hour's paddle in the waves of Waikiki beach in Hawaii on his way to the Clinton summit in October 1997, many believed he was seeking to display his fitness for political battle. Jiang breaststroked in a red and white cap, pink-framed tinted goggles, and black trunks accompanied by a gaggle of bodyguards and China's ambassador to the United States, Li Daoyu. The swim elicited comparisons with high-profile dips by Mao in the Yangtze River in 1966 and by Deng at the Beidaihe resort in 1992. But the event was not given any media coverage in China and even the foreign press was kept away from the scene. Jiang was merely doing his daily exercises. The Wen Wei Po reported that he wanted to swim for another hour but was told to come ashore by his bodyguards.[7] "I will not surrender myself to old age," he later told a group of Hawaii residents. "You have to be young in spirit to maintain your vigour."[8] While resting in the Mexican resort town of Cancún a month later, Jiang again took to the seas, although this time for only half an hour because of an impending welcoming banquet.

Apart from thinning hair, which is creating a shiny bald spot on his crown, slightly worsening eyes, and a rounding belly, Jiang remains energetic and stout. Rarely does he miss an engagement because of illness. That is probably indication enough that his health will not get in the way of his ambitions to lead China into the new century. Jiang is emerging into the post-Deng era both politically and physically healthy. If he remains in position until 2002 and continues to exert a significant influence for, say five to ten years after that, there is therefore every reason to take seriously his vision of China's future. As noted, the destination toward which China's transition seems to be heading may broadly be defined as similar to the "developmental dictatorships" found elsewhere in Asia. Jiang is not the only Chinese leader who advocates this mixture of economic and social freedoms with political authoritarianism. Zhu Rongji and Li Ruihan, for example, for all their alleged liberal instincts, appear to remain firmly convinced of the party's destiny to lead China into its future, even if that future will involve more economic freedom and checks on party power. China's emergence as a powerful new player in Asian and world politics, backed by its strong state and its surging economy, thus seems unlikely to be thwarted by internal politics.

The "fourth generation" of Chinese Communist leaders, especially Hu Jintao and Wen Jiabao, meanwhile, do not share exactly the same generational characteristics as Jiang and his cohorts. Their lack of experience in the era of the war against Japan and the civil war give them a less visceral nationalistic mentality. Jiang's patriotism campaign may not outlast him. Nor do they harbor Maoist concern for the poor, farmers, and intellectuals, concern that brought far more suffering than benefits to these groups in Mao's day, but that nonetheless set the tone for many of Jiang's national policies. Jiang's revival of such Maoist concern also may not last. For the rest, though, in particular the overall thrust of China's transition toward a postcommunist "developmental dictatorship," little is likely to be altered by the "fourth generation." They share the basic economic and political beliefs on which such a state would be based.

Merely by virtue of its size—China's population will reach 1.4 billion by 2010, while its economy, now the world's seventh largest, could overtake that of Germany and become the third largest (behind the United States and Japan) by 2020—this direction has important implications for Asia and the world. In essence, it implies that the Cold War–style confrontation between China and the United States is unlikely to abate, since the mainland's authoritarian state will remain impervious to major change. At the same time, the economic growth that is not only an aim but also a justification for that authoritarianism will continue to draw foreign investors and traders to China. They will exert an increasingly strong counterinfluence to those who seek to isolate and confront China. This would suggest that the balance of world opinion will continue to shift in favor of a more inclusive and cooperative treatment of China in international affairs.

Although Jiang's official retirement has been planned, he will be anything but a lameduck leader in the approach to the sixteenth congress of 2002.[9] His enhanced hold on power following the fifteenth congress and the March 1998 meeting of the national parliament will instead give him greater scope than ever to implement the tenets of his governing philosophy. The policies he sets in motion will set the tone for Communist rule in China in the twenty-first century. His plans to hand over formal power to a "fourth generation" of leaders in 2002, if successful, would mark the first bloodless succession in Communist China's history. This would not only add to Jiang's claim as a significant leader in Chinese history but would also enhance his stature as China's patriarch after 2002. Unlike Zhao Ziyang and Hua Guofeng, Jiang would take leave of his formal posts while still enjoying the support of his successors. Provided his health holds up and popular protest can be confined, Jiang can anticipate a lengthy period as China's acknowledged new emperor.

Jiang Zemin, then, will be counted as a significant leader in Chinese history for several reasons: for his role in reestablishing stability and growth in China after the 1989 Tiananmen Square massacre; for his wise approach to the shortcomings and excesses of the reform era under Deng Xiaoping; for his role in outlining a future Chinese state combining economic and social freedom with authoritarian government; and for the probable enhancement of China's role in the world of the early twenty-first century by that combination.

It is an impressive record for one who, it is probably fair to say, had greatness thrust upon him in 1989.

Notes

ACRONYMS AND ABBREVIATIONS

AFP   Agence France-Presse

AP   Associated Press

APEC   Asia-Pacific Economic Cooperation forum

AWSJ   *Asian Wall Street Journal*

CASS   Chinese Academy of Social Sciences

CDIC   Central Discipline Inspection Commission

CMC   Central Military Commission

CNN   Cable News Network

CNS   Zhongguo xinwen she (China News Service)

CPPCC   Chinese People's Political Consultative Conference

CR   *China Review* (Hong Kong: Chinese University Press)

DXP2   Deng Xiaoping, *Selected Works,* vol. 2: 1975–1982 (Beijing: Foreign Languages Press, 1984)

DXP3   Deng Xiaoping, *Selected Works,* vol. 3: 1982–1992 (Beijing: Foreign Languages Press, 1994)

FBIS   United States Foreign Broadcast Information Service, China Daily Report

FEER   *Far Eastern Economic Review*

HKCNA   Xianggang Zhongguo tongxun she (Hong Kong China News Agency)

JPRS   United States Foreign Broadcast Information Service, Joint Publications Research Service

Kyodo   Kyodo News Service (Japan)

LD   *Jiefang ribao* (Liberation Daily)

LWHW   *Liaowang haiwaiban* (Outlook Weekly, overseas edition, Beijing)

Ming Pao   *Ming bao* (*Ming Pao* Daily News, Hong Kong)

NPC   National People's Congress (parliament)

PAP   People's Armed Police (paramilitary police)

PD   *Renmin ribao* (People's Daily)

PLA   People's Liberation Army

PLAD   *Jiefangjun bao* (PLA Daily)

Reuters   Reuters News Agency

Rmb   renminbi: yuan, the currency of the People's Republic of China
             (U.S.$1 = Rmb8.28 in December 1997)

SCMP   *South China Morning Post* (Hong Kong)

SEZ   special economic zone

SWB   British Broadcasting Corporation, Summary of World Broadcasts,
             Far East

TKP   *Da gong bao* (*Ta Kung Pao*, Hong Kong)

WA   *Guangjiaojing* (Wide Angle, Hong Kong)

WWP   *Wen hui bao* (*Wen Wei Po*, Hong Kong)

Xinhua   New China News Agency

PREFACE

1. One potential source of confusion for biographers is that there was another engineer named Jiang Zemin (spelled with the same Chinese characters), who lived from 1903 to 1989 and also spent time at the Changchun auto works. This other Jiang Zemin was a director and academic supervisor (from 1956 to 1978) and then vice president (1978 to 1989) of the Society for Mechanical Engineering and an advisor to the First Ministry of Machine-Building Industry from 1978 to 1982.

CHAPTER 1. LEAVING YANGZHOU

1. Based on official 1980–1997 figures and 1998 forecasts.
2. Tie Lin, "Yishi xingtai wenti" (The Issue of Ideology), in Xu Ming, ed., *Guanjian shike* (Critical Moment) (Beijing: Jinri Zhongguo chubanshe [Today's China Publishing], 1997), pp. 54–85.
3. For a discussion of China's transitional processes, see *China Quarterly*, December 1995.

4. It is said among some people in Yangzhou that Jiang was actually born in Gaoyou county, which lies just north of Yangzhou along the Grand Canal. I was unable to confirm this.

5. Wu Yueqing was from a peasant family in nearby Changwei village (in present-day Jiangdu county just outside Yangzhou), probably sold into marriage by her impoverished family.

6. Author's visit to Changwei, October 1996.

7. The village of Jiang is now part of Baidi township in Jingde county.

8. The town of Xiannu is in today's Jiangdu county.

9. *Nantong ribao* (Nantong Daily), 4 June 1995, p. 6.

10. Ibid.

11. Yang Shuying, "Qiushan hongye zou zhengtu: Ji geming lieshi Jiang Shangqing" (Setting off on a Journey amid Autumn Hills and Red Leaves: Revolutionary Martyr Jiang Shangqing), *Zhuanji wenxue* (Biographical Literature), 1995, no. 11, p. 4. Hereafter cited as "Yang Shuying."

12. *Nantong ribao*, 4 June 1995, p. 6. The article refers to the institution as Yangzhou Middle School, but it did not take that name until 1927.

13. Ibid.

14. Ibid.

15. Yang Shuying.

16. Wang Zhijuan, "Geming lieshi Jiang Shangqing" (Revolutionary Martyr Jiang Shangqing). Hereafter cited as "Wang Zhijuan." In Wang Yu, ed., *Yangzhou lidai mingren* (Famous Yangzhou People through the Ages) (Nanjing: Jiangsu guji chubanshe [Jiangsu Ancient Books Publishing House], 1992), pp. 341–47. Hereafter cited as "Wang Yu."

17. Wang Zhijuan, p. 346.

18. *TKP*, 1 June 1990, p. 4; a modern version of the Three Character Classic (*sanzijing*) was published by the Guangzhou Children's Publishing House in 1995.

19. *Liaoning ribao* (Liaoning Daily), 4 September 1993, pp. 1–2.

20. Today the school is a "key" primary school of the city and the only one allowed to experiment with the basic curriculum.

21. *LWHW*, 12 March 1990, pp. 3–5.

22. *LWHW*, 17 July 1991, p. 15.

23. Shanghai Radio, 11 March 1994, quoted in FBIS, 14 March 1994, p. 22.

24. *WWP*, 2 April 1992, p. 2.

25. Number 16 Dongquanmen (now Dongquanmen Street) still stands, split inside and inhabited by two separate families. The only indication of its earlier tenants, as noted, is a fading tile sign that tells of the street's history.

26. Hu Zhihong, "Jiang Shangqing lieshi xunnan ji" (On the Just Death of Martyr Jiang Shangqing), *Zhuanji wenxue* (Biographical Literature), 1992, no. 2, p. 32. Hereafter "Hu Zhihong."

27. Immanuel Hsu, *The Rise of Modern China,* 5th ed. (New York: Oxford University Press, 1995), p. 563.

28. "Jiang Zemin yu Shen Junshan de sanci tanhua" (Three Talks between Jiang Zemin and Shen Chun-shan), *Jiushi niandai* (Nineties Monthly) (Hong Kong), August 1996, p. 69. Hereafter cited as "Shen Chun-shan talks."

29. For this period, see Yang Shuying, Wang Zhijuan, and Hu Zhihong.

30. Shen Chun-shan talks, p. 74.

31. Wang Xiaopeng, *Wo yanzhongde zhongguo lingdaoren* (Chinese Leaders in My Eyes) (Dalian: Liaoning daxue chubanshe [Liaoning University Press], 1993), pp. 1–18. Hereafter cited as "Wang Xiaopeng 1993."

32. The actual figures were 332 of 3,257 in 1936 and 425 of 4,015 in 1937. *Jiangsu sheng Yangzhou zhongxue jian xiao jiushi zhounian jiniance* (Ninetieth Anniversary Souvenir Book of Yangzhou Middle School, Jiangsu Province) (Yangzhou: n.p., 1992), p. 3. Hereafter cited as "Yangzhou Middle School Souvenir Book."

33. Based on counts of several class photos from the 1910s, 1920s, and 1930s in Yangzhou Middle School Souvenir Book.

34. Yangzhou Middle School Souvenir Book, p. 79.

35. Author's interview with the school principal, Shen Yiwen, 17 October 1996.

36. Yangzhou Middle School Souvenir Book, p. 86.

37. Ibid., p. 81.

38. Xinhua, 12 May 1991.

39. *Asahi Shimbun*, 13 August 1995, p. 1, in FBIS, 14 August 1995, p. 1.

40. WA, 16 July 1989, pp. 10–13.

41. Yangzhou Middle School Souvenir Book, p. 88.

42. Ibid., p. 78.

43. Shen Chun-shan talks, p. 69.

44. *LWHW*, 12 March 1990, pp. 3–5.

45. Xinhua, 5 September 1994.

46. China Central Television, 3 August 1996, in FBIS, 3 August 1996, documents 96–158.

47. HKCNA, 1 June 1990.

48. Bai Shouyi, ed., *An Outline History of China: 1919–1949* (Beijing: Foreign Languages Press, 1993), p. 259.

49. Wang Yu, p. 325.

50. Jiang Zemin wrote the inscriptions when a statue of Zhu Ziqing was unveiled at Yangzhou Middle School in 1988 and when his former residence in Yangzhou was opened as a public museum in 1992. Jiang could claim close personal links to Zhu, although it is doubtful whether they ever met. Zhu's son, Zhu Runsheng, was his classmate at Yangzhou Middle School and attended Jiaotong University at the same time. Zhu's stepbrother, Zhu Guohua, taught Jiang at Jiaotong. "I am a Yangzhou person," Zhu often declared in his writings, and the city was the setting for many of his works. See Wang Xiaopeng, *Zhongguo dangdai lingdaoren* (China's Current Leaders) (Beijing: Zhonggong dangshi chubanshe [Chinese Communist Party History Publishing House], 1994), p. 11. Hereafter "Wang Xiaopeng 1994."

51. WA, 16 October 1989, p. 11.

52. "Louis Cha Meets Jiang Zemin," *Ming bao yuekan* (*Ming Pao* Monthly), 1 June 1993, pp. 81–91, quoted in FBIS, 11 June 1993, p. 17. Hereafter "Louis Cha talks."

53. WA, March 1995, p. 21.

54. An example is shown in Yangzhou Middle School Souvenir Book, p. 88.

55. Jiang Shufeng remained in Yangzhou in the early years of occupation and eventually went to work for Gu Minyuan. From the winter of 1940 until he took up a teaching post at Haifu Teachers College in late 1943, he headed the propaganda offices in several districts liberated, and then administered, by the New Fourth Army in Qidong county of Jiangsu province, headed by Gu.

56. It was named the Jiangdu Cultural Preservation Association Mobile Publicity Group after the Jiang family's adopted home of Jiangdu county outside Yangzhou.

57. For details, see Yang Shuying, Hu Zhihong, and Wang Zhijuan.

58. Hu Zhihong, p 32.

59. Yang Shuying, p. 8.

60. HKCNA, 1 June 1990.

61. *WWP*, 17 July 1989, p. 5.

62. Cited in Yang Zhongmei, *Jiang Zemin zhuan* (Biography of Jiang Zemin) (Taipei: Shih pao wen hua ch'u pan she ch'i yeh [*China Times* Publishing], 1996), p. 49. Hereafter cited as "Yang Zhongmei."

63. Shen Chun-shan talks, p. 69.

64. Ibid., p. 69.

65. PD, 29 March 1993, p. 3.

66. See, e.g., Xinhua, 2 November 1987, and *Beijing Review*, 10 July 1989.

67. *Qianshao* (Frontline Magazine, Hong Kong), August 1996, pp. 18–19.

68. *Jiaotong daxue xiaoshi* (History of Jiaotong University, 1896–1949) (Shanghai: Shanghai jiaoyu chubanshe [Shanghai Education Press], 1986), p. 442. Hereafter cited as "History of Jiaotong."

69. *LWHW*, 12 March 1990, pp. 3–5.

70. Li Hongyuan, "Jiang zongshuji he tade tongxue" (General Secretary Jiang and His Classmate), *Zhongguo laonian* (China's Elderly), November 1994, pp. 4–6. Hereafter cited as "Li Hongyuan."

71. Li Hongyuan, p. 5.

72. *WWP*, 11 March 1998, p. 4.

73. *WWP*, 20 May 1996, p. 2.

74. WA, 16 July 1989, p. 74. The words are those of Cheng Xiaogang, who became chancellor in 1948.

75. Shanghai Jiaotong daxue dangwei xuanchuanbu (Propaganda Department of the Party Committee of Jiaotong University), "Zai dier tiao zhanxianshang: Jiefang zhanzhang shiqi Jiaotong daxue xuesheng yundong" (On the Second Battlefront: The Student Movement at Jiaotong University during the War of Liberation) (Neibu faxing [internal circulation], 1981) p. 3. Hereafter cited as "Second Battlefront."

76. Li Guoqiang, *Jiang Zemin pouxi* (Jiang Zemin in Depth) (Hong Kong: Guangjiaojing chubanshe [Wide Angle Press], 1989), p. 94. Hereafter cited as "Li Guoqiang."

77. Yang Zhongmei, p. 55.

78. Cited in Zheng Yi, *Jiang Zemin zhuanji* (Biography of Jiang Zemin), 4th ed. (Hong Kong: Mingchuang chubanshe [Mingchuang Publishing], 1994) p. 32. Hereafter cited as "Zheng Yi."

79. Shen Chun-shan talks, p. 69.

80. *Zuzhi renshi bao* (Organisation and Personnel News), 22 August 1996, p. 4.

81. Li Guoqiang, p. 92.

82. See, e.g., Second Battlefront, p. 83.

83. Wang Xiaopeng 1993, p. 4.

84. Li Hongyuan, p. 5.

85. Zheng Yi, p. 30. Second Battlefront gives a figure of "over 1,000" party members and other "activists" at Jiaotong in early 1946 (p. 26).

86. I borrow liberally in what follows from Li Guoqiang and from Jeffrey Wasserstrom, *Student Protests in Twentieth Century China: The View from Shanghai* (Stanford: Stanford University Press, 1991), chs. 6 and 9. Hereafter "Wasserstrom."

87. Zheng Yi, p. 35.

88. Li Guoqiang, p. 115.

89. Ibid., p. 109.

90. Shen Chun-shan talks, p. 70.

91. Wasserstrom, p. 266.

92. Li Guoqiang, p. 118.

93. Lei fled to Hong Kong, where he joined the party and took a post with its students' federation. Years later, he would return to teach at the Dalian College of Science and Engineering, where the two men would meet after nearly half a century. *Liaoning ribao*, 4 September 1993, in FBIS, 20 September 1993, p. 29.

94. Hsu, *Rise of Modern China*, p. 631; and see also Hu Sheng, ed., *A Concise History of the Communist Party of China* (Beijing: Foreign Languages Press, 1994), p. 332. Hereafter cited as "Hu Sheng."

95. Wasserstrom, p. 268.

96. Zheng Yi, p. 15.

97. *Current Biography*, May 1995, p. 30.

98. Laszlo Ladany, *The Communist Party of China and Marxism, 1921–1985* (London: C. Hurst & Co., 1988), p. 136.

99. Cited in Yang Zhongmei, p. 58.

100. Li Guoqiang, p. 119. The argument that Jiang was merely a participant and not an organizer of the student protests is also made in He Ruohan, *Jiang Zemin shidai* (The Era of Jiang Zemin) (Hong Kong: Tiandi tushu [Cosmos Books], 1997), p. 46.

101. See History of Jiaotong and Second Battlefront. On Shanghai's underground movement itself, see Gongqingtuan Shanghai shiwei (Communist Youth League Shanghai Party Committee), *Chuntiande yaolan* (Cradle of Spring) (Shanghai: Zhongguo qingnian chubanshe [China Youth Press], 1982).

CHAPTER 2. MAO'S CHINA

1. WA, 16 July 1989, p. 75.

2. *Xinjiang ribao* (Xinjiang Daily), 5 September 1990, p. 1.

3. Li Guoqiang, p. 142.

4. *Beijing Review*, 10–16 July 1989, p. 17.

5. Li Guoqiang, p. 128.

6. Cited in Zheng Yi, p. 44.

7. *Qianshao* (Frontline Magazine, Hong Kong), August 1996, p. 3.

8. WA, 16 July 1989, p. 75.

9. Zheng Yi, p. 46.

10. *Jiushi niandai* (Nineties Monthly, Hong Kong), January 1991, in JPRS, 30 April 1991, p. 8.

11. Ibid.

12. *Liaoning ribao* (Liaoning Daily), 30 June 1995, pp. 1–2.

13. It became the Shanghai Detergents Factory in 1955.

14. Most references give the date of Jiang's wedding as December 1949, although in *Jing bao*, October 1994, pp. 58–59, he is said to have married Wang Yeping "in the early 1950s," an imprecision that suggests ignorance.

15. WWP, 18 July 1989, p. 3.

16. WA, December 1991, p. 7. Also Shi Jian and Hu Nan, *Jiang Zemin xiyou-ji* (Jiang Zemin's Journey to the West) (Brampton: Mingjing chubanshe [Mirror Books], 1997), pp. 100–101.

17. WA, December 1991, p. 7.

18. WA, December 1995, p. 42.

19. *Nongmin ribao* (Farmers' Daily), 24 February 1990, p. 6.

20. Several references to the mother-in-law crop up through Jiang's later life, including that cited in the preceding note.

21. Various versions of the given names of the sons circulated after Jiang came to power in 1989. After the fifteenth party congress in September 1997, these definitive versions were given in Jiang's official biography. Xinhua, 19 September 1997.

22. Hu Sheng, p. 447.

23. Ibid., pp. 424–98 passim.

24. Interviews with family sources, October 1996.

25. Yang Shuying, p. 8.

26. Xinhua, 17 May 1991.

27. Xinhua, 14 July 1991.

28. Guang Yu, "Jiang Zemin zai Changchun yiqi" (Jiang Zemin at the Changchun Number One Vehicle Plant), *Zhonghua ernu* (Sons and Daughters of China), June 1994, pp. 35–39. Hereafter cited as "Guang Yu."

29. Guang Yu, p. 37.

30. WWP, 21 April 1997, p. 4.

31. AFP, 11 November 1997.

32. Xinhua, 17 May 1991. See also *Chung Kuo shih pao* (China Times, Taipei), 19 December 1997.

33. PD, 14 March 1990, p. 1.

34. Guang Yu, passim.

35. SCMP, 20 May 1996, p. 17. Guang Yu says the flat had three rooms rather than the two reported by the SCMP.

36. Guang Yu, p. 36.

37. Ibid.

38. Hei Lin, "Zongshuji jiejie qingpin yi jiu" (The Party General Secretary's Sister Is as Poor as Ever), *Nanfang ribao* (Nanfang Daily), 3 August 1994, p. 8.

39. Ibid.

40. Hu Sheng, p. 495.

41. *SCMP*, 20 May 1996, p. 17.

42. The power office had been a mere section (*ke*) level organ in the arcane government grading system, but the power plant was equivalent to an office (*zheng chu*) in a central government ministry. Jiang had skipped right past the junior office (*chu*) level.

43. *SCMP*, 20 May 1996, p. 17.

44. *Jingji daobao* (Economic Reporter, Hong Kong), 24 August 1992, p. 22.

45. *SCMP*, 20 May 1996, p. 17.

46. Xinhua, 20 January 1990; Jilin Radio, 27 March 1990, in FBIS 4 April 1990, p. 19.

47. This section follows Guang Yu, p. 37.

48. Guang Yu, p. 37.

49. Cheng Hai, "Jiang Zemin zai renmin qunzhongzhong" (Jiang Zemin among the People), *Zhonghua yingcai* (China's Talents), 31 July 1993, p. 14.

50. Ibid. See also Zou Aiguo and He Ping, eds., *Disandai lingdaorende zuji* (The Footprints of the Third Generation Leaders)(Beijing: Zhonggong zhongyang dangxiao chubanshe [Central Party School Publishing House], 1992), pp. 56–57.

51. Guang Yu, pp. 35–36.

52. *Dangdai* (Contemporary Monthly, Hong Kong), 28 April 1990, in FBIS 4 May 1990, p. 24.

53. *Nongmin ribao* (Farmers' Daily), 24 February 1990, p. 6.

54. Yang Zhongmei, p. 83.

55. Wang Xiaopeng 1993, p. 6.

56. *Nongmin ribao* (Farmers' Daily), 24 February 1990, p. 6.

57. All details based on interviews with school officials, October 1996.

58. *Shaanxi ribao* (Shaanxi Daily), 3 August 1991, p. 11.

59. Ibid.

60. Ibid.

61. Ibid.

62. *WWP*, 9 February 1990, p. 4.

63. *Shaanxi ribao*, 3 August 1991, p. 11.

64. Wang Xiaopeng 1993, p. 7.

65. Ibid., p. 7.

66. *Shaanxi ribao*, 3 August 1991, p. 11.

67. Wang Xiaopeng 1993, p. 6.

68. Yang Zhongmei, p. 24.

69. Ibid.

70. *WWP*, 9 February 1990, p. 4.

71. *Shaanxi ribao*, 3 August 1991, p. 11.

72. Harry Harding, "The Chinese State in Crisis," in *The Politics of China, 1949–89*, ed. Roderick MacFarquhar (New York: Cambridge University Press, 1993), p. 244.

73. Ho Pin and Gao Xin, *Princes and Princesses of Red China* (Toronto: Canada Mirror Books, 1993), p. 294. Hereafter cited as "Ho and Gao."

CHAPTER 3. FOOT SOLDIER FOR DENG

1. *WWP*, 9 February 1990, p. 4.
2. Cited in "Quarterly Chronicle and Documentation," *China Quarterly*, October–December 1966, pp. 149–52.
3. For details of ministry personnel changes, see Malcolm Lamb, *Directory of Officials and Organisations in China: A Quarter-Century Guide* (London and Armonk, N.Y.: M. E. Sharpe, 1994), pp. 478–80. Hereafter cited as "Lamb."
4. Yang Zhongmei, p. 86.
5. PLAD, 10 November 1996, p. 1.
6. *Jiushi niandai* (Nineties Monthly, Hong Kong), 1 November 1990, p. 60.
7. *AWSJ*, 6 February 1995, p. 1.
8. Xinhua, 1 July 1996.
9. Zhong Xu, "Xinren zongshuji Jiang Zemin ceying" (A Profile of the New Party General Secretary, Jiang Zemin), *Zhuanji wenxue* (Biographical Literature), 1989, no. 4, p. 4. Hereafter cited as "Zhong Xu."
10. Xinhua, 1 July 1996.
11. Shen Chun-shan talks, p. 69.
12. See Kenneth Lieberthal, *Governing China: From Revolution through Reform* (New York: Norton, 1995), table 7.1, p. 210.
13. Interview with Jiang office official, Beijing, May 1997.
14. The visiting American was eventually told that the colleague was not in Beijing at the time. Zhong Xu, p. 5.
15. This section follows Fan Shuo, *Ye Jianying zai 1976* (Ye Jianying in 1976), rev. ed. (Beijing: Zhonggong zhongyang dangxiao chubanshe [Central Party School Publishing House], 1995), pp. 402–8.
16. The first confirmation of this came in LD, 7 August 1989, p. 2. It is also mentioned in Li Guoqiang, p. 143. See also the article on Peng Chong in *Zhonghua ernu* (Sons and Daughters of China), 1997, no. 9, p. 48.
17. Xi Xuan and Jin Chunming, *Wenhua da geming jianshi* (A Short History of the Cultural Revolution) (Beijing: Zhonggong dangshi chubanshe [Party History Publishing House], 1996), p. 340.
18. This section follows Yang Zhongmei, pp. 104–5.
19. Yang Zhongmei (p. 107) makes the mistake of confusing Jiang with his namesake, who was made an advisor to the ministry in 1978. Yang concludes that Jiang was forced to stand down for unknown political reasons. In fact, it was a different person who was made an advisor, and Jiang continued as director of the ministry's Foreign Affairs Bureau.
20. *CR* 1996, p. 325, and *CR* 1994, p. 11.5.
21. In practice, the two bodies—the State Foreign Investment Control Commission and the State Import/Export Control Commission—were virtually indistinguishable. Vice-premier Gu Mu was the chairman of both.
22. WA, 16 July 1989, in JPRS, 13 November 1989, p. 11. Zhou Jiannan took over as executive vice-chairman of both. Jiang was also made secretary general of the commissions in charge of day-to-day affairs.
23. DXP2, p. 199.
24. This and following quotes from *WWP*, 28 September 1990, p. 1.

25. Chen Yun, *Collected Works* (Beijing: Foreign Languages Press, 1986), pp. 276–77.

26. It was created out of the former Fourth Machine-Building Ministry.

27. WA, 16 July 1989, in JPRS, 13 November 1989, p. 10.

28. According to family sources in Shanghai, he began using the phrase when he was made minister of electronics, although it only became widely known when he later became mayor of the city.

29. *Mechanical and Electronic Industries Yearbook of China, 1985* (Beijing: Ministry of Electronics, n.d.), pp. 41–51.

30. *Jingji ribao* (Economic Daily), 27 August 1983, p. 1.

31. *WWP*, 30 March 1983, p. 2.

32. Jiang also visited Harvard at this time. Shi Jian and Hu Nan, *Jiang Zemin xiyouji* (Jiang Zemin's Journey to the West) (Brampton: Mingjing chubanshe [Mirror Books]), 1997, p. 229.

33. *Jingji ribao* (Economic Daily), 27 August 1983, p. 1.

34. Xinhua, 21 February 1984.

35. *WWP*, 30 March 1982, p. 2.

36. Ibid.

37. *Chungang ilbo* (South Korea), 22 July 1996, pp. 3–4, in FBIS, 23 July 1996, FBIS-CHI-96–141.

38. Lowell Dittmer, "Chinese Informal Politics," *China Journal*, July 1995, pp. 1–34.

39. Luo Chenglie et al., eds., *Kongzi mingyan* (A Collection of the Sayings of Confucius) (Jinan: Qilu shushe [Qilu Press], 1989), p. 72.

40. PD, 4 March 1989, p. 1.

41. WA, 16 July 1989, in JPRS, 13 November 1989, p. 12.

42. PD, 29 May 1984, p. 5.

43. WA, 16 July 1989, in JPRS, 13 November 1989, p. 13.

CHAPTER 4. SHANGHAI'S CHIEF CLERK

1. Lynn T. White III, *Shanghai Shanghaied? Uneven Taxes in Reform China* (Hong Kong: Centre of Asian Studies, University of Hong Kong, 1989), table 13. Hereafter cited as "Lynn White."

2. DXP3, p. 353.

3. Lynn White, table 6.

4. WA, 16 July 1989, in JPRS, 13 November 1989, p. 11.

5. Wang Xiaopeng 1993, p. 7.

6. Ibid.

7. Wang Xiaopeng 1994, p. 1.

8. Li Guoqiang, p. 60.

9. Jiang Zemin, 1986 speech on fire prevention (Xinhua, 8 November 1996).

10. Hu Sheng, p. 272.

11. *WWP*, 16 June 1985, p. 1.

12. Shanghai Radio, 29 July 1985, in SWB, 12 August 1983, p. 3.

13. Ibid.

14. WA, 16 July 1989, in FBIS, 13 November 1989, p. 8.

15. *Washington Post*, 14 December 1986, p. C1.

16. Ibid.

17. WA, 16 July 1989, in JPRS, 13 November 1989, p. 9.

18. PD (Overseas Edition), 5 April 1987, p. 3.

19. Jiang Zefen quoted in Hei Lin, "Zongshuji jiejie qingpin yi jiu" (The Party General Secretary's Sister Is as Poor as Ever), *Nanfang ribao*, 3 August 1994, p. 8.

20. *Shaanxi ribao* (Shaanxi Daily), 3 August 1991, p. 11.

21. Wang Yu, p. 347.

22. A tablet almost ten feet high was erected, inscribed on the front by Zhang and on the back by several veterans of the New Fourth Army, in which Jiang Shangqing had served.

23. His foster sisters, Jiang Zeling and Jiang Zehui, attended, bringing along the then frail Wang Zhelan. Jiang's uncle, Jiang Shufeng, the younger brother of Jiang Shangqing, also attended and contributed a poem. But there is no evidence of Jiang's presence. Yang Shuying, p. 8.

24. *Sihong xian zhi* (Annals of Sihong County, Jiangsu Province) (Nanjing: Jiangsu renmin chubanshe [Jiangsu People's Publishing House], 1994), p. 974 and photo.

25. WWP, 17 July 1989, p. 1.

26. WA, March 1995, p. 21.

27. WWP, 18 July 1989, p. 1.

28. CNS, 3 July 1989.

29. *Ottawa Citizen*, 25 June 1989, p. D1.

30. Shanghai shiwei (Shanghai Municipal Party Committee), *Shanghai nianjian 1988* (Shanghai Statistical Yearbook 1988) (Shanghai tongji chubanshe [Shanghai Statistics Publishing House], 1989), p. 298.

31. *Washington Post*, 16 June 1985, p. F3.

32. Shanghai Radio, 10 August 1985, in SWB, 13 August 1985, p. 1.

33. Richard Baum, *Burying Mao: Chinese Politics in the Age of Deng Xiaoping* (Princeton: Princeton University Press, 1994), p. 191. Hereafter cited as "Baum."

34. *San Francisco Chronicle*, 18 December 1985, p. C3.

35. Shanghai Radio, 29 October 1985, in SWB, 5 November 1985, p. 2.

36. DXP2, p. 332.

37. DXP3, p. 54.

38. I prefer the translation "spiritual culture" rather than the more literal "spiritual civilization" for the phrase *jingshen wenming*, since the latter is awkward and ambiguous.

39. Both cited in Baum, pp. 200–201.

40. CNS, 23 December 1986.

41. Yang Zhongmei, p. 208.

42. Details from personal interviews in Shanghai (January 1996) as well as the sources listed below.

43. AFP, 23 December 1986.

44. AFP, 22 December 1986.

45. Yang Zhongmei, p. 212.
46. Li Guoqiang, p. 69.
47. Ibid.
48. Xinhua, 21 December 1986.
49. Shanghai Radio, 22 December 1986, in FBIS, 22 December 1986, p. 7.
50. AFP, 23 December 1986.
51. *Ming Pao*, 25 December 1986, p. 1.
52. Xinhua, 21 December 1986.
53. *Washington Post*, 23 December 1986, p. A13.
54. The lower figure is from Xinhua, 21 December 1986. The higher figure is from Kyodo News Service, 20 December 1986, in SWB, 22 December 1986, p. 1.
55. AFP, 22 December 1986.
56. "Jiang Zemin yu Shen Junshan de sanci tanhua" (Three Talks Between Jiang Zemin and Shen Chun-shan), *Jiushi niandai* (Nineties Monthly, Hong Kong), August 1996, p. 78. Hereafter cited as "Shen Chun-shan talks."
57. Ibid.
58. Ibid.
59. Shanghai Radio, 22 December 1986, in SWB, 23 December 1986, p. 13.
60. Kyodo, 20 December 1986.
61. *China Daily* (Beijing), 25 December 1986, p. 4.
62. Shen Chun-shan talks, p. 78.
63. Shanghai Radio, 22 December 1986, in SWB, 23 December 1986, p. 13.
64. Xinhua, 21 December 1986.
65. AP, 21 December 1986.
66. *Los Angeles Times*, 22 December 1986, p. 1.
67. AFP, 21 December 1986.
68. CNS, 23 December 1986.
69. Yang Zhongmei, p. 214.
70. Xinhua, 21 December 1986.
71. AFP, 22 December 1986.
72. Shanghai Radio, 22 December 1986, in SWB, 22 December 1986, p. 6.
73. Ibid., p. 7.
74. CNS, 23 December 1986.
75. Shanghai Radio, 23 December 1986, in SWB, 24 December 1986, p. 4.
76. CNS, 23 December 1986.
77. Reuters, 24 December 1986.
78. Shen Chun-shan talks, p. 78.
79. Xinhua, 25 December 1986.
80. CNS, 25 December 1986.
81. *Ming Pao*, 28 December 1986, p. 6.
82. It may be that Deng was misinformed about sentiments in Shanghai by those eager to discredit Hu. Two party elders who allegedly favored Hu's dismissal, Chen Yun and Li Xiannian, for example, were both reporting to Beijing from Shanghai at the time of the protests. See Ruan Ming, *Deng Xiaoping: Chronicle of an Empire* (Boulder, Colo.: Westview Press, 1992), p. 175.
83. Ruan Ming, p. 176.
84. Shanghai Radio, 7 January 1987, in SWB, 9 January 1987.

85. See Lei Yue, "Shijie jingji daobao shijian zhenxiang buyi" (Addendum to the Truth about the World Economic Herald Incident), *Zhongguo jizhe* (China Journalist), September 1989, p. 12.

86. Shanghai Radio, 7 March 1987, in SWB, 10 March 1987 p. 4.

87. Li Guoqiang, p. 70.

88. LD, 7 November 1986, pp. 1–2.

89. Li Guoqiang, p. 55.

90. WA, 16 July 1989, in JPRS, 13 November 1989, p. 9.

91. Wang Xiaopeng 1993, p. 13.

92. Speech released by Xinhua, 8 November 1996.

93. Ibid.

94. Xu Jingen, "Shibi gongqin de ling yimian" (The Other Side of Doing Things Yourself), PD, 6 July 1987, p. 1.

95. Wang Xiaopeng 1993, p. 14, and WA, 16 July 1989, in JPRS, 13 November 1989, p. 9.

96. *Seattle Times*, 21 July 1989, p. A3.

97. *Current Biography* (New York, H. W. Wilson Co.), May 1995, p. 31.

98. Li retained his mayorship, however.

99. The proportion dropped from 8 percent in the seventh Central Committee (1945–56) to 2 percent in the eleventh (1977–82) and just 1 percent in the twelfth (1992–97). See Peter Cheung, "The Political Context of Shanghai's Economic Development," in *Shanghai: Transformation and Modernization under China's Open Policy,* ed. Y. M. Yeung and Sung Yun-wing (Hong Kong: Chinese University Press, 1996), p. 62. Hereafter cited as "*Shanghai,* ed. Yeung and Sung."

100. I owe this point to Maurice Brosseau of the Chinese University of Hong Kong.

101. LD, 7 November 1986, p. 1.

102. Ibid., pp. 1–2.

103. Gao Xin and He Pin, "Zhu Rongji zhuan" (Biography of Zhu Rongji), *Lian he bao* (United Daily News, Hong Kong), part 5, 5 October 1993, p. 2.

104. Both examples taken from ibid.

105. It was not until Zhao Ziyang visited Shanghai in early January 1988, with Jiang and Zhu flanking him at every turn, that the Shanghai people were let in on the identity of their future mayor. Although only a deputy party secretary of the city for another four months, Zhu effectively took over as mayor at the beginning of the year.

106. WA, 16 July 1989, in JPRS, 13 November 1989, p. 12.

107. The policies were approved by the State Council in August 1986 and announced by Jiang a month later. The program offered many of the same incentives available to foreign investors in the SEZs: lower taxes and land-use fees, accelerated depreciation allowances, preferential access to bank loans and scare materials, and the freedom to hire and fire workers with a minimum of fuss. See *Wall Street Journal*, 23 September 1986, p. 5.

108. Sung Yun-wing, "Dragon Head of China's Economy?" in *Shanghai*, ed. Yeung and Sung, p. 184.

109. Ibid., p. 186.

110. AP, 24 June 1989.

111. *China Daily*, 1 February 1988, p. 1.

112. James Tyson, "Shanghai Battles Troubled Times," *Christian Science Monitor*, 11 July 1988.

113. Xinhua, 23 January 1988.

114. PD (Overseas), 14 March 1988, p. 4.

115. HKCNA, 10 March 1988.

116. WA, 16 July 1989, in JPRS, 13 November 1989, p. 10.

117. Xinhua, 5 December 1987.

118. *Wenhui bao* (Shanghai), 17 February 1988, p. 1.

119. LD, 14 March 1988, p. 1.

120. Yabuki Susumu, *China's New Political Economy* (Boulder, Colo.: Westview Press, 1995), p. 130.

121. Shanghai shiwei (Shanghai Municipal Party Committee), *Shanghai nianjian* 1989 (Shanghai Statistical Yearbook 1989) (Shanghai tongji chubanshe [Shanghai Statistics Publishing House], 1990), p. 341.

122. Rebecca Chiu, "Housing," in *Shanghai*, ed. Yeung and Sung, p. 369.

123. *China Daily*, 28 April 1988, p. 1.

124. AP, 3 December 1988.

125. PLAD, 1 January 1991, pp. 1–2.

126. Hu Sheng, p. 789.

127. Party Research Center of the Chinese Communist Party, *History of the Chinese Communist Party: A Chronology of Events, 1919–1990* (Beijing: Foreign Languages Press, 1991), p. 490.

128. For example, see Jiang's speech on Shanghai's econony, LD, 5 January 1988, pp. 1–2.

129. LD, 12 October 1988, p. 1.

130. Li Guoqiang, p. 67.

131. Zhao Ziyang zibian shu (Zhao Ziyang Self-Defense Statement), *Xinbao yuekan* (Hong Kong Economic Journal Monthly), July 1994, p. 134.

132. *San Francisco Chronicle*, 26 June 1989, p. A1.

133. *Washington Post*, 14 December 1986, p. C1.

134. *Chicago Sun-Times*, 8 September 1985, p. 16.

135. *San Francisco Chronicle*, 26 June 1989, p. A1.

CHAPTER 5. TIANANMEN

1. Pang Pang, *The Death of Hu Yaobang* (Honolulu: University of Hawaii Press, 1989), p. 10.

2. Shanghai Radio, 17 April 1989, in SWB, 20 April 1989, p. B2/1.

3. *WWP*, 20 April 1989, p. 1.

4. James Tong, "The 1989 Democracy Movement in China: A Preliminary Spatial Analysis" (Chinese University of Hong Kong, Universities Service Centre Seminar Series, no. 9, 1994).

5. LD, 21 September 1989, p. 1.

6. Xinhua, 18 August 1989.

7. *Zhongguo jizhe* (China Journalist), September 1989, pp. 11–12.

8. Li Cheng and Lynn T. White III, "China's Technocratic Movement and the 'World Economic Herald,'" *Modern China*, July 1991, p. 351. Hereafter cited as "Li and White."

9. *New York Times* Service, 24 April 1989.

10. This was issue no. 439 of the *Herald*.

11. *Zhengming* (*Cheng Ming*, Hong Kong), September 1996, p. 27.

12. Yang Zhongmei, p. 240.

13. Kate Wright, "The Political Fortunes of Shanghai's 'World Economic Herald,'" *Australian Journal of Chinese Affairs*, January 1990, p. 123. Hereafter cited as "Wright."

14. Yang Zhongmei, p. 249; Wright, p. 124.

15. Wright, p. 123.

16. Xinhua, 18 August 1989.

17. Wright, p. 126.

18. George Black and Robin Munro, *Black Hands of Beijing: Lives of Defiance in China's Democracy Movement* (New York: John Wiley & Sons, 1993), p. 146.

19. Xinhua, 18 August 1989.

20. Rephrased from Wright, p. 126.

21. See Li and White.

22. CNS, 18 May 1989.

23. *Zhongguo jizhe* (China Journalist), September 1989, p. 11.

24. Wright, p. 127.

25. Wright, p. 128.

26. CNS, 26 April 1989.

27. Beijing Radio, 27 April 1989, in SWB, 29 April 1989, p. B2/6. For an example of the early overseas press reports, see *New York Times* Service, 24 April 1989.

28. Xinhua, 18 August 1989.

29. *Washington Post* Service, 19 May 1989.

30. Xinhua, 18 August 1989.

31. CNS, 15 May 1989.

32. *Ming Pao*, 7 May 1989.

33. CNS, 6 May 1989.

34. Voice of Pujiang Radio, 5 May 1989, in SWB, 9 May 1989, p. B2/3.

35. Yang Zhongmei, p. 246.

36. Voice of Pujiang Radio, 5 May 1989, in SWB, 9 May 1989, p. B2/3.

37. *Zhongguo jizhe* (China Journalist), September 1989, p. 12.

38. Xinhua, 18 August 1989.

39. PD, 5 May 1989, p. 1.

40. Xinhua, 18 August 1989.

41. See, e.g., *Ming Pao*, 14 May 1989, p. 1.

42. CNS, 17 May 1989.

43. *Ming Pao*, 14 May 1989.

44. CNS, 17 May 1989.

45. CNS, 18 May 1989.

46. CNS, 18 May 1989.

47. *New York Times* Service, 18 April 1991.

48. Voice of Pujiang Radio, 19 April 1991, in SWB 22 April 1991, p. B2/8.
49. Shanghai Radio, 17 May 1989, in SWB, 20 May 1989, p. B2/5.
50. *SCMP*, 24 May 1989, p. 1.
51. Shanghai Radio, 18 May 1989, in SWB, 20 May 1989, p. B2/4.
52. Ibid., p. B2/13.
53. Ibid., 19 May 1989, in FBIS, 22 May 1989, p. 91.
54. *New York Times* Service, 18 May 1989.
55. Beijing Television, 26 September 1989, in FBIS, 26 September 1989, p. 12.
56. Shanghai Radio, 20 May 1989, in FBIS, 22 May 1989, p. 90.
57. Ibid., 21 May 1989, in FBIS, 22 May 1989, p. 90.
58. Ibid., in FBIS, 23 May 1989, p. 65.
59. *WWP*, 25 May 1989, p. 1.
60. Zhao Wei, *Biography of Zhao Ziyang* (Hong Kong: Educational and Cultural Press, 1987), p. 261.
61. *WWP*, 25 June 1989, p. 1.
62. *TKP*, 26 March 1984, p. 1.
63. WA, 16 July 1989, in JPRS, 13 November 1989, p. 11.
64. Yang Zhongmei, p. 223.
65. WA, 16 July 1989 in JPRS 13 November 1989, p. 11.
66. I borrow liberally in what follows from WA, 16 July 1989, in JPRS, 13 November 1989; Li Guoqiang, pp. 1–70 passim; and *WWP*, 25 June 1989, p. 1.
67. DXP3, p. 288.
68. *Jing bao,* January 1990, p. 49.
69. Li Guoqiang, p. 4.
70. *WWP*, 25 June 1989, p. 1.
71. Xinhua, 19 October 1992.
72. *WWP*, 25 June 1989, p. 1.
73. Wang Xiaopeng 1993, p. 2.
74. Xinhua, 19 October 1992.
75. *WWP*, 25 June 1989, p. 1.
76. This is according to China's top representative in Hong Kong at the time, Xu Jiatun, quoted in *Kaifang* (Open Magazine, Hong Kong), June 1997, p. 22. The Asahi News Service, 30 July 1989, said Jiang went to the square dressed as an artist.
77. *Kaifang*, June 1997, p. 22.
78. Jiang Zemin, conversation with Professor Chao Hao-sheng of Yale University, in *TKP*, 22 September 1989, p. 1. Hereafter cited as "Chao Hao-sheng talks."
79. *Jing bao,* October 1994, pp. 58–59.
80. Chao Hao-sheng talks.
81. LD, 7 August 1989, p. 2.
82. Chao Hao-sheng talks.
83. Kaifang, February 1998, p. 36.
84. Chao Hao-sheng talks.
85. *TKP*, 12 November 1989.
86. Ho Pin and Gao Xin, *Zhonggong taizi dang* (China's Princelings) (Toronto: Canada Mirror Books, 1993), p. 422. The first official report on

Zeng's transfer to Beijing was in *WWP*, 4 August 1989, p. 2. It was made official in November.

87. Richard Baum, *Burying Mao: Chinese Politics in the Age of Deng Xiaoping* (Princeton: Princeton University Press, 1994), p. 268.

88. *Jing bao,* 10 August 1989.

89. Ibid.

90. Xinhua, 25 May 1989.

91. Shanghai Radio, 26 May 1989, in FBIS, 2 June 1989, p. 45.

92. Xinhua, 27 May 1989.

93. CNS, 30 May 1989.

94. Mention of his speech is made in Shanghai Radio, 3 June 1989, in FBIS, 12 June 1989, p. 78.

95. Gao Xin and Ho Pin, "Zhu Rongji," *Lianhe bao* (United Daily News, Hong Kong), 10 October 1993, in JPRS, 17 August 1994, p. 22.

96. DXP3, p. 288

97. DXP3, pp. 291–92.

98. Li Guoqiang, pp. 6, 10, 45.

99. Figures cited in Baum, *Burying Mao*, pp. 276, 283.

100. See *Jiushi niandai* (Nineties Monthly, Hong Kong), June and September 1994.

101. Reuters, 12 December 1996.

102. LD, 30 May 1989, p. 1; interviews with family members in Shanghai, September 1995.

103. Interview with Jiang office official in Beijing, May 1997.

104. Shen Chun-shan talks, p. 71.

105. Xinhua, 25 February 1997.

106. *U.S. News & World Report,* 12 March 1990, pp. 50–54.

107. Letter to American students, Xinhua, 18 June 1990.

108. The investigation into Zhao would be formally called off at the party congress of 1992, allowing him to retain his party membership.

109. Shen Chun-shan talks, p. 78.

110. This point comes out clearly in the 1995 film documentary *The Gate of Heavenly Peace* directed by Carma Hinton and Richard Gordon.

111. Cited in Baum, *Burying Mao*, p. 276.

112. Beijing TV, 26 September 1989, in FBIS, 26 September 1989, p. 10.

113. Shen Chun-shan talks, p. 71.

114. *Qiushi* (Seeking Truth), May 1990, p. 5.

115. Xinhua, 25 May 1990.

116. PLAD, 3 January 1994, p. 1.

117. Shen Chun-shan talks, p. 71.

118. *Ming Pao,* 3 November 1997, p. 7. See also the author's article in *AWSJ*, 3 November 1997.

119. Shen Chun-shan talks, p. 70.

120. Shanghai Radio, 4 June 1989, in FBIS, 5 June 1989, p. 101.

121. Ibid., 5 June 1989, in FBIS, 5 June 1989, p. 109.

122. Ibid., 4 June 1989, in FBIS, 5 June 1989, p. 109.

123. Ibid., 7 June 1989, in SWB, 9 June 1989, p. B2/8.

124. *WWP*, 25 June 1989, p. 3.

125. Shanghai Radio, 6 June 1989, in SWB, 7 June 1989, p. B2/10.

126. Ibid., p. B2/11.

127. Beijing TV, 8 June 1989, in FBIS, 8 June 1989, p. 14; CNS, 8 June 1989.

128. Shanghai Radio, 8 June 1989, in FBIS, 9 June 1989, pp. 45–47.

129. WWP, 15 June 1989, p. 3.

130. Related in Shen Chun-shan talks, p. 78.

131. Xinhua, 27 June 1989.

132. DXP3, p. 301.

133. DXP3, p. 301.

134. DXP3, p. 304.

135. AP, 24 June 1989.

136. *Issues and Studies* (Taipei), July 1989, p. 2.

137. *Jing bao,* 5 October 1992, pp. 34–36.

138. Yang and Li promoted the military propagandist Shao Huaze to be chief editor, while Qiao installed the hard-line Jilin province party chief Gao Di as director. *Jing bao,* 5 October 1992, pp. 34–36.

139. Xinhua, 18 June 1989.

140. WWP, 25 June 1989.

141. *Washington Post* Service, 20 July 1989.

142. WA, 16 July 1989, in JPRS, 13 November 1989, p. 14.

143. DXP3, p. 292.

144. Chao Hao-sheng talks.

CHAPTER 6. THE GREAT RECONCILIATION

1. Beijing Television, 28 June 1989, in FBIS, 28 June 1989, p. 9; and PD, 29 June 1989, p. 1.

2. As revealed by Wang Zhen to a visiting Japanese politician, Kyodo, 20 August 1989. See the Beidaihe photograph from the summer of 1989 by Yang Shaoming (Yang Shangkun's son) in *Kaifang* (Open Magazine, Hong Kong), June 1997, p. 21.

3. *Jing bao*, 10 September 1989, p. 23.

4. Reuters, 26 June 1989.

5. Cited in Richard Baum, *Burying Mao: Chinese Politics in the Age of Deng Xiaoping* (Princeton: Princeton University Press, 1994), p. 290.

6. Beijing Radio, 27 November 1989.

7. PD, 29 June 1989, p. 1.

8. Shen Chun-shan talks, p. 78.

9. *Jing bao,* 10 August 1989.

10. Xinhua, 6 July 1989.

11. Ibid., 2 July 1989.

12. Chao Hao-sheng talks, p. 1.

13. Beijing TV, 26 September 1989, in FBIS, 26 September 1989, p. 11.

14. *LWHW*, 12 March 1990, pp. 3–5.

15. Xinhua, 26 August 1989; and Beijing Radio, 26 August 1989, in SWB, 29 August 1989, p. B2/1.

16. *LWHW*, 2 March 1990, pp. 3–5.

17. Xinhua, 16 October 1989.

18. Baum, *Burying Mao*, p. 316; Xinhua, 22 October 1992.

19. Two versions of the speech exist: Beijing Radio, 29 November 1989, in SWB, 2 December 1989, pp. B2/1–3; and *Qiushi* (Seeking Truth), no. 3 (March 1990).

20. *CR* 1991, p. 20.7.

21. *WWP*, 22 December 1989.

22. See Kwan Ha Yim, ed., *China under Deng* (New York: Facts on File, 1991), pp. 292–302.

23. *China's Economic Dilemmas in the 1990s*, ed. Joint Economic Committee of the Congress of the United States (New York: M. E. Sharpe, 1993), p. 748; and Yabuki Susumu, *China's New Political Economy* (Boulder, Colo.: Westview Press, 1995), p. 165.

24. China Statistical Yearbook, 1990.

25. Meeting with Ghulam Nabi Azad, Xinhua, 6 July 1989.

26. Xinhua, 16 October 1989; WA, 16 October 1989.

27. *LWHW*, 12 March 1990, p. 5.

28. WA, 16 October 1989; also see AP, 11 July 1989.

29. Kwan, ed., *China under Deng*, p. 293.

30. AP, 19 December 1989.

31. Shen Chun-shan talks, p. 70. Jiang and Nixon are reputed to have stood shoulder to shoulder and recited the Gettysburg Address like two schoolboys.

32. *New York Times*, 18 May 1990, p. 31.

33. *U.S. News & World Report*, 12 March 1990, pp. 50–54.

34. Xinhua, 18 June 1990; *Los Angeles Times*, 18 June 1990.

35. Shen Chun-shan talks, pp. 73, 78.

36. Xinhua, 24 July 1989.

37. *Dang jian* (Party Building), nos. 7 and 8 (combined), July 1989.

38. *LWHW*, 7 August 1989, p. 8.

39. *Zhonghua yingcai* (China's Talents), no. 66 (1993): 14.

40. Wang Xiaopeng 1994, p. 34; *Hainan ribao* (Hainan Daily), 23 May 1990, p. 1, in FBIS, 16 July 1990, p. 29.

41. PD, 13 April 1991, p. 3.

42. Cited in Baum, *Burying Mao*, p. 317.

43. PD, 10 March 1990, p. 1.

44. 21 August 1989 speech reported by Xinhua, 16 October 1989.

45. PD (Overseas), 17 August 1989, p. 1.

46. WA, October 1989.

47. *Qiushi*, 16 June 1989.

48. Beijing Television, 29 September 1989, in SWB, 2 October 1989, pp. C1/1–C1/10.

49. *U.S. News & World Report*, 12 March 1990, pp. 50–54.

50. SCMP, 28 October 1997, p. 10.

51. The only picture available of the couple and their baby daughter was printed in *Changjiang ribao* (Yangtze Daily), 5 April 1996, p. 13.

52. *Ottawa Citizen*, 5 July 1989, p. E8.

53. *Yao Yao: Disandai lingdao waijiao shilu* (Record of the Diplomacy of the Third Generation Leadership) (Beijing: Zhongguo Yanshi chubanshe [China Yanshi Publishing], 1997), p. 43.

54. ABC television interview, broadcast 18 May 1990.

55. AP, 30 June 1989.

56. *Dongxiang* (Trend Magazine), August 1996, pp. 22–25.

57. Some reports said he also consulted for the U.S. investment banking and securities brokerage firm Bear Stearns & Co., and spent time in Canada (*Qianshao* [Frontline], August 1995, p. 13; *Mirror*, October 1994, pp. 58–59).

58. *Zhongguo jizhe* (China Journalist) 4, no. 15 (April 1990): 8, says Jiang's grandson is four years old. Since the Chinese begin counting from conception, I assume that the child was aged three in Western terms and was therefore born in 1987.

59. *Time* (U.S. edition), 27 October 1997, p. 58.

60. WWP, 18 July 1989.

61. *Mirror*, October 1994, pp. 58–59.

62. Xinhua, 2 April 1992; WWP, 2 April 1992.

63. *Zhongguo jiancai bao* (China Building Materials Daily), July 1994, quoted in *Eastern Express* (Hong Kong), 13 October 1994, p. 9.

64. Hei Lin, p. 8.

65. Ibid.

66. In 1989 it was still believed that Jiang Shangqing had been killed on 29 August 1939. Later historical research showed the date to have been 29 July 1939, as used in this narrative.

67. The following is from WA, December 1991, pp. 6–8.

68. Wang Xiaopeng 1993, p. 18.

69. The anecdote that follows is based on interviews in Yangzhou, October 1996.

70. Interview with Anhui Foreign Affairs Department official, September 1995. WWP, 8 March 1998, p. 3.

71. DXP3, p. 307.

72. DXP3, p. 323.

73. *Jing bao,* 10 January 1990, p. 51.

74. DXP3, p. 315.

75. *WWP*, 20 November 1989. The same talk contained in DXP3, pp. 305–11, makes the language much less animated.

76. You Ji, *China Information*, Fall 1991, p. 20.

77. DXP3, p. 315.

78. When the appointments were voted on by the National People's Congress five months later (a formality that creates a state body to mirror the party one) Jiang received 99 percent of the votes, while 10 members of the parliament voted against him and 26 abstained. Two deputies with a sense of humor wrote in the names of Deng and Yang.

79. Deng Maomao, *Deng Xiaoping: My Father* (New York: Basic Books, 1995), p. 2.

80. Li Guoqiang, p. 78.

81. PLAD, 27 January 1990, p. 1.

82. Its share of GDP would continue to fall. Foreign estimates put the actual figure at between two and three times the published one.

83. Xinhua, 26 March 1990.

84. PLAD, 27 March 1990, p. 1.

85. *Jing bao,* 10 January 1990.

86. Japan Economic Newswire, 13 November 1989.

87. PD, 14 November 1989, p. 1.

88. Li Guoqiang, p. 76.

89. *U.S. News & World Report,* 12 March 1990, pp. 50–54.

90. CNS, 11 January 1990.

91. Xinhua, 25 January 1990.

92. WWP, 22 December 1989, p. 3.

93. Xinhua, 24 May 1990.

94. Beijing Radio, 14 March 1990, in FBIS, 15 March 1990, p. 4.

95. PD, 31 December 1989, p. 1.

96. PD (Overseas), 4 June 1990.

97. Central Radio, 26 March 1990, in SWB, 28 March 1990, p. C2/1.

98. *Jing bao,* October 1990, p. 31.

99. Ibid., May 1990, p. 33

100. Xinhua, 6 July 1990; and Kyodo, 6 July 1990.

101. *Jing bao,* September 1990, p. 36.

102. Ibid.

103. Ibid.

104. Xinhua, 11 July 1990.

105. *Jing bao,* 10 November 1990, p. 40.

106. Ibid., 10 October 1990, p. 41.

107. Pudong would be showered with Rmb1 billion in direct grants and Rmb5.5 billion in loans from central coffers during the five-year plan 1991 to 1995. Thomas Chan, "The Policy of Opening and SEZs," *CR* 1991, p. 11.12.

108. *Jing bao,* 10 March 1991.

109. Ibid., 10 November 1990, p. 41.

110. WA, 16 January 1991, p. 10.

111. *Jing bao,* 10 May 1991, in SWB, 11 May 1991, p. B2/3.

112. WA, 16 January 1991, p. 12.

113. *Jing bao,* 10 May 1991, in SWB, 11 May 1991, p. B2/3.

114. DXP3, p. 351.

115. Deng used the proverb in a 1962 speech entitled "Restore Agricultural Production." The original refers to yellow and black cats rather than white and black cats. See Deng Xiaoping, *Selected Works,* vol. 1: 1938–65 (Beijing: Foreign Languages Press, 1992), p. 293.

116. Central TV, 14 February 1991, in SWB, 16 February 1991, p. B2/1.

117. *Jing bao,* 10 May 1991, in SWB, 11 May 1991, p. B2/2.

118. Ibid., 10 June 1991, in SWB, 18 June 1991, p. B2/8.

119. PD, 24 April 1991, p. 1.

120. *Jing bao,* 10 June 1991, in SWB, 20 June 1991, p. B2/2.

121. Ibid., 5 January 1992, in SWB, 17 January 1992, p. B2/3.

122. PLAD, 24 April 1991, p. 1.

123. Xinhua, 14 June 1991.

124. *Jing bao,* 5 January 1992, in SWB, 17 January 1992, p. B2/4.

125. *Washington Times,* 31 October 1991, p. A1.

126. W. J. F. Jenner, *The Tyranny of History: The Roots of China's Crisis* (London: Allen Lane, Penguin Books, 1992), p. 93.

127. Xinhua, 30 September 1990.

128. Wang Xiaopeng 1994, p. 31.

129. *LWHW,* 13 August 1990, in SWB, 21 August 1990, p. B2/5.

130. *Shidai chao* (Tide of the Times Magazine) (Beijing: *Renmin ribao*), April 1997, p. 7.

131. Louis Cha talks, FBIS, 11 June 1993, p. 18.

132. Xinhua, 29 July 1990.

133. Tibet TV, 8 August 1990, in SWB, 21 August 1989, p. B2/4.

134. *Xinjiang ribao* (Xinjiang Daily), 7 September 1990, p. 1.

135. Interviews with China Islamic Association officials, October 1993.

136. *LWHW,* 17 June 1991; PLAD, 10 November 1996, p. 1.

137. Yunnan Radio, 23 November 1989, in FBIS, 27 November 1989, p. 17.

138. *Xinjiang ribao,* 5 September 1990, pp. 1–2.

139. This anecdote taken from *Ban yue tan* (Semi-Monthly Talks), 25 November 1994, pp. 4–7.

140. James Kung, "Peasants in a Hot Pot," *CR* 1994, p. 11.5.

141. Liu Yunhua, "The Rural Economy of China," *CR* 1995 (Hong Kong, 1995), p. 22.12.

142. World Bank, "Poverty in China: What Do the Numbers Say?" (unpublished background note, October 1996).

143. Guangxi Radio, 28 November 1990, in FBIS, 29 November 1990, pp. 19–20.

144. Guizhou Radio, 27 December 1991, in FBIS, 3 January 1992, p. 28.

145. Details on the trip from Niu Zhengwu, '92: *Deng Xiaoping nanxun jishi* (1992: Deng Xiaoping's Southern Inspection Tour) (Guangzhou: Huacheng chuban she [Huacheng Publishing], 1992); Jiang Xinghong et al., *Deng Xiaoping yu 1992 nian* (Deng Xiaoping and 1992) (Beijing: Zhonggong zhongyang dangxiao chubanshe [Central Party School Publishers], 1993); and speeches printed in *Beijing Review,* 7 February 1994, pp. 9–20.

146. *Jing bao,* 5 January 1992, in SWB, 17 January 1992, p. B2/2.

147. Niu Zhengwu, pp. 4–5.

148. Ibid., p. 1.

149. Xinhua, 19 January 1992.

150. Ibid., 25 January 1992.

151. Niu Zhengwu, p. 6.

152. China Central TV, 3 February 1992, in FBIS, 3 February 1992, p. 38.

153. The first reports were carried in *Ming Pao* on 21 January 1992. Others in Hong Kong followed the next day.

154. E.g., Niu Zhengwu, p. 103.

155. *Ming Pao,* 8 March 1992, p. 13.

156. Xinhua, 4 February 1992.

157. *Ming Pao*, 14 February 1992; WWP, 17 February 1992, 18 February 1992.

158. Xinhua, 2 April 1992; WWP, 2 April 1992.

159. *Jing bao*, 5 April 1992, p. 41.

160. Ibid., 6 June 1992 in SWB 17 June 1992, p. B2/1.

161. Ibid., 5 April 1992, p. 46.

162. In Chinese, *gaige kaifang danzi yao da yixie*.

163. WWP, 26 May 1992, in SWB, 28 May 1992, p. B2/1.

164. *Renmin luntan* (People's Forum), 5 September 1992, p. 21.

165. *TKP*, 23 July 1992, in SWB, 30 July 1992, p. B2/1.

166. *China Daily*, 16 June 1992, p. 4.

167. WWP, 16 January 1996, p. 2. WA, September 1997, p. 19, confirms that the speaker was Zhu Rongji.

168. Jiang Xinghong et al., p. 40.

169. *Jingji daobao* (Economic Reporter), 30 November 1992, p. 23.

170. *Jing bao*, 16 August 1992, pp. 6–9.

171. Wang Xiaopeng 1993, p. 1.

172. Xinhua, 19 October 1992.

CHAPTER 7. THE PRESIDENT'S MEN

1. See Tai Ming Cheung's articles in *FEER*, 15 June 1991 and 29 October 1992, and *CR* 1993, ch. 6.

2. PLAD, 20 March 1991, p. 1.

3. *Jing bao*, December 1992, p. 37, says that Yang Shangkun revived the slogan first, and that it was later taken up by Yang Baibing.

4. PD, 29 July 1992, p. 1.

5. *Ming Pao*, 24 November 1992 and 29 November 1992, in SWB, 2 December 1992, pp. B2/1–2; also *Jing bao*, December 1992, p. 36.

6. WWP, 15 December 1992, p. 2.

7. PLAD, 14 October 1992, p. 1.

8. Xinhua, 29 December 1992.

9. WWP, 15 December 1992, p. 2.

10. PLAD, 6 December 1992, p. 1.

11. Xinhua, 29 December 1992.

12. Jiang An, "Jiang in Firm Control of the Military," *Straits Times*, 27 June 1996, p. 46.

13. Li Guoqiang, p. 13; WA, 16 March 1993, p. 6.

14. China Central TV, 19 October 1992, in SWB, 21 October 1992, p. B2/1.

15. *Jing bao*, March 1993, p. 35.

16. Xinhua, 21 January 1993.

17. Xinhua, 15 January 1993.

18. PLAD, 24 April 1991, p.1.

19. WA, 16 March 1993, p. 7.

20. *Jing bao*, May 1990, p. 32.

21. Ibid., January 1995.

22. Ibid.

23. See Tai Ming-cheung, "The PAP: First Line of Defence" (unpublished paper read at *China Quarterly* / Council for Advanced Policy Studies conference in Hong Kong, July 1995).

24. Liu Ji, *Xiazhong jiansheng* (The Arrow Sound in the Little Box) (Shanghai: Shanghai renmin chubanshe [Shanghai People's Publishing], 1994), p. 7.

25. The section on Jiang's Hubei trip of 20–23 December 1992 is based on *Zhonghua yingcai* (China's Talents), no. 84 (1983): 6–8; Xinhua, 26 December 1992; and Hubei Radio, 27 December 1992, in FBIS, 31 December 1992, pp. 27–29.

26. *Nongmin ribao* (Farmers' Daily), 19 March 1993, p. 1.

27. *LWHW*, no. 14 (1995): 32.

28. CNS, 30 October 1994.

29. Xinhua, 18 October 1993.

30. WA, 16 March 1993, p. 6.

31. Details from WA, 16 August 1993, pp. 10–12.

32. WA, 16 August 1993, p. 11.

33. WA, 16 July 1993, p. 6.

34. *Jing bao,* 5 August 1993, p. 36.

35. WA, 16 July 1993, p. 8.

36. *Zhongguo jizhe* (China Journalist), March 1996, p. 31.

37. Xinhua, 3 October 1993.

38. PD, 9 November 1993, p. 1.

39. PD, 19 August 1993, p. 1.

40. See author's article in *Asia Inc.,* January 1993, pp. 56–63.

41. Xinhua, 25 October 1992.

42. *Nanfang ribao* (Nanfang Daily), 1 September 1995, p. 11.

43. *Jing bao,* 5 October 1993, p. 36.

44. Ibid., pp. 35–39.

45. Xinhua, 30 June 1993.

46. *WWP,* 14 August 1993, p. 2.

47. Jing bao, 5 October 1993, p. 37.

48. Xinhua, 5 March 1994.

49. PD, 17 January 1995.

50. Xinhua, 8 March 1993.

51. Xinhua, 17 November 1993.

52. Xinhua, 23 May 1993.

53. Interview with senior board member of Hong Kong Shipowners Association, 30 September 1993.

54. Worldnet interview (USIS, Hong Kong), 4 November 1993.

55. *Jing bao,* 5 January 1994, p. 38.

56. Based on interviews with U.S. officials in Hong Kong, July 1996.

57. CNS, 26 November 1993.

58. *Jing bao,* 5 January 1994, p. 39.

59. *Seattle Post-Intelligencer,* 19 November 1993, p. A1.

60. *Sacramento Bee,* 21 November 1993, p. A32; *Los Angeles Times,* 21 November 1993, P. 7.

61. Central TV, 1 December 1993, in FBIS, 2 December 1993, p. 22; AP, 2 December 1993.

62. *Jing bao,* March 1993, p. 31. The military commission salary is according to Tai Ming-cheung.

63. Interview with Lufthansa Airlines official in Beijing, December 1995.

64. *Jiushi niandai* (Nineties Monthly, Hong Kong), 1 March 1991, p. 14.

65. Interview with Jiang Office official in Beijing, May 1997.

66. WA, March 1996, pp. 74–76; *Zheng ming* (Cheng Ming, Hong Kong), March 1996, pp. 32–34.

67. *Ming Pao,* 9 November 1996, p. A11.

68. See Gao Xin, *Jiang Zemin de muliao* (Jiang Zemin's Counselors) (Mississauga: Mingjing chuban she [Canada Mirror Books], 1996), pp. 238–76.

69. *Washington Post,* 19 October 1997, pp. 1, 22.

70. Gao Xin, *Jiang Zemin de muliao,* cover

71. WA, 16 June 1994, p. 6.

72. *Jing bao,* 5 October 1994, pp. 58–59.

73. *Kaifang* (Open Magazine, Hong Kong), June 1997, p. 25.

74. WWP, 2 April 1992.

75. *Jing bao,* 5 October 1994, pp. 58–59.

CHAPTER 8. GLAD AND AT EASE

1. Xinhua, 28 September 1993.

2. *China Daily,* 8 October 1993, p. 4.

3. *Jing bao,* 5 December 1993, p. 32.

4. WWP, 24 November 1993, p. 2.

5. WWP, 29 November 1993, p. 2.

6. CR, 1994, pp. 2.43–2.46.

7. Xinhua, 19 January 1994.

8. Xinhua, 4 February 1994.

9. PD, 23 May 1994, p. 1.

10. PLAD, 3 January 1994, p. 1.

11. WA, 16 May 1994, p. 42.

12. Xinhua, 12 May 1994; *Selected Readings from the Works of Mao Tsetung* (Beijing: Foreign Languages Press, 1971), p. 472.

13. Sichuan Radio, 20 October 1994, in FBIS, 24 October 1994, p. 37.

14. Xinhua, 15 March 1994.

15. Li Peng's government work report to the 1995 NPC, Xinhua, 4 March 1995.

16. *Business Week,* 20 May 1996, p. 23.

17. WA, 16 March 1994, p. 18.

18. *Straits Times,* 27 June 1996, p. 46.

19. Zhang, who had already been sent out of the capital to the Chengdu regional command in 1992, was pulled out of active duty altogether and retired to a military academy.

20. *Ming Pao,* 2 June 1993, p. 8; Western diplomats in Hong Kong confirm the link between the two events, interview, February 1997.

21. See articles published in PLAD, 2 August 1993, 17 August 1993, and 30 July 1994.

22. *Jing bao*, 5 October 1993, p. 29.

23. WA, 16 August 1994, p. 10.

24. Xinhua, 14 March 1994.

25. PLAD, 28 January 1995, p. 1.

26. I owe these figures to the Chinese military analyst Tai Ming-cheung of Kim Eng Securities in Hong Kong.

27. PLAD, 23 July 1993, p. 1.

28. *Jing bao*, 5 October 1994, p. 24.

29. Xinhua, 3 January 1994.

30. *Jing bao*, 5 April 1994, p. 37.

31. *Lianhe bao* (United Daily News, Hong Kong), 30 March 1994, p. 2.

32. PD, 29 September 1994, p. 1.

33. PD, 11 November 1994, p. 1.

34. Xinhua, 3 July 1995, SCMP, 4 July 1995.

35. AFP, 31 January 1995.

36. Xinhua, 22 March 1995; Reuters, 23 March 1995.

37. *Chungang ilbo* (South Korea), 22 July 1996, pp. 3–4, in FBIS, 22 July 1996, FBIS-CHI-96–141; Shen Chun-shan talks, p. 96.

38. Samuel P. Huntington, *The Clash of Civilizations and the Remaking of World Order* (1989; reprint New York: Simon & Schuster, 1996); *Chungang ilbo* (South Korea), 22 July 1996, pp. 3–4, in FBIS, 22 July 1996, FBIS-CHI-96–141.

39. Shen Chun-shan talks, p. 88.

40. PLAD, 10 November 1996, p. 1.

41. *Business Week*, 20 May 1996, p. 23.

42. *Xinwen zhanxian* (News Frontline), July 1994, p. 3.

43. You Ji, "Jiang Zemin," *China Review* 1996, p. 23.

44. *Jing bao*, March 1997, p. 25.

45. Interview with Jiang office source in Beijing. The original reads: "Mao Zedong yi ju ding yi wan ju; Deng Xiaoping yi ju ding 63 ju, Jiang Zemin yi ju ding yi ju." The 63 refers to the senior leaders in the early 1990s including CAC standing committee members.

46. Quoted in *Jing bao*, 1 January 1996, p. 26.

47. *Zhongguo jizhe* (China Journalist), April 1990, p. 7.

48. WA, 16 August 1994, p. 62.

49. AP, 6 July 1995.

50. Author's translation. Based on Mao Zedong, *Poems* (Beijing: Foreign Languages Press, 1976), p. 37.

51. CNS, 30 November 1989.

52. *Pravda*, 30 April 1990, in SWB, 1 May 1990, p. C2/1.

53. *Zhonghua yingcai* (China's Talents), 1993, no. 66, p. 10.

54. Xinhua, 14 September 1989.

55. Xinhua, 19 October 1989.

56. *LWHW*, 6 November 1989.

57. Ibid.

CHAPTER 9. INDEPENDENT KINGDOMS

1. Hu Sheng, p. 629.
2. *Zhongguo huashang bao* (China Business Times), 19 January 1996, p. 4.
3. *Nanfang zhoumo* (Southern Weekend), 29 December 1995, p. 1.
4. *Wenzhai bao* (Press Digest), 15 November 1996, p. 1.
5. Xinhua, 1 March 1995.
6. *Qianshao* (Frontline Magazine, Hong Kong), May 1995, pp. 20–23.
7. Reuters, 30 April 1995.
8. *Jing bao,* June 1995, p. 28. CNS, 10 March 1998.
9. *WWP,* 4 March 1995, p. 2.
10. *Jing bao,* June 1995, pp. 24–25. There was no evidence that the bribes came from the Hong Kong investors, the biggest of whom was the tycoon Li Ka-shing. But that was less important than who took them.
11. CNS, 4 July 1995.
12. *Beijing ribao* (Beijing Daily), 11 April 1995, p. 1.
13. *Jing bao,* June 1995, p. 25.
14. *WWP,* 29 April 1995, p. 6.
15. AFP, 8 August 1997; CNS, 30 April 1995.
16. You Ji, "Jiang Zemin," *CR* 1996, p. 16.
17. Xinhua, 29 February 1996.
18. Fang Wen, *Tiannu* (Heaven's Wrath) (Hohhot, Inner Mongolia: Yuanfang chubanshe [Yuanfang Publishing], 1996). The ban was confirmed by CNS, 17 June 1997.
19. Xinhua, 8 November 1995.
20. *Lianhe bao* (United Daily News, Hong Kong), 30 January 1996, p. 1.
21. Shen Chun-shan talks, p. 103.
22. Shen Chun-shan is now president of Taiwan's Tsinghua University.
23. Shen Chun-shan talks, p. 87.
24. Ibid., p. 63.
25. Ibid., p. 75, p. 93.
26. Huang Jiashu, *Taiwan neng duli ma?* (Can Taiwan Achieve Independence?) (Haikou: Nanhai Chubanshe [South Seas Publishing], 1994).
27. Zheng Langping, *Yi jiu jiu wu run ba yue* (T-Day: Warning of Taiwan Strait War) (Taipei: Shang-chou wen-hwa [Commercial Week Publishing], 1994).
28. *Hsin hsin-wen* (The Journalist, Taipei), 22 October 1994, p. 16.
29. *Jing bao,* 1 January 1996, p. 26.
30. WA, 16 December 1994, p. 11.
31. Xinhua, 14 November 1994.
32. Xinhua, 30 January 1995.
33. *Jianchuan zhishi* (Naval and Merchant Ships), 6 January 1997, p. 11.
34. *Jing bao,* September 1995, pp. 18–19.
35. Ibid., September 1995, p. 19.
36. WA, August 1995, p. 47. See also *Kaifang* (Open Magazine), January 1998, pp. 16–18.
37. Xinhua, 30 June 1995.
38. *WWP,* 14 March 1995, p. 3.

39. See reports in *Zhonghua yingcai* (China's Talents), 1996, no. 2, pp. 6–9; ibid., 1995, no. 24, pp. 4–6; *Xinwen yu chengcai* (News and Self-Cultivation), 1996, no. 8, pp. 6–7.

40. Xinhua, 18 October 1995.

41. *LWHW*, 6 November 1995, p. 7.

42. Interview with Western diplomats in Hong Kong, February 1996.

43. *WWP*, 3 December 1995.

44. WA, August 1995, p. 48.

45. Xinhua, 17 October 1995.

46. Xinhua, 25 October 1995.

47. In private, they even began to organize a lobbying effort in the U.S. Congress that would eventually end in scandal. *AWSJ*, 11 March 1997, p. 1.

48. Reuters, 12 March 1996.

49. Reuters, 19 March 1996.

50. *WWP*, 21 March 1996, p. A2.

51. PD, 16 March 1996, p. 1.

52. Xinhua, 24 March 1996.

53. *Jing bao*, January 1996, p. 28.

54. *Newsweek*, 23 May 1996.

55. *Sankei shimbun*, 28 April 1996, p. 2, in FBIS 28 April 1996.

56. PLAD, 8 May 1996, p. 1.

57. Wu Yu et al., *Yangzhou* (Beijing: New World Press, 1989), p. 10.

58. Marcel Proust, *Remembrance of Things Past*, trans. C. K. Scott Moncrieff and Terence Kilmartin (London: Penguin Books, 1981), 1: 594.

59. Xinhua, 27 March 1993.

60. *Nongmin ribao* (Farmers' Daily), 15 November 1995, p. 1.

61. *Zhengming* (Cheng Ming Magazine, Hong Kong), August 1996, p. 36.

62. Reuters, 25 June 1996, 27 June 1996.

63. *Kaifang* (Open Magazine, Hong Kong), August 1996, p. 89.

64. *Dongxiang* (Trend Magazine, Hong Kong), July 1996, p. 47.

CHAPTER 10. JIANG THOUGHT

1. *Jing bao*, April 1997, pp. 42–43.

2. Xinhua, 8 May 1995.

3. *Gongren ribao* (Workers' Daily), 18 September 1996, p. 8.

4. *Jing bao*, April 1997, p. 43.

5. *Yazhou zhoukan* (Asia Week), 14 January 1996, pp. 22–28. No one knew who had written the document. The author was given as Li Yanming, a pen name that could be translated as "a clear voice from the common people." It was most likely produced by a group of writers associated with Deng Liqun, although he claimed when asked to have had nothing to do with it. Reuters, 17 September 1996.

6. *Jingji gongzuo yuekan* (Economic Work Monthly) (Guizhou), July 1996, reprinted in *Ming Pao*, 16 August 1996, p. E6.

7. *Zhongguo shehui bao* (China Society News), 25 July 1996, pp. 1, 3.

8. *Jing bao,* March 1996, p. 29.

9. Ibid., p. 25.

10. Jiang even appointed a party secretariat member, Wen Jiabao, as his emissary to assuage the querulous leftists, many of whom held influential posts in the propaganda and party theory apparatus. *Jing bao,* 1 July 1996, pp. 26–28.

11. Xinhua, 30 June 1995.

12. Xinhua, 17 January 1996.

13. *Zhenli de zhuiqiu* (Pursuit of Truth), March 1996, p. 7.

14. *Shenxing shibao* (Shenzhen Shenxing Daily), 5 March 1996, p. 4.

15. Xinhua, 30 June 1996.

16. WA, February 1996, p. 10.

17. Xinhua, 30 June 1996.

18. WWP, 23 September 1996, p. 6.

19. *Tansuo yu zhengming* (Exploration and Contention) (Beijing), April 1996, p. 5; WA, October 1996, p. 8.

20. *Chung kung yan chiu* (Studies in Communist China) (Taipei), March 1996, p. 16.

21. *Jing bao,* September 1996, p. 26.

22. Xinhua, 23 June 1996.

23. *Jing bao,* April 1997, p. 43.

24. WA, August 1996, p. 7.

25. Louis Cha talks, *Ming bao yuekan* (*Ming Pao* Monthly), 1 June 1993, p. 85.

26. Xinhua, 10 June 1996.

27. Xinhua, 27 December 1996.

28. *Xinwen yu chengcai* (Journalism and Self Cultivation, Beijing), June 1996, p. 4.

29. *Jing bao,* 1 November 1996, p. 35.

30. AFP, 22 July 1996.

31. WWP, 10 March 1995, p. 2.

32. *Jing bao,* March 1996, p. 25.

33. PD, 22 September 1995, p. 1.; *Jing bao,* March 1996, p. 25.

34. AFP, 17 July 1996.

35. Xinhua, 9 April 1996.

36. Xinhua, 18 July 1996.

37. AP, 23 October 1996.

38. *LWHW,* 16 July 1990, p. 13.

39. Xinhua, 31 May 1991.

40. *Jing bao,* 1 July 1996, p. 28.

41. WA, August 1996, pp. 6–8.

42. Xinhua, 26 May 1997.

43. Xinhua, 11 March 1996.

44. WA, November 1996, p. 6.

45. Xinhua, 11 March 1996; PLAD, 26 August 1996, p. 1.

46. PLAD, 23 May 1996, p. 1.

47. Xinhua, 29 July 1996.

48. Xinhua, 17 April 1996.

49. WA, September 1996, p. 12.

50. Interview with U.S. official in Hong Kong, 30 August 1996.

51. Xinhua, 13 February 1996.

52. *WWP*, 8 March 1996, p. 3.

53. CNS, 4 March 1996.

54. Reuters, 24 December 1996.

55. *Chung kuo shih pao* (China Times Magazine, Taipei), 2 July 1995, p. 31.

56. Wang Huning, *Zhengzhide rensheng* (A Political Life) (Shanghai: Shanghai renmin chubanshe [Shanghai People's Publishing], 1995), p. 133. Hereafter cited as "Wang Huning."

57. LD, 7 August 1989, p. 2.

58. Wang Huning, pp. 135–44.

59. Author's interview with the Fudan professor Qiu Bosheng, 3 April 1995.

60. Xinhua, 8 October 1995.

61. Jiang Zemin, conversation with U.S. Senator Max Baucus (D, Montana), *SCMP*, 30 May 1997, p. 9.

62. Xinhua, 7 March 1996.

63. *Zhongguo shuiwu bao* (China Tax News), 17 January 1997, p. 1; *Jingji ribao* (Economic Daily), 10 May 1997, p. 1.

64. *Jingji guanli* (Economic Management), 5 July 1996, p. 16.

65. *CR* 1995, p. 20.11.

66. Xinhua, 9 March 1996.

67. Xinhua, 15 July 1996.

68. PD, 15 July 1996.

69. World Bank, "Poverty in China: What Do the Numbers Say?" (unpublished background note, October 1996). The report uses a world poverty standard of U.S.$1 a day of income rather than China's U.S.$0.60 a day and reduces China's official GDP figures using purchasing power–based exchange rates.

70. Xinhua, 22 September 1996.

71. Xinhua, 5 November 1996.

72. PD, 22 April 1996, p. 1.

73. Xinhua, 27 June 1995.

74. *Jing bao*, September 1996, p. 25.

75. Quoted by Central News Agency, Taipei, 7 December 1995.

76. *Xinwen jizhe* (News Journalist), October 1995, p. 5.

77. *China Daily*, 11 May 1997.

78. Xinhua, 23 April 1996.

79. *Dongxiang* (Trend Magazine, Hong Kong), February 1996, pp. 24–25.

80. There was an official report that he had written a book on the history of Tai Shan Mountain in Shandong province. But there have been no other references to this work, suggesting the report was mistaken. See Shandong Radio, 3 September 1993, in FBIS, 8 September 1993, p. 43.

81. Xinhua, 8 November 1996.

82. Weng Jieming et al., eds., *Yu zongshuji tanxin* (Talking Heart-to-Heart with the General Secretary) (Beijing: Zhongguo shehui kexue yuan chubanshe [CASS Publishing], 1996), p. 4.

83. WA, November 1996, p. 16.

84. CNS, 8 November 1996.

85. Xu Ming, ed., *Guanjian shike* (Critical Moment) (Beijing: Jinri zhong-guo chubanshe [Today's China Publishing], 1997), p. 3 (preface). Hereafter cited as "Xu Ming."

86. Ibid. (editor's note).

87. *Zhenli de zhuiqiu* (Search for Truth), March 1997, pp. 12–15, in FBIS-CHI-97-113.

88. Fang Hsueh-chun, "Chiang Tse-min's Ideology, Ability and Leadership Style," *Issues and Studies* (Taipei), October 1990, p. 17.

89. *Zhongguo qingnian* (China Youth), 1 February 1997, pp. 8–11.

90. *Ming Pao*, 24 February 1997, p. 3.

91. Roxana Witke, *Comrade Chiang Ch'ing* (Boston: Little, Brown, 1977).

92. *WWP*, 28 August 1996, p. 2.

CHAPTER 11. THE EMPEROR'S MANDATE

1. *Jing bao*, September 1996, p. 27.

2. Ibid., March 1997, p. 38; *Yangcheng wanbao* (Yangcheng Evening News), 23 February 1997, p. 1.

3. *Yangcheng wanbao* (Yangcheng Evening News), 23 February 1997, p. 1.

4. *Jing bao*, March 1997, p. 38.

5. Reuters, 13 January 1997; FEER, 16 January 1997, pp. 20–21.

6. Xinhua, 5 February 1997.

7. *Jing bao*, March 1997, p. 38.

8. *Pingguo ribao* (Apple Daily, Hong Kong), 15 February 1997, p. 1.

9. Reuters, 16 February 1997.

10. *Xingdao ribao* (*Sing Tao Daily News*, Hong Kong), 27 February 1997, p. 1.

11. *WWP*, 1 March 1997, p. 3.

12. *Beijing qingniun bao* (Beijing Youth Daily), 4 April 1997, p. 1.

13. Xinhua, 4 March 1997.

14. CNS, 26 February 1997.

15. *Jing bao*, April 1997, p. 28.

16. Ibid., June 1997, p. 29.

17. Ibid., April 1997, p. 27.

18. Reuters, 20 May 1997.

19. The new quasi-alliance was in fact little more than a continuation of the warming in ties with Russia initiated by China in 1994. When Jiang visited Moscow in that year, the two sides had agreed to begin a "constructive part-nership." That was upgraded to a "strategic partnership" when Yeltsin returned the visit in early 1996. The two ideas were now being rolled into one.

20. *Xingdao ribao* (*Sing Tao Daily News*, Hong Kong), 18 April 1997, p. 6.

21. Xinhua, 22 February 1997.

22. Xinhua, 11 May 1997.

23. Xinhua, 15 May 1997.

24. Xinhua, 29 May 1997.

25. CNS, 1 July 1996.

26. Xinhua, 26 January 1996.

27. *Jing bao,* May 1997, p. 29; ibid., June 1997, p. 24.

28. Li Xiaozhuang, *Dong Jianhua* (Tung Chee-hwa) (Beijing: Shishi chuban-she [Shishi Publishing], 1996), p. 209. Hereafter cited as "Li Xiaozhuang."

29. Shen Chun-shan talks, p. 72.

30. Li Xiaozhuang, p. 51.

31. Xinhua, 11 July 1989.

32. Xu Jiatun memoirs in *Lianhe bao* (United Daily News, Hong Kong), 21 September 1993, in JPRS, 17 March 1994, p. 15.

33. Louis Cha talks, *Ming bao yuekan* (*Ming Pao* Monthly), 1 June 1993, p. 18.

34. *Jing bao,* December 1996, p. 26.

35. Ibid., June 1997, p. 22.

36. Xinhua, 9 May 1997.

37. Xinhua, 1 July 1997.

38. Ibid.

39. *Lianhe bao* (United Daily News, Hong Kong), 17 March 1994, p. 10.

40. *Hong Kong Standard*, 9 December 1995.

41. Interview with U.S. scholar, Hong Kong, June 1997. Jiang would make the same argument that he was not a "tyrant" in an interview with Canada's *Globe & Mail* newspaper, 1 December 1997, p. 1.

42. *Jing bao,* September 1996, p. 22.

43. The first mention of this plan, which set off a wave of speculation in the foreign press, was in *Jing bao,* June 1996, p. 29.

44. PD, 15 May 1997, p. 9.

45. *Financial Times*, 11 September 1996, p. 3.

46. *Jing bao,* June 1996, p. 28.

47. *Jing bao,* March 1997, p. 24.

48. *Jing bao,* September 1997, p. 26.

49. WWP, 19 September 1997, p. 3.

50. *Jing bao,* October 1997, p. 26.

51. Kyodo, 30 September 1997.

52. Ibid.

53. *Jing bao,* September 1997, p. 25.

54. AFP, 11 July 1997.

55. *Jing bao,* October 1997, p. 27.

56. *Jing bao,* September 1997, p. 26, January 1998, pp. 34–35.

57. This is suggested in Michael Swaine, *The Role of the Chinese Military in National Security Policymaking* (Santa Monica, Calif.: Rand National Defense Research Institute, 1996), p. 77.

58. See Zhu's humorous question-and-answer session at the annual meeting of the International Monetary Fund and World Bank in Hong Kong in WWP, 23 September 1997, p. 6. Also see his sarcastic remarks to local cadres in *Jing bao,* October 1997, pp. 34–35.

59. Zeng Peiyan was head of the general office of the party's leading group on finance and the economy, as well as minister of the new State Development Planning Commission. See CNS, 3 September 1997.

60. Party elder Wan Li said at the time that the selection and training of a "fourth generation" of leaders was in full swing as a "key item" on the party agenda (*Jing bao*, January 1994, p. 39).

61. Huang and Wu assisted Hu Jintao in training young cadres (WA, October 1994, p. 9).

62. WWP, 20 September 1997, p. 1.

63. The reduction had been agreed in principle in 1993 (WWP, 16 September 1997, p. 5).

64. *Jing bao*, October 1997, p. 27.

65. WA, May 1997, p. 27.

66. *Jing bao*, December 1996, p. 29.

67. Xinhua, 1 July 1997; *Chunggang ilbo*, 22 July 1996, pp. 3–4, in FBIS-CHI-96-141, 22 July 1996.

68. Xinhua, 25 September 1997.

69. WA, May 1997, p. 12.

70. WA, November 1996, p. 12.

71. *Xinbao* (Hong Kong Economic Journal), 7 May 1997, p. 15.

72. WWP, 11 November 1993, p. 3.

73. Xinhua, 4 February 1997.

74. *Jing bao*, April 1997, p. 34.

75. *Zhenlide zhuiqiu* (Search for Truth), April 1997, pp. 6–10.

76. *Xinbao* (Hong Kong Economic Journal), 20 June 1997, p. 19.

77. WWP, 13 July 1997, p. 2.

78. WWP, 3 September 1997, p. 2. A different figure of 76 percent for the "public sector" (state and collective) share of 1996 GDP, versus the 72 percent here, was given in WWP, 14 September 1997, p. 1.

79. WWP, 28 August 1997, p. 6.

80. *Jingji ribao* (Economic Daily), 19 August 1997.

81. World Bank, *China 2020: Development Challenges in the New Century* (Washington, D.C.: World Bank Group, 1997), p. 100.

82. WWP, 12 May 1997, p. 4.

83. WWP, 15 September 1997, p. 3.

84. Ibid.

85. WA, September 1997, p. 19.

86. WWP, 6 September 1997, p. 4.

87. World Bank, *China 2020*, p. 21.

88. *Jing bao*, April 1997, p. 35.

89. Xinhua, 5 August 1997.

90. WWP, 15 September 1997, p. 5.

91. *Jing bao*, August 1997, p. 30.

92. *Jing bao*, May 1996, p. 29.

93. Xinhua, 17 March 1997.

94. PD, 21 March 1997, p. 1.

95. AFP, 8 September 1997.

96. CNS, 1 September 1997.

97. Li Li in *Guanjian shike* (Critical Moment), ed. Xu Ming (Beijing: Jinri zhongguo chubanshe [Today's China Publishing], 1997), p. 328.

98. *Jing bao*, June 1997, p. 34.

99. Xu Ming, pp. 310–30.

100. CNS, 22 August 1997.

101. *Jing bao*, April 1997, p. 31.

102. Ibid., p. 32.

103. See FEER, 7 December 1995, pp. 35–36. See also Jonathan Unger and Anita Chan, "Corporatism in China," in *China After Socialism*, ed. Barrett McCormick and Jonathan Unger (Armonk, N.Y.: M. E. Sharpe, 1996), pp. 95–129; Chen Jie et al., "Assessing Political Support in China," *Journal of Contemporary China* 6, no. 16 (1997): 551–66; and Andrew Walder, "Does China Face an Unstable Future? On the Political Impact of Rapid Growth," *CR* 1997, pp. 327–48.

104. See, e.g., Ju Yanan, *Understanding China* (Albany: State University of New York Press, 1996), ch. 4.

105. CNS, 28 July 1997.

106. *Jing bao*, September 1997, p. 30.

107. Ibid., p. 31.

108. See, e.g., *Banyuetan* (Semi-Monthly Talks), 1997, no. 15, pp. 6–13.

109. CNS, 26 August 1997.

110. *Jing bao*, July 1997, p. 55.

111. Xinhua, 31 August 1997.

112. Xinhua, 19 September 1997. The English version is incomplete.

113. WA, June 1997, p. 7.

114. Reuters, 27 November 1996.

115. Kyodo, 4 June 1997.

116. Reuters, 25 October 1997.

117. *Jing bao*, January 1996, p. 28.

118. AFP, 9 May 1997; *Time* (U.S. edition), 27 October 1997, pp. 54–58; *Washington Post*, 19 October 1997, pp. 1, 22.

119. *New York Times*, 25 October 1997, p. 1.

120. Ibid., p. 6.

121. *SCMP*, 4 November 1997, p. 1.

122. *Washington Post* Service, 2 November 1997.

123. Jiang's name recognition abroad was still remarkably low. Shortly before the Washington summit, in a Reuters report from Singapore (12 September 1997), China's president was identified as "Jingo Semen." Jiang's name had obviously been changed by a spell-checker, and editors failed to notice the mistake.

124. Reuters, 26 November 1997.

CONCLUSION

1. Xinhua, 26 October 1997; also Xinhua 16 March 1998.

2. *Jing bao*, April 1997, p. 29.

3. *Dongxiang* (Trend Magazine, Hong Kong), December 1995 and August 1996; *Zhengming* (*Cheng Ming*, Hong Kong), June 1991.

4. *Time* (U.S. edition), 27 October 1997, p. 58.
5. Interview with family sources, Yangzhou, October 1996.
6. *Chunggang ilbo*, 22 July 1996, pp. 3–4, in FBIS-CHI-96-141, 22 July 1996.
7. WWP, 28 October 1997, p. 3.
8. *SCMP*, 28 October 1997, p. 10.
9. *Jing bao,* January 1998, p. 35; March 1998, p. 23.

Select Bibliography

Items listed in quotation marks are shorthand titles used in the notes.

Baum, Richard. *Burying Mao: Chinese Politics in the Age of Deng Xiaoping.* Princeton: Princeton University Press, 1994.

Bernstein, Richard, and Ross H. Munro. *The Coming Conflict with China.* New York: Alfred A. Knopf, 1997.

Black, George, and Robin Munro. *Black Hands of Beijing: Lives of Defiance in China's Democracy Movement.* New York: John Wiley & Sons, 1993.

"Chao Hao-sheng talks." Jiang Zemin, conversation with Professor Chao Hao-sheng of Yale University. *Ta Kung Pao* (Hong Kong), 22 September 1989, p. 1.

Evans, Richard. *Deng Xiaoping and the Making of Modern China.* New York: Viking, 1994.

Gao Xin. *Jiang Zemin de muliao* (Jiang Zemin's Counselors). Mississauga: Mingjing chubanshe (Canada Mirror Books), 1996.

Gongqingtuan Shanghai shiwei (Communist Youth League Shanghai Party Committee), *Chuntiande yaolan* (Cradle of Spring). Shanghai: Zhongguo qingnian chubanshe (China Youth Press), 1982.

Guang Yu. "Jiang Zemin zai Changchun yiqi" (Jiang Zemin at the Changchun Number One Vehicle Plant). In *Zhonghua ernu* (Sons and Daughters of China), no. 6 (1994): 35–39.

He Ruohan. *Jiang Zemin shidai* (The Era of Jiang Zemin). Hong Kong: Tiandi tushu (Cosmos Books), 1997.

Hei Lin. "Zongshuji jiejie qingpin yi jiu" (The Party General Secretary's Sister Is as Poor as Ever). *Nanfang ribao* (Nanfang Daily), 3 August 1994, p. 8.

"History of Jiaotong." *Jiaotong daxue xiaoshi* (History of Jiaotong University, 1896–1949). Shanghai: Shanghai jiaoyu chubanshe (Shanghai Education Press), 1986.

Ho Pin and Gao Xin. *Princes and Princesses of Red China.* Toronto: Canada Mirror Books, 1993.
———. *Zhonggong taizi dang* (China's Princelings). Toronto: Canada Mirror Books, 1993.
Hsu, Immanuel. *The Rise of Modern China.* 5th ed. New York: Oxford University Press, 1995.
Hu Sheng. *A Concise History of the Communist Party of China.* Beijing: Foreign Languages Press, 1994.
Hu Zhihong. "Jiang Shangqing lieshi xunnan ji" (On the Just Death of the Martyr Jiang Shangqing). *Zhuanji wenxue* (Biographical Literature), February 1992, pp. 28–32.
Jenner, W. J. F. *The Tyranny of History: The Roots of China's Crisis.* London: Allen Lane, Penguin Books, 1992.
Jiang Xinghong et al. *Deng Xiaoping yu 1992 nian* (Deng Xiaoping and 1992). Beijing: Zhonggong zhongyang dangxiao chubanshe (Central Party School Publishing House), 1993.
Joint Economic Committee of the Congress of the United States, ed. *China's Economic Dilemmas in the 1990s.* New York: M. E. Sharpe, 1993.
Ju Yanan. *Understanding China.* Albany: State University of New York Press, 1996.
Kemenade, Willem van. *China, Hong Kong, Taiwan, Inc.* Translated from the Dutch by Diane Webb. New York: Alfred A. Knopf, 1997.
Kwan Ha Yim, ed. *China under Deng.* New York: Facts on File, 1991.
Ladany, Laszlo. *The Communist Party of China and Marxism, 1921–1985.* London: C. Hurst & Co., 1988.
Lamb, Malcolm. *Directory of Officials and Organizations in China: A Quarter-Century Guide.* London and Armonk, N.Y.: M. E. Sharpe, 1994.
Lieberthal, Kenneth. *Governing China: From Revolution through Reform.* New York: Norton, 1995.
Lieberthal, Kenneth, and David M. Lampton, eds. *Bureaucracy, Politics, and Decision Making in Post-Mao China.* Berkeley: University of California Press, 1992.
Li Cheng and Lynn T. White III. "China's Technocratic Movement and the 'World Economic Herald.'" *Modern China,* July 1991, pp. 342–88.
Li Guoqiang. *Jiang Zemin pouxi* (Jiang Zemin in Depth). Hong Kong: Guangjiaojing chubanshe (Wide Angle Press), 1989.
Li Hongyuan, "Jiang zongshuji he tade tongxue" (General Secretary Jiang and His Classmate). *Zhongguo laonian* (China's Elderly), November 1994, pp. 4–6.
"Louis Cha talks." *Ming bao yuekan* (Ming Pao Monthly), 1 June 1993, pp. 81–91, in FBIS, 11 June 1993, pp. 15–20.
McCormick, Barrett, and Jonathan Unger, eds. *China After Socialism.* Armonk, N.Y.: M. E. Sharpe, 1996.
MacFarquhar, Roderick, ed. *The Politics of China, 1949–89.* New York: Cambridge University Press, 1993.
Meisner, Maurice J. *The Deng Xiaoping Era: An Inquiry into the Fate of Chinese Socialism, 1978–1994.* New York: Hill and Wang, 1996.

"*Nantong ribao.*" "Jiang zongshuji yijia yu Nantong" (General Secretary Jiang's Family and Nantong). *Nantong ribao* (Nantong Daily), 4 June 1995, p. 6.

Nathan, Andrew J. *China's Transition.* New York: Columbia University Press, 1997.

Niu Zhengwu. '92: *Deng Xiaoping nanxun jishi* (1992: Deng Xiaoping's Southern Inspection Tour). Guangzhou: Huacheng chubanshe (Huacheng Publishing), 1992.

Overholt, William H. *The Rise of China: How Economic Reform Is Creating a New Superpower.* New York: Norton, 1993.

Party Research Center of the Chinese Communist Party. *History of the Chinese Communist Party: A Chronology of Events, 1919–1990.* Beijing: Foreign Languages Press, 1991.

Schell, Orville. *Discos and Democracy: China in the Throes of Reform.* New York: Pantheon, 1988.

———. *Mandate of Heaven: A New Generation of Entrepreneurs, Dissidents, Bohemians, and Technocrats Lays Claim to China's Future.* New York: Simon & Schuster, 1994.

———. *To Get Rich is Glorious: China in the Eighties.* New York: Pantheon, 1984.

Shambaugh, David, ed. *Deng Xiaoping: Portrait of a Chinese Statesman.* Oxford and New York: Oxford University Press, 1995.

Shanghai Jiaotong daxue dangwei xuanchuanbu (Propaganda Department of the Party Committee of Jiaotong University). "Zai dier tiao zhanxianshang: Jiefang zhanzhang shiqi Jiaotong daxue xuesheng yundong" (On the Second Battlefront: The Student Movement at Jiaotong University during the War of Liberation). Neibu faxing (internal circulation), 1981. Cited as "Second Battlefront."

Shanghai shiwei (Shanghai Municipal Party Committee). *Shanghai nianjian* (Shanghai Statistical Yearbook). Shanghai tongji chubanshe (Shanghai Statistics Publishing House), various years.

"Shen Chun-shan talks." "Jiang Zemin yu Shen Junshan de sanci tanhua" (Three Talks between Jiang Zemin and Shen Chun-shan). *Jiushi niandai* (Nineties Monthly, Hong Kong), August 1996, pp. 60–111.

Wang Huning. *Zhengzhide rensheng* (A Political Life). Shanghai: Shanghai renmin chubanshe (Shanghai People's Publishing), 1995.

Wang Xiaopeng. *Wo yanzhongde zhongguo lingdaoren* (Chinese Leaders in My Eyes). Dalian: Liaoning daxue chubanshe (Liaoning University Press), 1993.

———. *Zhongguo dangdai lingdaoren* (China's Current Leaders). Beijing: Zhonggong dangshi chubanshe (Chinese Communist Party History Publishing House), 1994.

Wang Yu, ed. *Yangzhou lidai mingren* (Famous Yangzhou People through the Ages). Nanjing: Jiangsu guji chubanshe (Jiangsu Ancient Books Publishing House), 1992. Cited as "Wang Yu."

Wang Zhijuan. "Geming lieshi Jiang Shangqing" (Revolutionary Martyr Jiang Shangqing). In Wang Yu, ed., *Yangzhou lidai mingren* (Famous Yangzhou People through the Ages), pp. 341–47. Nanjing: Jiangsu guji chubanshe (Jiangsu Ancient Books Publishing House), 1992.

Wasserstrom, Jeffrey. *Student Protests in Twentieth-Century China: The View from Shanghai*. Stanford: Stanford University Press, 1991.

Weng Jieming et al., eds. *Yu zongshuji tanxin* (Talking Heart-to-Heart with the General Secretary). Beijing: Zhongguo shehui kexue yuan chubanshe (CASS Publishing), 1996.

White, Lynn T., III. *Shanghai Shanghaied? Uneven Taxes in Reform China*. Centre of Asian Studies Occasional Papers and Monographs, no. 84. Hong Kong: Centre of Asian Studies, University of Hong Kong, 1989.

Witke, Roxane. *Comrade Chiang Ch'ing*. Boston: Little, Brown, 1977.

Wright, Kate, "The Political Fortunes of Shanghai's 'World Economic Herald.'" *Australian Journal of Chinese Affairs*, January 1990, pp. 121–32.

Xu Ming, ed. *Guanjian shike* (Critical Moment). Beijing: Jinri Zhongguo chubanshe (Today's China Publishing), 1997.

Yabuki Susumu. *China's New Political Economy*. Boulder, Colo.: Westview Press, 1995.

Yang Shuying. "Qiushan hongye zou zhengtu: ji geming lieshi Jiang Shangqing" (Setting off on a Journey amid Autumn Hills and Red Leaves: Revolutionary Martyr Jiang Shangqing). *Zhuanji wenxue* (Biographical Literature), no. 11 (1995): 4.

Yang Zhongmei. *Jiang Zemin zhuan* (Biography of Jiang Zemin). Taipei: Shih pao wen hua ch'u pan she ch'i yeh (*China Times* Publishing), 1996.

"Yangzhou Middle School Souvenir Book." *Jiangsu sheng Yangzhou zhongxue jian xiao jiushi zhounian jiniance* (Ninetieth Anniversary Souvenir Book of Yangzhou Middle School, Jiangsu Province). Yangzhou: n.p., 1992.

Yeung, Y. M., and Sung Yun-wing, eds. *Shanghai: Transformation and Modernization under China's Open Policy*. Hong Kong: Chinese University Press, 1996.

You Ji. *Jiang Zemin's Leadership and Chinese Elite Politics after 4 June 1990*. Canberra: Strategic and Defence Studies Centre, Research School of Pacific Studies, Australian National University, 1990.

Zhang Cangcang, Song Qiang, Qiao Bian et al. *Zhongguo keyi shuo bu* (China Can Say No). Bejing: Zhonghuo gongshang lianhe chubanshe (China Industrial and Commercial United Publishing), 1996.

Zheng Yi. *Jiang Zemin zhuanji* (Biography of Jiang Zemin). 4th ed. Hong Kong: Mingchuang chubanshe (Mingchuang Publishing), 1994.

Zhong Xu. "Xinren zongshuji Jiang Zemin ceying" (A Profile of the New Party General Secretary, Jiang Zemin). *Zhuanji wenxue* (Biographical Literature), no. 4 (1989): 4–5.

Zou Aiguo and He Ping, eds. *Disandai lingdaorende zuji* (The Footprints of the Third-Generation Leaders). Beijing: Zhonggong zhongyang dangxiao chubanshe (Central Party School Publishing House), 1992.

Index

Unless otherwise indicated, all cities, events, and organizations are in China.

Jiang Shangqing (*continued*)
163, 351nn.22–23; publishing activities of, 11–12, 95; revolutionary activities of, 9
Jiang Shijun (Jiang Zemin's father), 6, 8, 10, 12, 17, 18, 54
Jiang Shixi (Jiang Zemin's grandfather), 7–8, 9, 11, 24
Jiang Shixiong (Jiang Zemin's uncle), 54
Jiang Shou, 64
Jiang Shufeng (Jiang Zemin's uncle), 9, 12, 17, 95, 345n.55, 351n.23
Jiang Thought, 267–74, 277–87; central power, 280; criticism of, 284–86; vs. Deng Xiaoping's policies, 286, 297–98; as guiding policy, 297, 320–21, 335; income redistribution, 279–80, 335; inland regions, 280; paying attention to politics, 267–69, 273–74, 277, 287; poverty relief, 281, 335; rural policies, 280–81; speeches/pronouncements, publication of, 282–86, 370n.80; spiritual culture, 269–74, 277; state enterprises, 281–82; twelve great relationships, 278–79, 282
Jiang Yiren, 102
Jiang Zefen (Jiang Zemin's sister), 42, 78, 79, 162
Jiang Zehui (Jiang Zemin's foster sister), 37–38, 163, 164, 351n.23
Jiang Zekuan (Jiang Zemin's brother), 38
Jiang Zeling (Jiang Zemin's foster sister), 79, 163, 351n.23
Jiang Zemin, 155–56, 359n.31; as adopted son of Jiang Shangqing, 19, 80–81; aides to, 215–18; appearance of, 4, 29, 35, 56, 214, 230, 259–60; assumes leadership at Deng Xiaoping's death, 3–4; attends Deng Xiaoping's funeral/memorial, 291–92, 293–94; attends Hu Yaobang's funeral, 117; birth of, 5–7, 343n.4; bourgeois lifestyle, suspected of, 51–53; on capitalism vs. Chinese-style socialism, 93–94; career of, 331–32, 334; caricatures by, 25; "Carry Out Party Rectification in a Thorough Way by Constantly Seeking Unity of Thinking," 73; on Central Committee, 72–73, 80, 99, 333; in Central Committee Shanghai Work Group, 63–64, 99; as Central Military Commission chairman, 164–68, 190, 225, 254, 360n.78; at Central University, 20; challenges to, following Deng Xiaoping's death, 295–96; in Changchun, 41, 47, 347n.35; at

Changchun power plant, 44, 45, 46–48, 348n.42; childhood of, 6, 9, 10–11; at China Soap Factory, 35; Communist conversion of, 20–21; as Communist Party branch chief, 34; as Communist Party deputy secretary, 69; Communist Party involvement, as student, 23–25, 28–29; as Communist Party secretary, 4, 132–36, 146–48, 150–51, 190; downfall scenarios for, 336; education of, 9–10, 12, 13–17, 20, 21–23; as electronics minister, 69–71, 350n.32; as "everyman's leader," 47–48, 56; family, 78–81, 162–64; at First Machine-Building Ministry, 37; at Foreign Affairs Bureau, 60–61, 62, 65, 349n.19; future of, 335–37, 339; grandchildren of, 160, 161, 359n.51, 360n.58; Guangdong visit, 102; hairstyle/hair combing of, 52–53, 56, 259–62; health of, 46–47, 337; income of, 214; inspection tours of frontiers by, 177–80; intellectualism of, 229–30, 233, 321, 331; at Jiaotong University, 21–25, 28–29, 344n.50; joins student protests, 22–23, 142–43; language skills of, 321; and Li Peng, 123, 133, 138, 150, 171, 228, 334; literary interests of, 15–16, 20; Mao Zedong, affinity with, 232–35, 269–70, 286, 322; marriage to Wang Yeping, 35–36, 347n.14 (*see also* Wang Yeping); as mayor of Shanghai, 75–78, 79, 81, 82, 95, 99–100; meaning of name Zemin, 6, 78, 230; at Ministry of Electronics Industry, 69; in Moscow, 39–40; musicianship of, 10, 25–26, 40, 98, 232–33; nationalism of, 14–15, 327; nicknames of, 69, 108–9, 321, 350n.28; nondictatorial style of, 304, 305, 372n.41; at Number One Vehicle Plant, 39, 40, 41–42, 43–44, 45, 47; personality of, 5, 34, 47–48, 56, 98, 230–33, 327, 332; in Politburo, 98, 100, 109, 333; as powerful leader, 196–98, 227–29, 322, 334–35; as president, 197–98; presidential style of, 213–15, 217–18, 231–32; public speaking of, 231; *The Rational Use of Electrical Power in Machine-Building Factories,* 45; in Romania, 61–62; roundtable discussions with Shanghai residents, 104; scientific interests of, 20, 24; at 7 May Cadres School, 60; at Shanghai design bureau, 35, 36; at Shanghai Electrical Equipment Re-

Compositor:	BookMasters
Text:	10/13 Sabon
Display:	Sabon
Printer and Binder:	Haddon Craftsmen